AIX PERFORMANCE TUNING

FRANK WATERS

Prentice Hall PTR
Upper Saddle River, New Jersey 07458

For book and bookstore information

http://www.prenhall.com

Waters, Frank (Frank C.H.)
    AIX performance tuning / Frank Waters. –1st ed.
        p. cm.
    Includes index.
    ISBN 0-13-386707-2
    1. AIX (Computer files) 2. Operating systems (Computers)
I. Title.
QA76.76.063W367 1995   95-40606
005.4'469--dc20   CIP

Editorial/production supervision: **Ann Sullivan**
Cover designer: **Design Source**
Cover manager: **Jerry Votta**
Manufacturing manager: **Alexis R. Heydt**
Acquisitions editor: **Gregory G. Doench**
Editorial assistant: **Meg Cowen**

Published by Prentice Hall PTR
Prentice-Hall, Inc.
A Simon and Schuster Company
Upper Saddle River, NJ 07458

The publisher offers discounts on this book when ordered in bulk quantities. For more information, contact:

Corporate Sales Department
Prentice Hall PTR
One Lake Street
Upper Saddle River, NJ 07458

Phone: 800-382-3419   Fax: 201-236-7141
email: corpsales@prenhall.com

This edition of *AIX Performance Tuning* applies to AIX Version 3.2.5 and 4.1 for the IBM RISC System/6000.
The following trademarks appear in this book:
AIX is a trademark of International Business Machines Corporation
BEST/1 is a trademark of BGS Systems, Inc.
Encina is a trademark of Transarc Corporation
IBM is a registered trademark of International Business Machines Corporation
KAP/C and KAP/FORTRAN are trademarks of Kuck and Associates, Inc.
NFS is a trademark of SUN Microsystems
RISC System/6000 is a trademark of international Business Machines Corporation
UNIX is a registered trademark licensed exclusively by X/Open Company
VAST is a trademark of Pacific Sierra Research

Printed in the United States of America

10 9 8 7 6 5 4

ISBN: 0-13-386707-2

Prentice-Hall International (UK) Limited, *London*
Prentice-Hall of Australia Pty. Limited, *Sydney*
Prentice-Hall Canada Inc., *Toronto*
Prentice-Hall Hispanoamericana, S.A., *Mexico*
Prentice-Hall of India Private Limited, *New Delhi*
Prentice-Hall of Japan, Inc., *Tokyo*
Simon & Schuster Asia Pte. Ltd., *Singapore*
Editora Prentice-Hall do Brasil, Ltda., *Rio de Janeiro*

Table of Contents

Table of Contents i

Preface xi
AIX Performance Management Structure xi
Performance Tools Packages and Their Documentation xii
    BEST/1 xii
    AIX Performance Diagnostic Tool (PDT) xii
    AIX Base Operating System (BOS) xii
    Performance Toolbox (PTX) xiii
    AIX Performance PMR Data Collection Tool (PerfPMR) xiv
Overview of Contents xiv
Highlighting xvi

Acknowledgments xvii

Performance Concepts 1
    How Fast Is That Computer in the Window? 1
    First, Understand the Workload 2
    Program Execution Dynamics 3
    System Dynamics 7
An Introduction to the Performance-Tuning Process 8
    Identifying the Workloads 9
    Setting Objectives 9
    Identifying the Critical Resources 9
    Minimizing Critical-Resource Requirements 11
    Reflecting Priorities in Resource Allocation 11
    Repeating the Tuning Steps 11
    Applying Additional Resources 12
Performance Benchmarking—the Inevitable Dirtiness of Performance Data 12

AIX Resource Management Overview 14
Performance Overview of the AIX CPU Scheduler 14
    AIX Version 4.1 Thread Support 14
    Scheduling Policy for Threads with Local or Global Contention Scope 15
    Process and Thread Priority 15
    AIX Scheduler Run Queue 16
    Scheduler CPU Time Slice 17

Performance Overview of the Virtual Memory Manager (VMM) 17
    Real-Memory Management 17
    VMM Memory Load Control Facility 21
    Allocation and Reclamation of Paging Space Slots 25
Performance Overview of AIX Management of Fixed-Disk Storage 25
    Sequential-Access Read Ahead 27
    Write Behind 28
    Memory Mapped Files and Write Behind 28
    Disk-I/O Pacing 29
    Disk Array 29

An Introduction to Multiprocessing **31**
Symmetrical Multiprocessor (SMP) Concepts and Architecture 32
    Symmetrical vs Asymmetrical Multiprocessors 32
    Data Serialization 33
    Lock Granularity 34
    Locking Overhead 35
    Cache Coherency 35
    Processor Affinity 35
    Memory and Bus Contention 36
SMP Performance Issues 36
    Workload Concurrency 36
    Throughput 36
    Response Time 37
Adapting Programs to an SMP Environment 37
SMP Workloads 37
Workload Multiprocessability 37
Multiprocessor Throughput Scalability 38
Multiprocessor Response Time 40
SMP Scheduling 40
    Default Scheduler Processing of Migrated Workloads 41
    Scheduling Algorithm Variables 41
Processor Affinity and Binding 42

Performance-Conscious Planning, Design, and Implementation **43**
    Identifying the Components of the Workload 44
    Documenting Performance Requirements 44
    Estimating the Resource Requirements of the Workload 45
Design and Implementation of Efficient Programs 53
    CPU-Limited Programs 53
    Design and Coding for Effective Use of Caches 53
    Registers and Pipeline 55
    Cache and TLBs 55
    Effective Use of Preprocessors and the XL Compilers 57
    Levels of Optimization 61
    XL C Options for string.h Subroutine Performance 62
    C and C++ Coding Style for Best Performance 62

Compiler Execution Time 63
Memory-Limited Programs 64
Performance-Related Installation Guidelines 66
AIX Pre-Installation Guidelines 66
CPU Pre-Installation Guidelines 66
Memory Pre-Installation Guidelines 67
Disk Pre-Installation Guidelines 67
Communications Pre-Installation Guidelines 71

System Monitoring and Initial Performance Diagnosis **72**
The Case for Continuous Performance Monitoring 72
Performance Monitoring Using iostat, netstat, vmstat 73
The Performance Diagnostic Tool 74
The AIX Performance Toolbox 74
Inference from the Kind of Performance Problem Reported 75
A Particular Program Runs Slowly 75
Everything Runs Slowly at a Particular Time of Day 76
Everything Runs Slowly at Unpredictable Times 76
Everything an Individual User Runs Is Slow 77
A Number of LAN-Connected Systems Slow Down Simultaneously 77
Everything That Uses a Particular Service or Device Slows Down at Times 78
Using PerfPMR for Performance Diagnosis 78
Check before You Change 80
Identifying the Performance-Limiting Resource 80
Starting with an Overview of System Performance 80
Determining the Limiting Factor for a Single Program 83
Disk or Memory? 84
Workload Management 87

Monitoring and Tuning CPU Use **88**
Using vmstat to Monitor CPU Use 88
Using the time Command to Measure CPU Use 89
time and timex Cautions 90
Using xmperf to Monitor CPU Use 91
Using ps to Identify CPU-Intensive Programs 91
Using tprof to Analyze Programs for CPU Use 94
A (Synthetic) Cautionary Example 95
Detailed Control Flow Analysis with stem 101
Basic stem Analysis 101
Restructuring Executables with fdpr 103
Controlling Contention for the CPU 104
Controlling the Priority of User Processes 104
Running a Command at a Nonstandard Priority with nice 104
Setting a Fixed Priority with the setpri Subroutine 105
Displaying Process Priority with ps 106
Modifying the Priority of a Running Process with renice 106
Clarification of nice/renice Syntax 107

Tuning the Process-Priority-Value Calculation with schedtune 107
Modifying the Scheduler Time Slice 109
CPU-Efficient User ID Administration 110

Monitoring and Tuning Memory Use **111**
How Much Memory Is Really Being Used? 111
    vmstat 111
    ps 112
    svmon 112
    Example of vmstat, ps, and svmon Output 113
    Memory-Leaking Programs 114
Analyzing Patterns of Memory Use with BigFoot 115
Assessing Memory Requirements via the rmss Command 115
    Two Styles of Using rmss 115
Tuning VMM Memory Load Control 124
    Memory-Load-Control Tuning—Possible, but Usually Inadvisable 124
Tuning VMM Page Replacement 126
    Choosing minfree and maxfree Settings 126
    Choosing minperm and maxperm Settings 128

Monitoring and Tuning Disk I/O **130**
    Pre-Installation Planning 130
    Building a Pre-Tuning Baseline 130
    Assessing Disk Performance after Installation 130
    Assessing Physical Placement of Data on Disk 131
    Reorganizing a Logical Volume or Volume Group 134
    Reorganizing a File System 135
    Performance Considerations of Paging Spaces 136
    Measuring Overall Disk I/O with vmstat 137
    Using filemon for Detailed I/O Analysis 137
    Disk-Limited Programs 140
    Expanding the Configuration 140
    Background Information 141
Tuning Sequential Read Ahead 141
Use Of Disk-I/O Pacing 142
    Example 143
Logical Volume Striping 144
    Designing a Striped Logical Volume 146
    Tuning for Striped Logical Volume I/O 146
File-System Fragment Size 147
Compression 147
Asynchronous Disk I/O 148
Using Raw Disk I/O 148
Using sync/fsync 149
Modifying the SCSI Device Driver max_coalesce Parameter 149
Setting SCSI-Adapter and Disk-Device Queue Limits 150
    Non-IBM Disk Drive 150

Non-IBM Disk Array 151
Disk Adapter Outstanding-Request Limits 151
Controlling the Number of System pbufs 152

Monitoring and Tuning Communications I/O 153
UDP/TCP/IP Performance Overview 153
Communication Subsystem Memory (mbuf) Management 155
Socket Layer 155
Relative Level of Function in UDP and TCP 156
IP Layer 161
IF Layer (Demux Layer in AIX Version 4) 162
LAN Adapters and Device Drivers 162
TCP and UDP Performance Tuning 163
Overall Recommendations 163
Tuning TCP Maximum Segment Size (MSS) 165
IP Protocol Performance Tuning Recommendations 167
Ethernet Performance Tuning Recommendations 168
Token Ring (4Mb) Performance Tuning Recommendations 168
Token Ring (16Mb) Performance Tuning Recommendations 168
FDDI Performance Tuning Recommendations 169
ATM Performance Tuning Recommendations 169
SOCC Performance Tuning Recommendations 169
HIPPI Performance Tuning Recommendations 169
AIX Version 3.2.5 mbuf Pool Performance Tuning 170
Overview of the mbuf Management Facility 170
When to Tune the mbuf Pools 171
How to Tune the mbuf Pools 173
UDP, TCP/IP, and mbuf Tuning Parameters Summary 175
thewall 175
sb_max 175
rfc1323 176
udp_sendspace 176
udp_recvspace 176
tcp_sendspace 177
tcp_recvspace 177
ipqmaxlen 177
xmt_que_size 178
rec_que_size 178
MTU 179
NFS Tuning 180
How Many biods and nfsds Are Needed for Good Performance? 180
Performance Implications of Hard or Soft NFS Mounts 182
Tuning to Avoid Retransmits 182
Tuning the NFS File-Attribute Cache 183
Disabling Unused NFS ACL Support 183
Tuning for Maximum Caching of NFS Data 183

Tuning Other Layers to Improve NFS Performance 184
Increasing NFS Socket Buffer Size 184
NFS Server Disk Configuration 184
Hardware Accelerators 185
Misuses of NFS That Affect Performance 185
Serving Diskless Workstations 186
How a Diskless System Is Different 186
NFS Considerations 186
When a Program Runs on a Diskless Workstation 187
Paging 189
Resource Requirements of Diskless Workstations 189
Tuning for Performance 190
Commands Performance 193
Case Study 1—An Office Workload 194
Case Study 2—A Software-Development Workload 196
Tuning Asynchronous Connections for High-Speed Transfers 200
Measurement Objectives and Configurations 200
Results 201
The 8/16 Async Port Adapter 202
The 64-Port Async Adapter 202
The 128-Port Async Adapter 203
Async Port Tuning Techniques 203
fastport for Fast File Transfers 204
Using netpmon to Evaluate Network Performance 205
Using iptrace to Analyze Performance Problems 207

DFS Performance Tuning **210**
DFS Caching on Disk or Memory? 210
DFS Cache Size 211
DFS Cache Chunk Size 211
Number of DFS Cache Chunks 211
Location of DFS Disk Cache 212
Cache Status-Buffer Size 212
Effect of Application Read/Write Size 212
Communications Parameter Settings for DFS 212
DFS File Server Tuning 213
DCE LFS Tuning for DFS Performance 213

Performance Analysis with the Trace Facility **214**
Understanding the Trace Facility 214
Limiting the Amount of Trace Data Collected 215
Starting and Controlling Trace 215
Formatting Trace Data 215
Viewing Trace Data 216
An Example of Trace Facility Use 216
Obtaining a Sample Trace File 216
Formatting the Sample Trace 216

Reading a Trace Report 217
Filtering of the Trace Report 218
Starting and Controlling Trace from the Command Line 218
Controlling Trace in Subcommand Mode 218
Controlling Trace by Commands 219
Starting and Controlling Trace from a Program 219
Controlling Trace with Trace Subroutine Calls 219
Controlling Trace with ioctl Calls 219
Adding New Trace Events 221
Possible Forms of a Trace Event Record 221
Trace Channels 222
Macros for Recording Trace Events 222
Use of Event IDs 223
Examples of Coding and Formatting Events 223
Syntax for Stanzas in the Trace Format File 225

Performance Diagnostic Tool (PDT) **229**
Structure of PDT 229
Scope of PDT Analysis 230
Sample PDT Report 232
Installing and Enabling PDT 234
Customizing PDT 234
Responding to PDT-Report Messages 238

Handling a Possible AIX Performance Bug **243**
Measuring the Baseline 243
Reporting the Problem 243
Obtaining and Installing AIX Version 3.2.5 PerfPMR 244
Installing AIX Version 4.1 PerfPMR 245
Problem-Analysis Data 245

AIX Performance Monitoring and Tuning Commands **248**
Performance Reporting and Analysis Commands 248
Performance Tuning Commands 250
schedtune Command 252
vmtune Command 255
pdt_config Script 258
pdt_report Script 259

Performance-Related Subroutines **260**

Cache and Addressing Considerations **261**
Disclaimer 261
Addressing 261
Cache Lookup 262
TLB Lookup 264
RAM Access 264
Implications 265

Efficient Use of the ld Command **266**
    Rebindable Executables 266
    Prebound Subroutine Libraries 266
    Examples 267

Performance of the Performance Tools **268**
    filemon 268
    fileplace 268
    iostat 268
    lsattr 268
    lslv 269
    netpmon 269
    netstat 269
    nfsstat 269
    PDT 269
    ps 269
    svmon 269
    tprof 269
    trace 269
    vmstat 270

Application Memory Management—malloc and realloc **271**

Performance Effects of Shared Libraries **273**
    Advantages and Disadvantages of Shared Libraries 273
    How to Build Executables Shared or Nonshared 273
    How to Determine If Nonshared Will Help 274

Accessing the ProcessorTimer **275**
    POWER-Architecture-Unique Timer Access 277
    Accessing Timer Registers in PowerPC-Architecture Systems 278
    Example Use of the second Routine 278

National Language Support— Locale vs Speed **280**
    Programming Considerations 280
    Some Simplifying Rules 281
    Controlling Locale 282

Summary of Tunable AIX Parameters **283**
    arpt_killc 283
    biod Count 283
    Disk Adapter Outstanding-Requests Limit 284
    Disk Drive Queue Depth 284
    dog_ticks 284
    fork() Retry Interval 285
    ipforwarding 285
    ipfragttl 285
    ipqmaxlen 286

ipsendredirects 286
loop_check_sum (3.2.5 only) 286
lowclust (3.2.5 only) 286
lowmbuf (3.2.5 only) 287
maxbuf 287
max_coalesce 287
maxfree 288
maxperm 288
maxpgahead 288
maxpin (4.1 only) 289
maxpout 289
maxttl 289
mb_cl_hiwat (3.2.5 only) 290
Memory-Load-Control Parameters 290
minfree 290
minperm 291
minpgahead 291
minpout 291
MTU 292
nfs_chars (3.2.5), nfs_socketsize (4.1) 292
nfsd Count 293
nfs_gather_threshold (4.1 only) 293
nfs_portmon (3.2.5), portcheck (4.1) 293
nfs_repeat_messages (4.1 only) 293
nfs_setattr_error (4.1 only) 294
nfsudpcksum (3.2.5), udpchecksum (4.1) 294
nonlocsrcroute 294
npskill (4.1 only) 294
npswarn (4.1 only) 295
numclust (4.1 only) 295
numfsbuf (4.1 only) 295
Paging Space Size 295
Process-Priority Calculation 296
rec_que_size 296
rfc1122addrchk 297
rfc1323 297
sb_max 297
subnetsarelocal 298
syncd Interval 298
tcp_keepidle 298
tcp_keepintvl 299
tcp_mssdflt 299
tcp_recvspace 299
tcp_sendspace 300
tcp_ttl 300

thewall 300
Time-Slice Expansion Amount 301
udp_recvspace 301
udp_sendspace 301
udp_ttl 302
xmt_que_size 302
Bibliography 303
Glossary 304
Index 309

Preface

This book provides information on concepts, tools, and techniques for assessing and tuning the performance of AIX on RISC System/6000. Topics covered include efficient system and application design and implementation, as well as post-implementation tuning of CPU use, memory use, disk I/O, and communications I/O. Most of the tuning recommendations were developed or validated on AIX Version 3.2.5. Information that applies only to AIX Version 4.1 is so identified in the text.

This book is intended for programmers, system managers, and end users concerned with performance tuning of AIX systems. You should be familiar with the AIX operating environment. Introductory sections are included to assist the less experienced and to acquaint experienced users with AIX performance-tuning terminology.

AIX Performance Management Structure

There are appropriate tools for each phase of AIX system performance management. Some of the tools are available from IBM; others are the products of third parties. The figure illustrates the phases of performance management in a simple LAN environment and some of the tools packages that apply in each phase.

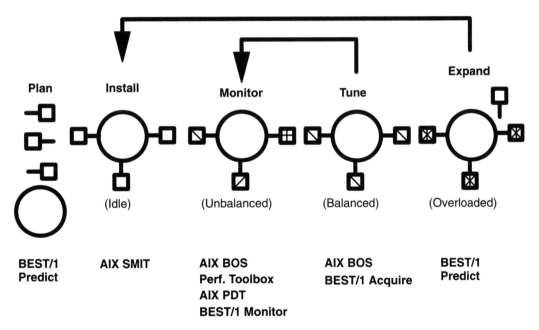

Figure 1. Performance Phases and Corresponding Tools

Performance Tools Packages and Their Documentation

The packaging of the performance tools lets the performance analyst install on any given system only those tools that are required to monitor and tune that system. This packaging changed for AIX Release 4.1. The revised packaging is reflected in the following summary.

BEST/1

BEST/1 is a capacity-planning tool that uses queuing models to predict the performance of a given configuration when processing a specific workload. The prediction can be based on:

- workload descriptions derived from an application design, or
- workload data acquired by monitoring existing systems.

BEST/1 has three main components:

Collect   Collects detailed information about the processing of a workload by an existing system.

Analyze   Transforms the detailed information into reports and a queuing model of the workload-processing activity.

Predict   Uses the queuing model to estimate the performance effects of changes in the workload or the configuration.

BEST/1 for UNIX is a product of BGS Systems, Inc. BGS Systems can be reached at 1-800-891-0000 (in the US).

AIX Performance Diagnostic Tool (PDT)

The Performance Diagnostic Tool, which is an optionally installable component of AIX Version 4.1, assesses the configuration of the system and tracks trends in resource use. If PDT detects an actual or potential performance problem, it reports the situation to the system administrator. This book contains detailed documentation of the functions of PDT, beginning on page 229.

AIX Base Operating System (BOS)

The AIX Base Operating System contains a number of monitoring and tuning tools that have historically been part of UNIX systems or that are required to manage the implementation-specific features of AIX. The BOS functions and commands most important to performance analysts are:

iostat   Reports CPU and I/O statistics.

lsattr   Displays the attributes of devices.

lslv   Displays information about a logical volume or the logical volume allocations of a physical volume.

netstat	Displays the contents of network-related data structures.
nfsstat	Displays statistics about Network File System (NFS) and Remote Procedure Call (RPC) activity.
nice	Runs a command at higher- or lower-than-normal priority.
no	Displays or sets network options.
ps	Displays the status of processes.
renice	Changes the priority of one or more processes.
reorgvg	Reorganizes the physical-partition allocation within a volume group.
sar	Collects and reports or records system-activity information.
time	Prints the elapsed execution time and the user and system processing time attributed to a command.
trace	Records and reports selected system events.
vmstat	Reports virtual-memory activity and other system statistics.

The documentation of the AIX BOS commands is the *AIX Commands Reference Manual*, IBM form number GBOF-1802.

Performance Toolbox (PTX)

The Performance Toolbox for AIX (PTX) contains tools for local and remote system-activity monitoring and tuning. This licensed product consists of two main components: the PTX Manager and the PTX Agent. The PTX Agent is available as a separate licensed product called the Performance Aide for AIX. The figure shows a simplified LAN configuration in which the PTX Manager is being used to monitor the activity of several systems.

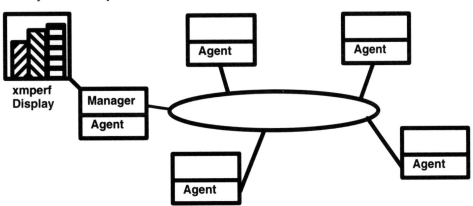

Figure 2. LAN Configuration Using Performance Toolbox

The main purpose of the PTX Manager is to collect and display data from the various systems in the configuration. The primary program for this purpose is **xmperf**. The primary program used by the Agent to collect and transmit data to the Manager is **xmservd**.

In addition to the main PTX components, in AIX Version 4.1 both the Performance Toolbox for AIX and the Performance Aide for AIX licensed products include a set of separate monitoring and tuning tools, most of which were part of the AIX Base Operating System in Version 3.2.5:

fdpr Optimizes an executable program for a particular workload.

filemon Uses the trace facility to monitor and report the activity of the AIX file system.

fileplace Displays the placement of a file's blocks within logical or physical volumes.

lockstat Displays statistics about contention for kernel locks.

lvedit Facilitates interactive placement of logical volumes within a volume group.

netpmon Uses the trace facility to report on network I/O and network-related CPU usage.

rmss Simulates systems with various sizes of memory for performance testing.

svmon Captures and analyzes information about virtual-memory usage.

syscalls Records and counts system calls.

tprof Uses the trace facility to report CPU usage at module and source-code-statement levels.

BigFoot Reports memory access patterns of processes (AIX Version 4.1 only).

stem Permits subroutine-level entry/exit instrumentation of existing executables (AIX Version 4.1 only).

The primary documentation of the commands and functions of PTX is the *AIX Performance Toolbox User's Guide*, IBM form number SC23-2625, although the syntax descriptions of the tools listed above are documented in the *AIX Version 4.1 Commands Reference*. Use of the listed commands is incorporated in various diagnosis and tuning scenarios in this book.

AIX Performance PMR Data Collection Tool (PerfPMR)

The AIX Performance PMR Data Collection Tool (PerfPMR) package is used to collect configuration and performance information to accompany a report of a suspected AIX performance defect. This book contains the primary, detailed documentation of the functions and use of PerfPMR.

Overview of Contents

This book contains the following chapters and appendixes:

- Chapter 1, "Performance Concepts," gives an introduction to the basic considerations of performance analysis. For those who are already experienced in performance tuning, this chapter will be of interest mainly as a guide to AIX terminology.

- Chapter 2, "AIX Resource Management Overview," describes the structures and principal algorithms of the main resource-management components of AIX.
- Chapter 3, "An Introduction to Multiprocessing," provides an overview of the performance aspects of multprocessor systems.
- Chapter 4, "Performance-Conscious Planning, Design, and Implementation," describes the performance considerations that should be taken into account in preparation for an application.
- Chapter 5, "System Monitoring and Initial Performance Diagnosis," explains how to prepare for the detection of performance problems and the preliminary steps to take when such a problem is encountered.
- Chapter 6, "Monitoring and Tuning CPU Use," describes techniques for ensuring that the CPU resource is being used efficiently.
- Chapter 7, "Monitoring and Tuning Memory Use," shows how to determine how much real and virtual storage is being used and how to avoid or detect some common inefficiencies.
- Chapter 8, "Monitoring and Tuning Disk I/O," explains the dynamics of disk I/O in AIX and how those dynamics can be affected by user choices.
- Chapter 9, "Monitoring and Tuning Communications I/O," gives tuning techniques for various forms of communications I/O.
- Chapter 10, "DFS Performance Tuning," describes various parameters of DFS operation that can affect performance.
- Chapter 11, "Performance Analysis with the Trace Facility," gives an extended explanation of the use of the trace facility, which is a powerful tool for detailed performance tuning and also is the base of a number of other tools discussed in this book.
- Chapter 12, "Performance Diagnostic Tool (PDT)," describes a new AIX Version 4.1 tool that assesses configurations for balance and maintains historical performance data to identify performance trends.
- Chapter 13, "Handling a Possible AIX Performance Bug," explains the process of reporting, and providing data about, a possible performance bug in AIX.
- Appendix A, "AIX Performance Monitoring and Tuning Commands," lists the AIX commands that are most helpful in carrying out performance monitoring and tuning tasks and provides detailed documentation of the syntax and functions of the **schedtune**, **vmtune**, **pdt_config**, and **pdt_report** commands.
- Appendix B, "Performance-Related Subroutines," describes several subroutines with performance-related uses.
- Appendix C, "Cache and Addressing Considerations," provides a conceptual discussion of the way caches operate and how they can affect the performance of programs.
- Appendix D, "Efficient Use of the ld Command," describes techniques for using the AIX binder.

- Appendix E, "Performance of the Performance Tools," documents the resource consumption and response time of the performance tools.
- Appendix F, "Application Memory Management," describes the distinction between the original and the current versions of the **malloc** and **realloc** subroutines.
- Appendix G, "Performance Effects of Shared Libraries," describes the performance advantages and disadvantages of shared libraries versus nonshared libraries.
- Appendix H, "Accessing the Processor Timer," describes methods of using the processor timer to compute elapsed-time values.
- Appendix I, "National Language Support—Locale versus Speed," explains the effect that use of the AIX National Language Support facility can have on performance.
- Appendix J, "Summary of Tunable AIX Parameters," documents the AIX operational parameters that can be changed by the user and that have a direct or indirect effect on performance.

Highlighting

The following highlighting conventions are used in this book:

Bold   Identifies commands, subroutines, keywords, files, structures, directories, and other items whose names are predefined by the system. Also identifies graphical objects such as buttons, labels, and icons that the user selects.

Italics   Identifies parameters whose actual names or values are to be supplied by the user.

Monospace   Identifies examples of specific data values, examples of text similar to what you might see displayed, examples of portions of program code similar to what you might write, messages from the system, or information you should actually type.

Acknowledgments

This book is a synthesis of the technical and literary contributions of many people—members of the AIX System Performance group, AIX developers, AIX Information Design and Development personnel, and IBMers around the world. I want to acknowledge particularly the work of Shirley Ackerman, my editor at IBM. Major technical contributors to the book include Matt Accapadi, Virgil Albaugh, Bill Alexander, Robert Berry, Bill Britton, Chij-Mehn Chang, Herman Dierks, Will Fiveash, Xander Fleming, Mike Fortin, Bill Hay, Rajiv Jauhari, Tom Keller, Don Kersch, Bill Maron, Augie Mena, Bret Olszewski, Robert Sur, Brian Twichell, Bob Urquhart, and David Whitworth. Most important, the consistent support of Jerry Kilpatrick and his System Performance management team made the creation of this book both possible and fun.

Frank C. H. Waters
Austin, Texas

1

Performance Concepts

Everyone who uses a computer has an opinion about its performance. Unfortunately, those opinions are often based on oversimplified ideas about the dynamics of program execution. Uninformed intuition can lead to expensive wrong guesses about the capacity of a system and the solutions to the perceived performance problems.

This chapter describes the dynamics of program execution and provides a conceptual framework for evaluating system performance.

How Fast Is That Computer in the Window?

Using words like "speed" and "fast" to describe contemporary computers, while condoned by precedent, is extreme oversimplification. There was a time when one could read a program, calculate the sum of the instruction times, and confidently predict how long it would take the computer to run that program. Thousands of programmers and engineers have spent the last 30 years making such straightforward calculations impossible, or at least meaningless.

Today's computers are more powerful than their ancestors, not just because they use integrated circuits instead of vacuum tubes and have far shorter cycle times, but because of innumerable hardware and software architectural inventions. Each advance in integrated-circuit density brings an advance in computer performance, not just because it allows the same logic to work in a smaller space with a faster system clock, but because it gives engineers more space in which to implement clever ideas. In short, computers have gained capacity by becoming more complex as well as quicker.

The complexity of modern computers and their operating systems is matched by the complexity of the environment in which they operate. In addition to the execution of individual programs, today's computer has to deal with varying numbers of unpredictably timed interrupts from I/O and communications devices. To the extent that the engineers' clever ideas were based on an assumption of a single program running in a standalone machine, they may be partly defeated by the randomness of the real world. To the extent that those ideas were intended to deal with randomness, they may win back some of the loss. The wins and losses change from program to program and from moment to moment.

The net of all these hardware and software wins and losses is the performance of the system. The "speed" of the system is the rate at which it can handle a specific sequence of demands. If the demands mesh well with the system's hardware and software architectures, we can say, "The system runs this workload fast." We can't say, "The system *is* fast"—or at least we shouldn't.

First, Understand the Workload

As you can see, an accurate and complete definition of the system's workload is critical to predicting or understanding its performance. A difference in workload can cause far more variation in the measured performance of a system than differences in CPU clock speed or RAM size. The workload definition must include not only the type and rate of requests to the system but also the exact software packages and in-house application programs to be executed.

Whenever possible, current users of existing applications should be observed to get authentic, real-world measurements of the rates at which users interact with their workstations or terminals.

Make sure that you include the work that your system is doing "under the covers." For example, if your system contains file systems that are NFS-mounted and frequently accessed by other systems, handling those accesses is probably a significant fraction of the overall workload, even though your system is not officially a "server."

A Risky Shortcut: Industry-Standard Benchmarks

A benchmark is a workload that has been standardized to allow comparisons among dissimilar systems. Any benchmark that has been in existence long enough to become "industry-standard" has been studied exhaustively by systems developers. Operating systems, compilers, and in some cases hardware, have been tuned to run the benchmark with lightning speed.

Unfortunately, few real workloads duplicate the exact algorithms and environment of a benchmark. Even those industry-standard benchmarks that were originally derived from real applications may have been simplified and homogenized to make them portable to a wide variety of hardware platforms. The environment in which they run has been constrained in the interests of reproducible measurements.

Bluntly, reasoning of the form "System A is rated at 50% more MegaThings than System B, so System A should run my program 50% faster than System B" may be a tempting shortcut, but it is wrong. There is no benchmark with such universal applicability. The only valid use for industry-standard benchmarks is to narrow the field of candidate systems that will be subjected to a serious evaluation. There is no substitute for developing a clear understanding of *your* workload and its performance in systems under consideration.

Performance Objectives

After defining the workload that the system will have to process, you can choose performance criteria and set performance objectives based on those criteria. The main overall performance criteria of computer systems are *response time* and *throughput*.

Response time is the time from the initiation of an operation until the initiator has enough information to resume work, while throughput is the *number* of workload operations that can be accomplished per unit of time. The relationship between these metrics is complex. In some cases you may have to trade off one against the other. In other situations, a single change can improve both.

In planning for or tuning any system, you should have clear objectives for both response time and throughput when processing the specified workload. Otherwise you risk spending analysis time and resource dollars improving an aspect of system performance that is of secondary importance.

Program Execution Dynamics

Normally, an application programmer thinks of the running program as an uninterrupted sequence of instructions that perform a specified function. Great amounts of inventiveness and effort have been expended on the operating system and hardware to ensure that programmers are not distracted from this idealized view by "irrelevant" space, speed, and multiprogramming/multiprocessing considerations. If the programmer is seduced by this comfortable illusion, the resulting program may be unnecessarily expensive to run—and may not meet its performance objectives.

To think clearly about the performance characteristics of a workload, we need a dynamic, rather than a static, model of program execution, as shown in the figure "Program Execution Hierarchy."

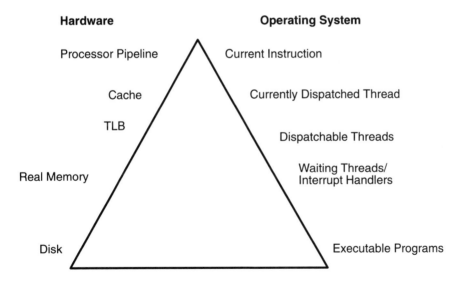

Figure 3. Program Execution Hierarchy

To run, a program must make its way up both the hardware and operating-system hierarchies, more or less in parallel. Each element in the hardware hierarchy is scarcer and more expensive than the element below it. Not only does the program have to contend with other programs for each resource, the *transition* from one level to the next takes time.

To understand the dynamics of program execution, we need to have a basic understanding of each of the levels.

Hardware Hierarchy

Usually, the time required to move from one hardware level to another consists primarily of the *latency* of the lower level—the time from the issuing of a request to the receipt of the first data.

Fixed Disks

By far the slowest operation for a running program (other than waiting on a human keystroke) is obtaining code or data from a disk:

- The disk controller must be directed to access the specified blocks (queuing delay).
- The disk arm must seek to the correct cylinder (seek latency).
- The read/write heads must wait until the correct block rotates under them (rotational latency).
- The data must be transmitted to the controller (transmission time) and then conveyed to the application program (interrupt handling time).

Disk operations can have many causes besides explicit read or write requests in the program. System tuning activities frequently turn out to be hunts for unnecessary disk I/O.

Real Memory

RAM is fast compared to disk, but much more expensive per byte. Operating systems try to keep in RAM the code and data that are currently in use, spilling any excess onto disk (or never bringing them into RAM in the first place).

RAM is not necessarily fast compared to the processor. In the RISC System/6000, a RAM latency of several processor cycles occurs between the time the hardware recognizes the need for a RAM access and the time the data or instruction is available to the processor.

If the access is to a page of virtual memory that has been spilled to disk (or has not been brought in yet), a *page fault* occurs, and the execution of the program is suspended until the page has been read in from disk.

Translation Lookaside Buffers (TLBs)

One of the ways programmers are insulated from the physical limitations of the system is the implementation of virtual memory. The programmer designs and codes the program as though the memory were very large, and the system takes responsibility for translating the program's virtual addresses for instructions and data into the real addresses that are needed to get the instructions and data from RAM. Since this address-translation process is time-consuming, the system keeps the real addresses of recently accessed virtual-memory pages in a cache called the translation lookaside buffer (TLB). As long as the running program continues to access a small set of program and data pages, the full virtual-to-real page-address translation does not need to be redone for each RAM access. When the program tries to access a virtual-memory page that does not have a TLB entry (a *TLB miss*), dozens of processor cycles (the *TLB-miss latency*) are usually required to perform the address translation.

Caches

To minimize the number of times the program has to experience the RAM latency, the RISC System/6000 incorporates caches for instructions and data. If the required instruction or data is already in the cache (a *cache hit*), it is available to the processor on the next cycle (that is, no delay occurs); otherwise (a *cache miss*), the RAM latency occurs.

In some systems there are two levels of cache, usually called L1 and L2. If a particular storage reference results in an L1 miss, L2 is checked. If L2 generates a miss, then the reference goes to RAM.

In the RISC System/6000, the cache sizes and structures vary by model, but the principles of using them efficiently are identical. Appendix C, "Cache and Addressing Considerations", contains a more detailed discussion of cache and TLB architectures for the benefit of the curious and those who envision very low-level program tuning.

Pipeline and Registers

The RISC System/6000's pipelined, superscalar architecture makes possible, under certain circumstances, the simultaneous processing of multiple instructions. Large sets of general-purpose registers and floating-point registers make it possible to keep considerable amounts of the program's data in registers, rather than continually storing and reloading.

The RISC System/6000 optimizing compilers are designed to take maximum advantage of these capabilities. The compilers' optimization functions should always be used when generating production programs, however small. The *Optimization and Tuning Guide for XL Fortran, XL C and XL C++* describes the ways in which programs can be tuned for maximum performance.

Software Hierarchy

To run, a program must also progress through a series of steps in the software hierarchy.

Executable Programs

When a user requests the execution of a program, AIX performs a number of operations to transform the executable program on disk to a running program. First, the directories in the user's current **PATH** environment variable must be scanned to find the correct copy of the program. Then, the system loader (not to be confused with **ld**, the binder) must resolve any external references from the program to shared libraries.

To represent the user's request, the operating system creates a *process*, which is a set of resources, such as a private virtual address segment, required by any running program.

In AIX Version 4.1, the operating system also automatically creates a single thread within that process. A *thread* is the current execution state of a single instance of a program. In AIX Version 4.1, access to the processor and other resources is allocated on a thread basis, rather than a process basis. Multiple threads can be created within a process by the application program. Those threads share the resources owned by the process within which they are running.

Finally, the system branches to the entry point of the program. If the program page that contains the entry point is not already in memory (as it might be if the program had been recently compiler, executed, or copied), the resulting page-fault interrupt causes the page to be read.

Interrupt Handlers

The mechanism for notifying the operating system that an external event has taken place is to interrupt the currently running thread and transfer control to an interrupt handler. Before the interrupt handler can run, enough of the hardware state must be saved to ensure that the system can restore the context of the thread after interrupt handling is complete. Newly invoked interrupt handlers experience all of the delays of moving up the hardware hierarchy (except page faults). Unless the interrupt handler was run very recently (or the intervening programs were very economical), it is unlikely that any of its code or data remains in the TLBs or the caches.

When the interrupted thread is dispatched again, its execution context (such as register contents) is *logically* restored, so that it functions correctly. However, the contents of the TLBs and caches must be reconstructed on the basis of the program's subsequent demands. Thus, both the interrupt handler and the interrupted thread can experience significant cache-miss and TLB-miss delays as a result of the interrupt.

Waiting Threads

Whenever an executing program makes a request that cannot be satisfied immediately, such as an I/O operation (either explicit or as the result of a page fault), that thread is put in a Wait state until the request is complete. Normally, this results in another set of TLB and cache latencies, in addition to the time required for the request itself.

Dispatchable Threads

When a thread is dispatchable, but not actually running, it is accomplishing nothing useful. Worse, other threads that *are* running may cause the thread's *cache lines* (the areas of the cache that contain the instructions and/or data of this thread—see Appendix C) to be re-used and real memory pages to be reclaimed, resulting in even more delays when the thread is finally dispatched.

Currently Dispatched Thread

The scheduler chooses the thread that has the strongest claim to the use of the processor. (The considerations that affect that choice are discussed in "Performance Overview of the AIX CPU Scheduler" on page 14.) When the thread is dispatched, the logical state of the processor is restored to that in effect when the thread was interrupted.

Current Instructions

Most of the machine instructions in a RISC System/6000 are capable of executing in a single processor cycle, *if* no TLB or cache miss occurs. In contrast, if a program branches rapidly to different areas of the executable and/or accesses data from a large number of different areas, causing high TLB and cache miss rates, the *average* number of processor cycles per instruction executed might be much greater than one. The program is said to exhibit poor "locality of reference." It might be using the minimum number of *instructions* necessary to do its job, but consuming an unnecessarily large number of *cycles*. In part because of this poor correlation between number of instructions and number of cycles, sitting down with a program listing to calculate "path length" no longer yields a time value directly. While a shorter path is *usually* faster than a longer path, the speed ratio can be very different from the path-length ratio.

The XL compilers rearrange code in very sophisticated ways to minimize the number of cycles required for the execution of the program. The programmer seeking maximum performance should be primarily concerned with ensuring that the compiler has all the information necessary to optimize effectively, rather than trying to second-guess the compiler's optimization techniques. (See "Effective Use of Preprocessors and the XL Compilers" on page 57.) The real measure of optimization effectiveness is the performance of an authentic workload.

System Dynamics

It's not enough to create the most efficient possible individual programs. In many cases, the actual programs being run were created outside of the control of the person who is responsible for meeting the organization's performance objectives. Further, most of the levels of the hierarchy we have just described are managed by one or more parts of AIX. In any case, once the application programs have been acquired, or implemented as efficiently as possible, further improvement in the overall performance of the system becomes a matter of system tuning. The main components that are subject to system-level tuning are:

Fixed Disk The Logical Volume Manager (LVM) controls the placement of file systems and paging spaces on the disk, which can significantly affect the amount of seek latency the system experiences.

The disk device drivers control the order in which I/O requests are acted on.

Real Memory The Virtual Memory Manager (VMM) controls the pool of free real-memory frames and determines when and from whom to steal frames to replenish the pool.

Running Thread The scheduler determines which dispatchable entity should receive control next. (In AIX Version 4.1 the dispatchable entity changes from a process to a thread. See "AIX Version 4.1 Thread Support" on page 14.)

Communications I/O

Depending on the type of workload and the type of communications link, it may be necessary to tune one or more of the communications device drivers, TCP/IP, or NFS.

Classes of Workload

Workloads tend to fall naturally into a small number of classes. The types that follow are sometimes used to categorize *systems*. However, since a single system often is called upon to process multiple classes, "workload" seems more apt in the context of performance.

Workstation   A workload that consists of a single user submitting work through the native keyboard and receiving results on the native display of the system. Typically, the highest-priority performance objective of such a workload is minimum response time to the user's requests.

Multiuser   A workload that consists of a number of users submitting work through individual terminals. Typically, the performance objectives of such a workload are either to maximize system throughput while preserving a specified worst-case response time or to obtain the best possible response time for a fairly constant workload.

Server   A workload that consists of requests from other systems. For example, a file-server workload is mostly disk read/write requests. In essence, it is the disk-I/O component of a multiuser workload (plus NFS or DFS activity), so the same objective of maximum throughput within a given response-time limit applies. Other server workloads consist of compute-intensive programs, database transactions, print jobs, etc.

When a single system is processing workloads of more than one type, there must be a clear understanding between the users and the performance analyst as to the relative priorities of the possibly conflicting performance objectives of the different workloads.

An Introduction to the Performance-Tuning Process

Performance tuning is primarily a matter of resource management and proper system parameter setting. Tuning the workload and the system for efficient resource use consists of the following steps:

1. Identifying the workloads on the system
2. Setting objectives:
   a. Determining how the results will be measured
   b. Quantifying and prioritizing the objectives
3. Identifying the "critical resources" that limit the system's performance
4. Minimizing the workload's critical-resource requirements:
   a. Using the most appropriate resource, if there is a choice
   b. Reducing the critical-resource requirements of individual programs or system functions
   c. Structuring for parallel resource use
5. Modifying the allocation of resources to reflect priorities
   a. Changing the priority or resource limits of individual programs
   b. Changing the settings of system resource-management parameters
6. Repeating steps 3–5 until objectives are met (or resources are saturated)
7. Applying additional resources, if necessary

Identifying the Workloads

It is essential that *all* of the work performed by the system be identified. Especially in LAN-connected systems, a complex set of cross-mounted file systems can easily develop with only informal agreement among the users of the systems. These must be identified and taken into account as part of any tuning activity.

With multiuser workloads, the analyst must quantify both the typical and peak request rates. It's also important to be realistic about the proportion of the time that a user is actually interacting with the terminal.

An important element of this stage is determining whether the measurement and tuning activity has to be done on the production system or can be accomplished on another system (or off-shift) with a simulated version of the actual workload. The analyst must weigh the greater authenticity of results from a production environment against the flexibility of the nonproduction environment, where the analyst can perform experiments that risk performance degradation or worse.

Setting Objectives

Objectives must be set in terms of measurable quantities, yet the actual desired result is often subjective, such as "satisfactory" response time. Further, the analyst must resist the temptation to tune what is measurable rather than what is important. If no system-provided measurement corresponds to the desired improvement, one must be devised.

The most valuable aspect of quantifying the objectives is not selecting numbers to be achieved, but making a public decision about the relative importance of (usually) multiple objectives. Unless these priorities are set in advance, and understood by all concerned, the analyst cannot make trade-off decisions without incessant consultation and is apt to be surprised by the reaction of users or management to aspects of performance that have been ignored. If the support and use of the system crosses organizational boundaries, a written service-level agreement between the providers and the users may be needed to ensure that there is a clear common understanding of the performance objectives and priorities.

Identifying the Critical Resources

In general, the performance of a given workload is determined by the availability and speed of one or two critical system resources. The analyst must identify those resources correctly or risk falling into an endless trial-and-error operation.

Systems have both real and logical resources. Critical real resources are generally easier to identify, since more system performance tools are available to assess the utilization of real resources. The real resources that most often affect performance are:

- CPU cycles
- Memory
- I/O bus

- Various adapters
- Disk arms
- Disk space
- Network access

Logical resources are less readily identified. Logical resources are generally programming abstractions that partition real resources. The partitioning is done to share and manage the real resource.

Some examples of real resources and the logical resources built on them are:

CPU

- Processor time slice

Memory

- Page frames
- Stacks
- Buffers
- Queues
- Tables
- Locks and semaphores

Disk Space

- Logical volumes
- File systems
- Files
- Partitions

Network Access

- Packets
- Channels

It is important to be aware of logical resources as well as real resources. Threads can be blocked by lack of logical resources just as for lack of real resources, and expanding the underlying real resource does not necessarily ensure that additional logical resources will be created. For example, consider the NFS block I/O daemon (**biod**, see "NFS Tuning" on page 179). A **biod** on the client is required to handle each pending NFS remote I/O request. The number of **biod**s therefore limits the number of NFS I/O operations that can be in progress simultaneously. When a shortage of **biod**s exists, system instrumentation may indicate that the CPU and communications links are only slightly utilized. You may have the false impression that your system is underutilized (and slow), when in fact you have a shortage of **biod**s that is constraining the rest of the resources. A **biod** uses processor cycles and memory, but you cannot fix this problem simply by adding real memory or converting to a faster CPU. The solution is to create more of the logical resource (**biod**s).

Logical resources and bottlenecks can be created inadvertently during application development. A method of passing data or controlling a device may, in effect, create a logical resource. When such resources are created by accident, there are generally no tools to monitor their use and no interface to control their allocation. Their existence may not be appreciated until a specific performance problem highlights their importance.

Minimizing Critical-Resource Requirements

Using the Appropriate Resource

The decision to use one resource over another should be done consciously and with specific goals in mind. An example of a resource choice during application development would be a trade-off of increased memory consumption for reduced CPU consumption. A common system configuration decision that demonstrates resource choice is whether to place files locally on an individual workstation or remotely on a server.

Reducing the Requirement for the Critical Resource

For locally developed applications, the programs can be reviewed for ways to perform the same function more efficiently or to remove unnecessary function. At a system-management level, low-priority workloads that are contending for the critical resource can be moved to other systems or run at other times.

Structuring for Parallel Use of Resources

Since workloads require multiple system resources to run, take advantage of the fact that the resources are separate and can be consumed in parallel. For example, the AIX system read-ahead algorithm detects the fact that a program is accessing a file sequentially and schedules additional sequential reads to be done in parallel with the application's processing of the previous data. Parallelism applies to system management as well. For example, if an application accesses two or more files at the same time, adding a disk drive may improve the disk-I/O rate if the files that are accessed at the same time are placed on different drives.

Reflecting Priorities in Resource Allocation

AIX provides a number of ways of prioritizing activities. Some, such as disk pacing, are set at the system level. Others, such as process priority, can be set by individual users to reflect the importance they attach to a specific task.

Repeating the Tuning Steps

A truism of performance analysis is that "there is always a next bottleneck." Reducing the use of one resource means that another resource limits throughput or response time. Suppose, for example, we have a system in which the utilization levels are:

CPU: 90%   Disk: 70%   Memory 60%

This workload is CPU-bound. If we successfully tune the workload so that the CPU load is reduced from 90 to 45%, we might expect a two-fold improvement in performance. Unfortunately, the workload is now I/O-limited, with utilizations of about:

CPU: 45%   Disk: 90%   Memory 60%

The improved CPU utilization allows the programs to submit disk requests sooner, but then we hit the ceiling imposed by the disk drive's capacity. The performance improvement is perhaps 30% instead of the 100% we had envisioned.

There is always a new critical resource. The important question is whether we have met the performance objectives with the resources at hand.

Applying Additional Resources

If, after all of the preceding approaches have been exhausted, the performance of the system still does not meet its objectives, the critical resource must be enhanced or expanded. If the critical resource is logical and the underlying real resource is adequate, the logical resource can be expanded for no additional cost. If the critical resource is real, the analyst must investigate some additional questions:

- How much must the critical resource be enhanced or expanded so that it ceases to be a bottleneck?
- Will the performance of the system then meet its objectives, or will another resource become saturated first?
- If there will be a succession of critical resources, is it more cost effective to enhance or expand all of them, or to divide the current workload with another system?

Performance Benchmarking—the Inevitable Dirtiness of Performance Data

When we attempt to compare the performance of a given piece of software in different environments, we are subject to a number of possible errors—some technical, some conceptual. The following section is mostly cautionary. Other sections of this book discuss the various ways in which elapsed and process–specific times can be measured.

When we measure the elapsed ("wall-clock") time required to process a system call, we get a number that consists of:

- The actual time during which the instructions to perform the service were executing
- Varying amounts of time during which the processor was stalled while waiting for instructions or data from memory (i.e., the cost of cache and/or TLB misses)
- The time required to access the "clock" at the beginning and end of the call
- Time consumed by periodic events such as system timer interrupts
- Time consumed by more or less random events such as I/O interrupts

To avoid reporting an inaccurate number, we normally measure the workload a number of times. Since all of the extraneous factors *add* to the actual processing time, the typical set of measurements has a curve of the form:

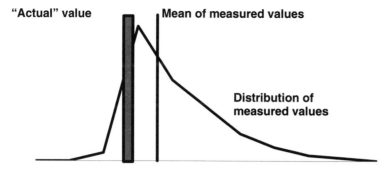

The extreme low end may represent a low-probability optimum caching situation or may be a rounding effect.

A regularly recurring extraneous event might give the curve a bimodal form (two maxima), such as:

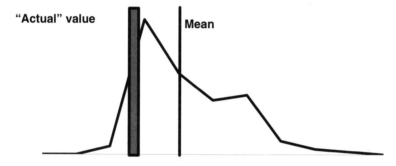

One or two time-consuming interrupts might skew the curve even further:

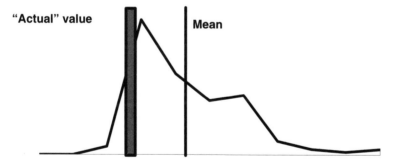

The distribution of the measurements about the "actual" value is not random, and the classic tests of inferential statistics can be applied only with great caution (or chutspah). Also, depending on the purpose of the measurement, it may be that neither the mean nor the "actual" value is an appropriate characterization of performance.

2

AIX Resource Management Overview

This chapter describes the components of AIX that manage the resources that have the most effect on system performance, and the ways in which these components can be tuned. Specific tuning recommendations appear in the chapters on tuning individual resources.

Performance Overview of the AIX CPU Scheduler

The addition of thread support to AIX Version 4.1 has resulted in extensive changes to the CPU scheduler. Conceptually, the scheduling algorithm and priority scheme are similar to those of AIX Version 3.2.5, but the addition of thread support required many detail-level changes. Although the net behavioral change for unchanged applications running on uniprocessors may be small, anyone concerned with performance tuning should understand the changes and the opportunities.

AIX Version 4.1 Thread Support

A *thread* can be thought of as a low-overhead process. It is a dispatchable entity that requires fewer resources to create than an AIX process. The fundamental dispatchable entity of the AIX Version 4.1 scheduler is the thread.

This does not mean that processes have ceased to exist. In fact, workloads migrated directly from earlier releases of AIX will create and manage processes as before. Each new process will be created with a single thread that has its parent process's priority and contends for the CPU with the threads of other processes. The process owns the resources used in execution; the thread owns only its current state.

When new or modified applications take advantage of AIX thread support to create additional threads, those threads are created within the context of the process. They share the process's private segment and other resources.

A user thread within a process has specified *contention scope*. If the contention scope is *global*, the thread contends for CPU time with all other threads in the system. (The thread that is created when a process is created has global contention scope.) If the contention scope is *local*, the thread contends with the other threads within the process to be the recipient of the process's share of CPU time.

The algorithm for determining which thread should be run next is called a scheduling policy.

Scheduling Policy for Threads with Local or Global Contention Scope

In AIX Version 4.1 there are three possible values for thread scheduling policy:

FIFO   Once a thread with this policy is scheduled, it runs to completion unless it is blocked, it voluntarily yields control of the CPU, or a higher-priority thread becomes dispatchable. Only fixed-priority threads can have a FIFO scheduling policy.

RR   This is similar to the AIX Version 3 scheduler round-robin scheme based on 10ms time slices. When a RR thread has control at the end of the time slice, it moves to the tail of the queue of dispatchable threads of its priority. Only fixed-priority threads can have a RR scheduling policy.

OTHER   This policy is defined by POSIX1003.4a as implementation-defined. In AIX version 4.1, this policy is defined to be equivalent to RR, except that it applies to threads with non-fixed priority. The recalculation of the running thread's priority value at each clock interrupt means that a thread may lose control because its priority value has risen above that of another dispatchable thread. This is the AIX Version 3 behavior.

Threads are primarily of interest for applications that currently consist of several asynchronous processes. These applications might impose a lighter load on the system if converted to a multithread structure.

Process and Thread Priority

The priority management tools in AIX Version 3.2.5 manipulate process priority. In AIX Version 4.1, process priority is simply a precursor to thread priority. When **fork()** is called, a process and a thread to run in it are created. The thread has the priority that would have been attributed to the process in Version 3.2.5. The following general discussion applies to both versions.

The kernel maintains a *priority value* (sometimes termed the *scheduling priority*) for each thread. The priority value is a positive integer and varies inversely with the importance of the associated thread. That is, a smaller priority value indicates a more important thread. When the scheduler is looking for a thread to dispatch, it chooses the dispatchable thread with the smallest priority value.

A thread can be *fixed-priority* or *nonfixed priority*. The priority value of a fixed-priority thread is constant, while the priority value of a nonfixed priority thread is the sum of the minimum priority level for user threads (a constant 40), the thread's *nice* value (20 by default, optionally set by the **nice** or **renice** command), and its CPU-usage penalty. The figure "How the Priority Value is Determined" illustrates some of the ways in which the priority value can change.

The nice value of a thread is set when the thread is created and is constant over the life of the thread, unless explicitly changed by the user via the **renice** command or the **setpri** , **setpriority**, or **nice** system calls.

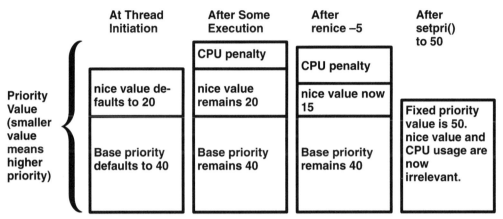

Figure 4. How the Priority Value is Determined

The CPU penalty is an integer that is calculated from the recent CPU usage of a thread. The recent CPU usage increases by 1 each time the thread is in control of the CPU at the end of a 10ms clock tick, up to a maximum value of 120. Once per second, the recent CPU usage values for all threads are reduced. The result is that:

- The priority of a nonfixed-priority thread decreases as its recent CPU usage increases and vice versa. This implies that, on average, the more time slices a thread has been allocated recently, the less likely it is that the thread will be allocated the next time slice.
- The priority of a nonfixed-priority thread decreases as its nice value increases, and vice versa.

The priority of a thread can be fixed at a certain value via the **setpri** subroutine. The priority value, nice value, and short-term CPU-usage values for a process can be displayed with the **ps** command.

See "Controlling Contention for the CPU" on page 104 for a more detailed discussion of the use of the **nice** and **renice** commands.

See "Tuning the Process-Priority-Value Calculation with **schedtune**" on page 107, for the details of the calculation of the CPU penalty and the decay of the recent CPU usage values.

AIX Scheduler Run Queue

The scheduler maintains a *run queue* of all of the threads that are ready to be dispatched. The figure labelled "Run Queue" depicts the run queue symbolically.

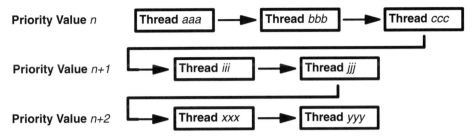

Figure 5. Run Queue

All the dispatchable threads of a given priority occupy consecutive positions in the run queue.

When a thread is moved to the "end of the run queue" (for example, when the thread has control at the end of a time slice), it is moved to a position after the last thread in the queue that has the same priority value.

Scheduler CPU Time Slice

The CPU time slice is the period between recalculations of the priority value. Normally, recalculation is done at each tick of the system clock, that is, every 10 milliseconds. The –t option of the **schedtune** command (see page 252) can be used to increase the number of clock ticks between recalculations, increasing the length of the time slice by 10 millisecond increments. Keep in mind that the time slice is not a *guaranteed* amount of processor time. It is the *longest* time that a thread can be in control before it faces the possibility of being replaced by another thread. There are many ways in which a thread can lose control of the CPU before it has had control for a full time slice.

Performance Overview of the Virtual Memory Manager (VMM)

The RISC System/6000 Virtual Address space is partitioned into segments (see Appendix C, "Cache and Addressing Considerations" for an extensive discussion of the virtual-addressing structure). A segment is a 256MB, contiguous portion of the virtual-memory address space into which a data object can be mapped. Process addressability to data is managed at the segment (or object) level so that a segment can be shared between processes or maintained as private. For example, processes can share code segments yet have separate and private data segments.

Real-Memory Management

Virtual-memory segments are partitioned into fixed-size units called *pages*. In AIX, the page size is 4096 bytes. Each page in a segment can be in real memory (RAM), or stored on disk until it is needed. Similarly, real memory is divided into 4096-byte *page frames*. The role of the VMM is to manage the allocation of real-memory page frames and to resolve references by the program to virtual-memory pages that are not currently in real memory or do not yet exist (for example, when a process makes the first reference to a page of its data segment).

Since the amount of virtual memory that is in use at any given instant may be larger than real memory, the VMM must store the surplus on disk. From the performance standpoint, the VMM has two, somewhat opposed, objectives:

- Minimize the overall processor-time and disk-bandwidth cost of the use of virtual memory.
- Minimize the response-time cost of page faults.

In pursuit of these objectives, the VMM maintains a *free list* of page frames that are available to satisfy a page fault. The VMM uses a *page-replacement algorithm* to determine which virtual-memory pages currently in memory will have their page frames reassigned to the free list. The page-replacement algorithm uses several mechanisms:

- Virtual-memory segments are classified into persistent segments or working segments.
- Virtual-memory segments are classified as containing computational or file memory.
- Virtual-memory pages whose access causes a page fault are tracked.
- Page faults are classified as new-page faults or as repage faults.
- Statistics are maintained on the rate of repage faults in each virtual-memory segment.
- User-tunable thresholds influence the page-replacement algorithm's decisions.

The following sections describe the free list and the page-replacement mechanisms in more detail.

Free List

The VMM maintains a list of free page frames that it uses to accommodate page faults. In most environments, the VMM must occasionally add to the free list by reassigning some page frames owned by running processes. The virtual-memory pages whose page frames are to be reassigned are selected by the VMM's page-replacement algorithm. The number of frames reassigned is determined by the VMM thresholds.

In AIX Version 3, the contents of page frames are not lost when the page frames are reassigned to the free list. If a virtual-memory page is referenced before the frame it occupies is actually used to satisfy a page fault, the frame is removed from the free list and reassigned to the faulting process. This is phenomenon is termed a *reclaim*. Reclaiming is not supported in AIX Version 4.1.

Persistent vs Working Segments

The pages of a *persistent segment* have permanent storage locations on disk. Files containing data or executable programs are mapped to persistent segments. Since each page of a persistent segment has a permanent disk storage location, the VMM writes the page back to that location when the page has been changed and can no longer be kept in real memory. If the page has not changed, its frame is simply reassigned to the free list. If the page is referenced again later, a new copy is read in from its permanent disk-storage location.

Working segments are transitory, exist only during their use by a process, and have no permanent disk-storage location. Process stack and data regions are mapped to working segments, as are the kernel text segment, the kernel-extension text segments and the shared-library text and data segments. Pages of working segments must also have disk-storage locations to occupy when they cannot be kept in real memory. The disk paging space is used for this purpose.

The figure "Persistent and Working Storage Segments" illustrates the relationship beween some of the types of segment and the locations of their pages on disk. It also shows the actual (arbitrary) locations of the pages when they are in real memory.

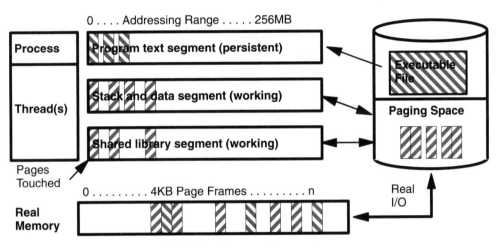

Figure 6. Persistent and Working Storage Segments

There are further classifications of the persistent-segment types. *Client segments* are used to map remote files (for example, files that are being accessed via NFS), including remote executables. Pages from client segments are saved and restored over the network to their permanent file location, not on the local-disk paging space. Journaled and deferred segments are persistent segments that must be atomically updated. If a page from a journaled or deferred segment is selected to be removed from real memory (*paged out*), it must be written to disk paging space unless it is in a state that allows it to be committed (written to its permanent file location).

Computational vs File Memory

Computational memory consists of the pages that belong to working-storage segments or program text segments. (A segment is considered to be a program text segment if an instruction cache miss occurs on any of its pages.) *File memory* consists of the remaining pages.

Repaging

A page fault is considered to be either a *new page fault* or a *repage fault*. A new page fault occurs when there is no record of the page having been referenced recently. A repage fault occurs when a page that is known to have been referenced recently is referenced again, and is not found in memory because the page has been replaced (and perhaps written to disk) since it was last accessed. A perfect (clairvoyant) page-replacement policy would eliminate repage faults entirely (assuming adequate real memory) by always stealing frames from pages that are not going to be referenced again. Thus, the number of repage faults is an inverse measure of the effectiveness of the page-replacement algorithm in keeping frequently reused pages in memory, thereby reducing overall I/O demand and potentially improving system performance.

In order to classify a page fault as new or repage, the VMM maintains a *repage history buffer* that contains the page IDs of the N most recent page faults, where N is the number of frames that the memory can hold. For example, a 16MB memory requires a 4096-entry repage history buffer. At page in, if the page's ID is found in the repage history buffer, it is counted as a repage. Also, the VMM estimates the computational-memory repaging rate and the file-memory repaging rate separately by maintaining counts of repage faults for each type of memory. The repaging rates are multiplied by 0.9 each time the page-replacement algorithm runs, so that they reflect recent repaging activity more strongly than historical repaging activity.

VMM Thresholds

Several numerical thresholds define the objectives of the VMM. When one of these thresholds is breached, the VMM takes appropriate action to bring the state of memory back within bounds. This section discusses the thresholds that can be altered by the system administrator via the **vmtune** command.

The number of page frames on the free list is controlled by:

minfree   Minimum acceptable number of real-memory page frames in the free list. When the size of the free list falls below this number, the VMM begins stealing pages. It continues stealing pages until the size of the free list reaches **maxfree**.

maxfree   Maximum size to which the free list will grow by VMM page stealing. The size of the free list may exceed this number as a result of processes terminating and freeing their working-segment pages or the deletion of files that have pages in memory.

The VMM attempts to keep the size of the free list greater than or equal to **minfree**. When page faults and/or system demands cause the free list size to fall below **minfree**, the page-replacement algorithm is run. The size of the free list must be kept above a certain level (the default value of **minfree**) for several reasons. For example, the AIX sequential-prefetch algorithm requires several frames at a time for each process that is doing sequential reads. Also, the VMM must avoid deadlocks within the operating system itself, which could occur if there were not enough space to read in a page that was required in order to free a page frame.

The following thresholds are expressed as percentages. They represent the fraction of the total real memory of the machine that is occupied by file pages—pages of noncomputational segments.

minperm   If the percentage of real memory occupied by file pages falls below this level, the page-replacement algorithm steals both file and computational pages, regardless of repage rates.

maxperm   If the percentage of real memory occupied by file pages rises above this level, the page-replacement algorithm steals only file pages.

When the percentage of real memory occupied by file pages is between **minperm** and **maxperm**, the VMM normally steals only file pages, but if the repaging rate for file pages is higher than the repaging rate for computational pages, computational pages are stolen as well.

The main intent of the page-replacement algorithm is to ensure that computational pages are given fair treatment; for example, the sequential reading of a long data file into memory should not cause the loss of program text pages that are likely to be used again soon. The page-replacement algorithm's use of the thresholds and repaging rates ensures that both types of pages get treated fairly, with a slight bias in favor of computational pages.

VMM Memory Load Control Facility

When a process references a virtual-memory page that is on disk, because it either has been paged out or has never been read, the referenced page must be paged in and, on average, one or more pages must be paged out, creating I/O traffic and delaying the progress of the process.

AIX attempts to steal real memory from pages that are unlikely to be referenced in the near future, via the page-replacement algorithm. A successful page-replacement algorithm allows the operating system to keep enough processes active in memory to keep the CPU busy. But at some level of competition for memory—depending on the total amount of memory in the system, the number of processes, the time-varying memory requirements of each process, and the page-replacement algorithm—no pages are good candidates for paging out to disk because they will all be reused in the near future by the active set of processes.

When this happens, continuous paging in and paging out occurs. This condition is called *thrashing*. Thrashing results in incessant I/O to the paging disk and causes each process to encounter a page fault almost as soon as it is dispatched, with the result that none of the processes make any significant progress. The most pernicious aspect of thrashing is that, although thrashing may have been triggered by a brief, random peak in workload (such as all of the users of a system happening to hit the Enter key in the same second), the system may continue thrashing for an indefinitely long time.

AIX has a memory load control algorithm that detects when the system is starting to thrash and then suspends active processes and delays the initiation of new processes for a period of time. Five parameters set rates and bounds for the algorithm. The default values of these parameters have been chosen to "fail safe" across a wide range of workloads. For special situations, a mechanism for tuning (or disabling) load control is available (see "Tuning VMM Memory Load Control" on page 124).

Memory Load Control Algorithm

The memory load control mechanism assesses, once a second, whether sufficient memory is available for the set of active processes. When a *memory overcommitment* condition is detected, some processes are suspended, decreasing the number of active processes and thereby decreasing the level of memory overcommitment. When a process is suspended, all of its threads are suspended when they reach a suspendable state. The pages of the suspended processes quickly become stale and are paged out via the page replacement algorithm, releasing enough page frames to allow the remaining active processes to progress. During the interval in which existing processes are suspended, newly created processes are also suspended, preventing new work from entering the system. Suspended processes are not reactivated until a subsequent interval passes during which no potential thrashing condition exists. Once this *safe interval* has passed, the threads of the suspended processes are gradually reactivated.

Memory load control parameters specify: the system memory overcommitment threshold; the number of seconds required to make a safe interval; the individual process's memory overcommitment threshold by which an individual process is qualified as a suspension candidate; the minimum number of active processes when processes are being suspended; and the minimum number of elapsed seconds of activity for a process after reactivation.

These parameters and their default values (shown in parentheses) are:

h *H*igh memory-overcommitment threshold (6)

w *W*ait to reactivate suspended processes (1 second)

p *P*rocess memory-overcommitment threshold (4)

m *M*inimum degree of multiprogramming (2)

e *E*lapsed time exempt from suspension (2 seconds)

All parameters are positive integer values.

The h Parameter

The h parameter controls the threshold defining memory overcommitment. Memory load control attempts to suspend processes when this threshold is exceeded during any one-second period. The threshold is a relationship between two direct measures: the number of pages written to paging space in the last second, and the number of page steals occurring in the last second. The number of page writes is *usually* much less than the number of page steals. Memory is considered overcommitted when:

$$\frac{\text{number of page writes in last second}}{\text{number of page steals in last second}} > \frac{1}{h}$$

As this fraction increases, thrashing becomes more likely. The default value of 6 for h means that the system is considered to be likely to thrash when the fraction of page writes to page steals exceeds 17%. A lower value of h (which can be as low as zero—the test is made without an actual division) raises the thrashing detection threshold; that is, the system is allowed to come closer to thrashing before processes are suspended. The above fraction was chosen as a thrashing threshold because it is comparatively configuration-independent. Regardless of the disk paging capacity and the number of megabytes of memory installed in the system, when the above fraction is low, thrashing is unlikely. For values near 1.0, thrashing is certain. Any period of time in which memory is not overcommitted we define as a safe period.

The w Parameter

The w parameter controls the number of one-second intervals during which the above fraction must remain below $1/h$ before suspended processes are reactivated. The default value of one second is close to the minimum value allowed, zero. A value of one second aggressively attempts to reactivate processes as soon as a one-second safe period has occurred. Large values of w run the risk of unnecessarily poor response times for suspended processes, while the processor is idle for lack of active processes to run.

The p Parameter

The p parameter determines whether a process is eligible for suspension. Analogous to the h parameter, the p parameter is used to set a threshold for the ratio of two measures that are maintained for every process. The two measures are the number of *repages* (defined in the earlier section on page replacement) that the process has accumulated in the last second and the number of page faults that the process has accumulated in the last second. A high ratio of repages to page faults means the individual process is thrashing. A process is considered eligible for suspension (it is thrashing or contributing to overall thrashing) when:

$$\frac{\text{number of repages in last second}}{\text{number of page faults in last second}} > \frac{1}{p}$$

The default value of p is 4, meaning that a process is considered to be thrashing (and a candidate for suspension) when the fraction of repages to page faults over the last second is greater than 25%. A low value of p (which can be as low as zero—the test is made without an actual division) results in a higher degree of individual process thrashing being allowed before a process is eligible for suspension. A value of zero means that no process can be suspended by memory load control.

The m Parameter

The m parameter determines a lower limit for the degree of multiprogramming. The degree of multiprogramming is defined as the number of active (not suspended) processes. (Each process is counted as one, regardless of the number of threads running in it.) Excluded from the count are the kernel process and processes with (1) fixed priorities with priority values less than 60, (2) pinned memory or (3) awaiting events, since no process in these categories is ever eligible for suspension. The default value of 2 ensures that at least two user processes are always able to be active. Lower values of m, while allowed, mean that at times as few as one user process may be active. High values of m effectively defeat the ability of memory load control to suspend processes. This parameter is very sensitive to configuration and workload. Too small a value of m in a large configuration results in overly aggressive suspension; too large a value of *m* for a small-memory configuration does not allow memory load control to be aggressive enough. The default value of 2 is a fail-safe value for small-memory configurations; it is likely to be suboptimal for large configurations in which many tens of processes can and should be active to exploit available resources.

For example, if one knows that for a particular configuration and a particular workload, approximately 25 concurrent processes can successfully progress, while more than 25 concurrent processes run the risk of thrashing, then setting *m* to 25 may be a worthwhile experiment.

The e Parameter

Each time a suspended process is reactivated, it is exempt from suspension for a period of *e* elapsed seconds. This is to ensure that the high cost (in disk I/O) of paging in a suspended process's pages results in a reasonable opportunity for progress. The default value of *e* is 2 seconds.

Once per second, the scheduler (process 0) examines the values of all the above measures that have been collected over the preceding one-second interval, and determines if processes are to be suspended or activated. If processes are to be suspended, every process eligible for suspension by the *p* and *e* parameter test is marked for suspension. When that process next receives the CPU in user mode, it is suspended (unless doing so would reduce the number of active processes below *m*). The user-mode criterion is applied so that a process is ineligible for suspension during critical system activities performed on its behalf. If, during subsequent one-second intervals, the thrashing criterion is still being met, additional process candidates meeting the criteria set by *p* and *e* are marked for suspension. When the scheduler subsequently determines that the safe-interval criterion has been met and processes are to be reactivated, some number of suspended processes are put on the run queue (made active) every second.

Suspended processes are reactivated (1) by priority and (2) by the order in which they were suspended. The suspended processes are not all reactivated at once. A value for the number of processes reactivated is selected by a formula that recognizes the number of then-active processes and reactivates either one-fifth of the number of then-active processes or a monotonically increasing lower bound, whichever is greater. This cautious strategy results in increasing the degree of multiprogramming roughly 20% per second. The intent of this strategy is to make the rate of reactivation relatively slow during the first second after the safe interval has expired, while steadily increasing the reintroduction rate in subsequent seconds. If the memory-overcommitment condition recurs during the course of reactivating processes, reactivation is halted; the "marked to be reactivated" processes are again marked suspended; and additional processes are suspended in accordance with the above rules.

The six parameters of the memory-load-control facility can be set by the system administrator via the **schedtune** command. Techniques for tuning the memory-load-control facility are described in Chapter 6, "Monitoring and Tuning Memory Use."

Allocation and Reclamation of Paging Space Slots

AIX supports two schemes for allocation of paging-space slots. Under the normal, *late-allocation* algorithm, a paging slot is allocated to a page of virtual memory only when that page is first read from or written into. That is the first time that the page's content is of interest to the executing program.

Many programs exploit late allocation by allocating virtual-memory address ranges for maximum-sized structures and then only using as much of the structure as the situation requires. The pages of the virtual-memory address range that are never accessed never require real-memory frames or paging-space slots.

This technique does involve some degree of risk. If all of the programs running in a machine happened to encounter maximum-size situations simultaneously, paging space might be exhausted. Some programs might not be able to continue to completion.

The second AIX paging-space-slot-allocation scheme is intended for use in installations where this situation is likely, or where the cost of failure to complete is intolerably high. Aptly called *early allocation*, this algorithm causes the appropriate number of paging-space slots to be allocated at the time the virtual-memory address range is allocated, for example, with **malloc**. If there are not enough paging-space slots to support the **malloc**, an error code is set. The early-allocation algorithm is invoked with:

```
export PSALLOC=early
```

This causes all future programs **exec**ed in the environment to use early allocation. It does not affect the currently executing shell.

Early allocation is of interest to the performance analyst mainly because of its paging-space size implications. Many existing programs make use of the "**malloc** a lot, use what you need" technique. If early allocation is turned on for those programs, paging-space requirements can increase many fold. Whereas the normal recommendation for paging-space size is at least twice the size of the system's real memory, the recommendation for systems that use PSALLOC=early is at least four times real memory size. Actually, this is just a starting point. You really need to analyze the virtual storage requirements of your workload and allocate paging spaces to accomodate them. As an example, at one time the AIXwindows server required 250MB of paging space when run with early allocation.

You should remember, too, that paging-space slots are only released by process (not thread) termination or by the **disclaim** system call. They are *not* released by **free**.

See "Placement and Sizes of Paging Spaces" on page 69 for more information on paging space allocation and monitoring.

Performance Overview of AIX Management of Fixed-Disk Storage

The figure "Organization of Fixed-Disk Data (Unmirrored)" illustrates the hierarchy of structures used by AIX to manage fixed-disk storage. Each individual disk drive, called a *physical volume* (PV), has a name, such as /dev/hdisk0. If the physical volume is in use, it belongs to a *volume group* (VG). All of the physical volumes in a volume group are divided into *physical partitions* or PPs of the same size (by default, 2MB in volume groups that include physical volumes smaller than 300MB; 4MB otherwise). For space-allocation purposes, each physical volume is divided into five regions (outer_edge, outer_middle, center, inner_middle, and inner_edge). The number of physical partitions in each region varies, depending on the total capacity of the disk drive.

Within each volume group, one or more *logical volumes* (LVs) are defined. Each logical volume consists of one or more logical partitions. Each logical partition corresponds to at least one physical partition. If mirroring is specified for the logical volume, additional physical partitions are allocated to store the additional copies of each logical partition. Although the logical partitions are numbered consecutively, the underlying physical partitions are not necessarily consecutive or contiguous.

Logical volumes can serve a number of system purposes, such as paging, but each logical volume that holds ordinary system or user data or programs contains a single journaled file system (JFS). Each JFS consists of a pool of page-size (4096-byte) blocks. When data is to be written to a file, one or more additional blocks are allocated to that file. These blocks may or may not be contiguous with one another and/or with other blocks previously allocated to the file.

In AIX Version 4.1, a given file system can be defined as having a fragment size of less than 4096 bytes. Fragment size can be 512, 1024, or 2048 bytes. This allows small files to be stored more efficiently.

For purposes of illustration, the figure shows a bad (but not the worst possible) situation that might arise in a file system that had been in use for a long period without reorganization. The file **/op/filename** is physically recorded on a large number of blocks that are physically distant from one another. Reading the file sequentially would result in many time-consuming seek operations.

While an AIX file is conceptually a sequential and contiguous string of bytes, the physical reality may be very different. *Fragmentation* may arise from multiple extensions to logical volumes as well as allocation/release/reallocation activity within a file system. We say a file system is fragmented when its available space consists of large numbers of small chunks of space, making it impossible to write out a new file in contiguous blocks.

Access to files in a highly fragmented file system may result in a large number of seeks and longer I/O response times (seek latency dominates I/O response time). For example, if the file is accessed sequentially, a file placement that consists of many, widely separated chunks requires more seeks than a placement that consists of one or a few large contiguous chunks. If the file is accessed randomly, a placement that is widely dispersed requires longer seeks than a placement in which the file's blocks are close together.

The effect of a file's placement on I/O performance diminishes when the file is buffered in memory. When a file is opened in AIX, it is mapped to a persistent data segment in virtual memory. The segment represents a virtual buffer for the file; the file's blocks map directly to segment pages. The VMM manages the segment pages, reading file blocks into segment pages upon demand (as they are accessed). There are several circumstances that cause the VMM to write a page back to its corresponding block in the file on disk; but, in general, the VMM keeps a page in memory if it has been accessed

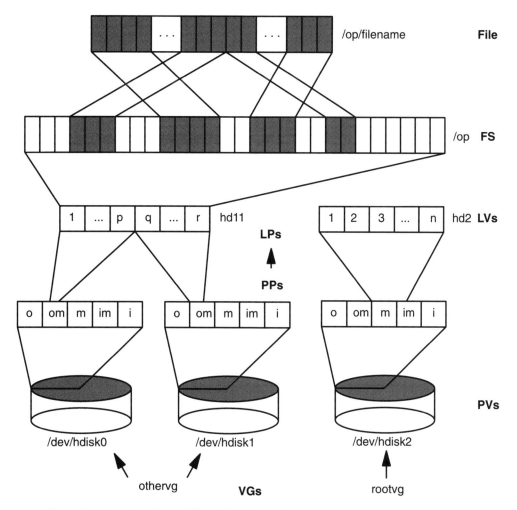

Figure 7. Organization of Fixed-Disk Data (Unmirrored)

recently. Thus, frequently accessed pages tend to stay in memory longer, and logical file accesses to the corresponding blocks can be satisfied without physical disk accesses.

At some point, the user or system administrator may choose to reorganize the placement of files within logical volumes and the placement of logical volumes within physical volumes to reduce fragmentation and to more evenly distribute the total I/O load. "Monitoring and Tuning Disk I/O" on page 130 contains an extensive discussion of detecting and correcting disk placement and fragmentation problems.

Sequential-Access Read Ahead

The VMM tries to anticipate the future need for pages of a sequential file by observing the pattern in which a program is accessing the file. When the program accesses two successive pages of the file, the VMM assumes that the program will continue to access the file sequentially, and the VMM schedules additional sequential reads of the file. These

27

reads are overlapped with the program processing, and will make the data available to the program sooner than if the VMM had waited for the program to access the next page before initiating the I/O. The number of pages to be read ahead is determined by two VMM thresholds:

minpgahead   Number of pages read ahead when the VMM first detects the sequential access pattern. If the program continues to access the file sequentially, the next read ahead will be for 2 times **minpgahead**, the next for 4 times **minpgahead**, and so on until the number of pages reaches **maxpgahead**.

maxpgahead   Maximum number of pages the VMM will read ahead in a sequential file.

If the program deviates from the sequential-access pattern and accesses a page of the file out of order, sequential read ahead is terminated. It will be resumed with **minpgahead** pages if the VMM detects a resumption of sequential access by the program. The values of **minpgahead** and **maxpgahead** can be set with the **vmtune** command. "Tuning Sequential Read Ahead" on page 141 contains a more extensive discussion of read ahead and the groundrules for changing the thresholds.

Write Behind

To increase write performance, limit the number of dirty file pages in memory, reduce system overhead, and minimize disk fragmentation, the file system divides each file into 16KB partitions. The pages of a given partition are not written to disk until the program writes the first byte of the next 16KB partition. At that point, the file system forces the four dirty pages of the first partition to be written to disk. The pages of data remain in memory until their frames are re-used, at which point no additional I/O is required. If a program accesses any of the pages before their frames are re-used, no I/O is required.

The size of the write-behind partitions can be changed with the **vmtune** command.

Memory Mapped Files and Write Behind

Normal AIX files are automatically mapped to segments to provide mapped files. This means that normal file access bypasses traditional kernel buffers and block I/O routines, allowing files to use more memory when the extra memory is available (file caching is not limited to the declared kernel buffer area).

Files can be mapped explicitly with **shmat** or **mmap**, but this provides no additional memory space for their caching. Applications that **shmat** or **mmap** a file explicitly and access it by address rather than by **read** and **write** may avoid some path length of the system-call overhead, but they lose the benefit of the system write-behind feature. When applications do not use the **write** subroutine, modified pages tend to accumulate in memory and be written randomly when purged by the VMM page-replacement algorithm or the sync daemon. This results in many small writes to the disk that cause inefficiencies in CPU and disk utilization, as well as fragmentation that may slow future reads of the file.

Disk-I/O Pacing

Prior to Version 3.2, users of AIX occasionally encountered long interactive-application response times when another application in the system was doing large writes to disk. Because most writes are asynchronous, FIFO I/O queues of several megabytes could build up, which could take several seconds to complete. The performance of an interactive process is severely impacted if every disk read spends several seconds working its way through the queue. In response to this problem, the VMM has an option called *I/O pacing* to control writes.

I/O pacing does not change the interface or processing logic of I/O. It simply limits the number of I/Os that can be outstanding against a file. When a process tries to exceed that limit, it is suspended until enough outstanding requests have been processed to reach a lower threshold. "Use of Disk-I/O Pacing" on page 142 describes I/O pacing in more detail.

Disk Array

A disk array is a set of disk drives that are managed as a group. Different management algorithms yield different levels of performance and/or data integrity. These management algorithms are identified by different RAID levels. (RAID stands for redundant array of independent disks.) The RAID levels that are architecturally defined are::

RAID0 Data is written on consecutive physical drives, with a fixed number of 512-byte blocks per write. This is analogous to the technique known as striping. It has the same data-integrity characteristics as ordinary independent disk drives. That is, data integrity is entirely dependent on the frequency and validity of backups. This level of function is analogous to the disk striping function described in "Performance Implications of Logical Volume Striping" on page 144.

RAID1 Data is striped, as in RAID0, but half of the drives are used to mirror the other drives. RAID1 resolves some of the data integrity and availability concerns with RAID0 if a single drive fails, but becomes equivalent to RAID0 when operating with one or more failed drives. Conscientious backup is still desirable. This level of function is analogous to the logical volume mirroring function of the logical volume manager

RAID3 Data is striped on a byte-by-byte basis across a set of data drives, while a separate parity drive contains a parity byte for each corresponding byte position on the data drives. If any single drive fails, its contents can be inferred from the parity byte and the surviving data bytes. The parity drive becomes the performance bottleneck in this technique, since it must be written on each time a write occurs to *any* of the other disks.

RAID5 Data is striped block by (512-byte) block, but portions of several (not necessarily all) of the drives are set aside to hold parity information. This spreads the load of writing parity information more evenly.

RAID devices should be considered primarily a data-integrity and data-availability solution, rather than a performance solution. Large RAID configurations tend to be limited by the fact that each RAID is attached to a single SCSI adapter. If performance is a concern, a given number of disk drives would be better supported by using multiple RAID devices attached to multiple SCSI adapters, rather than a single, maximum-sized RAID.

3

An Introduction to Multiprocessing

The old saying, "Many hands make light work," expresses the premise that leads to the development of multiple-processor systems. At any given time, there is a technological limit on the speed with which a single processor chip can operate. If a system's workload cannot be handled satisfactorily by a single processor, one response is to apply multiple processors to the problem.

The success of this response depends not only on the skill of the system designers but also on whether the workload is amenable to multiprocessing. In terms of human tasks, adding "hands" may be a good idea if the task is answering calls to an "800" number, but is dubious if the task is driving a car.

If improved performance is the objective of a proposed migration from a uniprocessor to a multiprocessor system, the following should all be true:

1. The workload is processor-limited and has saturated its uniprocessor system.
2. The workload contains multiple processor-intensive elements, such as transactions or complex calculations, that can be performed simultaneously and independently.
3. The existing uniprocessor cannot be upgraded or replaced with another uniprocessor of adequate power.
4. One or more considerations, such as a centralized database, preclude dividing the workload among multiple uniprocessor systems.

In general, a uniprocessor solution is preferable when possible, because the presence of multiple processors gives rise to performance concerns that are minimal or nonexistent in uniprocessor systems. In particular, if point 2 is not true, the performance of a multiprocessor can sometimes actually be worse than that of a comparable uniprocessor.

Although unchanged single-thread applications normally function correctly in a multiprocessor environment, their performance often changes in unexpected ways. Migration to a multiprocessor can improve the throughput of a system, and sometimes can improve the execution time of complex, multithread applications, but seldom improves the response time of individual, single-thread commands.

Getting the best possible performance from a multiprocessor system requires an understanding of the operating-system and hardware-execution dynamics that are unique to the multiprocessor environment.

Symmetrical Multiprocessor (SMP) Concepts and Architecture

As with any change that increases the complexity of the system, the use of multiple processors generates design considerations that must be addressed for satisfactory operation and performance. The additional complexity gives more scope for hardware/software tradeoffs and requires closer hardware/software design coordination than in uniprocessor systems. The different combinations of design responses and tradeoffs give rise to a wide variety of multiprocessor system architectures.

This section describes the main design considerations of multiprocessor systems and the responses of AIX and the RISC System/6000 to those considerations.

Perhaps the most fundamental decision in designing a multiprocessor system is whether the system will be symmetrical or asymmetrical.

Symmetrical vs Asymmetrical Multiprocessors

In an asymmetrical multiprocessor system, the processors are assigned different roles. One processor may handle I/O, while others execute user programs, and so forth. Some of the advantages and disadvantages of this approach are:

- By restricting certain operations to a single processor, some forms of data serialization and cache coherency problems (see below) can be reduced or avoided. Some parts of the software may be able to operate as though they were running in a uniprocessor.
- In some situations, I/O-operation or application-program processing may be faster because it does not have to contend with other parts of the operating system or the workload for access to a processor.
- In other situations, I/O-operation or application-program processing can be slowed because not all of the processors are available to handle peak loads.
- The existence of a single processor handling specific work creates a unique point of failure for the system as a whole.

In a symmetrical multiprocessor system, all of the processors are essentially identical and perform identical functions:

- All of the processors work with the same virtual and real address spaces.
- Any processor is capable of running any thread in the system.
- Any processor can handle any external interrupt. (Each processor handles the internal interrupts generated by the instruction stream it is executing.)
- Any processor can initiate an I/O operation.

This interchangeability means that all of the processors are potentially available to handle whatever needs to be done next. The cost of this flexibility is primarily borne by the hardware and software designers, although symmetry also makes the limits on the multiprocessability of the workload more noticeable, as we shall see.

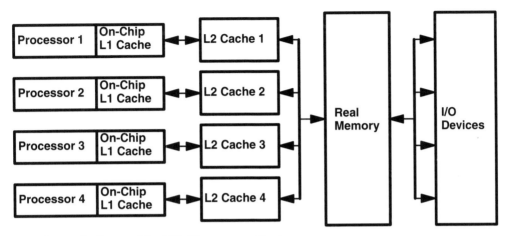

Figure 8. Symmetrical Multiprocessor System

The RISC System/6000 family contains, and AIX Version 4.1 supports, only symmetrical multiprocessors, one form of which is shown in the figure "Symmetrical Multiprocessor System." Different systems may have different cache configurations.

Although RISC System/6000 multiprocessor systems are technically symmetrical, a minimal amount of asymmetry is introduced by the software. A single processor is initially in control during the boot process. This first processor to be started is designated as the "master processor." To ensure that user-written software continues to run correctly during the transition from uniprocessor to multiprocessor environments, device drivers and kernel extensions that do not explicitly describe themselves as able to run safely on multiple processors are forced to run only on the master processor. This constraint is called "funnelling."

Data Serialization

Any storage element that can be read or written by more than one thread may change while the program is running. This is generally true of multiprogramming environments as well as multiprocessing environments, but the advent of multiprocessors adds to the scope and importance of this consideration in two ways:

- Multiprocessors and thread support make it attractive and easier to write applications that share data among threads.
- The kernel can no longer solve the serialization problem simply by disabling interrupts.

To avoid disaster, programs that share data must arrange to access that data *serially*, rather than in parallel. Before a program touches a shared data item, it must ensure that no other program (including another copy of itself running on another thread) will change the item.

The primary mechanism that is used to keep programs from interfering with one another is the *lock*. A lock is an abstraction that represents permission to access one or more data items. Lock and unlock requests are atomic; that is, they are implemented in such a way that neither interrupts nor multiprocessor access affect the outcome. All programs that access a shared data item must obtain the lock that corresponds to that data item before manipulating it. If the lock is already held by another program (or another thread running the same program), the requesting program must defer its access until the lock becomes available.

Besides the time spent waiting for the lock, serialization adds to the number of times a thread becomes nondispatchable. While the thread is nondispatchable, other threads are probably causing the nondispatchable thread's cache lines to be replaced, which will result in increased memory-latency costs when the thread finally gets the lock and is dispatched.

The AIX kernel contains many shared data items, so it must perform serialization internally. This means that serialization delays can occur even in an application program that does not share data with other programs, because the kernel services used by the program have to serialize on shared kernel data.

Lock Granularity

A programmer working in a multiprocessor environment must decide how many separate locks should be created for shared data. If there is a single lock to serialize the entire set of shared data items, lock contention is comparatively likely. If each distinct data item has its own lock, the probability of two threads contending for that lock is comparatively low. Each additional lock and unlock call costs processor time, however, and the existence of multiple locks makes a deadlock possible. At its simplest, deadlock is the situation shown in the figure "Deadlock," in which Thread 1 owns Lock A and is waiting for Lock B, while Thread 2 owns Lock B and is waiting for Lock A. Neither program will ever reach the **unlock** call that would break the deadlock. The usual preventive for deadlock is to establish a protocol by which all of the programs that use a given set of locks must always acquire them in exactly the same sequence.

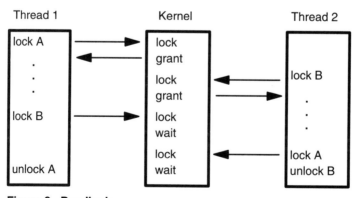

Figure 9. Deadlock

Locking Overhead

Requesting locks, waiting for locks, and releasing locks add processing overhead in several ways:

- A program that supports multiprocessing always does the same lock and unlock processing, even though it is running in a uniprocessor or is the only user in a multiprocessor system of the locks in question.
- When one thread requests a lock held by another thread, the requesting thread may spin for a while or be put to sleep and, if possible, another thread dispatched. This consumes processor time.
- The existence of widely used locks places an upper bound on the throughput of the system. For example, if a given program spends 20% of its execution time holding a mutual-exclusion lock, at most 5 instances of that program can run simultaneously, *regardless of the number of processors* in the system. In fact, even 5 instances would probably never be so nicely synchronized as to avoid waiting on one another (see "Multiprocessor Throughput Scalability" on page 38).

Cache Coherency

In designing a multiprocessor, engineers give considerable attention to ensuring cache coherency. They succeed; but their success is not free. To understand why cache coherency has a performance cost, we need to understand the problem being attacked:

> If each processor has a cache (see the "Symmetrical Multiprocessor System" figure on page 33), which reflects the state of various parts of memory, it is possible that two or more caches may have copies of the same line. It is also possible that a given line may contain more than one lockable data item. If two threads make appropriately serialized changes to those data items, the result could be that both caches end up with different, incorrect versions of the line of memory; that is, the system's state is no longer coherent — the system contains two different versions of what is supposed to be the content of a specific area of memory.

The solutions to the cache coherency problem usually include invalidating all but one of the duplicate lines. Although the invalidation is done by the hardware, without any software intervention, any processor whose cache line has been invalidated will have a cache miss, with its attendant delay, the next time that line is addressed.

For a detailed background discussion of RISC System/6000 addressing architecture and cache operation, see Appendix C. "Cache and Addressing Considerations."

Processor Affinity

If a thread is interrupted and later redispatched to the same processor, there may still be lines in that processor's cache that belong to the thread. If the thread is dispatched to a different processor, it will probably experience a series of cache misses until its cache working set has been retrieved from RAM. On the other hand, if a dispatchable thread has to wait until the processor it was previously running on is available, the thread may experience an even longer delay.

Processor affinity is the dispatching of a thread to the processor that was previously executing it. The degree of emphasis on processor affinity should vary directly with the size of the thread's cache working set and inversely with the length of time since it was last dispatched.

In AIX Version 4.1, processor affinity can be achieved by *binding* a thread to a processor. A thread that is bound to a processor can run only on that processor, regardless of the status of the other processors in the system.

Memory and Bus Contention

In a uniprocessor, contention for some internal resources, such as banks of memory and I/O or memory buses, is usually a minor component processing time. In a multiprocessor these effects can become more significant, particularly if cache-coherency algorithms add to the number of accesses to RAM.

SMP Performance Issues

Workload Concurrency

The primary performance issue that is unique to SMP systems is *workload concurrency*, which can be expressed as, "Now that we've got n processors, how do we keep them all usefully employed?" If only one processor in a four-way multiprocessor system is doing useful work at any given time, it is no better than a uniprocessor— possibly worse, because of the extra code to avoid interprocessor interference.

Workload concurrency is the complement of serialization. To the extent that the system software or the application workload—or the interaction of the two—require serialization, workload concurrency suffers.

Workload concurrency may also be decreased, more desirably, by increased processor affinity. The improved cache efficiency gained from processor affinity may result in quicker completion of the program. Workload concurrency is reduced (unless there are more dispatchable threads available), but response time is improved.

A component of workload concurrency, *process concurrency*, is the degree to which a multithread process has multiple dispatchable threads at all times.

Throughput

The throughput of an SMP system is mainly dependent on:

- A *consistently* high level of workload concurrency. More dispatchable threads than processors at some times cannot compensate for idle processors at other times.
- The amount of lock contention.
- The degree of processor affinity.

Response Time

The response time of a particular program in an SMP system is dependent on:

- The process-concurrency level of the program. If the program consistently has two or more dispatchable threads, its response time will probably improve in an SMP environment. If the program consists of a single thread, its response time will be, at best, comparable to that in a uniprocessor of the same speed.
- The amount of lock contention of other instances of the program or with other programs that use the same locks.
- The degree of processor affinity of the program. If each dispatch of the program is to a different processor that has none of the program's cache lines, the program may run more slowly than in a comparable uniprocessor.

Adapting Programs to an SMP Environment

The following terms are used to describe the extent to which an existing program has been modified, or a new program designed, to operate in an SMP environment:

SMP safe   Avoidance in a program of any action, such as unserialized access to shared data, that would cause functional problems in an SMP environment. This term, when used alone, usually refers to a program that has undergone only the minimum changes necessary for correct functioning in an SMP environment.

SMP efficient   Avoidance in a program of any action that would cause functional or performance problems in an SMP environment. A program that is described as SMP efficient is generally assumed to be SMP safe as well. An SMP-efficient program has usually undergone additional changes to minimize incipient bottlenecks.

SMP exploiting   Adding features to a program that are specifically intended to make effective use of an SMP environment, such as multithreading. A program that is described as SMP exploiting is generally assumed to be SMP safe and SMP efficient as well.

SMP Workloads

The effect of additional processors on performance is dominated by certain characteristics of the specific workload being handled. The following sections discuss those critical characteristics and their effects.

Workload Multiprocessability

Multiprogramming operating systems like AIX running heavy workloads on fast computers like the RISC System/6000 give our human senses the impression that several things are happening simultaneously. In fact, many demanding workloads do not have large numbers of dispatchable threads at any given instant, even when running on a single-processor system where serialization is less of a problem. Unless there are always at least as many dispatchable threads as there are processors, one or more processors will be idle part of the time.

The number of dispatchable threads is:

The total number of threads in the system,
> minus the number of threads that are waiting for I/O,
> minus the number of threads that are waiting for a shared resource,
> minus the number of threads that are waiting for the results of another

thread,
> minus the number of threads that are sleeping at their own request.

A workload can be said to be *multiprocessable* to the extent that it presents at all times as many dispatchable threads as there are processors in the system. Note that this does not mean simply an *average* number of dispatchable threads equal to the processor count. If the number of dispatchable threads is zero half the time and twice the processor count the rest of the time, the average number of dispatchable threads will equal the processor count, but any given processor in the system will be working only half the time.

Increasing the multiprocessability of a workload involves one or both of:

- Identifying and resolving any bottlenecks that cause threads to wait
- Increasing the total number of threads in the system

These solutions are not independent. If there is a single, major system bottleneck, increasing the number of threads of the existing workload that pass through the bottleneck will simply increase the proportion of threads waiting. If there is not currently a bottleneck, increasing the number of threads may create one.

Multiprocessor Throughput Scalability

All of these factors contribute to what is called the *scalability* of a workload. Scalability is the degree to which workload throughput benefits from the availability of additional processors. It is usually expressed as the quotient of the throughput of the workload on a multiprocessor divided by the throughput on a comparable uniprocessor. For example, if a uniprocessor achieved 20 requests per second on a given workload and a four-processor system achieved 58 requests per second, the scaling factor would be 2.9. That workload is highly scalable. A workload that consisted exclusively of long-running, compute-intensive programs with negligible I/O or other kernel activity and no shared data might approach that level. Most real-world workloads would not. Scalability is very difficult to estimate. Whenever possible, scalability assumptions should be based on measurements of authentic workloads.

The figure "Multiprocessor Scaling" illustrates the problems of scaling. The workload consists of a series of commands. Each command is about one-third normal processing, one-third I/O wait, and one-third processing with a lock held. On the uniprocessor, only one command can actually be processing at a time, regardless of whether or not the lock is held. In the time interval shown (five times the standalone execution time of the command), the uniprocessor handles 7.67 of the commands.

On the multiprocessor, there are two processors to handle program execution, but there is still only one lock. For simplicity, all of the lock contention is shown affecting processor B. In the period shown, the multiprocessor handles 14 commands. The scaling factor is thus 1.83. We stop at two processors because more would not change the situation. The lock is now in use 100% of the time. In a four-way multiprocessor, the scaling factor would be 1.83 or less.

Real programs are seldom as symmetrical as the commands in the illustration. Remember, too, that we have only taken into account one dimension of contention—locking. If we had included cache-coherency and processor-affinity effects, the scaling factor would almost certainly be lower yet.

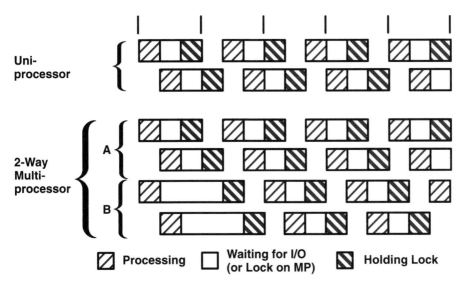

Figure 10. Multiprocessor Scaling

The point of this example is that workloads often cannot be made to run faster simply by adding processors. It is also necessary to identify and minimize the sources of contention among the threads.

Some published benchmark results imply that high levels of scalability are easy to achieve. Most such benchmarks are constructed by running combinations of small, CPU-intensive programs that use almost no kernel services. These benchmark results represent an upper bound on scalability, not a realistic expectation.

Multiprocessor Response Time

A multiprocessor can only improve the execution time of an individual program to the extent that the program can run multithreaded. There are several ways to achieve parallel execution of parts of a single program:

- Making explicit calls to **libpthreads** subroutines (or, in older programs, to **fork()**) to create multiple threads that run simultaneously.
- Processing the program with a parallelizing compiler or preprocessor that detects sequences of code that can be executed simultaneously and generates multiple threads to run them in parallel.
- Making use of a software package that is itself multithreaded.

Unless one or more of these techniques is used, the program will run no faster in a multiprocessor system than in a comparable uniprocessor. In fact, since it may experience more locking overhead and delays due to being dispatched to different processors at different times, it may be significantly slower.

Even if all of the applicable techniques are exploited, the maximum improvement is limited by a rule that has been called Amdahl's Law:

If a fraction x of a program's uniprocessor execution time, t, can only be processed sequentially, the improvement in execution time in an n-way multiprocessor over execution time in a comparable uniprocessor (the *speed-up*) is given by the equation:

$$\text{speed-up} = \frac{\text{uniprocessor time}}{\text{seq time} + \text{mp time}} = \frac{t}{xt + \frac{(x-1)t}{n}} = \frac{1}{x + \frac{x}{n}}$$

$$\lim_{n \to \infty} \text{speed-up} = \frac{1}{x}$$

As an example, if 50% of a program's processing must be done sequentially, and 50% can be done in parallel, the maximum response-time improvement is less than a factor of 2 (in an otherwise-idle 4-way multiprocessor, at most 1.6)

SMP Scheduling

Thread support, added to AIX in Version 4.1, divides program-execution control into two elements:

- A *process* is a collection of physical resources required to run the program, such as memory and access to files.
- A *thread* is the execution state of an instance of the program, such as the current contents of the   instruction-address register and the general-purpose registers. Each thread runs within the context of a given process, and uses that process's resources. Multiple threads can run within a single process, sharing its resources.

In previous versions of AIX, the CPU scheduler dispatched processes. In AIX Version 4, the scheduler dispatches threads.

In the SMP environment, the availability of thread support makes it easier and less expensive to implement SMP-exploiting applications. Forking multiple processes to create multiple flows of control is cumbersome and expensive, since each process has its own set of memory resources and requires considerable system processing to set up. Creating multiple threads within a single process requires less processing and uses less memory.

Thread support exists at two levels: **libpthreads.a** support in the application program environment and kernel thread support. In AIX Version 4.1, scheduling of threads is almost entirely a function of kernel thread support.

Default Scheduler Processing of Migrated Workloads

The new division between processes and threads is invisible to existing programs. In fact, workloads migrated directly from earlier releases of AIX create processes as before. Each new process is created with a single thread (the *initial thread*) that contends for the CPU with the threads of other processes. The default attributes of the initial thread, in conjunction with the new scheduler algorithms, minimize changes in system dynamics for unchanged workloads.

Priorities can be manipulated with the **nice** and **renice** commands and the **setpri** system call, as before. The scheduler allows a given thread to run for at most one time slice (normally 10ms) before forcing it to yield to the next dispatchable thread of the same or higher priority.

Scheduling Algorithm Variables

Several variables affect the scheduling of threads. Some are unique to thread support; others are elaborations of process-scheduling considerations:

- Priority. A thread's priority value is the basic indicator of its precedence in the contention for processor time.
- Scheduler run queue position. A thread's position in the scheduler's queue of dispatchable threads reflects a number of preceding conditions.
- Scheduling policy. This thread attribute determines what happens to a running thread at the end of the time slice.
- Contention scope. A thread's contention scope determines whether it competes only with the other threads within its process or with all threads in the system.
- Processor affinity. The degree to which affinity is enforced affects performance.

The combinations of these considerations can seem complex, but there are essentially three distinct approaches from which to choose in managing a given process:

- Default. The process has one thread, whose priority varies with CPU consumption and whose scheduling policy, SCHED_OTHER, is comparable to the AIX Version 3 algorithm.
- Process-level control. The process can have one or more threads, but the scheduling policy of those threads is left as the default SCHED_OTHER, which

41

permits the use of the existing AIX Version 3 methods of controlling nice values and fixed priorities. All of these methods affect all of the threads in the process identically. If **setpri()** is used, the scheduling policy of all of the threads in the process is set to SCHED_RR.

- Thread-level control. The process can have one or more threads. The scheduling policy of these threads is set to SCHED_RR or SCHED_FIFO, as appropriate. The priority of each thread is fixed, and is manipulated with thread-level subroutines.

Processor Affinity and Binding

Other things being equal, it is desirable to dispatch a thread on the processor it last used. This dispatching criterion is called *processor affinity*. The level of emphasis on processor affinity can vary.

The highest possible degree of processor affinity is to *bind* a thread to a specific processor. Binding means that the thread will be dispatched to that processor only, regardless of the availability of other processors. The **bindprocessor** command and subroutine bind the thread (or threads) of a specified process to a particular processor.

This technique can be useful for CPU-intensive programs that experience few interrupts. It can sometimes be counterproductive for ordinary programs, because it may delay the redispatch of a thread after an I/O until the processor to which the thread is bound becomes available. If the thread has been blocked for the duration of an I/O operation, it is unlikely that much of its processing context remains in the caches of the processor to which it is bound. It would probably be better served if it were dispatched to the next available processor.

4

Performance-Conscious Planning, Design, and Implementation

A program that does not perform acceptably is not functional.

Every program has to satisfy a set of users—admittedly, sometimes a large and diverse set. If the performance of the program is truly unacceptable to a significant group of those users, it will not be used. A program that is not being used is not performing its intended function.

This is true of licensed software packages as well as user-written applications, although most developers of software packages are aware of the effects of poor performance and take pains to make their programs run as fast as possible. Unfortunately, they can't anticipate all of the environments and uses that their programs will experience. Final responsibility for acceptable performance falls on the people who select or write, plan for, and install software packages.

This chapter attempts to describe the stages by which a programmer or system administrator can ensure that a newly written or purchased program has acceptable performance. (Wherever the word programmer appears alone, the term includes system administrators and anyone else who is responsible for the ultimate success of a program.)

The way to achieve acceptable performance in a program is to identify and quantify acceptability at the start of the project and never lose sight of the measures and resources needed to achieve it. This prescription borders on banal, but some programming projects consciously reject it. They adopt a policy that might be fairly described as "design, code, debug, maybe document, and if we have time, fix up the performance."

The only way that programs can *predictably* be made to function in time, not just in logic, is by integrating performance considerations in the software planning and development process. Advance planning is perhaps more critical when existing software is being installed, because the installer has fewer degrees of freedom than the developer.

Although the detail of this process may seem burdensome for a small program, remember that we have a second agenda. Not only must the new program have satisfactory performance; we must also ensure that the addition of that program to an existing system does not cause the performance of other programs run on that system to become unsatisfactory.

Identifying the Components of the Workload

Whether the program is new or purchased, small or large, the developers, the installers, and the prospective users have assumptions about the use of the program, such as:

- Who will be using the program
- Situations in which the program will be run
- How often those situations will arise and at what times of the hour, day, month, year
- Whether those situations will also require additional uses of existing programs
- Which systems the program will run on
- How much data will be handled, and from where
- Whether data created by or for the program will be used in other ways

Unless these ideas are elicited as part of the design process, they will probably be vague, and the programmers will almost certainly have different assumptions than the prospective users. Even in the apparently trivial case in which the programmer is also the user, leaving the assumptions unarticulated makes it impossible to compare design to assumptions in any rigorous way. Worse, it is impossible to identify performance requirements without a complete understanding of the work being performed.

Documenting Performance Requirements

In identifying and quantifying performance requirements, it is important to identify the reasoning behind a particular requirement. Users may be basing their statements of requirements on assumptions about the logic of the program that do not match the programmer's assumptions. At a minimum, a set of performance requirements should document:

- The maximum satisfactory response time that will be experienced most of the time for each distinct type of user-computer interaction, along with a definition of "most of the time." Remember that response time is measured from the time that the user performs the action that says "Go" until the user receives enough feedback from the computer to continue the task. It is the user's subjective wait time. It is not "from entry to my subroutine until the first write statement."

  If the user denies interest in response time and indicates that only the answer is of interest, you can ask whether (ten times your current estimate of stand-alone execution time) would be acceptable. If the answer is "yes," you can proceed to discuss throughput. Otherwise, you can continue the discussion of response time with the user's full attention.

- The response time that is just barely tolerable the rest of the time. Anything longer and people start thinking the system is down—or at least blaming the computer for a loss of productivity and becoming averse to using it. You also need to specify "rest of the time;" the peak minute of a day, 1% of interactions, etc. This should also be in user-subjective terms at first. For example, response time degradations may be more costly or painful at a particular time of the day.

- The typical throughput required and the times it will be taking place. Again, this should not be shrugged aside. For example, the requirement for one program might be: "This program only runs twice a day—at 10:00 a.m. and 3:15 p.m." If this is a CPU-limited program that runs for 15 minutes and is planned to run on a multiuser system, some negotiation is in order.

- The size and timing of maximum-throughput periods.

- The mix of requests expected and how the mix varies with time.

- The number of users per machine and total number of users, if this is a multiuser application. This description should include the times these users log on and off, as well as their assumed rates of keystrokes, completed requests, and think times. You may want to investigate whether think times vary systematically with the preceding and/or following request.

- Any assumptions the user is making about the machines the workload will run on. If the user has a specific existing machine in mind, you should know that *now*. Similarly, if the user is assuming a particular type, size, cost, location, interconnection, or any other variable that will constrain your ability to satisfy the preceding requirements, that assumption becomes part of the requirements as well. Satisfaction will probably not be assessed on the system where the program is developed, tested, or first installed.

Estimating the Resource Requirements of the Workload

Unless you are purchasing a software package that comes with detailed resource-requirement documentation, resource estimation can be the most difficult task in the performance-planning process. The difficulty has several causes:

- In AIX there are several ways to do anything. One can write a C (or other HLL) program, a shell script, an **awk** script, a **sed** script, an AIXwindows dialog, etc. Some techniques that may seem particularly suitable for the algorithm and for programmer productivity are extraordinarily expensive from the performance perspective.

  A useful guideline is that, the higher the level of abstraction, the more caution is needed to ensure that one doesn't receive a performance surprise. One must think very carefully about the data volumes and number of iterations implied by some apparently harmless constructs.

- In AIX it is difficult to define the precise cost of a single process. This difficulty is not merely technical; it is philosophical. If multiple instances of a given program run by multiple users are sharing pages of program text, which process should be charged with those pages of memory? The operating system leaves recently used file pages in memory to provide a caching effect for programs that reaccess that data. Should programs that reaccess data be charged for the space that was used to keep the data around? The granularity of some measurements such as the system clock can cause variations in the CPU time attributed to successive instances of the same program.

There are two approaches to dealing with resource-report ambiguity and variability. The first is to ignore the ambiguity and to keep eliminating sources of variability until the measurements become acceptably consistent. The second approach is to try to make the measurements as realistic as possible and describe the results statistically. We prefer the latter, since it yields results that have some correlation with production situations.

- AIX systems are rarely dedicated to the execution of a single instance of a single program. There are almost always daemons running, frequently communications activity, often workload from multiple users. These activities seldom combine additively. For example, increasing the number of instances of a given program may result in few new program text pages being used, because most of the program was already in memory. However, the additional process may result in more contention for the processor's caches, so that not only do the other processes have to share processor time with the newcomer, but *all* processes may experience more cycles per instruction—in effect, a slowdown of the processor—as a result of more frequent cache misses.

Our recommendation is to keep your estimate as close to reality as the specific situation allows:

- If the program exists, measure the existing installation that most closely resembles your own requirements.
- If no suitable installation is available, do a trial installation and measure a synthetic workload.
- If it is impractical to generate a synthetic workload that matches the requirements, measure individual interactions and use the results as input to a simulation.
- If the program doesn't exist yet, find a comparable program that uses the same language and general structure, and measure it. Again, the more abstract the language, the more care is needed in determining comparability.
- If no comparable program exists, prototype the main algorithms in the planned language, measure the prototype, and model the workload.
- If, and only if, measurement of any kind is impossible or infeasible should you make an educated guess. If it is necessary to guess at resource requirements during the planning stage, it is even more important than usual that the actual program be measured at the earliest possible stage of its development.

In resource estimation, we are primarily interested in four dimensions (in no particular order):

CPU time   Processor cost of the workload

Disk accesses   Rate at which the workload generates disk reads or writes

Real memory   Amount of RAM the workload requires

LAN traffic Number of packets the workload generates and the number of bytes of data exchanged

The following sections describe, or refer you to descriptions of, the techniques for determining these values in the various situations just described.

Measuring Workload Resources

If the real program, a comparable program, or a prototype is available for measurement, the choice of technique depends on:

- Whether or not the system is processing other work in addition to the workload we want to measure.
- Whether or not we have permission to use tools that may degrade performance (for example, is this system in production or is it dedicated to our use for the duration of the measurement?).
- The degree to which we can simulate or observe an authentic workload.

Measuring a Complete Workload on a Dedicated System

This is the ideal situation because it allows us to use measurements that include system overhead as well as the cost of individual processes.

To measure CPU and disk activity, we can use **iostat.** The command

```
$ iostat 5 >iostat.output
```

gives us a picture of the state of the system every 5 seconds during the measurement run. Remember that the first set of **iostat** output contains the cumulative data from the last boot to the start of the **iostat** command. The remaining sets are the results for the preceding interval, in this case 5 seconds. A typical set of **iostat** output on a large system looks like this:

```
tty:      tin      tout     cpu:   % user   % sys    % idle   % iowait
          1.2      1.6              60.2     10.8     23.4     5.6
Disks:         % tm_act    Kbps      tps   Kb_read   Kb_wrtn
hdisk1           0.0       0.0       0.0        0         0
hdisk2           0.0       0.0       0.0        0         0
hdisk3           0.0       0.0       0.0        0         0
hdisk4           0.0       0.0       0.0        0         0
hdisk11          0.0       0.0       0.0        0         0
hdisk5           0.0       0.0       0.0        0         0
hdisk6           0.0       0.0       0.0        0         0
hdisk7           3.0      11.2       0.8        8        48
hdisk8           1.8       4.8       1.2        0        24
hdisk9           0.0       0.0       0.0        0         0
hdisk0           2.0       4.8       1.2       24         0
hdisk10          0.0       0.0       0.0        0         0
```

To measure memory, we would use **svmon.** The command **svmon –G** gives a picture of overall memory use. The statistics are in terms of 4KB pages:

```
$ svmon -G
          m e m o r y              i n  u s e            p i n      p g  s p a c e
     size inuse  free  pin  work  pers  clnt   work  pers  clnt  size   inuse
    24576 24366   210 2209 15659  6863  1844   2209     0     0 40960   26270
```

47

This machine's 96MB memory is fully used. About 64% of RAM is in use for working segments—the read/write memory of running programs. If there are long-running processes that we are interested in, we can review their memory requirements in detail. The following example determines the memory used by one of user xxxxxx's processes.

```
$ ps -fu xxxxxx
    USER   PID  PPID   C    STIME     TTY  TIME CMD
  xxxxxx 28031 51445  15 14:01:56  pts/9  0:00 ps -fu xxxxxx
  xxxxxx 51445 54772   1 07:57:47  pts/9  0:00 -ksh
  xxxxxx 54772  6864   0 07:57:47      -  0:02 rlogind

$ svmon -P 51445
 Pid                         Command       Inuse       Pin       Pgspace
51445                            ksh        1668         2          4077

Pid:   51445
Command:  ksh

Segid  Type  Description       Inuse  Pin  Pgspace Address Range
8270   pers  /dev/fslv00:86079     1    0        0  0..0
4809   work  shared library     1558    0     4039  0..4673 : 60123..65535
9213   work  private              37    2       38  0..31 : 65406..65535
 8a1   pers  code,/dev/hd2:14400   72    0        0  0..91
```

The working segment (9213), with 37 pages in use, is the cost of this instance of **ksh**. The 1558-page cost of the shared library and the 72-page cost of the **ksh** executable are spread across all of the running programs and all instances of **ksh**, respectively.

If we believe that our 96MB system is larger than necessary, we can use the **rmss** command to reduce the effective size of the machine and remeasure the workload. If paging increases significantly or response time deteriorates, we have reduced memory too far. This technique can be continued until we find a size that just runs our workload without degradation. See "Assessing Memory Requirements via the rmss Command" beginning on page 115 for more information on this technique.

The primary command for measuring network usage is **netstat**. The following example shows the activity of a specific Token-Ring interface:

```
$ netstat -I tr0 5
    input   (tr0)    output            input  (Total)   output
  packets errs packets errs colls   packets errs packets errs colls
 35552822 213488 30283693    0    0  35608011 213488 30338882    0    0
      300      0      426     0    0       300      0      426     0    0
      272      2      190     0    0       272      2      190     0    0
      231      0      192     0    0       231      0      192     0    0
      143      0      113     0    0       143      0      113     0    0
      408      1      176     0    0       408      1      176     0    0
```

The first line of the report shows the cumulative network traffic since the last boot. Each subsequent line shows the activity for the preceding 5-second interval.

Measuring a Complete Workload on a Production System

The techniques of measurement on production systems are similar to those on dedicated systems, but we must take pains to avoid degrading system performance. For example, the **svmon –G** command is very expensive to run. The one shown earlier took about 5 seconds of CPU time on a Model 950. Estimates of the resource costs of the most frequently used performance tools are shown in Appendix E, "Performance of the Performance Tools."

Probably the most cost-effective tool is **vmstat**, which supplies data on memory, I/O, and CPU usage in a single report. If the **vmstat** intervals are kept reasonably long, say 10 seconds, the average cost is low—about .01 CPU seconds per report on a model 950. See "Identifying the Performance-Limiting Resource" on page 80 for more information on the use of **vmstat**.

Measuring a Partial Workload on a Production System

By partial workload we mean measuring a part of the production system's workload for possible transfer to or duplication on a different system. Because this is a production system, we must be as unobtrusive as possible. At the same time, we have to analyze the workload in more detail to distinguish between the parts we are interested in and those we aren't. To do a partial measurement we need to discover what the workload elements of interest have in common. Are they:

- The same program or a small set of related programs?
- Work performed by one or more specific users of the system?
- Work that comes from one or more specific terminals?

Depending on the commonality, we could use one of the following:

```
ps -ef | grep pgmname
ps -fuusername, . . .
ps -ftttyname, . . .
```

to identify the processes of interest and report the cumulative CPU time consumption of those processes. We can then use **svmon** (judiciously!) to assess the memory use of the processes.

Measuring an Individual Program

There are many tools for measuring the resource consumption of individual programs. Some of these programs are capable of more comprehensive workload measurements as well, but are too intrusive for use on production systems. Most of these tools are discussed in depth in the chapters that discuss tuning for minimum consumption of specific resources. Some of the more prominent are:

time   measures the elapsed execution time and CPU consumption of an individual program. Discussed in "Using the time Command to Measure CPU Use" on page 89.

tprof   measures the relative CPU consumption of programs, subroutine libraries, and the AIX kernel. Discussed in "Using tprof to Analyze Programs for CPU Use" on page 94.

| svmon | measures the real memory used by a process. Discussed in "How Much Memory Is Really Being Used" on page 111. |
| vmstat –s | can be used to measure the I/O load generated by a program. Discussed in "Measuring Overall Disk I/O with vmstat" on page 137. |

Estimating the Resources Required by a New Program

It is impossible to make precise estimates of unwritten programs. The invention and redesign that take place during the coding phase defy prediction, but the following rules of thumb may help you to get a general sense of the requirements. As a starting point, a minimal program would need:

- CPU time
  - About 50 milliseconds, mostly system time.
- Real Memory
  - One page for program text
  - About 15 pages (of which 2 are pinned) for the working (data) segment
  - Access to **libc.a**. Normally this is shared with all other programs and is considered part of the base cost of the operating system.
- Disk I/O
  - About 12 page-in operations, if the program has not been compiled, copied, or used recently; 0 otherwise.

Add to that basic cost allowances for demands implied by the design (the CPU times given are for a Model 580):

- CPU time
  - The CPU consumption of an ordinary program that does not contain high levels of iteration or costly subroutine calls is almost unmeasurably small.
  - If the proposed program contains a computationally expensive algorithm, the algorithm should be prototyped and measured.
  - If the proposed program uses computationally expensive library subroutines, such as X or Motif constructs or **printf**, measure their CPU consumption with otherwise trivial programs.
- Real Memory
  - Allow (*very* approximately) 350 lines of code per page of program text. That is about 12 bytes per line. Keep in mind that coding style and compiler options can make a factor of two difference in either direction. This allowance is for pages that are touched in your typical scenario. If your design places infrequently executed subroutines at the end of the executable, those pages will not normally take up real memory.
  - References to shared libraries other than **libc.a** will increase the memory requirement only to the extent that those libraries are not shared with other programs or instances of the program being estimated. To measure the size of these libraries, write a trivial, long-running program that references them and use **svmon –P** against the process.
  - Estimate the amount of storage that will be required by the data structures identified in the design. Round up to the nearest page.

- In the short run, each disk I/O operation will use one page of memory. Assume that the page has to be available already. Don't assume that the program will wait for another program's page to be freed.
- Disk I/O
  - For sequential I/O, each 4096 bytes read or written causes one I/O operation, unless the file has been accessed recently enough that some of its pages are still in memory.
  - For random I/O, each access, however small, to a different 4096-byte page causes one I/O operation, unless the file has been accessed recently enough that some of its pages are still in memory.
  - Under laboratory conditions, each sequential read or write of a 4KB page in a large file takes about 140+/–20 microseconds of CPU time. Each random read or write of a 4KB page takes about 350+/–40 microseconds of CPU time. Remember that real files are not necessarily stored sequentially on disk, even though they are written and read sequentially by the program. Consequently, the typical CPU cost of an actual disk access will be closer to the random-access cost than to the sequential-access cost.
- Communications I/O
  - If disk I/O is actually to AFS or NFS remote-mounted file systems, the disk I/O is performed on the server, but the client experiences higher CPU and memory demands.
  - RPCs of any kind contribute substantially to the CPU load. The proposed RPCs in the design should be minimized, batched, prototyped, and measured in advance.
  - Under laboratory conditions, each sequential NFS read or write of an 4KB page takes about 670+/–30 microseconds of client CPU time. Each random NFS read or write of a 4KB page takes about 1000+/–200 microseconds of client CPU time.

Transforming Program-Level Estimates to Workload Estimates

The best method for estimating peak and typical resource requirements is to use a queuing model such as BEST/1. Static models can be used, but you run the risk of overestimating or underestimating the peak resource. In either case, you need to understand how multiple programs in a workload interact from the standpoint of resource requirements.

If you are building a static model, use a time interval that is the specified worst-acceptable response time for the most frequent or demanding program (usually they are the same). Determine, based on your projected number of users, their think time, their key entry rate, and the anticipated mix of operations, which programs will typically be running during each interval.

- CPU time
  - Add together the CPU requirements for the all of the programs that are running during the interval. Include the CPU requirements of the disk and communications I/O the programs will be doing.
  - If this number is greater than 75% of the available CPU time during the interval, consider fewer users or more CPU.

- Real Memory
  - Start with 6 to 8MB for the operating system itself. The lower figure is for a standalone system. The latter for a system that is LAN-connected and uses TCP/IP and NFS.
  - Add together the working segment requirements of all of the instances of the programs that will be running during the interval, including the space estimated for the program's data structures.
  - Add to that total the memory requirement of the text segment of each distinct program that will be running (one copy of the program text serves all instances of that program). Remember that any (and only) subroutines that are from unshared libraries will be part of the executable—but the libraries themselves will not be in memory.
  - Add to the total the amount of space consumed by each of the shared libraries that will be used by any program in the workload. Again, one copy serves all.
  - To allow adequate space for some file caching and the free list, your total memory projection should not exceed 80% of the size of the machine to be used.
- Disk I/O
  - Add the number of I/Os implied by each instance of each program. Keep separate totals for I/Os to small files or randomly to large files versus purely sequential reading or writing of large files (more than 32KB)
  - Subtract those I/Os that you believe will be satisfied from memory. Any record that was read or written in the previous interval is probably still available in the current interval. Beyond that, you need to look at the size of the proposed machine versus the total RAM requirements of the machine's workload. Any space left over after the operating system's requirement and the workload's requirements probably contains the most recently read or written file pages. If your application's design is such that there is a high probability of reuse of recently accessed data, you can calculate an allowance for the caching effect. Remember that the reuse is at the page level, not at the record level. If the probability of reuse of a given record is low, but there are a lot of records per page, it is likely that some of the records needed in any given interval will fall in the same page as other, recently used, records.
  - Compare the net I/O requirements to the table on page 68 showing the approximate capabilities of current disk drives. If the random or sequential requirement is greater than 75% of the total corresponding capability of the disks that will hold application data, tuning and possibly expansion will be needed when the application is in production.
- Communications I/O
  - Calculate the bandwidth consumption of the workload. If the total bandwidth consumption of all of the nodes on the LAN is greater than 70% of nominal bandwidth (50% for Ethernet) there is cause for concern.
  - You should carry out a similar analysis of CPU, memory, and I/O requirements of the added load that will be placed on the server.

Remember that these guidelines for a "back of an envelope" estimate are intended for use only when no extensive measurement is possible. Any application-specific measurement that can be used in place of a guideline will improve the accuracy of the estimate considerably.

Design and Implementation of Efficient Programs

If you are sure that you know which resource will limit the speed of your program, you can go directly to the section that discusses appropriate techniques for minimizing the use of that resource. Otherwise, you should assume that the program will be balanced and that all of the recommendations in this chapter may apply. Once the program is implemented, you will want to proceed to "Identifying the Performance-Limiting Resource" on page 80.

CPU-Limited Programs

The maximum speed of a truly processor-limited program is determined by:

- The algorithm used
- The source code and data structures created by the programmer
- The sequence of machine-language instructions generated by the compiler
- The sizes and structures of the processor's caches
- The architecture and clock rate of the processor itself

If the program is CPU-limited simply because it consists almost entirely of numerical computation, obviously the algorithm that has been chosen will have a major effect on the performance of the program. A discussion of alternative algorithms is beyond the scope of this book. It is assumed that computational efficiency has been considered in choosing the algorithm.

Given an algorithm, the only items in the preceding list that the programmer can affect are the source code, the compiler options used, and possibly the data structures. The following sections deal with techniques that can be used to improve the efficiency of an individual program for which the user has the source code. If the source code is not available, tuning or workload-management techniques should be tried.

Design and Coding for Effective Use of Caches

In "Performance Concepts," beginning on page 1, we indicated that the RISC System/6000 processors have a multi-level hierarchy of memory:

1. The instruction pipeline and the CPU registers
2. The instruction and data cache(s) and the corresponding translation lookaside buffers
3. RAM
4. Disk

As instructions and data move up the hierarchy, they move into storage that is faster than the level below it, but also smaller and more expensive. To obtain the maximum possible performance from a given machine, therefore, the programmer's objective must be to make the most effective use of the available storage at each level.

Effective use of storage means keeping it full of instructions and data that are likely to be used. An obstacle to achieving this objective is the fact that storage is allocated in fixed-length blocks such as cache lines and real memory pages that usually do not correspond to boundaries within programs or data structures. Programs and data structures that are designed without regard to the storage hierarchy often make inefficient use of the storage allocated to them, with adverse performance effects in small or heavily loaded systems.

Taking the storage hierarchy into account does not mean programming for a particular page or cache-line size. It means understanding and adapting to the general principles of efficient programming in a cached or virtual-memory environment. There are repackaging techniques that can yield significant improvements without recoding, and, of course, any new code should be designed with efficient storage use in mind.

Two terms are essential to any discussion of the efficient use of hierarchical storage: "locality of reference" and "working set." The *locality of reference* of a program is the degree to which its instruction-execution addresses and data references are clustered in a small area of storage during a given time interval. The *working set* of a program during that same interval is the set of storage blocks that are in use, or, more precisely, the code or data that occupy those blocks. A program with good locality of reference will have a minimal working set, since the blocks that are in use are tightly packed with executing code or data. A functionally equivalent program with poor locality of reference will have a larger working set, since more blocks are needed to accommodate the wider range of addresses being accessed.

Since each block takes a significant amount of time to load into a given level of the hierarchy, the objective of efficient programming for a hierarchical-storage system is to design and package code in such a way that the working set remains as small as practical.

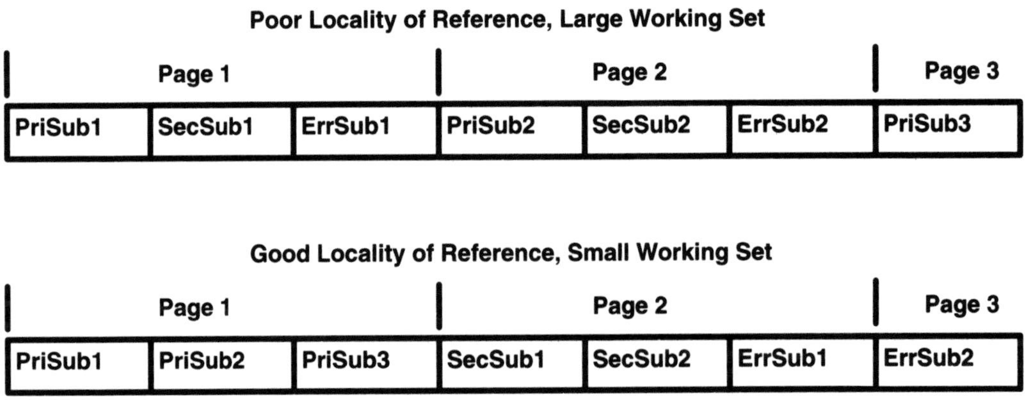

Figure 11: Locality of Reference

The figure "Locality of Reference" illustrates good and bad practice at a subroutine level. The first version of the program is packaged in the sequence in which it was probably written—a sort of programming "stream of consciousness." The first subroutine **PriSub1** contains the entry point of the program. It always uses primary subroutines **PriSub2** and **PriSub3**. Some infrequently used functions of the program require secondary subroutines **SecSub1** and **2**. On very rare occasions, the error subroutines **ErrSub1** and **2** are needed. This version of the program has poor locality of reference because it takes three pages of memory to run in the normal case. The secondary and error subroutines separate the main path of the program into three, physically distant sections.

The improved version of the program moves the primary subroutines to be adjacent to one another, puts the low-frequency function next, and leaves the necessary but practically never-used error subroutines to the end of the executable. The most common functions of the program can now be handled with only one disk read and one page of memory instead of the three that were required before.

Remember that locality of reference and working set are defined with respect to time. If a program works in stages, each of which takes a significant time and uses a different set of subroutines, one should try to minimize the working set of each stage.

Registers and Pipeline

In general, the allocation and optimization of register space and keeping the pipeline full are the responsibilities of the compilers. The main obligation of the programmer is to avoid structures that defeat compiler-optimization techniques. For example, if you use one of your subroutines in one of the critical loops of your program, it may be appropriate for the compiler to inline that subroutine to minimize execution time. If the subroutine has been packaged in a different **.c** module, however, it cannot be inlined by the compiler.

Cache and TLBs

Depending on the architecture (POWER, POWER 2, or PowerPC) and model, RISC System/6000 processors have from one to several caches to hold:

- Parts of executing programs.
- Data used by executing programs.
- Translation lookaside buffers (TLBs), which contain the mapping from virtual address to real address of recently used pages of instruction text or data.

If a cache miss occurs, loading a complete cache line can take a dozen or more processor cycles. If a TLB miss occurs, calculating the virtual-to-real mapping of a page can take several dozen cycles. The exact cost is implementation-dependent. See Appendix C for a more detailed discussion of cache architectures.

Even if a program and its data fit in the caches, the more lines or TLB entries used (that is, the lower the locality of reference), the more CPU cycles it takes to get everything loaded in. Unless the instructions and data are reused many times, the overhead of loading them is a significant fraction of total program execution time, resulting in degraded system performance.

In cached machines, a good style of programming is to keep the main-line, typical-case flow of the program as compact as possible. The main procedure and all of the subroutines it calls frequently should be contiguous. Low-probability conditions, such as obscure errors, should only be tested for in the main line. If the condition actually occurs, its processing should take place in a separate subroutine. All such subroutines should be grouped together at the end of the module. This reduces the probability that low-usage code will take up space in a high-usage cache line. In large modules it is even possible that some or all of the low-usage subroutines may occupy a page that almost never has to be read into memory.

The analogous principle applies to data structures, although it is sometimes necessary to change the code to compensate for the compiler's rules about data layout. An example of this kind of problem was detected during the development of AIX Version 3. Some matrix operations, such as matrix multiplication, involve algorithms that, if coded simplistically, have very poor locality of reference. Matrix operations generally involve accessing the matrix data sequentially, such as row elements acting on column elements. Each compiler has specific rules about the storage layout of matrices. The XL FORTRAN compiler lays out matrices in column-major format (that is, all of the elements of column 1, followed by all the elements of column 2, and so forth) The XL C compiler lays out matrices in row-major format. If the matrices are small, the row and column elements can be contained in the data cache, and the processor and floating-point unit can run at full speed. However, as the size of the matrices increases, the locality of reference of such row/column operations deteriorates to a point where the data can no longer be maintained in the cache. In fact, the natural access pattern of the row/column operations generates a thrashing pattern for the cache where a string of elements accessed is larger than the cache, forcing the initially accessed elements out and then repeating the access pattern again for the same data. The general solution to such matrix access patterns is to partition the operation into blocks, so that multiple operations on the same elements can be performed while they remain in the cache. This general technique is given the name *strip mining*. A group experienced in numerical analysis was asked to code versions of the matrix-manipulation algorithms that made use of strip mining and other optimization techniques. The result was a 30-fold improvement in matrix-multiplication performance. The tuned routines are in the AIX Basic Linear Algebra Subroutines (BLAS) library, **/usr/lib/libblas.a**. A larger set of performance-tuned subroutines is the Engineering and Scientific Subroutine Library (ESSL) licensed program, which is documented in the *IBM Engineering and Scientific Subroutine Library Guide and Reference*, IBM form number SC23-0184.

The functions and interfaces of the Basic Linear Algebra Subroutines are documented in *AIX Version 4.1 Technical Reference, Volume 2: Base Operating System and Extensions*. The FORTRAN run-time environment must be installed to use the library. Users should generally use this library for their matrix and vector operations because its subroutines are tuned to a degree that non-numerical-analyst users are unlikely to achieve by themselves.

If the data structures are under the control of the programmer, other efficiencies are possible. The general principle is to pack frequently used data together whenever possible. If a structure contains frequently accessed control information and occasionally accessed detailed data, make sure that the control information is allocated in consecutive bytes.

This will increase the probability that the control information will all be loaded into the cache with a single, or at least with the minimum number of, cache misses.

Effective Use of Preprocessors and the XL Compilers

The programmer who wants to obtain the highest possible performance from a given program running on a given machine must deal with several considerations:

- There are preprocessors that can rearrange some source code structures to form a functionally equivalent source module that can be compiled into more efficient executable code.
- Just as there are several variants of the POWER architecture, there are several compiler options to allow optimal compilation for a specific variant or set of variants.
- The programmer can use the **#pragma** feature to inform the XL C compiler of certain aspects of the program that will allow the compiler to generate more efficient code by relaxing some of its worst-case assumptions.
- There are several levels of optimization that give the compiler different degrees of freedom in instruction rearrangement.

For programmers who lack the time or interest for experiment, there is a simple rule—*always optimize*. The difference in performance between optimized and unoptimized code is almost always so large that at least basic optimization (the **–O** option of the **cc** or **xlc** or **xlf** command) should be used as a matter of course. The only exceptions are testing situations in which there is a specific need for straightforward code generation, such as statement-level performance analysis using the **tprof** tool.

The other techniques yield additional performance improvement for some programs, but the determination of which combination yields the very best performance for a specific program may require considerable recompilation and measurement.

The following sections summarize the techniques for efficient use of the compilers. A much more extensive discussion appears in *Optimization and Tuning Guide for XL Fortran, XL C and XL C++*, IBM form number SC09-1705.

Source Code Preprocessors

There are several source-code preprocessors available for the RISC System/6000. Three with which there is some experience at this time are:

- KAP/C and KAP/FORTRAN (from Kuck and Associates)
- VAST (from PSR)

Among the techniques used by these preprocessors is recognition of code that is mathematically equivalent to one of the subroutines in the ESSL or BLAS libraries, mentioned earlier. The preprocessor replaces the original computational code with a call to the corresponding performance-tuned subroutine. Preprocessors also attempt to modify data structures in ways that work more efficiently in RISC System/6000 machines.

Architecture-Specific Compilation

The **–qarch** compiler option allows you to specify which of the three POWER architectures (POWER, POWER 2, PowerPC) the executable program will be run on. The possible values are:

–qarch=COM

> Compile for the common subset of the three instruction sets. Programs compiled with this option will run correctly on all three architectures. This is the default.

–qarch=PWR Compile for the POWER architecture of the original RISC System/6000. Programs compiled with this option will run correctly on all three architectures, but some instructions may be simulated on PowerPC systems, to the detriment of performance.

–qarch=PWRX

> Compile specifically for the POWER2 architecture. Programs that use double-precision floating point or floating-point square root extensively may show performance improvement. The executable should be run only on POWER2 systems.

–qarch=PPC Compile specifically for the PowerPC architecture. Programs that use single-precision floating point extensively may show performance improvement. The executable should be run only on PowerPC systems.

The **–qtune** compiler option allows you to give the compiler a hint as to the architecture that should be favored by the compilation. Unlike the **–qarch** option, **–qtune** does not result in the generation of architecture-specific instructions. It simply tells the compiler, when there is a choice of techniques, to choose the technique most appropriate for the specified architecture. The possible values for **–qtune** are:

–qtune=PWR Assume that the program will run predominantly on a POWER system.

–qtune=PWRX Assume that the program will run predominantly on a POWER2 system.

–qtune=601 Assume that the program will run predominantly on a PowerPC 601 system.

The figure "Combinations of **–qarch** and **–qtune**" shows the valid combinations of values of these options and the default values of **–qtune** for specified values of **–qarch**. If neither option is specified, the default is **–qarch=COM –qtune=PWR**.

	–qtune=PWR	–qtune=PWRX	–qtune=601	–qtune default
–qarch=COM	Valid	Valid	Valid	PWR
–qarch=PWR	Valid	Valid	Valid	PWR
–qarch=PWRX	Valid	Valid	Invalid	PWRX
–qarch=PPC	Valid	Invalid	Valid	601

Figure 12: Combinations of –qarch and –qtune

Use of the #pragma Directive

In some situations, the optimizer can be inhibited by the need to generate code that is correct in the worst-case situation. The **#pragma** directive can be used to indicate to the compiler that some constraints can be relaxed, thus permitting more efficient code to be generated.

A *pragma* is an implementation-defined instruction to the compiler. Pragmas have the general form:

```
#pragma character_sequence ...
```

The following pragmas in XL C may have a significant effect on the performance of a program whose source code is otherwise unchanged:

- `disjoint`
- `isolated_call`

#pragma disjoint

The `#pragma disjoint` directive lists the identifiers that are not aliases to each other within the scope of their use.

```
#pragma disjoint ( { identifier | *identifier }
                  [,{ identifier | *identifier } ] ... )
```

The directive informs the compiler that none of the identifiers listed shares the same physical storage, which provides more opportunity for optimizations. If any of the identifiers listed do actually share physical storage, the program might produce incorrect results.

The pragma can appear anywhere in the source program. An identifier in the directive must be visible at the point in the program where the pragma appears. The identifiers listed cannot refer to:

- A member of a structure or union
- A structure or union tag
- An enumeration constant
- A label

The identifiers must be declared before they are used in the pragma. A pointer in the identifier list must not have been used as a function argument before appearing in the directive.

The following example shows the use of the **#pragma disjoint** directive. Because external pointer `ptr_a` does not share storage with and never points to the external variable b, the compiler can assume that the assignment of 7 to the object that `ptr_a` points to will not change the value of b. Likewise, external pointer `ptr_b` does not share storage with and never points to the external variable a. The compiler can then assume that the argument to `another_function` has the value 6.

```
int a, b, *ptr_a, *ptr_b;

#pragma disjoint(*ptr_a, b)      /* ptr_a never points to b */
#pragma disjoint(*ptr_b, a)      /* ptr_b never points to a */
one_function()
{
    b = 6;
    *ptr_a = 7; /* Assignment will not change the value of b */
    another_function(b);      /* Argument "b" has the value 6 */
}
```

#pragma isolated_call

The **#pragma isolated_call** directive lists functions that do not alter data objects visible at the time of the function call.

```
#pragma isolated_call ( identifier [ , identifier ] ... )
```

The pragma must appear before any calls to the functions in the identifier list. The identifiers listed must be declared before they are used in the pragma. Any functions in the identifier list that are called before the pragma is used are not treated as isolated calls. The identifiers must be of type function or a typedef of function.

The pragma informs the compiler that none of the functions listed has side effects. For example, accessing a volatile object, modifying an external object, modifying a file, or calling a function that does any of these can be considered side effects. Essentially, any change in the state of the run-time environment is considered a side effect. Passing function arguments by reference is one side effect that is allowed, but in general, functions with side effects can give incorrect results when listed in **#pragma isolated_call** directives.

Marking a function as isolated indicates to the optimizer that external and static variables cannot be changed by the called function and that references to storage can be deleted from the calling function where appropriate. Instructions can be reordered with more freedom, which results in fewer pipeline delays and faster execution. Note that instruction reordering might, however, result in code that requires more values of general purpose and/or floating-point registers to be maintained across the isolated call. When the isolated call is not located in a loop, the overhead of saving and restoring extra registers might not be worth the savings that result from deleting the storage references.

Functions specified in the identifier list are permitted to examine external objects and return results that depend on the state of the run-time environment. The functions can also modify the storage pointed to by any pointer arguments passed to the function; that is, calls by reference. Do not specify a function that calls itself or relies on local static storage. Listing such functions in the **#pragma isolated_call** directive can give unpredictable results.

The following example shows the use of the **#pragma isolated_call** directive. Because the function this_function does not have side effects, the compiler can assume that a call to it will not change the value of the external variable a. The compiler can then assume that the argument to other_function has the value 6.

```
int a, this_function(int);   /* Assumed to have no side effects */

#pragma isolated_call(this_function)

that_function()
{
   a = 6;
   this_function(7);     /* Call does not change the value of a */
   other_function(a);          /* Argument "a" has the value 6 */
}
```

Levels of Optimization

The levels of optimization in the XL compilers have changed from earlier versions. The new levels are:

No Optimization

In the absence of any version of the **–O** flag, the compiler generates straightforward code with no instruction reordering or other attempt at performance improvement.

–O or –O2

These (equivalent) flags cause the compiler to optimize on the basis of conservative assumptions about code reordering. Only explicit relaxations such as the **#pragma** directives just discussed are used. This level no longer performs software pipelining, loop unrolling, or simple predictive commoning. It also constrains the amount of memory the compiler can use.

The result of these changes is that large or complex routines may have poorer performance when compiled with the **–O** option than they achieved on earlier versions of the compilers.

–O3

Directs the compiler to be aggressive about the optimization techniques used and to use as much memory as necessary for maximum optimization.

This level of optimization may result in functional changes to the program if the program is sensitive to:

- Floating-point exceptions
- The sign of zero
- Precision effects of reordering calculations

These side-effects can be avoided, at some performance cost, by using the **–qstrict** option in combination with **–O3**.

The **–qhot** option, in combination with **–O3**, enables predictive commoning and some unrolling.

The result of these changes is that large or complex routines should have the same or better performance with the **–O3** option (possibly in conjunction with **–qstrict** or **–qhot**) that they had with the **–O** option in earlier versions of the compiler.

XL C Options for string.h Subroutine Performance

AIX provides the ability to embed the string subroutines in the application program rather than using them from **libc.a**. This saves the Call/Return linkage time. To have the string subroutines embedded, the source code of the application must have the statement:

```
#include <string.h>
```

prior to the use of the subroutine(s). In Version 3.1, the only subroutines that would be embedded via this technique were:

- **strcpy()**
- **strcmp()**

Currently, the additional routines are:

- **strlen()**
- **strchr()**
- **strrchr()**
- **strcat()**
- **strncat()**
- **strncpy()**
- **strncmp()**
- **index()**
- **rindex()**
- **memchr()**
- **memcpy()**
- **memccpy()**
- **memmove()**
- **memcmp()**
- **memset()**

If you want to return to the Version 3.1 level of embedding, you should precede the `#include <string.h>` statement with:

```
#define __STR31__
```

C and C++ Coding Style for Best Performance

In many cases, the performance cost of a C construct is not obvious, and sometimes is even counter-intuitive. The following paragraphs document some of these situations.

- Whenever possible, use `int` instead of `char` or `short`.

  In most cases, `char` and `short` data items take more instructions to manipulate. The extra instructions cost time, and, except in large arrays, any space that is saved by using the smaller data types is more than offset by the increased size of the executable.

- If you have to use a char, make it unsigned, if possible.

  A signed char takes another two instructions more than an unsigned char each time the variable is loaded into a register.
- Use local (automatic) variables rather than global variables whenever possible.

  Global variables take more instructions to access than local variables. Also, in the absence of information to the contrary, the compiler assumes that any global variable may have been changed by a subroutine call. This has an adverse effect on optimization because the value of any global variable used after a subroutine call will have to be reloaded.
- When it is necessary to access a global variable (that is not shared with other threads), copy the value into a local variable and use the copy.

  Unless the global variable is accessed only once, it is more efficient to use the local copy.
- Use binary codes rather than strings to record and test for situations.

  Strings use up both data and instruction space. For example, the sequence:

```
#define situation_1 1
#define situation_2 2
#define situation_3 3
int situation_val;

situation_val = situation_2;
. . .
if (situation_val == situation_1)
. . .
```

is much more efficient than:

```
char situation_val[20];

strcpy(situation_val,"situation_2");
. . .
if ((strcmp(situation_val,"situation_1"))==0)
. . .
```

- When strings are really necessary, use fixed-length strings rather than null-terminated variable-length strings wherever possible.

  The **mem*()** family of routines, such as **memcpy()**, are faster than the corresponding **str*()** routines, such as **strcpy()**, because the **str*()** routines have to check each byte for null and the **mem*()** routines don't.

Compiler Execution Time

In AIX, the C compiler can be invoked by two different commands: **cc** and **xlc**. The **cc** command, which has historically been used to invoke the system's C compiler, causes the XL C compiler to run in langlevel=extended mode. This allows the compilation of existing C programs that are not ANSI-compliant. It also consumes processor time.

If the program being compiled is, in fact, ANSI-compliant, it is more efficient to invoke the XL C compiler via the **xlc** command.

Use of the **–O3** flag implicitly includes the **–qmaxmem** option. This allows the compiler to use as much memory as necessary for maximum optimization. This can have two effects:

- On a multiuser system, a large **–O3** compilation may take up enough memory to have an adverse effect on the performance experienced by other users.
- On a system with small real memory, a large **–O3** compilation may take up enough memory to cause high paging rates, making compilation very slow.

Memory-Limited Programs

To programmers accustomed to struggling with the addressing limitations of, for instance, the DOS environment, the 256MB virtual memory segments in the RISC System/6000 environment seem effectively infinite. The programmer is tempted to ignore storage constraints and code for minimum path length and maximum simplicity. Unfortunately, there is a drawback to this attitude. Virtual memory is large, but it is variable-speed. The more memory used, the slower it becomes, and the relationship is not linear. As long as the total amount of virtual storage actually being touched by all programs (that is, the sum of the working sets) is slightly less than the amount of unpinned real memory in the machine, virtual memory performs at about the speed of real memory. As the sum of the working sets of all executing programs passes the number of available page frames, memory performance degrades very rapidly (if VMM memory load control is turned off) by up to two orders of magnitude. When the system reaches this point, it is said to be *thrashing*. It is spending almost all of its time paging, and no useful work is being done because each process is trying to steal back from other processes the storage necessary to accommodate its working set. If VMM memory load control is active, it can avoid this self-perpetuating thrashing, but at the cost of significantly increased response times.

The degradation caused by inefficient use of memory is much greater than that from inefficient use of the caches because the difference in speed between memory and disk is so much higher than the difference between cache and memory. Where a cache miss can take a few dozen CPU cycles, a page fault typically takes 20 milliseconds or more, which is at least 400,000 CPU cycles.

Although the presence of VMM memory load control in AIX ensures that incipient thrashing situations do not become self-perpetuating, unnecessary page faults still exact a cost in degraded response time and/or reduced throughput.

Structuring of Pageable Code

To minimize the code working set of a program, the general objective is to pack code that is frequently executed into a small area, separating it from infrequently executed code. Specifically:

- Do not put long blocks of error-handling code in line. Put them in separate subroutines, preferably in separate source-code modules. This applies not only to error paths, but to any functional option that is infrequently used.
- Do not structure load modules arbitrarily. Try to ensure that frequently called object modules are located as close to their callers as possible. Object modules consisting (ideally) of infrequently called subroutines should be concentrated at the end of the load module. The pages they inhabit will seldom be read in.

Structuring of Pageable Data

To minimize the data working set, try to concentrate the frequently used data and avoid unnecessary references to virtual-storage pages. Specifically:

- Only **malloc** or **calloc** as much space as you really need. Never **malloc** and then initialize a maximum-sized array when the typical real-world situation uses only a fraction of it. When you touch a new page to initialize the array elements, you effectively force the VMM to steal a page of real memory from someone. Later, this results in a page fault when the process that owned that page tries to access it again. Remember that the difference between **malloc** and **calloc** is not just in the interface. Because **calloc** zeroes the allocated storage, it touches every page that is allocated, whereas **malloc** touches only the first page. If you **calloc** a large area and then use only a small portion at the beginning, you put a large, unnecessary load on the system. Not only do the pages have to be initialized; if their real-memory frames are reclaimed, the initialized and never-to-be-used pages must be written out to paging space. This wastes both I/O and paging-space slots.
- Linked lists of large structures (such as buffers) can result in similar problems. If your program does a lot of chain following looking for a particular key, consider maintaining the links and keys separately from the data or using a hash-table approach instead.
- Locality of reference means locality in time, not just in address space. Data structures should be initialized just before they are used (if at all). In a heavily loaded system, data structures that are resident for a long time between initialization and use risk having their frames stolen. Your program would then experience an unnecessary page fault when it began to use the data structure.
- Similarly, if a large structure is used early and then left untouched for the remainder of the program, it should be released. It is not sufficient to **free** the space that was **malloc**ed or **calloc**ed. **free** releases only the address range that the structure occupied. In order to release the real memory and paging space, you must **disclaim** the space as well.

Misuse of Pinned Storage

To avoid circularities and time-outs, a small fraction of the system has to be pinned in real memory. For this code and data, the concept of working set is meaningless, since all of the pinned information is in real storage all the time, whether it is used or not. Any program (such as a user-written device driver) that pins code or data must be carefully designed (or scrutinized, if ported) to ensure that only minimal amounts of pinned storage are used. Some cautionary examples are:

- Code is pinned on a load-module (executable file) basis. If a component has some object modules that must be pinned and others that can be pageable, the pinned object modules should be packaged in a separate load module.
- Pinning a module or a data structure just in case there might be a problem is irresponsible. The designer should understand the conditions under which the information could be required and whether a page fault could be tolerated at that point.
- Pinned structures whose required size is load-dependent, such as buffer pools, should be tunable by the system administrator.

Performance-Related Installation Guidelines

This topic provides recommendations for actions you should take (or not take) before and during the installation process.

AIX Pre-Installation Guidelines

Installing AIX on a New System

Before you begin the installation process, be sure that you have made decisions about the size and location of disk file systems and paging spaces, and that you understand how to communicate those decisions to AIX.

Installing a New Level of AIX on an Existing System

If you are upgrading to a new level of AIX, you should:

- Identify all uses in your present environment of the release-specific performance tools **schedtune** and **vmtune**. Since these tools can only be run by root, their use should not be widespread.
- If these programs are used during system boot, such as from **/etc/inittab**, they should be temporarily removed or bypassed until you are convinced by documentation or experiment that your use of these tools works correctly in the new release.

CPU Pre-Installation Guidelines

We do not recommend any *a priori* changes from the default CPU scheduling parameters, such as the time-slice duration. Unless you have extensive monitoring and tuning experience with the same workload on a nearly identical configuration, you should leave these parameters unchanged at installation time.

See "Monitoring and Tuning CPU Use" on page 88 for post-installation recommendations.

Memory Pre-Installation Guidelines

If the system you are installing is larger than 32MB and is expected to support more than five active users at one time, you may want to consider raising the minimum level of multiprogramming of the VMM memory-load-control mechanism. As an example, if your conservative estimate is that four of your most memory-intensive applications should be able to run simultaneously, leaving at least 16MB for the operating system and 25% of real memory for file pages, you could increase the minimum multiprogramming level from the default of 2 to 4 with the command:

```
# schedtune -m 4
```

All other memory threshold changes should wait until you have had experience with the response of the system to the real workload.

See "Monitoring and Tuning Memory Use" on page 111 for post-installation recommendations.

Disk Pre-Installation Guidelines

General Recommendations

Although the mechanisms for defining and expanding logical volumes attempt to make the best possible default choices, satisfactory disk-I/O performance is much more likely if the installer of the system tailors the size and placement of the logical volumes to the expected data storage and workload requirements. Our recommendations are:

- If possible, the default volume group, **rootvg**, should consist only of the physical volume on which the system is initially installed. One or more other volume groups should be defined to control the other physical volumes in the system. This recommendation has system management as well as performance advantages.
- If a volume group consists of more than one physical volume, you may gain performance by:
  - Initially defining the volume group with a single physical volume.
  - Defining a logical volume within the new volume group. This causes the allocation of the volume group's journal logical volume on the first physical volume.
  - Adding the remaining physical volumes to the volume group.
  - Defining the high-activity file systems on the newly added physical volumes.
  - Defining only very-low-activity file systems, if any, on the physical volume containing the journal logical volume.

This approach separates journaling I/O activity from the high-activity data I/O, increasing the probability of overlap. This technique can have an especially significant effect on NFS server performance, because both data and journal writes must be complete before NFS signals I/O complete for a write operation,

- At the earliest opportunity, define or expand the logical volumes to their maximum expected sizes. To maximize the probability that performance-critical logical volumes will be contiguous and in the desired location, define or expand them first.

- High-usage logical volumes should occupy parts of multiple disk drives. If the "RANGE of physical volumes" option on **smit**'s Add a Logical Volume screen (fast path **smit mklv**) is set to **maximum**, the new logical volume will be divided among the physical volumes of the volume group (or the set of physical volumes explicitly listed).

- If the system has drives of different types (or you are trying to decide which drives to order), consider the following guidelines:

  - Large files that are normally accessed sequentially should be on the fastest available disk drive. At this writing, the sequential and random performance ranking of the disk drives we have measured (from slowest to fastest) is:

Drive Capacity	SCSI Adapter	Random Pages per Second	Sequential Pages per Second
200MB	Model 250 Integrated	approx. 40	approx. 250
400MB	SCSI II	approx. 50	approx. 375
857MB	SCSI II	approx. 60	approx. 550
2.4GB	SCSI II	approx. 65*	approx. 525
1.37GB	SCSI II	approx. 70	approx. 800
540MB	SCSI II	approx. 85	approx. 975
1.0GB†	SCSI II	approx. 85	approx. 1075
2.0GB	SCSI II	approx. 85	approx. 950

* per accessor (there are two)
† This 1.0GB drive (part number 45G9464) replaced an earlier 1.0GB drive (part number 55F5206) in late 1993.

Note: These numbers are derived from the results of laboratory measurements under ideal conditions. They represent a synthesis of a number of different measurements, not the results of a single benchmark. They are provided to give you a general sense of the relative speeds of the disk drives. They will change with time due to improvements in the drives, adapters, and software.

  - If you expect frequent sequential accesses to large files on the fastest disk drives, you should limit the number of disk drivers per disk adapter. Our recommendation for the 540MB, 1.0GB, and 2.0GB drives described above is:

Disk Adapter	Disk Drives per Adapter
Original RISC System/6000 SCSI adapter	1
SCSI-2 High Performance Controller	2
SCSI-2 Fast Adapter (8-bit)	2
SCSI-2 Fast/Wide Adapter (16-bit)	3

- When possible, attach drives with critical, high-volume performance requirements to a SCSI-2 adapter. These adapters have features, such as back-to-back write capability, that are not available on other RISC System/6000 disk adapters.
- On the 200MB, 540MB, and 1.0GB disk drives, logical volumes that will hold large, frequently accessed sequential files should be allocated in the outer_edge of the physical volume. These disks have more blocks per track in their outer sections, which improves sequential performance.
- On a SCSI bus, the highest-numbered drives (those with the numerically largest SCSI addresses, as set on the physical drives) have the highest priority. In most situations this effect is not noticeable, but large sequential file operations have been known to exclude low-numbered drives from access to the bus. You should probably configure the disk drives holding the most response-time-critical data at the highest addresses on each SCSI bus. The command **lsdev –Cs scsi** reports on the current address assignments on each SCSI bus. For the original SCSI adapter, the SCSI address is the first number in the fourth pair of numbers in the output. In the output example below, the 400MB disk is at SCSI address 0, the 320MB disk at address 1, and the 8mm tape drive at address 5.

```
hdisk0  Available  00-01-00-00  400 MB SCSI Disk Drive
hdisk1  Available  00-01-00-10  320 MB SCSI Disk Drive
rmt0    Defined    00-01-00-50  2.3 GB 8mm Tape Drive
```

- Large files that are heavily used and are normally accessed randomly, such as data bases, should be spread across two or more physical volumes.

See "Monitoring and Tuning Disk I/O" on page 130 for post-installation recommendations.

Placement and Sizes of Paging Spaces

The general recommendation is that the sum of the sizes of the paging spaces should be equal to at least twice the size of the real memory of the machine, up to a memory size of 256MB (512MB of paging space). For memories larger than 256MB, we recommend:

total paging space = 512MB + (memory size – 256MB) * 1.25

Ideally, there should be several paging spaces of roughly equal size, each on a different physical disk drive. If you decide to create additional paging spaces, create them on physical volumes that are more lightly loaded than the physical volume in **rootvg**. When allocating paging space blocks, the VMM allocates four blocks, in round-robin fashion, from each of the active paging spaces that has space available. While the system is booting, only the primary paging space (hd6) is active. Consequently, all paging-space blocks allocated during boot are on the primary paging space. This means that the primary paging space should be somewhat larger than the secondary paging spaces. The secondary paging spaces should all be of the same size to ensure that the round-robin algorithm can work effectively.

The **lsps –a** command gives a snapshot of the current utilization level of all the paging spaces on a system. The **psdanger()** subroutine can also be used to determine how closely paging-space utilization is approaching dangerous levels. As an example, the following program uses **psdanger()** to provide a warning message when a threshold is exceeded:

```
/* psmonitor.c
   Monitors system for paging space low conditions. When the condition is
   detected, writes a message to stderr.

   Usage:    psmonitor [Interval [Count]]

   Default:  psmonitor 1 1000000
*/

#include <stdio.h>
#include <signal.h>

main(int argc,char **argv)
{
  int interval = 1;         /* seconds */
  int count = 1000000;      /* intervals */
  int current;              /* interval */
  int last;                 /* check */
  int kill_offset;          /* returned by psdanger() */
  int danger_offset;        /* returned by psdanger() */

  /* are there any parameters at all? */
  if (argc > 1) {
    if ( (interval = atoi(argv[1])) < 1 ) {
      fprintf(stderr,"Usage: psmonitor [ interval [ count ] ]\n");
      exit(1);
    }
    if (argc > 2) {
      if ( (count = atoi( argv[2])) < 1 ) {
        fprintf(stderr,"Usage: psmonitor [ interval [ count ] ]\n");
        exit(1);
      }
    }
  }
  last = count -1;
  for(current = 0; current < count; current++) {
    kill_offset = psdanger(SIGKILL); /* check for out of paging space */
    if (kill_offset < 0)
      fprintf(stderr,
          "OUT OF PAGING SPACE! %d blocks beyond SIGKILL threshold.\n",
          kill_offset*(-1));
    else {
      danger_offset = psdanger(SIGDANGER); /* check for paging sp. low */
      if (danger_offset < 0) {
        fprintf(stderr,
     "WARNING: paging space low. %d blocks beyond SIGDANGER threshold.\n",
            danger_offset*(-1));
        fprintf(stderr,
     "                         %d blocks below SIGKILL threshold.\n",
            kill_offset);
      }
    }
      if (current < last)
```

```
        sleep(interval);
    }
}
```

Performance Implications of Disk Mirroring

If mirroring is being used and Mirror Write Consistency is on (as it is by default), you may want to locate the copies in the outer region of the disk, since the Mirror Write Consistency information is always written in Cylinder 0. From a performance standpoint, mirroring is costly, mirroring with Write Verify is costlier still (extra disk rotation per write), and mirroring with both Write Verify and Mirror Write Consistency is costliest of all (disk rotation plus a seek to Cylinder 0). To avoid confusion, we should point out that although an **lslv** command will usually show Mirror Write Consistency to be on for non-mirrored logical volumes, no actual processing is incurred unless the COPIES value is greater than one. Write Verify, on the other hand, defaults to off, since it does have meaning (and cost) for nonmirrored logical volumes.

Communications Pre-Installation Guidelines

See the summary of communications tuning recommendations in "UDP, TCP/IP, and mbuf Tuning Parameters Summary" on page 175.

5

System Monitoring and Initial Performance Diagnosis

This chapter describes tools and techniques for monitoring performance-related system activity and diagnosing performance problems.

The Case for Continuous Performance Monitoring

In some installations, monitoring of performance activity is done on a demand basis. When a performance problem is reported, the performance analyst runs one or more commands in an attempt to determine why the problem occurred. In some cases, explicit recreation of the problem is needed in order to collect analysis data. The result is that users experience every performance problem twice.

It is usually more effective to monitor performance continuously, preferably with automatic collection of additional data if performance deteriorates. The costs of continuous monitoring are outweighed by the advantages, such as:

- Monitoring can sometimes detect incipient problems before they have an adverse effect.
- Monitoring can detect problems that happen to users who are reluctant to complain and problems that are not quite severe enough to complain about—but are affecting productivity and morale.
- Monitoring can collect data when a problem occurs for the first time.

Successful monitoring involves five main activities:

1. Periodically obtaining performance-related information from the operating system
2. Storing the information for future use in problem diagnosis
3. Displaying the information for the benefit of the system administrator

4. Detecting situations that require additional data collection or responding to directions from the system administrator to collect such data, or both
5. Collecting and storing the necessary detail data

The following sections discuss several approaches to continuous monitoring. These approaches are not mutually exclusive, but use of more than one may involve some redundancy.

Performance Monitoring Using iostat, netstat, vmstat

The **iostat**, **netstat**, and **vmstat** commands have functional characteristics that make them useful for continuous monitoring of system performance:

- They can produce reports at a fixed interval indefinitely.
- They report on activity that varies with different types of load.
- They report on activity since the last previous report, so changes in activity are easy to detect.

The following example shows samples of the periodic reports produced by these programs.

```
$ iostat 5 2

tty:      tin        tout      cpu:   % user    % sys     % idle    % iowait
          0.0        0.0              0.0       0.2       99.6      0.1

Disks:        % tm_act    Kbps      tps    Kb_read    Kb_wrtn
hdisk0          0.1       0.3       0.0     18129      56842
cd0             0.0       0.0       0.0         0          0

tty:      tin        tout      cpu:   % user    % sys     % idle    % iowait
          0.0        0.0              23.1      9.0       65.9      2.0

Disks:        % tm_act    Kbps      tps    Kb_read    Kb_wrtn
hdisk0          2.4       6.4       1.6         0         32
cd0             0.0       0.0       0.0         0          0


$ vmstat 5 2
procs     memory                  page                    faults          cpu
----- ----------- ------------------------ ------------- -----------
 r  b   avm    fre   re  pi  po  fr   sr  cy  in   sy  cs us sy id wa
 0  0  2610   1128    0   0   0   0    0   0 112    1  19  0  0 99  0
 0  0  2505   1247    0   0   0   0    0   0 125 1056  37 22  9 67  2


$ netstat -I tr0 5
    input    (tr0)      output              input    (Total)      output
 packets   errs  packets  errs colls    packets   errs  packets  errs colls
  532099   1664      985     0     0     532111   1664      997     0     0
      45      0        6     0     0         45      0        6     0     0
      44      1        5     0     0         44      1        5     0     0
```

Remember that the first report from each of these programs is for cumulative activity since the last system boot. The second report shows activity for the first 5-second interval. Even this small sample shows that the activity in the first interval was significantly higher than the average.

These commands are the basic foundation on which a performance-monitoring mechanism can be constructed. Shell scripts can be written to perform data reduction on ***stat** command output and warn of performance problems or record data on the status of the system when a problem is occurring. For example, a shell script could test the CPU idle percentage for zero and execute another shell script when that CPU-saturated condition occurred. A script such as:

```
$ ps -ef | egrep -v "STIME|$LOGNAME" | sort +3 -r | head -n 15
```

would record the 15 active processes that had consumed the most CPU time recently (other than the processes owned by the user of the script).

Depending on the required level of sophistication, creating such a family of shell scripts can be a substantial project. Fortunately, there are packages available that require less development and setup and have considerably more function than the typical installation would want to implement locally.

The Performance Diagnostic Tool

The Performance Diagnostic Tool (PDT) is a new tool in AIX Version 4.1. PDT collects configuration and performance information and attempts to identify potential problems, both current and future.

PDT is an optionally installable component of the AIX Base Operating System. Its name is **bos.perf.diag_tool**. After PDT has been installed, it must be activated with the **pdt_config** command. This causes appropriate entries to be made in the **crontab** file, which causes PDT to run periodically, recording data and looking for new trends.

In assessing the configuration and the historical record of performance measurements, PDT attempts to identify:

- Resource imbalances—asymmetrical aspects of configuration or device utilization
- Usage trends—changes in usage levels that will lead to saturation
- New consumers of resources—expensive processes that haven't been observed before
- Inappropriate system parameter values—settings that may cause problems
- Errors—hardware or software problems that may lead to performance problems

Extensive documentation on PDT is given in "Performance Diagnostic Tool (PDT)" beginning on page 229.

The AIX Performance Toolbox

The Performance Toolbox for AIX (PTX) is a licensed product that allows graphic display of a variety of performance-related metrics. Among the advantages of PTX over ASCII reporting programs is that it is much easier to check current performance with a glance at the graphic monitor than by looking at a screen full of numbers. PTX also facilitates the combination of information from multiple performance-related AIX commands.

PTX is described in detail in the *Performance Toolbox 1.2 and 2.1 for AIX: User's Guide*, IBM form number SC23-2625.

Inference from the Kind of Performance Problem Reported

When a performance problem is reported, the kind of performance problem will often help the performance analyst to narrow the list of possible culprits.

A Particular Program Runs Slowly

This may seem to be the trivial case, but there are still questions to be asked:

- Has the program always run slowly?

  If the program has just started running slowly, a recent change may be the cause.

- Has the source code been changed or a new version installed?

  If so, check with the programmer or vendor.

- Has something in the environment changed?

  If a file used by the program (including its own executable) has been moved, it may now be experiencing LAN delays that weren't there before; or files may be contending for a single disk accessor that were on different disks before.

  If the system administrator has changed system-tuning parameters, the program may be subject to constraints that it didn't experience before. For example, if the **schedtune –r** command has been used to change the way priority is calculated, programs that used to run rather quickly in the background may now be slowed down, while foreground programs have speeded up.

- Is the program written in the **awk**, **csh**, or some other interpretive language?

  While they allow programs to be written quickly, interpretive languages have the problem that they are not optimized by a compiler. Also, it is easy in a language like **awk** to request an extremely compute- or I/O-intensive operation with a few characters. It is often worthwhile to perform a desk check or informal peer review of such programs with the emphasis on the number of iterations implied by each operation.

- Does the program always run at the same speed, or is it sometimes faster?

  The AIX file system uses some of system memory to hold pages of files for future reference. If a disk-limited program is run twice in quick succession, it will normally run faster the second time than the first. Similar phenomena may be observed with programs that use NFS and DFS. This can also occur with large programs, such as compilers. The program's algorithm may not be disk-limited, but the time needed to load a large executable may make the first execution of the program much longer than subsequent ones.

- If the program has always run slowly, or has slowed down without any obvious change in its environment, we need to look at its dependency on resources.

  "Identifying the Performance-Limiting Resource" on page 80 describes techniques for finding the bottleneck.

Everything Runs Slowly at a Particular Time of Day

Most people have experienced the rush-hour slowdown that occurs because a large number of people in the organization habitually use the system at one or more particular times each day. This phenomenon is not always simply due to a concentration of load. Sometimes it is an indication of an imbalance that is (at present) only a problem when the load is high. There are also other sources of periodicity in the system that should be considered.

- If you run **iostat** and **netstat** for a period that spans the time of the slowdown (or have previously captured data from your monitoring mechanism), are some disks much more heavily used than others? Is the CPU Idle percentage consistently near zero? Is the number of packets sent or received unusually high?

  If the disks are unbalanced, look at "Monitoring and Tuning Disk I/O" on page 130.

  If the CPU is saturated, use **ps** to identify the programs being run during this period. The script given in "Performance Monitoring Using iostat, netstat, vmstat" simplifies the search for the CPU hogs.

  If the slowdown is counter-intuitive, such as paralysis during lunch time, look for a pathological program such as a graphic Xlock or game program. Some versions of Xlock are known to use huge amounts of CPU time to display graphic patterns on an idle display. It is also possible that someone is running a program that is a known CPU burner and is trying to run it at the least intrusive time.

- Unless your **/var/adm/cron/cron.allow** file is null, you may want to check the contents of the **/var/adm/cron/crontab** directory for expensive operations. For example, users have been known to request an hourly copy of all of their home directory files to an NFS-mounted backup directory.

If you find that the problem stems from conflict between foreground activity and long-running, CPU-intensive programs that are, or should be, run in the background, you should consider using **schedtune −r −d** to give the foreground higher priority. See "Tuning the Process-Priority-Value Calculation with schedtune" on page 107.

Everything Runs Slowly at Unpredictable Times

The best tool for this situation is an overload detector, such as **xmperf**'s **filtd** program (a component of PTX). **filtd** can be set up to execute shell scripts or collect specific information when a particular condition is detected. You can construct a similar, but more specialized, mechanism using shell scripts containing **vmstat**, **netstat**, and **ps**.

If the problem is local to a single system in a distributed environment, there is probably a pathological program at work, or perhaps two that intersect randomly.

Everything an Individual User Runs Is Slow

Sometimes a system seems to "pick on" an individual.

- Quantify the problem. Ask the user which commands are used frequently, and run them with the **time** command, as in the following example:

```
$ time cp .profile testjunk
real     0m0.08s
user     0m0.00s
sys      0m0.01s
```

Then run them under a satisfactory userid. Is there a difference in the reported real time?

- A program should not show much CPU time (user+sys) difference from run to run, but may show a real time difference because of more or slower I/O. Are the user's files on an NFS-mounted directory? On a disk that has high activity for other reasons?
- Check the user's .profile file for strange $PATH specifications. For example, if you always search a couple of NFS-mounted directories (fruitlessly) before searching /usr/bin, everything will take longer.

A Number of LAN-Connected Systems Slow Down Simultaneously

There are some common problems that arise in the transition from independent systems to distributed systems. They usually result from the need to get a new configuration running as soon as possible, or from a lack of awareness of the cost of certain functions. In addition to tuning the LAN configuration in terms of MTUs and mbufs (see the Monitoring and Tuning Communications I/O chapter), we should look for LAN-specific pathologies or nonoptimal situations that may have evolved through a sequence of individually reasonable decisions.

- Some types of software or firmware bugs can sporadically saturate the LAN with broadcast or other packets.

  When a broadcast storm occurs, even systems that are not actively using the network can be slowed by the incessant interrupts and by the CPU resource consumed in receiving and processing the packets. These bugs are better detected and localized with LAN analysis devices than with normal AIX performance tools.

- Do you have two LANs connected via an AIX system?

  Using an AIX system as a router consumes large amounts of CPU time to process and copy packets. It is also subject to interference from other work being processed by the AIX system. Dedicated hardware routers and bridges are usually a more cost-effective and robust solution to the need to connect LANs.

- Is there a clearly defensible purpose for each NFS mount?

  At some stages in the development of distributed configurations, NFS mounts are used to give users on new systems access to their home directories on their original systems. This simplifies the initial transition, but imposes a continuing data communication cost. It is not unknown to have users on system A interacting primarily with data on system B and vice versa.

  Access to files via NFS imposes a considerable cost in LAN traffic, client and server CPU time, and end-user response time. The general principle should be that user and data should normally be on the same system. The exceptions are those situations in which there is an overriding concern that justifies the extra expense and time of remote data. Some examples are a need to centralize data for more reliable backup and control, or a need to ensure that all users are working with the most current version of a program.

  If these and other needs dictate a significant level of NFS client-server interchange, it is better to dedicate a system to the role of server than to have a number of systems that are part-server, part-client.

- Have programs been ported correctly (and justifiably) to use remote procedure calls (RPCs)?

  The simplest method of porting a program into a distributed environment is to replace program calls with RPCs on a 1:1 basis. Unfortunately, the disparity in performance between local program calls and RPCs is even greater than the disparity between local disk I/O and NFS I/O. Assuming that the RPCs are really necessary, they should be batched whenever possible.

Everything That Uses a Particular Service or Device Slows Down at Times

Make sure you have followed the configuration recommendations in the appropriate subsystem manual and/or the recommendations in the appropriate "Monitoring and Tuning" chapter of this book.

Using PerfPMR for Performance Diagnosis

The PerfPMR package was developed to ensure that reports of suspected performance problems in AIX were accompanied by enough data to permit problem diagnosis by IBM. This makes the shell scripts in PerfPMR useful to other performance analysts as well. PerfPMR is an optionally installable part of the AIX Version 4.1 Base Operating System. It is located in **/usr/sbin/perf/pmr**. See the discussion in "Installing AIX Version 4.1 PerfPMR" on page 245 . A version of PerfPMR is also available for AIX Version 3.2.5. See "Obtaining and Installing AIX Version 3.2.5 PerfPMR" on page 244.

The script **perfpmr** is the highest-level script of the package, but it collects data, such as configuration information, that a local performance analyst probably knows already. The lower-level script **monitor** collects a coordinated set of performance information for a specified number of seconds and summarizes the data. The syntax of **monitor** is:

> **monitor** *seconds* [**–n**] [**–p**]

The *seconds* parameter must be at least 60. If *seconds* is 600 or less, the interval for the periodic reports is 10 seconds; otherwise, the interval is 60 seconds. The **–n** flag suppresses collection of **netstat** and **nfsstat** data. The **–p** flag suppresses collection of process-profile data (see below). The **monitor** script should not be run at the same time as any other operation that uses the system trace facility.

A single **monitor** request creates:

- A **monitor.int** file containing:
  - Combined output of **ps –elk** and **ps gv** commands run at the beginning and end of the monitoring period.
  - Output of a **sar –A** command with the appropriate interval.
  - Output of an **iostat** command with the appropriate interval. The initial, cumulative report is omitted.
  - Output of a **vmstat** command with the appropriate interval. The initial, cumulative report is omitted.
- A **monitor.sum** file containing:
  - For those processes that were active at both the beginning and end of the monitor run, the differences between end and start values of various resource-use statistics.
  - The "Average" lines from the **sar –A** command output.
  - Averages of the **iostat** interval statistics.
  - Averages of the **vmstat** interval statistics.
  - The "after – before" differences of the statistics produced by the **vmstat –s** command.
- If the **–n** option was *not* specified, a **netstat.int** file containing:
  - The output at the beginning of the monitor run of the following commands:
    > **netstat –v**
    > **netstat –m**
    > **netstat –rs**
    > **netstat –s**
  - The output of a **netstat** command with the appropriate interval.
  - The output at the end of the monitor run of the following commands:
    > **netstat –v**
    > **netstat –m**
    > **netstat –rs**
    > **netstat –s**
- If the **–n** option was *not* specified, an **nfsstat.int** file containing:
  - The output at the beginning and end of the monitor run of a **nfsstat –csnr** command.
- If the **–p** option was *not* specified, a pair of files named **Pprof.stt** and **Pprof.flow. Pprof.stt** contains the starting and ending times of the run. **Pprof.flow** contains process-profile data. The columns in the **Pprof.flow** file are:

1 Process name

2 Process ID

3 Time of first occurrence of the process within the measurement period

4 Time of last occurrence of the process

5 Total process execution time

6 Begin/end flag (sum of Begin + End, below). Describes the beginning and ending state of the process.

Begin:

execed:	0
forked:	1
Alive at Start:	2

End:

Alive at end:	0
execed away:	4
Exited:	8

7 Parent process ID

Check before You Change

One particularly important use of the PerfPMR package is the creation of a configuration and performance baseline prior to a significant change in system hardware or software. Just as you probably back up critical files before such a change, you should make a record of the configurations and the performance they were providing. If a performance degradation should occur after the change, you will have detailed data that will let you perform a rigorous before-and-after analysis of the system.

To get the most complete data possible, you should run:

```
$ perfpmr 3600
```

during the busiest hour of the day. The output files from this measurement run will appear in directory **/var/perf/tmp**. (If you are running on a pre-Version 4 system, the output files will appear in the current working directory.) Be sure to move these files to a safe haven before beginning the configuration change.

Identifying the Performance-Limiting Resource

Starting with an Overview of System Performance

Perhaps the best tool for an overall look at resource utilization while running a multiuser workload is the **vmstat** command. The **vmstat** command reports CPU and disk-I/O activity as well as memory utilization data. The command

```
$ vmstat 5
```

causes the **vmstat** command to begin writing a one-line summary report of system activity every 5 seconds. Since no count was specified following the interval, reporting continues until the command is cancelled.

The following **vmstat** report was made on a system running AIXwindows and several synthetic applications (some low-activity intervals have been removed):

procs		memory		page						faults			cpu			
r	b	avm	fre	re	pi	po	fr	sr	cy	in	sy	cs	us	sy	id	wa
0	0	8793	81	0	0	0	1	7	0	125	42	30	1	2	95	2
0	0	8793	80	0	0	0	0	0	0	155	113	79	14	8	78	0
0	0	8793	57	0	3	0	0	0	0	178	28	69	1	12	81	6
0	0	9192	66	0	0	16	81	167	0	151	32	34	1	6	77	16
0	0	9193	65	0	0	0	0	0	0	117	29	26	1	3	96	0
0	0	9193	65	0	0	0	0	0	0	120	30	31	1	3	95	0
0	0	9693	69	0	0	53	100	216	0	168	27	57	1	4	63	33
0	0	9693	69	0	0	0	0	0	0	134	96	60	12	4	84	0
0	0	10193	57	0	0	0	0	0	0	124	29	32	1	3	94	2
0	0	11194	64	0	0	38	201	1080	0	168	29	57	2	8	62	29
0	0	11194	63	0	0	0	0	0	0	141	111	65	12	7	81	0
0	0	5480	755	3	1	0	0	0	0	154	107	71	13	8	78	2
0	0	5467	5747	0	3	0	0	0	0	167	39	68	1	16	79	5
0	1	4797	5821	0	21	0	0	0	0	191	192	125	20	5	42	33
0	1	3778	6119	0	24	0	0	0	0	188	170	98	5	8	41	46
0	0	3751	6139	0	0	0	0	0	0	145	24	54	1	10	89	0

The columns of interest for this initial assessment are pi and po in the page category and the four columns in the cpu category.

- Entries pi and po are the paging-space page ins and page outs, respectively. If any paging-space I/O is taking place, the workload is approaching (or is beyond) the system's memory limits.
- If the sum of us and sy (user and system) CPU-utilization percentages is greater than 80% in a given 5-second interval, the workload was approaching the CPU limits of the system during that interval.
- If the wa (I/O wait) percentage is nonzero (and pi and po are zero), a significant amount of time is being spent waiting on nonoverlapped file I/O, and some part of the workload is I/O-limited.

By "approaching its limits," we mean that some parts of the workload are already experiencing a slowdown due to the critical resource. The longer response times may not be subjectively significant yet, but an increase in that element of the workload will cause a rapid deterioration of performance.

If **vmstat** indicates a significant amount of I/O wait time, an **iostat** will give more detailed information. The command

```
$ iostat 5 3
```

causes **iostat** to begin writing summary reports of I/O activity and CPU utilization every 5 seconds. Since a count of 3 was specified following the interval, reporting will stop after the third report.

The following **iostat** report was made on a system running the same workload as the **vmstat** reports above, but at a different time. The first report is for the cumulative activity since the preceding boot, while subsequent reports are for activity during the preceding 5-second interval:

tty:	tin	tout	cpu:	% user	% sys	% idle	%iowait
	0.0	4.3		0.2	0.6	98.8	0.4

Disks:	% tm_act	Kbps	tps	msps	Kb_read	Kb_wrtn
hdisk0	0.0	0.2	0.0		7993	4408
hdisk1	0.0	0.0	0.0		2179	1692
hdisk2	0.4	1.5	0.3		67548	59151
cd0	0.0	0.0	0.0		0	0

tty:	tin	tout	cpu:	% user	% sys	% idle	%iowait
	0.0	30.3		8.8	7.2	83.9	0.2

Disks:	% tm_act	Kbps	tps	msps	Kb_read	Kb_wrtn
hdisk0	0.2	0.8	0.2		4	0
hdisk1	0.0	0.0	0.0		0	0
hdisk2	0.0	0.0	0.0		0	0
cd0	0.0	0.0	0.0		0	0

tty:	tin	tout	cpu:	% user	% sys	% idle	%iowait
	0.0	8.4		0.2	5.8	0.0	93.8

Disks:	% tm_act	Kbps	tps	msps	Kb_read	Kb_wrtn
hdisk0	0.0	0.0	0.0		0	0
hdisk1	0.0	0.0	0.0		0	0
hdisk2	98.4	575.6	61.9		396	2488
cd0	0.0	0.0	0.0		0	0

The first report, which displays cumulative activity since the last boot, shows that the I/O on this system is unbalanced. Most of the I/O (86.9% of kilobytes read and 90.7% of kilobytes written) is to hdisk2 , which contains both the operating system and the paging space. The cumulative CPU utilization since boot statistic is usually meaningless, unless the system is used consistently 24 hours a day.

The second report shows a small amount of disk activity reading from hdisk0, which contains a separate file system for the system's primary user. The CPU activity arises from two application programs and **iostat** itself. Although **iostat**'s output is redirected to a file, the output is not voluminous, and the system is not sufficiently memory-constrained to force any output during this interval.

In the third report, we have artificially created a near-thrashing condition by running a program that allocates, and stores into, a large amount of memory (about 26MB in this example). hdisk2 is active 98.4% of the time, which results in 93.8% I/O wait. The fact that a single program that uses more than three-fourths of the system's memory (32MB) can cause the system to thrash reminds us of the limits of VMM memory load control (see page 124). Even with a more homogeneous workload, we need to understand the memory requirements of the components.

If **vmstat** indicates that there is a significant amount of CPU idle time when the system seems subjectively to be running slowly, you may be experiencing delays due to kernel lock contention. In AIX Version 4.1, this possibility can be investigated with the **lockstat** command if the Performance Toolbox is installed on your system.

Determining the Limiting Factor for a Single Program

If you are the sole user of a system, you can get a general idea of whether a program is I/O or CPU dependent by using the **time** command as follows:

```
$ time cp foo.in foo.out

real  0m0.13s
user  0m0.01s
sys   0m0.02s
```

Note: Examples of the **time** command here and elsewhere in this book use the version that is built into the Korn shell. The official **time** command (**/usr/bin/time**) reports with a lower precision and has other disadvantages.

In this example, the fact that the real, elapsed time for the execution of the **cp** (.13 seconds) is significantly greater than the sum (.03 seconds) of the user and system CPU times indicates that the program is I/O bound. This occurs primarily because foo.in has not been read recently. Running the same command a few seconds later against the same file gives:

```
real  0m0.06s
user  0m0.01s
sys   0m0.03s
```

Most or all of the pages of foo.in are still in memory because there has been no intervening process to cause them to be reclaimed and because the file is small compared with the amount of RAM on the system. A small foo.out would also be buffered in memory, and a program using it as input would show little disk dependency.

If you are trying to determine the disk dependency of a program, you have to be sure that its input is in an authentic state. That is, if the program will normally be run against a file that has not been accessed recently, you must make sure that the file used in measuring the program is not in memory. If, on the other hand, a program is usually run as part of a standard sequence in which it gets its input from the output of the preceding program, you should *prime* memory to ensure that the measurement is authentic. For example,

```
$ cp foo.in /dev/null
```

would have the effect of priming memory with the pages of foo.in.

The situation is more complex if the file is large compared to RAM. If the output of one program is the input of the next and the entire file won't fit in RAM, the second program will end up reading pages at the head of the file, which displace pages at the end. Although this situation is very hard to simulate authentically, it is nearly equivalent to one in which no disk caching takes place.

The case of a file that is (perhaps just slightly) larger than RAM is a special case of the RAM versus disk analysis discussed in the next section.

Disk or Memory?

Just as a large fraction of real memory is available for buffering files, the system's page space is available as temporary storage for program working data that has been forced out of RAM. Suppose that you have a program that reads little or no data and yet shows the symptoms of being I/O dependent. Worse, the ratio of real time to user + system time does not improve with successive runs. The program is probably memory-limited, and its I/O is to, and possibly from, the paging space. A way to check on this possibility is shown in the following vmstatit shell script. The vmstatit script summarizes the voluminous **vmstat –s** report, which gives cumulative counts for a number of system activities since the system was started:

```
vmstat -s >temp.file    # cumulative counts before the command
time $1                 # command under test
vmstat -s >>temp.file   # cumulative counts after execution
grep "pagi.*ins" temp.file >>results   # extract only the data
grep "pagi.*outs" temp.file >>results  # of interest
```

If the shell script is run as follows:

```
$ vmstatit "cp file1 file2"  2>results
```

the result in results is:

```
real  0m0.03s
user  0m0.01s
sys   0m0.02s
    2323 paging space page ins
    2323 paging space page ins
    4850 paging space page outs
    4850 paging space page outs
```

The fact that the before-and-after paging statistics are identical confirms our belief that the **cp** command is not paging bound. An extended variant of the vmstatit shell script can be used to show the true situation:

```
vmstat -s >temp.file
time $1
vmstat -s >>temp.file
echo "Ordinary Input:"                   >>results
grep "^[ 0-9]*page ins"    temp.file >>results
echo "Ordinary Output:"                  >>results
grep "^[ 0-9]*page outs"   temp.file >>results
echo "True Paging Output:"               >>results
grep "pagi.*outs"          temp.file >>results
echo "True Paging Input:"                >>results
grep "pagi.*ins"           temp.file >>results
```

Because all ordinary I/O in the AIX operating system is processed via the VMM, the **vmstat –s** command reports ordinary program I/O as page ins and page outs. When the above version of the `vmstatit` shell script was run against the **cp** command of a large file that had not been read recently, the result was:

```
real  0m2.09s
user  0m0.03s
sys   0m0.74s
Ordinary Input:
    46416 page ins
    47132 page ins
Ordinary Output:
   146483 page outs
   147012 page outs
True Paging Output:
     4854 paging space page outs
     4854 paging space page outs
True Paging Input:
     2527 paging space page ins
     2527 paging space page ins
```

The **time** command output confirms the existence of an I/O dependency. The increase in page ins shows the I/O necessary to satisfy the **cp** command. The increase in page outs indicates that the file is large enough to force the writing of dirty pages (not necessarily its own) from memory. The fact that there is no change in the cumulative paging-space-I/O counts confirms that the **cp** command does not build data structures large enough to overload the memory of the test machine.

The order in which this version of the `vmstatit` script reports I/O is intentional. Typical programs read file input and then write file output. Paging activity, on the other hand, typically begins with the writing out of a working-segment page that does not fit. The page is read back in only if the program tries to access it. The fact that the test system has experienced almost twice as many `paging space page outs` as `paging space page ins` since it was booted indicates that at least some of the programs that have been run on this system have stored data in memory that was not accessed again before the end of the program. "Memory-Limited Programs" on page 64 provides more information. See also "Monitoring and Tuning Memory Use" beginning on page 111.

To show the effects of memory limitation on these statistics, the following example observes a given command in an environment of adequate memory (32MB) and then artificially shrinks the system using the **rmss** command (see "Assessing Memory Requirements via the rmss Command" on page 115). The command sequence

```
$ cc -c ed.c
$ vmstatit "cc -c ed.c" 2>results
```

first primes memory with the 7944-line source file and the executable file of the C compiler, then measures the I/O activity of the second execution:

```
real  0m7.76s
user  0m7.44s
sys   0m0.15s
Ordinary Input:
    57192 page ins
    57192 page ins
Ordinary Output:
   165516 page outs
   165553 page outs
True Paging Output:
    10846 paging space page outs
    10846 paging space page outs
True Paging Input:
     6409 paging space page ins
     6409 paging space page ins
```

Clearly, this is not I/O limited. There is not even any I/O necessary to read the source code.

If we then issue the command

```
# rmss -c 8
```

to change the effective size of the machine to 8MB, and perform the same sequence of commands, we get:

```
real  0m9.87s
user  0m7.70s
sys   0m0.18s
Ordinary Input:
    57625 page ins
    57809 page ins
Ordinary Output:
   165811 page outs
   165882 page outs
True Paging Output:
    11010 paging space page outs
    11061 paging space page outs
True Paging Input:
     6623 paging space page ins
     6701 paging space page ins
```

The symptoms of I/O dependency are present:

- Elapsed time longer than total CPU time

- Significant amounts of ordinary I/O on the nth execution of the command

The fact that the elapsed time is longer than in the memory-unconstrained situation, and the existence of significant amounts of paging-space I/O, make it clear that the compiler is being hampered by insufficient memory.

Note: This example illustrates the effects of memory constraint. No effort was made to minimize the use of memory by other processes, so the absolute size at which the compiler was forced to page in this environment does not constitute a meaningful measurement.

To avoid working with an artificially shrunken machine until the next restart, run

```
# rmss -r
```

to release back to the operating system the memory that the **rmss** command had sequestered, thus restoring the system to its normal capacity.

Workload Management

When you have exhausted the program performance-improvement and system-tuning possibilities, and performance is still unsatisfactory at times, you have three choices:

- Live with the situation.
- Upgrade the performance-limiting resource.
- Adopt workload-management techniques.

If you adopt the first approach, some of your less stoic users will experience increasing frustration and decreasing productivity. If you choose to upgrade, you have to justify the expenditure to someone. That someone will undoubtedly want to know if you have exhausted all possibilities with the current system, which means you need to investigate the possibilities of workload management.

Workload management simply means assessing the components of the workload to determine whether they are all needed as soon as possible. Usually, there is work that can wait for a while; for example, a report that is needed first thing in the morning. That report is equally useful when run at 3 a.m. as at 4 p.m. on the preceding day. The difference is that at 3 a.m. it uses CPU cycles and other resources that would otherwise be idle. The **at** command or **crontab** command can be used to request the running of a program at a specific time or at regular intervals.

Similarly, some programs that do have to be run during the day can be run at reduced priority. They will take longer to complete, but they will be less in competition with really time-critical processes.

A related technique is moving work from one machine to another; for example, running a compilation on the machine where the source code resides. This kind of workload balancing requires more planning and monitoring, because reducing the load on the network and increasing the CPU load on a server may result in a net loss.

6

Monitoring and Tuning CPU Use

The processing unit in a RISC System/6000 is one of the fastest components of the system. It is comparatively rare for a single program to keep the CPU 100% busy for more than a few seconds at a time. Even in heavily loaded multiuser systems, there are occasional 10ms periods that end with everything in a wait state. If a monitor shows the CPU 100% busy (that is, 0% idle and 0% wait) for an extended period, there is a good chance that some program is in an infinite loop. Even if the program is "merely" expensive, rather than broken, it needs to be identified and dealt with.

This chapter deals with techniques for detecting runaway or CPU-intensive programs and minimizing their adverse effect on performance.

Readers who are not familiar with AIX CPU scheduling may want to look at "Performance Overview of the AIX CPU Scheduler," beginning on page 14, before continuing.

Using vmstat to Monitor CPU Use

As a CPU monitor, **vmstat** is superior to **iostat** in that its one-line-per-report output is easier to scan as it scrolls. **vmstat** also gives you general information about memory use, paging, and ordinary disk I/O at a glance. The following example can help you identify situations in which a program has run away or is too CPU intensive to run in a multiuser environment.

```
$ vmstat 2
procs     memory              page                    faults          cpu
----- ----------- ------------------------ ------------ -----------
 r  b   avm   fre  re  pi  po  fr    sr  cy   in   sy   cs us sy id wa
 1  0 22478  1677   0   0   0   0     0   0  188 1380 157 57 32  0 10
 1  0 22506  1609   0   0   0   0     0   0  214 1476 186 48 37  0 16
 0  0 22498  1582   0   0   0   0     0   0  248 1470 226 55 36  0  9
```

```
2  0 22534  1465  0  0  0  0   0  0 238  903 239 77 23  0  0
2  0 22534  1445  0  0  0  0   0  0 209 1142 205 72 28  0  0
2  0 22534  1426  0  0  0  0   0  0 189 1220 212 74 26  0  0
3  0 22534  1410  0  0  0  0   0  0 255 1704 268 70 30  0  0
2  1 22557  1365  0  0  0  0   0  0 383  977 216 72 28  0  0

2  0 22541  1356  0  0  0  0   0  0 237 1418 209 63 33  0  4
1  0 22524  1350  0  0  0  0   0  0 241 1348 179 52 32  0 16
1  0 22546  1293  0  0  0  0   0  0 217 1473 180 51 35  0 14
```

This output shows the effect of introducing a program in a tight loop to a busy multiuser system. The first three reports (the summary has been removed) show the system balanced at 50–55% user, 30–35% system, and 10–15% I/O wait. When the looping program begins, all available CPU cycles are consumed. Since the looping program does no I/O, it can absorb all of the cycles previously unused because of I/O wait. Worse, it represents a process that is always ready to take over the CPU when a useful process relinquishes it. Since the looping program has a priority equal to that of all other foreground processes, it will not necessarily have to give up the CPU when another process becomes dispatchable. The program runs for about 10 seconds (five reports), and then the activity reported by vmstat returns to a more normal pattern.

Using the time Command to Measure CPU Use

The **time** command is a simple but useful tool for understanding the performance characteristics of a single program. **time** reports the elapsed time from beginning to end of the program, the `real` time. It also reports the amount of CPU time used by the program. The CPU time is divided into `user` and `sys`. The `user` value is the time used by the program itself and any library subroutines it calls. The `sys` value is the time used by system calls invoked by the program (directly or indirectly).

The sum of `user` + `sys` is total direct CPU cost of executing the program. This does not include the CPU costs of parts of the kernel that can be said to run on behalf of the program, but which do not actually run on its thread. For example, the cost of stealing page frames to replace the page frames taken from the free list when the program started is not reported as part of the program's CPU consumption.

The difference between the `real` time and the total CPU time, that is:

```
real - (user + sys)
```

is the sum of all of the factors that can delay the program, plus the program's own unattributed costs. In roughly the order of diminishing size, these factors may be:

- I/O required to bring in the program's text and data
- I/O required to acquire real memory for the program's use
- CPU time consumed by other programs
- CPU time consumed by the operating system

In the following example, the program used in the preceding section has been compiled with –O3 to make it quicker. There is very little difference between the real (wall-clock) time required to run the program and the sum of its user and system CPU times. The program is getting all the time it wants—probably at the expense of other programs in the system.

```
$ time looper
real    0m3.58s
user    0m3.16s
sys     0m0.04s
```

In the next example, we run the program at a lower priority by adding 10 to its nice value. It takes almost twice as long to run, but other programs are getting a chance to do their work too:

```
$ time nice -10 looper
real    0m6.54s
user    0m3.17s
sys     0m0.03s
```

Note that we placed the **nice** command within the **time** command, rather that the reverse. If we had entered

```
$ nice -10 time looper
```

we would have gotten a different **time** command (**/usr/bin/time**) with a lower-precision report, rather than the version of **time** we have been using, which is built into **ksh**. If the **time** command comes first, you will get the built-in version, unless you specify the fully qualified name of **/usr/bin/time**. If **time** is invoked from another command, you will get **/usr/bin/time**.

time and timex Cautions

There are several considerations that you should take into account when using **time** or its variant **timex**:

- The use of the **/usr/bin/time** and **/usr/bin/timex** commands is not recommended. When possible, use the **time** subcommand of the Korn or C shell. In AIX 3.2.5, **/usr/bin/time** incorrectly reports the CPU time used by a shell script containing a sequence of commands connected by pipes (the CPU time of all but the last command in the sequence is lost). This is because **/usr/bin/time** uses the system default shell. In AIX 3.2.5, the system default is the Bourne shell, which **exec**s the commands in the sequence in such a way that only the CPU consumption of the last can be measured. In AIX 4.1, the system default shell is the Korn shell, which does not exhibit this phenomenon.
- The **timex –s** command uses **sar** to acquire additional statistics. Since **sar** is intrusive, **timex –s** is too. Especially for brief runs, the data reported by **timex –s** may not precisely reflect the behavior of a program in an unmonitored system.
- Because of the length of the system clock tick (10 milliseconds) and the rules used by the scheduler in attributing CPU time use to threads, the results of the **time** command are not completely deterministic. There is a certain amount of unavoidable variation between successive runs. This variation is in terms of

clock ticks. Obviously, the shorter the run time of the program, the larger the variation will loom as a percentage of the reported result.

- Use of the **time** or **timex** command, whether from **/usr/bin** or via the built-in shell **time** function, to measure the user or system time of a sequence of commands connected by pipes, entered on the command line, is not recommended. One potential problem is that syntax oversights can cause **time** to measure only one of the commands, without any indication of a user error. The syntax is technically correct; it just doesn't produce the answer the user intended.

Using xmperf to Monitor CPU Use

Using **xmperf** to display CPU use in the system is even more attention-grabbing. If you display CPU as a moving skyline chart and display User CPU in bright red, a runaway program is immediately obvious from across a room. **xmperf** is described in detail in the *Performance Toolbox 1.2 and 2.1 for AIX: User's Guide*, IBM form number SC23-2625.

Using ps to Identify CPU-Intensive Programs

Three of the possible **ps** output columns report CPU use, each in a different way.

Column	Value Is:
C	Recently used CPU time for the process.
TIME	Total CPU time used by the process since it started.
%CPU	Total CPU time used by the process since it started divided by the elapsed time since the process started. This is a measure of the CPU dependence of the program.

The shell script:

```
$ps -ef | egrep -v "STIME|$LOGNAME" | sort +3 -r | head -n 15
```

is a tool for focusing on the most CPU-intensive user processes in the system. If we had used that script in the situation described in "Using vmstat to Monitor CPU Use" on page 88, its output would have appeared as follows (the header line has been reinserted for clarity):

```
 USER    PID  PPID   C   STIME    TTY   TIME CMD
waters 45742 54701 120 15:19:05 pts/29  0:02 ./looper
  root 52121     1  11 15:32:33 pts/31 58:39 xhogger
  root  4250     1   3 15:32:33 pts/31 26:03 xmconsole allcon
  root 38812  4250   1 15:32:34 pts/31  8:58 xmconstats 0 3 30
  root 27036  6864   1 15:18:35      -  0:00 rlogind
  root 47418 25925   0 17:04:26      -  0:00 coelogin <d29dbms:0>
  bick 37651 43538   0 16:58:40  pts/4  0:00 /bin/ksh
  bick 43538     1   0 16:58:38      -  0:07 aixterm
   luc 60061 27036   0 15:18:35 pts/18  0:00 -ksh
```

Recent CPU use is the fourth column ("C"). The looping program's process easily heads the list. Observe that the C value may understate the looping process's CPU usage, since the scheduler stops counting at 120.

The **ps** command is a very flexible tool for identifying the programs that are running in the system and the resources they are using. The individual options and columns are described in the formal documentation of **ps** in the *AIX Version 4.1 Commands Reference*.

Most of the flags of **ps** belong to one of two groups:

1. Flags that specify which processes are to be included in the output
2. Flags that specify what information is to be displayed about each process

The following two tables are intended to simplify the task of choosing **ps** flags by summarizing the effects of the flags. In each table, the flags specified with a minus sign are on the left side of the table; the flags specified without a minus sign are on the right side. You cannot mix types. If the first flag is specified with a minus sign, all other flags in that **ps** command must be from the minus-sign group.

Process-Specifying Flags:

Processes Listed Are:	−A	−a	−d	−e	−G −g	−k	−p	−U −t	−u	a	g	t	x
All processes	Y	-	-	-	-	-	-	-	-	-	Y	-	-
Not process-group leaders and not associated with a terminal	-	Y	-	-	-	-	-	-	-	-	-	-	-
Not process-group leaders	-	-	Y	-	-	-	-	-	-	-	-	-	-
Not kernel processes	-	-	-	Y	-	-	-	-	-	-	-	-	-
Members of specified process groups	-	-	-	-	Y	-	-	-	-	-	-	-	-
Kernel processes	-	-	-	-	-	Y	-	-	-	-	-	-	-
Those specified in process number list	-	-	-	-	-	-	Y	-	-	-	-	-	-
Those associated with TTY(s) in the list	-	-	-	-	-	-	-	Y (n TTYs)	-	-	-	Y (1 TTY)	-
Specified user's processes	-	-	-	-	-	-	-	-	Y	-	-	-	-
Processes with terminals	-	-	-	-	-	-	-	-	-	Y	-	-	-
Not associated with a TTY	-	-	-	-	-	-	-	-	-	-	-	-	Y

If the **ps** command is issued without a process-specifying flag, the processes owned by the user issuing the **ps** command are displayed.

Column-Selecting Flags:

–U

Column:	Default1	–f	–l	–u	Default2	e	l	s	u	v
PID	Y	Y	Y	Y	Y	Y	Y	Y	Y	Y
TTY	Y	Y	Y	Y	Y	Y	Y	Y	Y	Y
TIME	Y	Y	Y	Y	Y	Y	Y	Y	Y	Y
CMD	Y	Y	Y	Y	Y	Y	Y	Y	Y	Y
USER	-	Y	-	-	-	-	-	-	Y	-
UID	-	-	Y	Y	-	-	Y	-	-	-
PPID	-	Y	Y	-	-	-	Y	-	-	-
C	-	Y	Y	-	-	-	Y	-	-	-
STIME	-	Y	-	-	-	-	-	-	Y	-
F	-	-	Y	-	-	-	-	-	-	-
S/STAT	-	-	Y	-	Y	Y	Y	Y	Y	Y
PRI	-	-	Y	-	-	-	Y	-	-	-
NI/NICE	-	-	Y	-	-	-	Y	-	-	-
ADDR	-	-	Y	-	-	-	Y	-	-	-
SZ/SIZE	-	-	Y	-	-	-	Y	-	Y	Y
WCHAN	-	-	Y	-	-	-	Y	-	-	-
RSS	-	-	-	-	-	-	Y	-	Y	Y
SSIZ	-	-	-	-	-	-	-	Y	-	-
%CPU	-	-	-	-	-	-	-	-	Y	Y
%MEM	-	-	-	-	-	-	-	-	Y	Y
PGIN	-	-	-	-	-	-	-	-	-	Y
LIM	-	-	-	-	-	-	-	-	-	Y
TSIZ	-	-	-	-	-	-	-	-	-	Y
TRS	-	-	-	-	-	-	-	-	-	Y
environment	-	-	-	-	-	Y	-	-	-	-

(following the command;
has no column heading)

If **ps** is given with no flags or with a process-specifying flag that begins with a minus sign, the columns displayed are those shown for Default1. If the command is given with a process-specifying flag that does not begin with minus, Default2 columns are displayed. The **–u** or **–U** flag is both a process-specifying and column-selecting flag.

The following are brief descriptions of the contents of the columns:

PID	Process ID
TTY	Terminal or pseudo-terminal associated with the process
TIME	Cumulative CPU time consumed, in minutes and seconds
CMD	Command the process is running
USER	Login name of the user to whom the process belongs
UID	Numeric user ID of the user to whom the process belongs
PPID	ID of this process's parent process
C	Recently used CPU time
STIME	Time the process started, if today. Otherwise the date the process started.

F	Eight-character hexadecimal value describing the flags associated with the process (see the detailed description of the **ps** command)
S/STAT	Status of the process (see the detailed description of the **ps** command)
PRI	Current priority value of the process
NI/NICE	Nice value for the process
ADDR	Segment number of the process stack
SZ/SIZE	Number of working-segment pages that have been touched, times 4.
WCHAN	Event on which the process is waiting
RSS	Sum of the numbers of working-segment and code-segment pages in memory, times 4
SSIZ	Size of the kernel stack
%CPU	Percentage of time since the process started that it was using the CPU.
%MEM	RSS value divided by the machine size in KB, times 100, rounded to the nearest full percentage point.
PGIN	Number of page-ins caused by page faults. Since all AIX I/O is classified as page faults, this is basically a measure of I/O volume.
LIM	Limit on RSS size. Displayed as "xx" if not set.
TSIZ	Size of the text section of the executable file
TRS	Number of code-segment pages, times 4
environment	Value of all the environment variables for the process

Using tprof to Analyze Programs for CPU Use

The typical program execution is a variable mixture of application code, library subroutines, and kernel services. Frequently, a program that has not yet been tuned is found to expend most of its CPU cycles in a few statements or subroutines. Quite often, these "hot spots" are a surprise to the implementor—they can be considered performance bugs. Our tool of choice for pinpointing the hot spots in a program is the trace-driven profiler—**tprof**. **tprof** can profile any program produced by one of the XL compilers: XL C, XL C++, and XL FORTRAN.

In AIX Version 4.1, the **tprof** program is packaged as part of the Performance Toolbox for AIX. To determine whether **tprof** is available, use:

```
lslpp -lI perfagent.tools
```

If this package has been installed, **tprof** is available.

The raw data for **tprof** is obtained via the Trace facility (see "Performance Analysis with the Trace Facility" on page 214). When a program is profiled, the Trace facility is activated and instructed to collect data from the trace hook (hook ID 234) that records the contents of the Instruction Address Register when a system-clock interrupt occurs—100 times a second. Several other trace hooks are also activated to allow **tprof** to track process and dispatch activity. The trace records are not written to a disk file; they are written to a pipe that is read by a program that builds a table of the unique program addresses that have been encountered and the number of times each one occurred. When the workload being profiled is complete, the table of addresses and their occurrence counts is written to disk. The data-reduction component of **tprof** then correlates the instruction addresses that were encountered with the ranges of addresses occupied by the various programs and reports the distribution of address occurrences ("ticks") across the programs involved in the workload.

The distribution of ticks is roughly proportional to the CPU time spent in each program (10 milliseconds per tick). Once the high-use programs have been identified, the programmer can take action to restructure their hot spots or minimize their use.

A detailed description of the **tprof** command appears in the *AIX Version 4.1 Commands Reference, Volume 4.*

A (Synthetic) Cautionary Example

The following C program initializes each byte of a large array of integers to 0x01, increments each int by a random constant, and prints out a randomly selected int. The program does nothing useful, but is representative of programs that process large arrays.

```
/*  Array Incrementer -- Version 1   */
#include <stdlib.h>
#define Asize 1024
#define RowDim InnerIndex
#define ColDim OuterIndex
main()
{  int Increment;
   int OuterIndex;
   int InnerIndex;
   int big [Asize][Asize];

   /* initialize every byte of the array to 0x01 */
   for(OuterIndex=0; OuterIndex<Asize; OuterIndex++)
   {
     for (InnerIndex=0; InnerIndex<Asize; InnerIndex++)
       big[RowDim][ColDim] = 0x01010101;
   }
   Increment = rand();
   /* increment every element in the array */
   for(OuterIndex=0; OuterIndex<Asize; OuterIndex++)
   {
     for (InnerIndex=0; InnerIndex<Asize; InnerIndex++)
     {
       big[RowDim][ColDim] += Increment;
       if (big[RowDim][ColDim] < 0)
         printf("Negative number. %d\n",big[RowDim][ColDim]);
     }
   }
   printf("Version 1 Check Num: %d\n",
          big[rand()%Asize][rand()%Asize]);
```

```
    return(0);
}
```

The program was compiled with the command:

```
$ xlc -g version1.c -o version1
```

The −g parameter causes the XL C compiler to generate the object module with symbolic debugging information for use by **tprof**. Although **tprof** can profile optimized modules, we have omitted the −O parameter to make the line numbers that **tprof** uses more precise. When the XL C compiler is optimizing, it often does enough rearrangement of code to make **tprof**'s output harder to interpret. On the test system, this program runs in about 5.97 seconds of elapsed time, of which more than 5.9 seconds is user CPU time. Clearly the program meets its objective of being CPU-limited.

If we **tprof** the program with the following command:

```
$ tprof -p version1 -x version1
```

we get a file called __version1.all (shown below) that reports how many CPU ticks each of the programs involved in the execution consumed.

Process	PID	Total	Kernel	User	Shared	Other
version1	33570480	793	30	763	0	0
bsh	33566383	8	8	0	0	0
/etc/init	1	6	0	6	0	0
/etc/syncd	3059	5	5	0	0	0
tprof	5038	4	2	2	0	0
rlogind	11345	2	2	0	0	0
PID.771	771	1	1	0	0	0
tprof	11940	1	1	0	0	0
tprof	11951	1	1	0	0	0
tprof	13987	1	1	0	0	0
bsh	16048	1	1	0	0	0
Total		823	52	771	0	0

Process	FREQ	Total	Kernel	User	Shared	Other
version1	1	793	30	763	0	0
bsh	2	9	9	0	0	0
/etc/init	1	6	0	6	0	0
/etc/syncd	1	5	5	0	0	0
tprof	4	7	5	2	0	0
rlogind	1	2	2	0	0	0
PID.771	1	1	1	0	0	0
Total	11	823	52	771	0	0

```
Total Ticks For version1(    USER) =    763
```

Subroutine	Ticks	%	Source	Address	Bytes
.main	763	92.7	version1.c	632	560

The first section of the report shows the number of ticks consumed by, or on behalf of, each process. `version1` used 763 ticks itself, and 30 ticks occurred in the kernel on behalf of `version1`'s process. Two processes running the Bourne shell were involved in the execution of `version1`. Four processes were running **tprof**-related code. The **init** process, the **sync** daemon, an **rlogin** process, and one other process accounted for 14 ticks.

Remember that the program associated with a given numerical process ID changes with each **exec** call. If one application program **exec**s another, both program names will appear in the **tprof** output associated with the same process ID.

The second section of the report summarizes the results by program, regardless of process ID. It shows the number (FREQ) of different processes that ran each program at some point.

The third section breaks down the user ticks associated with the executable program being profiled. It reports the number of ticks used by each function in the executable, and the percentage of the total run's CPU ticks (823) that each function's ticks represent.

Up to this point, none of the **tprof** processing has required access to the specially compiled version of the program. We could have done the preceding analysis on a program for which we did not have access to the source code.

It is clear from this report that the preponderance (92.7%) of CPU consumption is in the program itself, not in the kernel nor in library subroutines that the program uses. We have to look at the program itself more closely.

Since we compiled `version1.c` with the **–g** option, the object file contains information that relates offsets in the program text to lines of source code. Consequently, **tprof** created an annotated version of the source file `version1.c`, called `__t.version1.c`, based on the offsets and line number information in the object module. The first column is simply the line number. The second column is the number of times the trace hook reported that the Timer interrupt occurred while the system was executing one of the instructions associated with that line.

```
Ticks Profile for main in version1.c

   Line    Ticks    Source

    14       34      for(OuterIndex=0; OuterIndex<Asize; OuterIndex++)
    15        -      {
    16       40        for (InnerIndex=0; InnerIndex<Asize; InnerIndex++)
    17      261          big[RowDim][ColDim] = 0x01010101;
    18        -      }
    19        -      Increment = rand();
    20        -
    21        -      /* increment every element in the array */
    22       70      for(OuterIndex=0; OuterIndex<Asize; OuterIndex++)
    23        -      {
    24        -        for (InnerIndex=0; InnerIndex<Asize; InnerIndex++)
    25        -        {
    26       69          big[RowDim][ColDim] += Increment;
    27       50          if (big[RowDim][ColDim] < 0)
    28      239            printf("Negative number.%d\n",
                                  big[RowDim][ColDim]);
    29        -        }
```

```
30      -          }
31      -          printf("Version 1 Check Num: %d\n",
32      -                  big[rand()%Asize][rand()%Asize]);
33      -          return(0);
34      -      }
```

763 Total Ticks for main in version1.c

This shows clearly that the largest numbers of ticks are associated with accessing elements of the array `big`, so we should be able to improve performance significantly by concentrating on the inner `for` loops. The first (initialization) `for` loop is a case of brute-force programming. It is very inefficient to initialize arrays one element at a time. If we were setting the array to 0, we should have used **bzero**. Since we are setting each byte to a specific character, we will use **memset** to replace the first `for` loop. (The very efficient **bzero** and **memset** functions, like the **str** functions, are written in assembler language and use hardware instructions that have no direct equivalent in the C language.)

We have to access the array one element at a time to increment the values, but we should ensure that the pattern of memory reference is to consecutive addresses, to maximize cache use. In this case, we have the row dimension changing faster than the column dimension. Since C arrays are arranged in row-major order, we are skipping over a complete row with each successive memory reference. Since the rows are 1024 `ints` long (4096 bytes), we are changing pages on every reference. The size of the array greatly exceeds both the data cache and data TLB capacities, so we have written a program for maximum cache and TLB thrashing. To fix this problem, we simply transpose the `#defines` to reverse the values of `RowDim` and `ColDim`.

The unoptimized form of the resulting program (`version2.c`) consumes about 2.7 CPU seconds, compared with 7.9 CPU seconds for `version1`.

The following file, `__t.version2.c`, is the result of a **tprof** run against the unoptimized form:

```
Ticks Profile for main in version2.c

  Line   Ticks   Source

   15      -         memset(big,0x01,sizeof(big));
   16      -         Increment = rand();
   17      -
   18      -         /* increment in memory order */
   19      60        for(OuterIndex=0; OuterIndex<Asize; OuterIndex++)
   20      -         {
   21      -           for (InnerIndex=0; InnerIndex<Asize; InnerIndex++)
   22      -           {
   23      67          big[RowDim][ColDim] += Increment;
   24      60          if (big[RowDim][ColDim] < 0)
   25      43           printf("Negative number.
%d\n",big[RowDim][ColDim]);
   26      -           }
   27      -         }
   28      -         printf("Version 2 Check Num: %d\n",
   29      -                 big[rand()%Asize][rand()%Asize]);
   30      -         return(0);
```

```
   31      -    }
```

230 Total Ticks for main in version2.c

By being aware of its CPU use pattern, we have improved the CPU speed of this program by a factor of almost three—for the unoptimized case. When we compile version1.c and version2.c with optimization and compare their performance, the "before and after" improvement due to our changes is a factor of 7.

In many cases, most of a program's CPU use will occur in the library subroutines it uses rather than in the program itself. If we take version2.c and remove the conditional test on line 24 and the printf entry on line 28, to create a version3.c that reads as follows:

```c
#include <string.h>
#include <stdlib.h>
#define Asize 256
#define RowDim OuterIndex
#define ColDim InnerIndex

main()
{
  int Increment;
  int OuterIndex;
  int InnerIndex;
  int big [Asize][Asize];

  /* Initialize every byte to 0x01 */
  memset(big,0x01,sizeof(big));
  Increment = rand();
  /* increment in memory order */
  for(OuterIndex=0; OuterIndex<Asize; OuterIndex++)
  {
    for (InnerIndex=0; InnerIndex<Asize; InnerIndex++)
    {
      big[RowDim][ColDim] += Increment;
      printf("RowDim=%d, ColDim=%d, Number=%d\n",
      RowDim, ColDim, big[RowDim][ColDim]);
    }
  }
  return(0);
}
```

the execution time becomes dominated by the **printf** statement. The command:

```
$ tprof -v -s -k -p version3 -x version3 >/dev/null
```

produces a __version3.all that includes profiling data for the kernel and the shared subroutine library libc.a (the only shared library this program uses):

Process	PID	Total	Kernel	User	Shared	Other
=======	===	=====	======	====	======	=====
version3	33568373	818	30	19	769	0
bsh	33567348	5	5	0	0	0
tprof	15987	3	1	2	0	0

tprof	7784	1	1	0	0	0
tprof	12905	1	1	0	0	0
bsh	13941	1	1	0	0	0
=======	===	=====	======	====	======	=====
Total		829	39	21	769	0

Process	FREQ	Total	Kernel	User	Shared	Other
=======	===	=====	======	====	======	=====
version3	1	818	30	19	769	0
bsh	2	6	6	0	0	0
tprof	3	5	3	2	0	0
=======	===	=====	======	====	======	=====
Total	6	829	39	21	769	0

Total Ticks For version3 (USER) =   19

Subroutine	Ticks	%	Source	Address	Bytes
=============	======	======	=======	=======	=====
.main	11	1.3	version3.c	632	320
.printf	8	1.0	glink.s	1112	36

Total Ticks For version3 (KERNEL) =   30

Subroutine	Ticks	%	Source	Address	Bytes
=============	======	======	=======	=======	=====
.sc_flih	7	0.8	low.s	13832	1244
.i_enable	5	0.6	low.s	21760	256
.vmcopyin	3	0.4	vmmove.c	414280	668
.xix_setattr	2	0.2	xix_sattr.c	819368	672
.isreadonly	2	0.2	disubs.c	689016	60
.lockl	2	0.2	lockl.s	29300	208
.v_pagein	1	0.1	v_getsubs1.c	372288	1044
.curtime	1	0.1	clock.s	27656	76
.trchook	1	0.1	noname	48168	856
.vmvcs	1	0.1	vmvcs.s	29744	2304
.spec_rdwr	1	0.1	spec_vnops.c	629596	240
.rdwr	1	0.1	rdwr.c	658460	492
.imark	1	0.1	isubs.c	672024	184
.nodev	1	0.1	devsw_pin.c	135864	32
.ld_findfp	1	0.1	ld_libld.c	736084	240

Total Ticks For version3 (SH-LIBs) =   769

Shared Object	Ticks	%	Source	Address	Bytes
=============	======	======	=======	=======	=====
libc.a/shr.o	769	92.0	/usr/lib	794624	724772

Profile: /usr/lib/libc.a shr.o

Total Ticks For version3 (/usr/lib/libc.a) =   769

Subroutine	Ticks	%	Source	Address	Bytes
._doprnt	476	56.9	doprnt.c	36616	7052
.fwrite	205	24.5	fwrite.c	50748	744
.strchr	41	4.9	strchr.s	31896	196
.printf	18	2.2	printf.c	313796	144
._moveeq	16	1.9	memcmp.s	36192	184
.strlen	10	1.2	strerror.c	46800	124
.isatty	1	0.1	isatty.c	62932	112
._xwrite	1	0.1	flsbuf.c	4240	280
.__ioctl	1	0.1	ioctl.c	57576	240

This confirms that most of the ticks are being used by the shared libraries—libc.a, in this case. The profile of libc.a shows that most of those ticks are being consumed by the **_doprnt** subroutine.

_doprnt is the processing module for **printf**, **sprintf**, etc. With a simple change, we have increased the run time from 2.7 seconds to 8.6 seconds, and our formatted printing now consumes about 60% of the CPU time. This makes it clear why formatting should be used judiciously. **_doprnt** performance is also affected by the locale. See Appendix I, "National Language Support—Locale vs Speed". These tests were run in the C locale—the most efficient.

Detailed Control Flow Analysis with stem

The **stem** instrumentation package can trace the flow of control through a wide range of software. It is available on AIX Version 4.1 systems as part of the Performance Toolbox for AIX. To determine whether **stem** is available on your system, use:

```
lslpp -lI perfagent.tools
```

If this package has been installed, **stem** is available.

Some of the most significant advantages of **stem** are:

- **stem** can instrument application programs that are:
  - stripped
  - optimized
  - running in multiple processes
  - in unstripped shared libraries
- **stem** entry and exit instrumentation subroutines can be:
  - **stem**-provided
  - user-provided

stem builds instrumented versions of the requested programs and libraries, and stores them in a directory called **/tmp/EXE**. When the user runs the instrumented program, **stem** creates a corresponding file called **stem_out**.

Basic stem Analysis

If we want to analyze the control flow of a simple application program, we would use:

```
stem -p stem_test_pgm
```

The output of that command would be:

```
************************************************************
Make.Stem does not exist, issuing make for stem_samples.o
make stem_samples.o
Target stem_samples.o is up to date.
*******************************************************
The instrumented stem_test_pgm is at /tmp/EXE/stem_test_pgm
Assuming AIX 3.2.5 or later, SVC_string=.sc_flih
```

The instrumentation of `stem_test_pgm` was successful, even though the program had been stripped. The instrumented form of the program has been placed in the directory **/tmp/EXE**. We then enter:

```
/tmp/EXE/stem_test_pgm
```

We get a file called **stem_out** in the current working directory. In this case, **stem_out** contains:

```
  Seconds.usecs   TID  Routine Names & Seconds.usecs since entering
routine.
767549539.847704   1 ->main
767549539.880523   1     ->setPI
767549539.880958   1     <-setPI   0.000435
767549539.881244   1     ->squareit
767549539.881515   1     <-squareit   0.000271
767549539.881793   1     ->printf
767549539.883316   1     <-printf   0.001523
767549539.883671   1     ->setPI
767549539.883944   1     <-setPI   0.000273
767549539.884221   1     ->squareit
767549539.884494   1     <-squareit   0.000273
767549539.884772   1     ->printf
767549539.885981   1     <-printf   0.001209
767549539.886330   1 <-main   0.038626
767549539.886647   1 ->exit
```

The call graph captures both calls to functions within the module (setPI and squareit) and calls to the **printf** subroutine in **libc.a**. The numbers to the right of the subroutine names represent the elapsed seconds and microseconds between the call and the return.

If we perform the same process on the **wc** command (**/usr/bin/wc**), the **stem_out** file (for a **wc** of a two-word file) contains:

```
  Seconds.usecs   TID  Routine Names & Seconds.usecs since entering
routine.
767548812.962031   1 ->main
767548812.993952   1     ->setlocale
767548812.995065   1     <-setlocale   0.001113
767548812.995337   1     ->catopen
767548812.995554   1     <-catopen   0.000217
767548812.995762   1     ->getopt
767548812.996101   1     <-getopt   0.000339
767548812.996345   1     ->open
767548812.996709   1     <-open   0.000364
```

```
767548812.996953    1      ->read
767548812.997209    1      <-read   0.000256
767548812.997417    1      ->read
767548812.997654    1      <-read   0.000237
767548812.997859    1      ->wcp
767548812.998113    1         ->printf
767548812.998586    1         <-printf  0.000473
767548812.998834    1      <-wcp   0.000975
767548812.999041    1      ->printf
767548813.000439    1      <-printf   0.001398
767548813.000720    1      ->close
767548813.000993    1      <-close   0.000273
767548813.001284    1      ->exit
```

This call graph, obtained almost effortlessly, shows the structure of an AIX command. The calls to **setlocale** and **catopen** ensure that the command process is running in the same National Language Support (NLS) locale and with the same message catalog as its parent process.

Although **stem**-instrumented programs can run in multiple processes, the call graph shows only the flow of control within the primary process.

Restructuring Executables with fdpr

The **fdpr** (feedback-directed program restructuring) program optimizes executable modules for faster execution and more efficient use of real memory. It is available on AIX Version 4.1 systems as part of the Performance Toolbox for AIX. To determine whether **fdpr** is available on your system, use:

```
lslpp -lI perfagent.tools
```

If this package has been installed, **fdpr** is available.

fdpr processing takes place in three stages:

- The executable module to be optimized is instrumented to allow detailed performance-data collection.
- The instrumented executable is run in a workload provided by the user, and performance data from that run is recorded.
- The performance data is used to drive a performance-optimization process that results in a restructured executable module that should perform *the workload that exercised the instrumented executable* more efficiently. It is critically important that the workload used to drive **fdpr** closely match the actual use of the program. The performance of the restructured executable with workloads that differ substantially from that used to drive **fdpr** is unpredictable, but can be worse than that of the original executable.

As an example, the command:

```
fdpr -p ProgramName -R3 -x test.sh
```

would use the testcase `test.sh` to run an instrumented form of program `ProgramName`. The output of that run would be used to perform the most aggressive optimization (R3) of the program to form a new module called, by default, `ProgramName.fdpr`. The degree to which the optimized executable performed better in production than its unoptimized predecessor would depend largely on the degree to which `test.sh` successfully imitated the production workload.

Warning: The **fdpr** program incorporates advanced optimization algorithms that sometimes result in optimized executables that do not function in the same way as the original executable module. It is **absolutely essential** that any optimized executable be exhaustively tested before being used in any production situation; that is, before its output is trusted.

In summary, users of **fdpr** should:

- Take pains to use a workload to drive **fdpr** that is representative of the intended use.
- Exhaustively test the functioning of the resulting restructured executable.
- Use the restructured executable only on the workload for which it has been tuned.

Controlling Contention for the CPU

Controlling the Priority of User Processes

User-process priorities can be manipulated using the **nice** or **renice** command or the **setpri** subroutine, and displayed with **ps**. An overview of priority is given in "Process and Thread Priority" on page 15.

Running a Command at a Nonstandard Priority with nice

Any user can run a command at a lower than normal priority by using **nice**. Only `root` can use **nice** to run commands at higher than normal priority.

With **nice**, the user specifies a value to be added to or subtracted from the standard nice value. The modified nice value is used for the process that runs the specified command. The priority of the process is still non-fixed. That is, the priority value is still recalculated periodically based on the CPU usage, nice value, and minimum user-process-priority value.

The standard nice value of a foreground process is 20; the standard nice value of a background process is 24. The nice value is added to the minimum user-process-priority level (40) to obtain the initial priority value of the process. For example, the command:

```
$ nice -5 vmstat 10 3 >vmstat.out
```

causes the **vmstat** command to be run with a nice value of 25 (instead of 20), resulting in a base priority value of 65 (before any additions for recent CPU use)

If we were `root`, we could have run the **vmstat** at a higher priority with:

```
# nice --5 vmstat 10 3 >vmstat.out
```

If we were not `root` and issued that **nice**, the **vmstat** command would still be run, but at the standard nice value of 20, and **nice** would not issue any error message.

Setting a Fixed Priority with the setpri Subroutine

An application that runs under the `root` userid can use the **setpri** subroutine to set its own priority or that of another process. For example:

```
retcode = setpri(0,59);
```

would give the current process a fixed priority of 59. If **setpri** fails, it returns −1.

The following program accepts a priority value and a list of process IDs and sets the priority of all of the processes to the specified value.

```
/*
fixprocpri.c
     Usage: fixprocpri priority PID . . .
*/

#include <sys/sched.h>
#include <stdio.h>
#include <sys/errno.h>

main(int argc,char **argv)
{
pid_t ProcessID;
int Priority,ReturnP;

if( argc < 3 ) {
     printf(" usage - setpri priority pid(s) \n");
     exit(1);
}

argv++;
Priority=atoi(*argv++);
if ( Priority < 50 ) {
     printf(" Priority must be >= 50 \n");
     exit(1);
}

while (*argv) {
     ProcessID=atoi(*argv++);
     ReturnP = setpri(ProcessID, Priority);
     if ( ReturnP > 0 )
          printf("pid=%d new pri=%d  old pri=%d\n",
             (int)ProcessID,Priority,ReturnP);
     else {
          perror(" setpri failed ");
          exit(1);
     }
}
}
```

Displaying Process Priority with ps

The –l (lower-case L) flag of the **ps** command displays the nice values and current priority values of the specified processes. For example, we can display the priorities of all of the processes owned by a given user with:

```
# ps -lu waters
      F S UID  PID PPID  C PRI NI ADDR    SZ    WCHAN   TTY  TIME CMD
 241801 S 200 7032 7287  0  60 20 1b4c   108            pts/2 0:00 ksh
 200801 S 200 7569 7032  0  65 25 2310    88  5910a58  pts/2 0:00
vmstat
 241801 S 200 8544 6495  0  60 20 154b   108            pts/0 0:00 ksh
```

The output shows the result of the **nice –5** command described earlier. Process 7569 has an effective priority of 65. (The **ps** command was run by a separate session in superuser mode, hence the presence of two TTYs.)

If one of the processes had used the **setpri** subroutine to give itself a fixed priority, the **ps –l** output format would be:

```
      F S UID   PID  PPID  C PRI NI ADDR    SZ    WCHAN   TTY  TIME CMD
 200903 S   0 10759 10500  0  59 -- 3438    40  4f91f98 pts/0 0:00
fixpri
```

Modifying the Priority of a Running Process with renice

Note: In the following discussion, the AIX Version 3 **renice** syntax is used. The next section discusses AIX Version 3 and 4 **nice** and **renice** syntax.

renice alters the nice value, and thus the priority, of one or more processes that are already running. The processes are identified either by process ID, process group ID, or the name of the user who owns the processes. **renice** cannot be used on fixed-priority processes.

To continue our example, we will **renice** the **vmstat** process that we started with **nice**.

```
# renice -5 7569
7569: old priority 5, new priority -5
# ps -lu waters
      F S UID  PID PPID  C PRI NI ADDR    SZ    WCHAN   TTY  TIME CMD
 241801 S 200 7032 7287  0  60 20 1b4c   108            pts/2 0:00 ksh
 200801 S 200 7569 7032  0  55 15 2310    92  5910a58  pts/2 0:00
vmstat
 241801 S 200 8544 6495  0  60 20 154b   108            pts/0 0:00 ksh
```

Now the process is running at a *higher* priority than the other foreground processes. Observe that **renice** does not add or subtract the specified amount from the old nice value. It replaces the old nice value with a new one. To undo the effects of all this playing around, we could issue:

```
# renice -0 7569
7569: old priority -5, new priority 0
# ps -lu waters
      F S UID  PID PPID  C PRI NI ADDR    SZ   WCHAN   TTY  TIME CMD
 241801 S 200 7032 7287  0  60 20 1b4c   108           pts/2 0:00 ksh
 200801 S 200 7569 7032  1  60 20 2310    92 5910a58   pts/2 0:00
vmstat
 241801 S 200 8544 6495  0  60 20 154b   108           pts/0 0:00 ksh
```

In these examples, **renice** was run by `root`. When run by an ordinary userid, there are two major limitations to the use of **renice**:

- Only processes owned by that userid can be specified.
- The priority of the process cannot be increased—not even to return the process to the default priority after lowering its priority with **renice**.

Clarification of nice/renice Syntax

AIX Version 3

The **nice** and **renice** commands have different ways of specifying the amount that is to be added to the standard nice value of 20.

With **nice**, the initial minus sign is required to identify the value, which is assumed to be positive. Specifying a negative value requires a second minus sign (with no intervening space).

With **renice**, the parameter following the command name is assumed to be the value, and it can be a signed or unsigned (positive) number. Thus the following pairs of commands are equivalent:

		Resulting nice Value	Resulting Priority Value
nice –5	renice 5	25	65
nice –5	renice +5	25	65
nice – –5	renice –5	15	55

AIX Version 4

For AIX Version 4, the syntax of **renice** has been changed to complement the alternative syntax of **nice**, which uses the **–n** flag to identify the nice-value increment. The following table is the AIX Version 4 version of the table in the preceding section:

		Resulting nice Value	Resulting Priority Value
nice –n 5	renice –n 5	25	65
nice –n +5	renice –n +5	25	65
nice –n –5	renice –n –5	15	55

Tuning the Process-Priority-Value Calculation with schedtune

A recent enhancement of **schedtune** and the AIX CPU scheduler permits changes to the parameters used to calculate the priority value for each process. This enhancement is part of AIX Version 4.1 and is available in a PTF for AIX Version 3.2.5. See "Process and Thread Priority" beginning on page 15 for background information on priority.

Briefly, the formula for calculating the priority value is:

$$\text{priority value} = \text{base priority} + \text{nice value} + \text{(CPU penalty based on recent CPU usage)}$$

The recent CPU usage value of a given process is incremented by 1 each time that process is in control of the CPU when the timer interrupt occurs (every 10 milliseconds). The recent CPU usage value is displayed as the "C" column in **ps** command output. The maximum value of recent CPU usage is 120.

The current algorithm calculates the CPU penalty by dividing recent CPU usage by 2. The *CPU-penalty-to-recent-CPU-usage ratio* is therefore .5. We will call this value R.

Once a second, the current algorithm divides the recent CPU usage value of every process by 2. The *recent-CPU-usage-decay factor* is therefore .5. We will call this value D.

For some users, the existing algorithm does not allow enough distinction between foreground and background processes. For example—ignoring other activity—if a system were running two compute-intensive user processes, one foreground (nice value = 20), one background (nice value = 24) that started at the same time, the following sequence would occur:

- The foreground process would be dispatched first. At the end of 8 time slices (80ms), its CPU penalty would be 4, which would make its priority value equal to that of the background process. The round-robin scheduling algorithm would cause the background process to be dispatched.
- After 2 further time slices, the background process's CPU penalty would be 1, making its priority value one greater than that of the foreground process. The foreground process would be dispatched.
- Another 2 time slices and the priority values of the processes would be equal again. The processes would continue to alternate every 2 time slices until the end of the second.
- At the end of the second, the foreground process would have had 54 time slices and the background would have had 46. After the decay factor was applied, the recent CPU usage values would be 27 and 23. In the second second of their competition, the foreground process would get only 4 more time slices than the background process.

Even if the background process had been started with **nice −20**, the distinction between foreground and background would be only slightly clearer. Although the scheduler stops counting time slices used after 120, this permits the CPU penalty to level off at 60—more than enough to offset the maximum nice value difference of 40.

To allow greater flexibility in prioritizing processes, the new feature permits user tuning of the ratio of CPU penalty to recent CPU usage (R) and the recent-CPU-usage-decay rate (D). The tuning is accomplished through two new options of the **schedtune** command: **−r** and **−d**. Each option specifies a parameter that is an integer from 0 through 32. The parameters are applied by multiplying the recent CPU usage value by the parameter value and then dividing by 32 (shift right 5). The default **r** and **d** values are 16, which yields the same behavior as the original algorithm ($D=R=16/32=.5$). The new range of values permits a far wider spectrum of behaviors. For example:

```
# schedtune -r 0
```

($R=0$, $D=.5$) would mean that the CPU penalty was always 0, making priority absolute. No background process would get any CPU time unless there were no dispatchable foreground processes at all. The priority values of the processes would effectively be constant, although they would not technically be fixed-priority processes.

```
# schedtune -r 5
```

($R=.15625$, $D=.5$) would mean that a foreground process would never have to compete with a background process started with **nice –20**. The limit of 120 CPU time slices accumulated would mean that the maximum CPU penalty for the foreground process would be 18.

```
# schedtune -r 6 -d 16
```

($R=.1875$, $D=.5$) would mean that, if the background process were started with **nice –20**, it would be at least one second before the background process began to receive any CPU time. Foreground processes, however, would still be distinguishable on the basis of CPU usage. Long-running foreground processes that should probably be in the background would ultimately accumulate enough CPU usage to keep them from interfering with the true foreground.

```
# schedtune -r 32 -d 32
```

($R=1$, $D=1$) would mean that long-running processes would reach a C value of 120 and stay there, contending on the basis of their nice values. New processes would have priority, regardless of their nice value, until they had accumulated enough time slices to bring them within the priority value range of the existing processes.

If you conclude that one or both parameters need to be modified to accommodate your workload, you can enter the **schedtune** command while logged on as `root`. The changed values will persist until the next **schedtune** that modifies them or until the next system boot. Values can be reset to their defaults with **schedtune –D**, but remember that *all* **schedtune** parameters are reset by that command, including VMM memory load control parameters. To make a change to the parameters that will persist across boots, you need to add an appropriate line at the end of the **/etc/inittab** file.

Modifying the Scheduler Time Slice

The length of the scheduler time slice can be modified with the **schedtune** command (see page 252). The syntax for this function is:

>   **schedtune –t** *increase*

where *increase* is the number of 10ms clock ticks by which the standard time slice (one 10ms tick) is to be increased. Thus, **schedtune –t 2** would set the time slice length to 30ms. **schedtune –t 0** would return the time slice length to the default.

In an environment in which the length of the time slice has been increased, some applications may not need or should not have the full time slice. These applications can give up the processor explicitly with the **yield** system call (as can programs in an unmodified environment). After a **yield** call, the calling thread is moved to the end of the dispatch queue for its priority level.

CPU-Efficient User ID Administration

To improve login response time and conserve CPU time in systems with many users, AIX can use a hashed version of the **/etc/passwd** file to look up userids. When this facility is used, the **/etc/passwd** file still exists, but is not used in normal processing. The hashed versions of the file (**/etc/passwd.dir** and **/etc/passwd.pag**) are built by the **mkpasswd** command. If the hashed versions are not current, login processing reverts to a slow, CPU-intensive sequential search through **/etc/passwd**.

Once the hashed password files have been built, if the **passwd**, **mkuser**, **chuser**, **rmuser** commands (or the **smit** equivalents, with fast paths of the same name) are used to administer user IDs, the hashed files are kept up to date automatically. If the **/etc/passwd** file is changed with an editor or with the **pwdadm** command, the hashed files must be rebuilt with the command:

```
# mkpasswd /etc/passwd
```

7

Monitoring and Tuning Memory Use

The memory of a RISC System/6000 is almost always full of something. If the currently executing programs don't take up all of memory, AIX retains in memory the text pages of programs that ran earlier and the files they used. It doesn't cost anything, because the memory would be unused anyway. In many cases, the program or file pages will be used again, which reduces disk I/O.

This caching technique improves the efficiency of the system but can make it harder to determine the actual memory requirement of a workload.

This chapter describes the ways in which memory use can be measured and modified.

Readers who are not familiar with AIX virtual-memory management may want to look at "Performance Overview of the Virtual Memory Manager (VMM)," beginning on page 17, before continuing.

How Much Memory Is Really Being Used?

Several performance tools provide reports of memory usage. The reports of most interest are from **vmstat**, **ps**, and **svmon**.

vmstat

vmstat summarizes the total "active" virtual memory used by all of the processes in the system, as well as the number of real-memory page frames on the free list. Active virtual memory is defined as the number of virtual-memory working-segment pages that have actually been touched. It is usually equal to the number of paging-space slots that have been assigned. This number can be larger than the number of real page frames in the machine, since some of the active virtual-memory pages may have been written out to paging space.

ps

ps provides several different reports of memory use, depending on the flag used. The most comprehensive comes with **ps v**, which displays the following memory-related columns:

SIZE
Virtual size in kilobytes of the data section of the process. (Displayed as SZ by other flags.) This number is equal to the number of working-segment pages of the process that have been touched (that is, the number of paging-space slots that have been allocated) times 4. If some working-segment pages are currently paged out, this number is larger than the amount of real memory being used.

RSS
Real-memory (resident set) size in kilobytes of the process. This number is equal to the sum of the number of working-segment and code-segment pages in memory times 4. Remember that code-segment pages are shared among all of the currently running instances of the program. If 26 **ksh** processes are running, only one copy of any given page of the **ksh** executable would be in memory, but **ps** would report that code-segment size as part of the RSS of *each* instance of **ksh**.

TSIZ
Size of text (shared-program) image. This is the size of the text section of the executable file. Pages of the text section of the executable are only brought into memory when they are touched, i.e., branched to or loaded from. This number represents only an upper bound on the amount of text that could be loaded.

TRS
Size of the resident set (real memory) of text. This is the number of code-segment pages times 4. As was noted earlier, this number exaggerates memory use for programs of which multiple instances are running.

%MEM
Calculated as the sum of the number of working-segment and code-segment pages in memory times 4 (that is, the RSS value), divided by the size of the real memory of the machine in KB, times 100, rounded to the nearest full percentage point. This value attempts to convey the percentage of real memory being used by the process. Unfortunately, like RSS, it tends the exaggerate the cost of a process that is sharing program text with other processes. Further, the rounding to the nearest percentage point causes all of the processes in the system that have RSS values under .005 times real memory size to have a %MEM of 0.0.

As you can see, reporting memory statistics in a format that was designed for earlier, simpler systems sometimes results in distorted data.

svmon

svmon provides both global, process-level, and segment-level reporting of memory use. For tuning purposes, the **–G** and **–P** options are most interesting.

–G
Summarizes the memory use for the entire system.

–P   Shows the memory use for one or more processes.

In AIX Version 4.1, the **svmon** command is packaged as part of the Performance Toolbox for AIX. To determine whether **svmon** is available, use:

```
lslpp -lI perfagent.tools
```

If this package has been installed, **svmon** is available.

Example of vmstat, ps, and svmon Output

The following example shows the output of these commands on a large system. **vmstat** was run in a separate window while **ps** and **svmon** were running consecutively. The **vmstat** summary (first) line has been removed:

```
$ vmstat 5
procs     memory              page                  faults         cpu
----- -----------  ------------------------  ------------  -----------
  r  b   avm   fre  re  pi  po  fr   sr  cy   in    sy  cs us sy id wa
  0  0 25270  2691   0   0   0   0    0   0  142  2012  41  4 11 86  0
  1  0 25244  2722   0   0   0   0    0   0  138  6752  39 20 70 10  0
  0  0 25244  2722   0   0   0   0    0   0  128    61  34  0  1 99  0
  0  0 25244  2722   0   0   0   0    0   0  137   163  41  1  4 95  0
```

The global **svmon** report below shows related numbers. The number that **vmstat** reports as Active Virtual Memory (avm) is reported by **svmon** as page-space slots in use (25270). The number of page frames on the free list (2691) is identical in both reports. The number of pages pinned (2157) is a separate report, since the pinned pages are included in the pages in use.

```
$ svmon -G
        m e m o r y            i n  u s e          p i n       p g  s p a c e
  size inuse  free   pin   work  pers  clnt  work  pers clnt size   inuse
 24576 21885  2691  2157  13172  7899   814  2157     0    0 40960   25270
```

Singling out a particular, long-running process on this machine, we can compare the **ps v** and **svmon –P** reports. The actual program has been renamed **anon**.

```
$ ps v 35851
   PID    TTY STAT   TIME PGIN  SIZE  RSS  LIM  TSIZ   TRS %CPU %MEM COMMAND
 35851      - S      0:03  494  1192 2696   xx  1147  1380  0.2  3.0 anon
```

The SIZE value (1192) is the **svmon** Pgspace number (298) times four. The RSS value (2696) is equal to the number of pages in the process private segment (329) plus the number of pages in the code segment (345) times four. The TSIZE number is not related to real-memory use. The TRS value (1380) is equal to the number of pages in use in the code segment (345) times four. The %MEM is the RSS value, divided by the size of real memory in KB, times 100, rounded to the nearest full percentage point.

```
$ svmon -P 35851
  Pid                          Command       Inuse        Pin     Pgspace
35851                          anon           2410          2        4624
Pid:   35851
Command:   anon
Segid  Type  Description        Inuse    Pin   Pgspace   Address Range
 18a3  pers  /dev/hd2:5150          1      0         0   0..0
 9873  pers  /dev/hd2:66256         1      0         0   0..0
 4809  work  shared library     1734      0      4326   0..4668 :
60123..65535
 748e  work  private             329      2       298   0..423 :
65402..65535
 2105  pers  code,/dev/hd2:4492   345      0         0   0..402
```

As we analyze various processes in the environment, we observe that the shared library is indeed shared among almost all of the processes in the system, so its memory requirement is part of overall system overhead. Segment 9873 is also widely used, so we can include its memory in overhead. If one were estimating the memory requirement for program **anon**, the formula would be:

> The total memory requirement for **anon** is equal to 345*4KB for program text (shared among all users) plus the estimated number of simultaneous users of **anon** times the sum of the working-segment size (329*4KB) and 4KB for the mapped segment (segment ID 18a3 in this example).

Memory-Leaking Programs

A *memory leak* is a program bug that consists of repeatedly allocating memory, using it, and then neglecting to free it. A memory leak in a long-running program, such as an interactive application, is a serious problem, because it can result in memory fragmentation and the accumulation of large numbers of mostly garbage-filled pages in real memory and page space. Systems have been known to run out of page space because of a memory leak in a single program.

A memory leak can be detected with **svmon**, by looking for processes whose working segment continually grows. Identifying the offending subroutine or line of code is more difficult, especially in AIXwindows applications, which generate large numbers of **malloc** and **free** calls. Some third-party programs exist for analyzing memory leaks, but they require access to the program source code.

Some uses of **realloc**, while not actually programming errors, can have the same effect as a memory leak. If a program frequently uses **realloc** to increase the size of a data area, the process's working segment can become increasingly fragmented if the storage released by **realloc** cannot be re-used for anything else. (Appendix F, "Application Memory Management" contains background information on **malloc** and **realloc**.)

In general, memory that is no longer required should be released with **free**, *if* the memory will probably be re-used by the program. On the other hand, it is a waste of CPU time to **free** memory after the last **malloc**. When the program terminates, its working segment is destroyed and the real-memory page frames that contained working-segment data are added to the free list.

Analyzing Patterns of Memory Use with BigFoot

Note: This section applies only to Version 4.1 (and later) of AIX.

The BigFoot tool is packaged as part of the Performance Toolbox for AIX. To determine whether BigFoot is available, use:

```
lslpp -lI perfagent.tools
```

If this package has been installed, BigFoot is available.

The BigFoot tool collects the memory footprint of a running program. It reports the virtual-memory pages touched by the process. BigFoot consists of two commands:

bf   collects information about pages touched during the execution of a program. It generates the complete data from the run in a file named **__bfrpt**.

bfrpt   filters the **__bfrpt** file to extract the storage references made by a given process.

The detailed descriptions of these commands appear in *AIX Version 4.1 Commands Reference*.

Assessing Memory Requirements via the rmss Command

rmss is an acronym for Reduced-Memory System Simulator. **rmss** provides you with a means to simulate RISC System/6000s with different sizes of real memories that are smaller than your actual machine, without having to extract and replace memory boards. Moreover, **rmss** provides a facility to run an application over a range of memory sizes, displaying, for each memory size, performance statistics such as the response time of the application and the amount of paging. In short, **rmss** is designed to help you answer the question: "How many megabytes of real memory does a RISC System/6000 need to run AIX and a given application with an acceptable level of performance?"—or in the multiuser context—"How many users can run this application simultaneously in a machine with X megabytes of real memory?"

In AIX Version 4.1, the **rmss** command is packaged as part of the Performance Toolbox for AIX. To determine whether **rmss** is available, use:

```
lslpp -lI perfagent.tools
```

If this package has been installed, **rmss** is available.

It is important to keep in mind that the memory size simulated by **rmss** is the total size of the machine's real memory, including the memory used by AIX and any other programs that may be running. It is not the amount of memory used specifically by the application itself. Because of the performance degradation it can cause, **rmss** can be used only by `root` or a member of the system group.

Two Styles of Using rmss

rmss can be invoked in two ways: (1) to change the memory size and exit; or (2) as a driver program, which executes a specified application multiple times over a range of memory sizes and displays important statistics that describe the application's performance at each memory size. The first invocation technique is useful when you want to get the look and feel of how your application performs at a given system memory size, when your application is too complex to be expressed as a single command, or when you want to run multiple instances of the application. The second invocation technique is appropriate when you have an application that can be invoked as an executable or shell script file.

Note: Before using **rmss**, it is a good idea to use the command **schedtune –h 0** (see page 124) to turn off VMM memory-load control. Otherwise, VMM memory-load control may interfere with your measurements at small memory sizes. When your experiments are complete, reset the memory-load-control parameters to the values that are normally in effect on your system (if you normally use the default parameters, use **schedtune –D**).

Using rmss to Change the Memory Size and Exit

To change the memory size and exit, use the **–c** flag:

```
# rmss -c memsize
```

For example, to change the memory size to 12MB, use:

```
# rmss -c 12
```

memsize is an integer or decimal fraction number of megabytes (for example, 12.25). Additionally, memsize must be between 4MB and the amount of physical real memory in your machine. Depending on the hardware and software configuration, **rmss** may not be able to change the memory size to less than 8MB, because of the size of inherent system structures such as the kernel. When **rmss** is unable to change to a given memory size, it displays an informative error message.

rmss reduces the effective memory size of a RISC System/6000 by stealing free page frames from the list of free frames that is maintained by the VMM. The stolen frames are kept in a pool of unusable frames and are returned to the free frame list when the effective memory size is to be increased. Also, **rmss** dynamically adjusts certain system variables and data structures that must be kept proportional to the effective size of memory.

It may take a short while (up to 15–20 seconds) to change the memory size. In general, the more you wish to reduce the memory size, the longer **rmss** takes to complete. When successful, **rmss** responds with the following message:

```
Simulated memory size changed to  12.00 Mb.
```

To display the current memory size, use the **–p** flag:

```
# rmss -p
```

To this, **rmss** responds:

```
Simulated memory size is  12.00 Mb.
```

Finally, if you wish to reset the memory size to the actual memory size of the machine, use the **–r** flag:

```
# rmss -r
```

No matter what the current simulated memory size, using the **–r** flag sets the memory size to be the physical real memory size of the machine. Since this example was run on was a 16MB machine, **rmss** responded:

```
Simulated memory size changed to  16.00 Mb.
```

Using the –c, –p, and –r Flags

The **–c**, **–p** and **–r** flags of **rmss** have an advantage over the other options in that they allow you to experiment with complex applications that cannot be expressed as a single executable or shell script file. On the other hand, the **–c**, **–p**, and **–r** options have a disadvantage in that they force you to do your own performance measurements. Fortunately, there is an easy way to do this. You can use **vmstat –s** to measure the paging-space activity that occurred while your application ran.

By running **vmstat –s**, running your application, then running **vmstat –s** again, and subtracting the number of paging-space page ins before from the number of paging-space page ins after, you can determine the number of paging-space page ins that occurred while your program ran. Furthermore, by timing your program, and dividing the number of paging-space page ins by the program's elapsed run time, you can obtain the average paging-space page-in rate.

It is also important to run the application multiple times at each memory size. There are two good reasons for doing so. First, when changing memory size, **rmss** often clears out a lot of memory. Thus, the first time you run your application after changing memory sizes it is possible that a substantial part of the run time may be due to your application reading files into real memory. But, since the files may remain in memory after your application terminates, subsequent executions of your application may result in substantially shorter elapsed times. Another reason to run multiple executions at each memory size is to get a feel for the *average* performance of the application at that memory size. The RISC System/6000 and AIX are complex systems, and it is impossible to duplicate the system state each time your application runs. Because of this, the performance of your application may vary significantly from run to run.

To summarize, you might consider the following set of steps as a desirable way to use this style of **rmss** invocation:

```
while there are interesting memory sizes to investigate:
  {
  change to an interesting memory size using rmss -c;
  run the application once as a warm-up;
  for a couple of iterations:
    {
    use vmstat -s to get the "before" value of paging-space page ins;
    run the application, while timing it;
    use vmstat -s to get the "after" value of paging-space page ins;
    subtract the "before" value from the "after" value to get the
        number of page ins that occurred while the application ran;
    divide the number of paging-space page ins by the response time
        to get the paging-space page-in rate;
    }
  }
run rmss -r to restore the system to normal memory size (or reboot)
```

117

The calculation of the (after – before) paging I/O numbers can be automated by using the **vmstat.sh** script that is part of the PerfPMR package.

Using rmss to Run a Command over a Range of Memory Sizes

The **–s**, **–f**, **–d**, **–n**, and **–o** flags are used in combination to invoke **rmss** as a driver program. As a driver program, **rmss** executes a specified application over a range of memory sizes and displays statistics describing the application's performance at each memory size. The syntax for this invocation style of **rmss** is given below:

rmss [**–s** *smemsize*] [**–f** *fmemsize*] [**–d** *memdelta*]
　　　[**–n** *numiterations*] [**–o** *outputfile*] *command*

The **–n** flag is used to specify the number of times to run and measure the command at each memory size. The **–o** flag is used to specify the file into which to write the **rmss** report, while *command* is the application that you wish to run and measure at each memory size. Each of these flags is discussed in detail below.

The **–s**, **–f**, and **–d** flags are used to specify the range of memory sizes. The **–s** flag specifies the starting size, the **–f** flag specifies the final size, and the **–d** flag specifies the difference between sizes. All values are in integer or decimal fractions of megabytes. For example, if you wanted to run and measure a command at sizes 24, 20, 16, 12 and 8MB, you would use the following combination:

```
-s 24 -f 8 -d 4
```

Likewise, if you wanted to run and measure a command at 16, 24, 32, 40, and 48MB, you would use the following combination:

```
-s 16 -f 48 -d 8
```

If the **–s** flag is omitted, **rmss** starts at the actual memory size of the machine. If the **–f** flag is omitted, **rmss** finishes at 8MB. If the **–d** flag is omitted, there is a default of 8MB between memory sizes.

What values should you choose for the **–s**, **–f**, and **–d** flags? A simple choice would be to cover the memory sizes of RISC System/6000s that are being considered to run the application you are measuring. However, increments of less than 8MB can be useful, because you can get an idea of how much "breathing room" you'll have when you settle on a given size. For instance, if a given application thrashes at 8MB but runs without page ins at 16MB, it would be useful to know where within the 8 to 16MB range the application starts thrashing. If it starts at 15MB, you may want to consider configuring the system with more than 16MB of memory, or you may want to try to modify the application so that there is more breathing room. On the other hand, if the thrashing starts at 9MB, you know that you have plenty of breathing room with a 16MB machine.

The **–n** flag is used to specify how many times to run and measure the command at each memory size. After running and measuring the command the specified number of times, **rmss** displays statistics describing the average performance of the application at that memory size. To run the command 3 times at each memory size, you would use the following:

```
-n 3
```

If the **–n** flag is omitted, **rmss** determines during initialization how many times your application must be run in order to accumulate a total run time of 10 seconds. **rmss** does this to ensure that the performance statistics for short-running programs will not be significantly skewed by transient outside influences, such as daemons.

Note: If you are measuring a very brief program, the number of iterations required to accumulate 10 seconds of CPU time can be very large. Since each execution of the program takes a minimum of about 2 elapsed seconds of **rmss** overhead, you should probably specify the **–n** parameter explicitly for short programs.

What are good values to use for the **–n** flag? If you know that your application takes much more than 10 seconds to run, then you can specify −n 1 so that the command is run and measured only once at each memory size. The advantage of using the **–n** flag is that **rmss** will finish sooner because it will not have to spend time during initialization to determine how many times to run your program. This can be particularly valuable when the command being measured is long-running and interactive.

It is important to note that **rmss** always runs the command once at each memory size as a warm-up before running and measuring the command. The warm-up is needed to avoid the I/O that occurs when the application is not already in memory. Although such I/O does affect performance, it is not necessarily due to a lack of real memory. The warm-up run is not included in the number of iterations specified by the **–n** flag.

The **–o** flag is used to specify a file into which to write the **rmss** report. If the **–o** flag is omitted, the report is written into the file rmss.out.

Finally, *command* is used to specify the application to be measured. *command* can be an executable or shell script, with or without command-line arguments. There are some limitations on the form of the command however. First, it cannot contain the redirection of input or output (for example, foo > output, foo < input). This is because **rmss** treats everything to the right of the command name as an argument to the command. If you wish to redirect, you must place the command in a shell script file.

Normally, if you want to store the **rmss** output in a specific file, you would use the **–o** option. If you want to redirect the stdout output of **rmss** (for example, to concatenate it to the end of an existing file) then, with the Korn shell, you need to enclose the **rmss** invocation in parentheses, as follows:

```
# (rmss -s 24 -f 8 foo) >> output
```

Interpreting rmss Results

This section gives suggestions on how to interpret performance statistics produced by **rmss**. Let's start out with some typical results.

The "Report Generated for the foo Program" example on page 120 was produced by running **rmss** on a real-life application program, although the name of the program has been changed to foo for anonymity. The specific command that would have been used to generate the report is:

```
# rmss -s 16 -f 8 -d 1 -n 1 -o rmss.out foo
```

```
Hostname:   widgeon.austin.ibm.com
Real memory size:   16.00 Mb
Time of day:  Thu Jan  8 19:04:04 1990
Command:  foo


Simulated memory size initialized to  16.00 Mb.


Number of iterations per memory size = 1 warm-up + 1 measured = 2.
```

Memory size (megabytes)	Avg. Pageins	Avg. Response Time (sec.)	Avg. Pagein Rate (pageins / sec.)
16.00	115.0	123.9	0.9
15.00	112.0	125.1	0.9
14.00	179.0	126.2	1.4
13.00	81.0	125.7	0.6
12.00	403.0	132.0	3.1
11.00	855.0	141.5	6.0
10.00	1161.0	146.8	7.9
9.00	1529.0	161.3	9.5
8.00	2931.0	202.5	14.5

The report consists of four columns. The leftmost column gives the memory size, while the Avg. Pageins column gives the average number of page ins that occurred when the application was run at that memory size. It is important to note that the Avg. Pageins column refers to all page in operations, including code, data, and file reads, from all programs, that completed while the application ran. The Avg. Response Time column gives the average amount of time it took the application to complete, while the Avg. Pagein Rate column gives the average rate of page ins.

First, concentrate on the Avg. Pagein Rate column. From 16MB to 13MB, the page-in rate is relatively small (< 1.5 page ins/sec). However, from 13MB to 8MB, the page-in rate grows gradually at first, and then rapidly as 8MB is reached. The Avg. Response Time column has a similar shape: relatively flat at first, then increasing gradually, and finally increasing rapidly as the memory size is decreased to 8MB.

Here, the page-in rate actually decreases when the memory size changes from 14MB (1.4 page ins/sec.) to 13MB (0.6 page ins/sec.). This should not be viewed with alarm. In a real-life system it is impossible to expect the results to be perfectly smooth. The important point is that the page-in rate is relatively low at both 14MB and 13MB.

Finally, there are a couple of deductions that we can make from the report. First of all, if the performance of the application is deemed unacceptable at 8MB (as it probably would be), then adding memory would improve performance significantly. Note that the response time rises from approximately 124 seconds at 16MB to 202 seconds at 8MB, an increase of 63%. On the other hand, if the performance is deemed unacceptable at 16MB, adding memory will not improve performance much, because page ins do not slow the program appreciably at 16MB.

Examples of Using the –s, –f, –d, –n, and –o Flags

To investigate the performance of a shell script named `ccfoo` that contains the command `cc -O -c foo.c` in memory sizes 16, 14, 12, 10, 8 and 6MB; run and measure the command twice at each memory size; and write the report to the file `cc.rmss.out`, enter:

```
# rmss -s 16 -f 6 -d 2 -n 2 -o cc.rmss.out ccfoo
```

Report for cc

The output is:

```
Hostname:  terran
Real memory size:    32.00 Mb
Time of day:  Mon Apr 20 16:23:03 1992
Command:  ccfoo


Simulated memory size initialized to  16.00 Mb.


Number of iterations per memory size = 1 warm-up + 2 measured = 3.
```

Memory size (megabytes)	Avg. Pageins	Avg. Response Time (sec.)	Avg. Pagein Rate (pageins / sec.)
16.00	0.0	0.4	0.0
14.00	0.0	0.4	0.0
12.00	0.0	0.4	0.0
10.00	0.0	0.4	0.0
8.00	0.5	0.4	1.2
6.00	786.0	13.5	58.4

```
Simulated final memory size.
```

This shows that we were too conservative. Clearly the performance degrades badly in a 6MB machine, but it is essentially unchanged for all of the larger sizes. We can redo the measurement with a narrower range of sizes and a smaller delta with:

```
rmss -s 11 -f 5 -d 1 -n 2 ccfoo
```

This gives us a clearer picture of the response-time curve of the compiler for this program:

```
Hostname:  terran
Real memory size:    32.00 Mb
Time of day:  Mon Apr 20 16:11:38 1992
Command:  ccfoo


Simulated memory size initialized to  11.00 Mb.


Number of iterations per memory size = 1 warm-up + 2 measured = 3.
```

Memory size (megabytes)	Avg. Pageins	Avg. Response Time (sec.)	Avg. Pagein Rate (pageins / sec.)
11.00	0.0	0.4	0.0
10.00	0.0	0.4	0.0
9.00	0.5	0.4	1.1
8.00	0.0	0.4	0.0
7.00	207.0	3.7	56.1
6.00	898.0	16.1	55.9
5.00	1038.0	19.5	53.1

Simulated final memory size.

Report for a 16MB Remote Copy

The following example illustrates a report that was generated (on a client machine) by running **rmss** on a command that copied a 16MB file from a remote (server) machine via NFS.

```
Hostname:  xray.austin.ibm.com
Real memory size:   48.00 Mb
Time of day:  Mon Aug 13 18:16:42 1990
Command:  cp /mnt/a16Mfile /dev/null

Simulated memory size initialized to  48.00 Mb.

Number of iterations per memory size = 1 warm-up + 4 measured = 5.
```

Memory size (megabytes)	Avg. Pageins	Avg. Response Time (sec.)	Avg. Pagein Rate (pageins / sec.)
48.00	0.0	2.7	0.0
40.00	0.0	2.7	0.0
32.00	0.0	2.7	0.0
24.00	1520.8	26.9	56.6
16.00	4104.2	67.5	60.8
8.00	4106.8	66.9	61.4

Note that the response time and page-in rate in this report start relatively low, rapidly increase at a memory size of 24MB, and then reach a plateau at 16 and 8MB. This report shows the importance of choosing a wide range of memory sizes when you use **rmss**. If this user had only looked at memory sizes from 24MB to 8MB, he or she might have missed an opportunity to configure the system with enough memory to accommodate the application without page ins.

Report for find / –ls >/dev/null

The next example is a report that was generated by running **rmss** on the shell script file findbench.sh, which contained the command find / -ls > /dev/null, which does an **ls** of every file in the system. The command that produced the report was:

```
# rmss -s 48 -d 8 -f 4.5 -n 1 -o find.out findbench.sh
```

A final memory size of 4.5MB was chosen because it happened to be the smallest memory size that was attainable by using **rmss** on this machine.

```
Hostname:   xray.austin.ibm.com
Real memory size:   48.00 Mb
Time of day:  Mon Aug 13 14:38:23 1990
Command:  findbench.sh

Simulated memory size initialized to  48.00 Mb.

Number of iterations per memory size = 1 warm-up + 1 measured = 2.
```

Memory size (megabytes)	Avg. Pageins	Avg. Response Time (sec.)	Avg. Pagein Rate (pageins / sec.)
48.00	373.0	25.5	14.6
40.00	377.0	27.3	13.8
32.00	376.0	27.5	13.7
24.00	370.0	27.6	13.4
16.00	376.0	27.3	13.8
8.00	370.0	27.1	13.6
4.50	1329.0	57.6	23.1

As in the first example, the average response times and page-in rate values remain fairly stable as the memory size decreases until we approach 4.5MB, where both the response time and page-in rate increase dramatically. However, the page-in rate is relatively high (approximately 14 page ins/sec.) from 48MB through 8MB. The lesson to be learned here is that with some applications, no practical amount of memory would be enough to eliminate page ins, because the programs themselves are naturally I/O-intensive. Common examples of I/O-intensive programs are programs that scan or randomly access many of the pages in very large files.

Hints for Using the –s, –f, –d, –n, and –o Flags

One helpful feature of **rmss**, when used in this way, is that it can be terminated (by the interrupt key, `Ctrl-C` by default) without destroying the report that has been written to the output file. In addition to writing the report to the output file, this causes **rmss** to reset the memory size to the physical memory size of the machine.

You can run **rmss** in the background, even after you have logged out, by using the **nohup** command. To do this, precede the **rmss** command by `nohup`, and follow the entire command with an & (ampersand):

```
# nohup rmss -s 48 -f 8 -o foo.out foo &
```

Important Rules to Consider When Running rmss

No matter which **rmss** invocation style you are using, it is important to recreate the end-user environment as closely as possible. For instance, are you using the same model CPU? same model disks? same network? Will the users have application files mounted from a remote node via NFS or some other distributed file system? This last point is particularly important, as pages from remote files are treated differently by the VMM than pages from local files.

Likewise, it is best to eliminate any system activity that is not related to the desired system configuration or the application you are measuring. For instance, you don't want to have people working on the same machine as **rmss** unless they are running part of the workload you are measuring.

Note: You cannot run multiple invocations of **rmss** simultaneously.

When you have completed all runs of **rmss**, it is best to shutdown and reboot the system. This will remove all changes that **rmss** has made to the system and will restore the VMM memory-load-control parameters to their normal settings.

Tuning VMM Memory Load Control

The VMM memory-load-control facility, described on page 21, protects an overloaded system from thrashing—a self-perpetuating paralysis in which the processes in the system are spending all their time stealing memory frames from one another and reading/writing pages on the paging device.

Memory-Load-Control Tuning—Possible, but Usually Inadvisable

Memory load control is intended to smooth out *infrequent* peaks in load that might otherwise cause the system to thrash. It is *not* intended to act continuously in a configuration that has too little RAM to handle its normal workload. It is a safety net, not a trampoline. The correct solution to a fundamental, persistent RAM shortage is to add RAM, not to experiment with memory load control in an attempt to trade off response time for memory. The situations in which the memory-load-control facility may really need to be tuned are those in which there is *more* RAM than the defaults were chosen for, not less—configurations in which the defaults are too conservative.

You should not change the memory-load-control parameter settings unless your workload is consistent and you believe the default parameters are ill-suited to your workload.

The default parameter settings shipped with the system are always in force unless changed; and changed parameters last only until the next system boot. All memory-load-control tuning activities must be done by `root`. The system administrator may change the parameters to "tune" the algorithm to a particular workload or to disable it entirely. This is done by running the **schedtune** command. The source and object code of **schedtune** are in **/usr/lpp/bos/samples**.

Warning: schedtune is in the **samples** directory because it is *very* VMM-implementation dependent. The **schedtune** code that accompanies each release of AIX was tailored specifically to the VMM in that release. Running the **schedtune** executable from one release on a different release might well result in an operating-system failure. It is also possible that the functions of **schedtune** may change from release to release. You should not propagate shell scripts or **inittab** entries that include **schedtune** to a new release without checking the **schedtune** documentation for the new release to make sure that the scripts will still have the desired effect. **schedtune** is not supported under SMIT, nor has it been tested with all possible combinations of parameters.

schedtune –? obtains a terse description of the flags and options. **schedtune** with no flags displays the current parameter settings, as follows:

```
        THRASH              SUSP        FORK        SCHED
-h      -p      -m      -w      -e      -f          -t
SYS     PROC    MULTI   WAIT    GRACE   TICKS   TIME_SLICE
6       4       2       1       2       10      0
```

(The **–f** and **–t** flags are not part of the memory-load-control mechanism. They are documented in the full syntax description of **schedtune**. The **–t** flag is also discussed in "Modifying the Scheduler Time Slice" on page 109.) After a tuning experiment, memory load control can be reset to its default characteristics by executing **schedtune –D**.

Memory load control is disabled by setting a parameter value such that processes are never suspended. **schedtune –h 0** effectively disables memory load control by setting to an impossibly high value the threshold that the algorithm uses to recognize thrashing.

In some specialized situations, it may be appropriate to disable memory load control from the outset. For example, if you are using a terminal emulator with a time-out feature to simulate a multiuser workload, memory-load-control intervention may result in some responses being delayed long enough for the process to be killed by the time-out feature. If you are using **rmss** to investigate the effects of reduced memory sizes, you will want to disable memory load control to avoid interference with your measurement.

If disabling memory load control results in more, rather than fewer, thrashing situations (with correspondingly poorer responsiveness), then memory load control is playing an active and supportive role in your system. Tuning the memory-load-control parameters then may result in improved performance—or you may need to add RAM.

Setting the minimum multiprogramming level, *m*, effectively keeps *m* processes from being suspended. Suppose a system administrator knew that at least ten processes must always be resident and active in RAM for successful performance, and suspected that memory load control was too vigorously suspending processes. If **schedtune –m 10** were issued, the system would never suspend so many processes that fewer than ten were competing for memory. The parameter *m* does not count the kernel, processes that have been pinned in RAM with the **plock** system call, fixed-priority processes with priority values less than 60, and processes awaiting events. The system default of *m*=2 ensures that the kernel, all pinned processes, and two user processes will always be in the set of processes competing for RAM.

While *m=2* is appropriate for a desktop, single-user configuration, it is frequently too small for larger, multiuser or server configurations with large amounts of RAM. On those systems, setting *m* to 4 or 6 may result in the best performance.

When you have determined the number of processes that ought to be able to run in your system during periods of peak activity, you can add a **schedtune** at the end of the **/etc/inittab** file, which ensures that it will be run each time the system is booted, overriding the defaults that would otherwise take effect with a reboot. For example, an appropriate **/etc/inittab** line for raising the minimum level of multiprogramming to 4 would be:

```
schedtune:2:wait:/usr/lpp/bos/samples/schedtune -m 4
```

Remember, this line should not be propagated to a new release of AIX without a check of the documentation.

While it is possible to vary other parameters that control the suspension rate of processes and the criteria by which individual processes are selected for suspension, it is impossible to predict with any confidence the effect of such changes on a particular configuration and workload. Deciding on the default parameters was a difficult task, requiring sophisticated measurement tools and patient observation of repeating workloads. Great caution should be exercised if memory-load-control parameter adjustments other than those just discussed are considered.

Tuning VMM Page Replacement

The memory-management algorithm, discussed on page 17, tries to keep the size of the free list and the percentage of real memory occupied by persistent-segment pages within specified bounds. These bounds can be altered with the **vmtune** command, which can only be run by `root`.

Warning: **vmtune** is in the **samples** directory because it is *very* VMM-implementation dependent. The **vmtune** code that accompanies each release of AIX was tailored specifically to the VMM in that release. Running the **vmtune** executable from one release on a different release might well result in an operating-system failure. It is also possible that the functions of **vmtune** may change from release to release. You should not propagate shell scripts or **inittab** entries that include **vmtune** to a new release without checking the **vmtune** documentation for the new release to make sure that the scripts will still have the desired effect.

Choosing minfree and maxfree Settings

The purpose of the free list is to keep track of real-memory page frames released by terminating processes and to supply page frames to requestors immediately, without forcing them to wait for page steals and the accompanying I/O to complete. The **minfree** limit specifies the free-list size below which page stealing to replenish the free list is to be started. **maxfree** is the size above which stealing will end.

The objectives in tuning these limits are:

- to ensure that any activity that has critical response-time objectives can always get the page frames it needs from the free list
- to ensure that the system does not experience unnecessarily high levels of I/O because of premature stealing of pages to expand the free list

If you have a short list of the programs you want to run fast, you could investigate their memory requirements with **svmon** (see "Finding Out How Much Memory Is Really Being Used" on page 111), and set **minfree** to the size of the largest. This technique risks being too conservative because not all of the pages that a process uses are acquired in one burst. At the same time, you may be missing dynamic demands that come from programs not on your list that may lower the average size of the free list when your critical programs run.

A less precise but more comprehensive tool for investigating an appropriate size for **minfree** is **vmstat**. The following is a portion of the **vmstat 1** output obtained while running an XLC compilation on an otherwise idle system. The first line has not been removed—observe that the first line contains summary CPU and other activity measures, but current memory statistics.

procs		memory		page						faults			cpu			
r	b	avm	fre	re	pi	po	fr	sr	cy	in	sy	cs	us	sy	id	wa
0	0	3085	118	0	0	0	0	0	0	115	2	19	0	0	99	0
0	0	3086	117	0	0	0	0	0	0	119	134	24	1	3	96	0
2	0	3141	55	2	0	6	24	98	0	175	223	60	3	9	54	34
0	1	3254	57	0	0	6	176	814	0	205	219	110	22	14	0	64
0	1	3342	59	0	0	42	104	249	0	163	314	57	43	16	0	42
1	0	3411	78	0	0	49	104	169	0	176	306	51	30	15	0	55
1	0	3528	160	1	0	10	216	487	0	143	387	54	50	22	0	27
1	0	3627	94	0	0	0	72	160	0	148	292	79	57	9	0	34
1	0	3444	327	0	0	0	64	102	0	132	150	41	82	8	0	11
1	0	3505	251	0	0	0	0	0	0	128	189	50	79	11	0	11
1	0	3550	206	0	0	0	0	0	0	124	150	22	94	6	0	0
1	0	3576	180	0	0	0	0	0	0	121	145	30	96	4	0	0
0	1	3654	100	0	0	0	0	0	0	124	145	28	91	8	0	1
1	0	3586	208	0	0	0	40	68	0	123	139	24	91	9	0	0

Because the compiler has not been run recently, the code of the compiler itself has to be read in. All told, the compiler acquires about 2MB in about 6 seconds. On this 32MB system **maxfree** is 64 and **minfree** is 56. The compiler almost instantly drives the free list size below **minfree**, and several seconds of frantic page-stealing activity take place. Some of the steals require that dirty working-segment pages be written to paging space, which shows up in the po column. If the steals cause the writing of dirty permanent-segment pages, that I/O does not appear in the **vmstat** report (unless you have directed **vmstat** to report on the I/O activity of the physical volume(s) to which the permanent pages are being written).

This example is not intended to suggest that you set minfree to 500 to accommodate large compiles. It points out how one can use **vmstat** to identify situations in which the free list has to be replenished while a program is waiting for space. In this case, about 2 seconds were added to the compiler execution time because there weren't enough page frames immediately available. If you observe the page frame consumption of your program, either during initialization or during normal processing, you will soon have an idea of the number page frames that need to be in the free list to keep the program from waiting for memory.

When you determine the appropriate size for the free list for your interactive workload, you can set **minfree** appropriately with **vmtune**. **maxfree** should be greater than **minfree** by at least 8 (or by **maxpgahead**, whichever is greater). If we concluded from the example above that **minfree** needed to be 128, and we had set **maxpgahead** to 16 to improve sequential performance, we would use the following **vmtune** command and receive the output shown:

```
# /usr/lpp/bos/samples/vmtune -f 128 -F 144

minperm   maxperm   minpgahead   maxpgahead   minfree   maxfree   numperm
   1392      5734            2           16        56        64      3106
number of memory frames = 8192    number of bad memory pages = 0
maxperm=70.0% of real memory
minperm=17.0% of real memory

minperm   maxperm   minpgahead   maxpgahead   minfree   maxfree   numperm
   1392      5734            2           16       128       144      3106
number of memory frames = 8192    number of bad memory pages = 0
maxperm=70.0% of real memory
minperm=17.0% of real memory
```

Choosing minperm and maxperm Settings

AIX takes advantage of the varying requirements for real memory by leaving in memory pages of files that have been read or written. If the file pages are requested again before their page frames are reassigned, this technique saves an I/O operation. (Even if a file page's page frame has been stolen and placed on the free list, if that file page is requested before the page frame is actually used for another purpose, it will be reclaimed from the free list.) These file pages may be from local or remote (for example, NFS) file systems.

The ratio of page frames used for files versus those used for computational (working or program text) segments is loosely controlled by the **minperm** and **maxperm** values.

In a particular workload, it may be worthwhile to emphasize the avoidance of file I/O. In another workload, keeping computational segment pages in memory may be more important. To understand what the ratio is in the untuned state, we use the **vmtune** command with no arguments.

```
# vmtune

minperm   maxperm   minpgahead   maxpgahead   minfree   maxfree   numperm
   1433      5734            2           16       128       144      3497
number of memory frames = 8192    number of bad memory pages = 0
maxperm=70.0% of real memory
minperm=17.5% of real memory
```

The default values are calculated by the following algorithm:

minperm (in pages) = ((number of memory frames) − 1024) * .2
maxperm (in pages) = ((number of memory frames) − 1024) * .8

The **numperm** column gives the number of file pages in memory, 3497. This is 42.7% of real memory. If we know that our workload makes little use of recently read or written files, we may want to constrain the amount of memory used for that purpose. The command:

```
# vmtune -p 15 -P 40
```

would set **minperm** to 15% and **maxperm** to 40% of real memory. This would ensure that the VMM would steal page frames only from file pages when the ratio of file pages to total memory pages exceeded 40%. On the other hand, if our application frequently references a small set of existing files (especially if those files are in an NFS-mounted file system), we might want to allow more space for local caching of the file pages with:

```
# vmtune -p 30 -P 60
```

8

Monitoring and Tuning Disk I/O

This chapter focuses on the performance of locally attached disk drives.

If you are not familiar with AIX's concepts of volume groups, logical and physical volumes, and logical and physical partitions, you may want to read "Performance Overview of AIX Management of Fixed-Disk Storage," beginning on page 25.

Pre-Installation Planning

File-system configuration has a large effect on overall system performance and is time-consuming to change after installation. Deciding on the number and types of hard disks, and the sizes and placements of paging spaces and logical volumes on those hard disks, is therefore a critical pre-installation process.

An extensive discussion of the considerations for pre-installation disk configuration planning appears in "Disk Pre-Installation Guidelines" beginning on page 67.

Building a Pre-Tuning Baseline

Before making significant changes in your disk configuration or tuning parameters, it is a good idea to build a baseline of measurements that record the current configuration and performance. In addition to your own measurements, you may want to create a comprehensive baseline with the PerfPMR package. See "Check Before You Change" on page 80.

Assessing Disk Performance after Installation

Begin the assessment by running **iostat** with an interval parameter during your system's peak workload period or while running a critical application for which you need to minimize I/O delays. The following shell script runs **iostat** in the background while a **cp** of a large file runs in the foreground so that there is some I/O to measure:

```
$ iostat 5 3 >io.out &
$ cp big1 /dev/null
```

This would leave the following three reports in `io.out`:

tty:	tin	tout	cpu:	% user	% sys	% idle	% iowait
	0.0	3.2		0.2	0.6	98.9	0.3

Disks:	% tm_act	Kbps	tps	msps	Kb_read	Kb_wrtn
hdisk0	0.0	0.3	0.0		29753	48076
hdisk1	0.1	0.1	0.0		11971	26460
hdisk2	0.2	0.8	0.1		91200	108355
cd0	0.0	0.0	0.0		0	0

tty:	tin	tout	cpu:	% user	% sys	% idle	% iowait
	0.0	0.4		0.6	9.7	50.2	39.5

Disks:	% tm_act	Kbps	tps	msps	Kb_read	Kb_wrtn
hdisk0	47.0	674.6	21.8		3376	24
hdisk1	1.2	2.4	0.6		0	12
hdisk2	4.0	7.9	1.8		8	32
cd0	0.0	0.0	0.0		0	0

tty:	tin	tout	cpu:	% user	% sys	% idle	% iowait
	0.6	56.6		0.2	2.0	93.2	4.6

Disks:	% tm_act	Kbps	tps	msps	Kb_read	Kb_wrtn
hdisk0	0.0	0.0	0.0		0	0
hdisk1	0.0	0.0	0.0		0	0
hdisk2	4.8	12.8	3.2		64	0
cd0	0.0	0.0	0.0		0	0

The first, summary, report shows the overall balance (or, in this case, imbalance) in the I/O to each of the hard disks. `hdisk1` is almost idle and `hdisk2` receives about 63% of the total I/O.

The second report shows the 5-second interval during which **cp** ran. The data must be viewed with care. The elapsed time for this **cp** was about 2.6 seconds. Thus, 2.5 seconds of high I/O dependency are being averaged with 2.5 seconds of idle time to yield the 39.5% `iowait` reported. A shorter interval would have given a more accurate characterization of the command itself, but this example demonstrates the considerations one must take into account in looking at reports that show average activity across intervals.

Assessing Physical Placement of Data on Disk

If the workload shows a significant degree of I/O dependency, you can investigate the physical placement of the files on the disk to determine if reorganization at some level would yield an improvement. To see the placement of the partitions of logical volume `hd11` within physical volume `hdisk0`, use:

```
$ lslv -p hdisk0 hd11
```

lslv then reports:

```
hdisk0:hd11:/home/op
USED   USED   USED   USED   USED   USED   USED   USED   USED   USED      1-10
USED   USED   USED   USED   USED   USED   USED                            11-17

USED   USED   USED   USED   USED   USED   USED   USED   USED   USED      18-27
USED   USED   USED   USED   USED   USED   USED                            28-34

USED   USED   USED   USED   USED   USED   USED   USED   USED   USED      35-44
USED   USED   USED   USED   USED   USED                                  45-50

USED   USED   USED   USED   USED   USED   USED   USED   USED   USED      51-60
0052   0053   0054   0055   0056   0057   0058                           61-67

0059   0060   0061   0062   0063   0064   0065   0066   0067   0068      68-77
0069   0070   0071   0072   0073   0074   0075                           78-84
```

The word USED means that the physical partition is in use by a logical volume other than hd11. The numbers indicate the logical partition of hd11 that is assigned to that physical partition.

We look for the rest of hd11 on hdisk1 with:

```
$ lslv -p hdisk1 hd11
```

which produces:

```
hdisk1:hd11:/home/op
0035   0036   0037   0038   0039   0040   0041   0042   0043   0044      1-10
0045   0046   0047   0048   0049   0050   0051                            11-17

USED   USED   USED   USED   USED   USED   USED   USED   USED   USED      18-27
USED   USED   USED   USED   USED   USED   USED                            28-34

USED   USED   USED   USED   USED   USED   USED   USED   USED   USED      35-44
USED   USED   USED   USED   USED   USED                                  45-50

0001   0002   0003   0004   0005   0006   0007   0008   0009   0010      51-60
0011   0012   0013   0014   0015   0016   0017                           61-67

0018   0019   0020   0021   0022   0023   0024   0025   0026   0027      68-77
0028   0029   0030   0031   0032   0033   0034                           78-84
```

We see that logical volume hd11 is fragmented within physical volume hdisk1, with its first logical partitions in the inner-middle and inner regions of hdisk1, while logical partitions 35–51 are in the outer region. A workload that accessed hd11 randomly would experience unnecessary I/O wait time as the disk's accessor moved back and forth between the parts of hd11. These reports also show us that there are no free physical partitions in either hdisk0 or hdisk1.

If we look at hd2 (the logical volume containing the **/usr** file system) on hdisk2 with:

```
$ lslv -p hdisk2 hd2
```

we find some physical partitions that are FREE:

```
hdisk2:hd2:/usr
USED   USED   USED   USED   FREE   FREE   FREE   FREE   FREE   FREE     1-10
FREE   FREE   FREE   FREE   FREE   FREE   FREE   FREE   FREE   FREE    11-20
FREE   FREE   FREE   FREE   FREE   FREE   FREE   FREE   FREE   FREE    21-30
FREE   FREE   FREE   FREE   FREE   FREE   FREE   FREE   FREE   FREE    31-40
FREE                                                                 41-41

USED   USED   USED   USED   USED   USED   USED   USED   USED   USED    42-51
USED   USED   USED   USED   USED   USED   FREE   FREE   FREE   FREE    52-61
FREE   FREE   FREE   FREE   FREE   FREE   FREE   FREE   FREE   FREE    62-71
FREE   FREE   FREE   FREE   FREE   FREE   FREE   FREE   FREE   FREE    72-81
FREE                                                                 82-82

USED   USED   0001   0002   0003   0004   0005   0006   0007   0008    83-92
0009   0010   0011   0012   0013   0014   0015   USED   USED   USED    93-102
USED   0016   0017   0018   0019   0020   0021   0022   0023   0024   103-112
0025   0026   0027   0028   0029   0030   0031   0032   0033   0034   113-122

0035   0036   0037   0038   0039   0040   0041   0042   0043   0044   123-132
0045   0046   0047   0048   0049   0050   0051   0052   0053   0054   133-142
0055   0056   0057   0058   0059   0060   0061   0062   0063   0064   143-152
0065   0066   0067   0068   0069   0070   0071   0072   0073   0074   153-162
0075                                                                163-163

0076   0077   0078   0079   0080   0081   0082   0083   0084   0085   164-173
0086   0087   0088   0089   0090   0091   0092   0093   0094   0095   174-183
0096   0097   0098   0099   0100   FREE   FREE   FREE   FREE   FREE   184-193
FREE   FREE   FREE   FREE   FREE   FREE   FREE   FREE   FREE   FREE   194-203
FREE                                                                204-204
```

There are several interesting differences from the previous reports. The hd2 logical volume is contiguous, except for four physical partitions (100–103). Other **lslv**s (not shown) tell us that these partitions are used for hd1, hd3, and hd9var (**/home**, **/tmp**, and **/var**, respectively).

If we want to see how the file copied earlier, big1, is stored on the disk, we can use the **fileplace** command:

```
$ fileplace -pv big1
```

The resulting report is:

```
File: big1  Size: 3554273 bytes  Vol: /dev/hd10 (4096 byte blks)
Inode: 19  Mode: -rwxr-xr-x  Owner: frankw  Group: system

Physical blocks (mirror copy 1)                     Logical blocks
-------------------------------                     --------------
01584-01591  hdisk0      8 blks,    32 KB,   0.9%   01040-01047
01624-01671  hdisk0     48 blks,   192 KB,   5.5%   01080-01127
01728-02539  hdisk0    812 blks,  3248 KB,  93.5%   01184-01995

  868 blocks over space of 956:  space efficiency = 90.8%
  3 fragments out of 868 possible:  sequentiality = 99.8%
```

This shows that there is very little fragmentation within the file, and those are small gaps. We can therefore infer that the disk arrangement of big1 is not affecting its sequential read time significantly. Further, given that a (recently created) 3.5MB file encounters this little fragmentation, it appears that the file system in general has not become particularly fragmented.

Note: If a file has been created by seeking to various locations and writing widely dispersed records, only the pages that contain records will take up space on disk and appear on a **fileplace** report. The file system does *not* fill in the intervening pages automatically when the file is created. However, if such a file is read sequentially, by the **cp** or **tar** commands, for example, the space between records is read as binary zeroes. Thus, the output of such a **cp** command can be *much* larger than the input file, although the data is the same.

In AIX Version 4.1, the **fileplace** command is packaged as part of the Performance Toolbox for AIX. To determine whether **fileplace** is available, use:

```
lslpp -lI perfagent.tools
```

If this package has been installed, **fileplace** is available.

Reorganizing a Logical Volume or Volume Group

If we found that a volume was sufficiently fragmented to require reorganization, we could use **smit** to run the **reorgvg** command (**smit –> Physical & Logical Storage –> Logical Volume Manager –> Volume Groups –> Set Characteristics of a Volume Group –> Reorganize a Volume Group**). The fast path is:

```
# smit reorgvg
```

Use of this command against `rootvg` on the test system, with no particular logical volumes specified, resulted in migration of all of the logical volumes on `hdisk2`. After the reorganization, the output of an

```
$ lslv -p hdisk2 hd2
```

was:

```
hdisk2:hd2:/usr
USED   USED   USED   USED   USED   USED   USED   USED   FREE   FREE      1-10
FREE   FREE   FREE   FREE   FREE   FREE   FREE   FREE   FREE   FREE     11-20
FREE   FREE   FREE   FREE   FREE   FREE   FREE   FREE   FREE   FREE     21-30
FREE   FREE   FREE   FREE   FREE   FREE   FREE   FREE   FREE   FREE     31-40
FREE                                                                  41-41

USED   USED   USED   USED   USED   USED   USED   USED   USED   USED     42-51
USED   USED   USED   USED   USED   USED   FREE   FREE   FREE   FREE     52-61
FREE   FREE   FREE   FREE   FREE   FREE   FREE   FREE   FREE   FREE     62-71
FREE   FREE   FREE   FREE   FREE   FREE   FREE   FREE   FREE   FREE     72-81
FREE                                                                  82-82

USED   USED   0001   0002   0003   0004   0005   0006   0007   0008     83-92
0009   0010   0011   0012   0013   0014   0015   0016   0017   0018     93-102
0019   0020   0021   0022   0023   0024   0025   0026   0027   0028    103-112
0029   0030   0031   0032   0033   0034   0035   0036   0037   0038    113-122
```

```
0039  0040  0041  0042  0043  0044  0045  0046  0047  0048  123-132
0049  0050  0051  0052  0053  0054  0055  0056  0057  0058  133-142
0059  0060  0061  0062  0063  0064  0065  0066  0067  0068  143-152
0069  0070  0071  0072  0073  0074  0075  0076  0077  0078  153-162
0079                                                        163-163

0080  0081  0082  0083  0084  0085  0086  0087  0088  0089  164-173
0090  0091  0092  0093  0094  0095  0096  0097  0098  0099  174-183
0100  FREE  FREE  FREE  FREE  FREE  FREE  FREE  FREE  FREE  184-193
FREE  FREE  FREE  FREE  FREE  FREE  FREE  FREE  FREE  FREE  194-203
FREE                                                        204-204
```

The physical-partition fragmentation within hd2 that was seen in the previous report has disappeared. However, we have *not* affected any fragmentation at the physical-block level that may exist within the **/usr** file system. Since most of the files in **/usr** are written once, during system installation, and are not updated thereafter, **/usr** is unlikely to experience much internal fragmentation. User data in the **/home** file system is another matter.

Reorganizing a File System

The test system has a separate logical volume and file system hd11 (mount point: /home/op) for potentially destructive testing. If we decide that hd11 needs to be reorganized, we start by backing up the data with:

```
# cd /home/op
# find . -print | pax -wf/home/waters/test_bucket/backuptestfile
```

which creates a backup file (in a different file system) containing all of the files in the file system to be reorganized. If the disk space on the system is limited, this backup could be done to tape.

Before the file system can be rebuilt, you must run **unmount**, as follows:

```
# unmount /home/op
```

If any processes are using /home/op or any of its subdirectories, they must be **kill**ed before the **unmount** can succeed.

To remake the file system on /home/op's logical volume, enter:

```
# mkfs /dev/hd11
```

You are prompted for confirmation before the old file system is destroyed. The name of the file system does not change. To restore the original situation (except that /home/op is empty), enter:

```
# mount /dev/hd11 /home/op
# cd /home/op
```

Now put the data back with:

```
# pax -rf/home/frankw/tuning.io/backuptestfile >/dev/null
```

Standard out is redirected to /dev/null to avoid displaying the name of each of the files restored, which can be very time-consuming.

If we look again at the large file inspected earlier, with:

```
# fileplace -piv big1
```

we see that it is now (nearly) contiguous:

```
File: big1  Size: 3554273 bytes  Vol: /dev/hd11 (4096 byte blks)
Inode: 8290  Mode: -rwxr-xr-x  Owner: frankw  Group: system

INDIRECT BLOCK: 60307

Physical blocks (mirror copy 1)                    Logical blocks
-------------------------------                    --------------
60299-60306  hdisk1     8 blks,    32 KB,  0.9%    08555-08562
60308-61167  hdisk1   860 blks,  3440 KB, 99.1%    08564-09423

  868 blocks over space of 869:  space efficiency = 99.9%
  2 fragments out of 868 possible:  sequentiality = 99.9%
```

The **–i** option that we added to the **fileplace** command shows us that the one-block gap between the first eight blocks of the file and the remainder contains the indirect block, which is required to supplement the i-node information when the length of the file exceeds eight blocks.

Performance Considerations of Paging Spaces

I/O to and from paging spaces is random, mostly one page at a time. **vmstat** reports indicate the amount of paging-space I/O taking place. Both of the following examples show the paging activity that occurs during a C compilation in a machine that has been artificially shrunk using **rmss**. The **pi** and **po** (paging-space page ins and paging-space page outs) columns show the amount of paging-space I/O (in terms of 4096-byte pages) during each 5-second interval. The first, summary, report has been removed. Notice that the paging activity occurs in bursts.

```
$ vmstat 5
procs    memory                page              faults          cpu
----- -----------  -------------------------  ------------  -----------
 r b   avm   fre  re  pi  po   fr    sr  cy  in   sy   cs us sy id wa
 0 0  2502   432   0   0   0    0     0   0 134   26   20  0  1 99  0
 0 0  2904   201   4   0   7   43  1524   0 129  227   38 64 12 15 10
 1 0  3043   136   0   0   0   17   136   0 117   46   24 92  6  0  2
 1 0  3019    90   3   0   0    0     0   0 126   74   34 84  6  0 10
 0 0  3049   178   2   0  15   28   876   0 148   32   32 85  6  0  9
 1 0  3057   216   0   1   6   11    77   0 121   39   25 93  5  0  2
 0 0  2502   599   2  15   0    0     0   0 142 1195   69 47  9 11 34
 0 0  2502   596   0   0   0    0     0   0 135   30   22  1  1 98  1
```

The following before and after **vmstat –s** reports show the accumulation of paging activity. Remember that it is the "paging space page ins" and ". . .outs" that represent true paging-space I/O. The (unqualified) "page ins" and "page outs" report total I/O—both paging-space I/O and the ordinary file I/O that is also performed by the paging mechanism. (The reports have been edited to remove lines that are irrelevant to this discussion.)

```
$ vmstat -s                          $ vmstat -s
       .                                    .
       .                                    .
  6602 page ins                        7022 page ins
  3948 page outs                       4146 page outs
   544 paging space page ins    ►       689 paging space page ins
  1923 paging space page outs          2032 paging space page outs
    71 total reclaims                    84 total reclaims
       .                                    .
       .                                    .
```

The fact that more paging-space page ins than page outs occurred during the compilation suggests that we had shrunk the system to the point of incipient thrashing. Some pages were being repaged because their frames were stolen before their use was complete (that is, before any change had been made).

Measuring Overall Disk I/O with vmstat

The technique just discussed can also be used to assess the disk I/O load generated by a program. If the system is otherwise idle, the sequence:

```
$ vmstat -s >statout
$ testpgm
$ sync
$ vmstat -s >> statout
$ egrep "ins|outs" statout
```

will yield a before and after picture of the cumulative disk activity counts, such as:

```
  5698 page ins
  5012 page outs
     0 paging space page ins
    32 paging space page outs
  6671 page ins
  5268 page outs
     8 paging space page ins
   225 paging space page outs
```

During the period when this command (a large C compile) was running, the system read a total of 981 pages (8 from paging space) and wrote a total of 449 pages (193 to paging space).

Using filemon for Detailed I/O Analysis

The **filemon** command uses the trace facility to obtain a detailed picture of I/O activity during a time interval. Since it uses the trace facility, **filemon** can be run only by root or by a member of the system group.

In AIX Version 4.1, the **filemon** command is packaged as part of the Performance Toolbox for AIX. To determine whether **filemon** is available, use:

```
lslpp -lI perfagent.tools
```

If this package has been installed, **filemon** is available.

Tracing is started by the **filemon** command, optionally suspended with **trcoff** and resumed with **trcon**, and terminated with **trcstop**. As soon as tracing is terminated,

filemon writes its report to **stdout**. The following sequence of commands gives a simple example of **filemon** use:

```
# filemon -o fm.test.out ; cp smit.log /dev/null ; trcstop
```

The report produced by this sequence, in an otherwise-idle system, was:

```
Wed Jan 12 11:28:25 1994
System: AIX alborz Node: 3 Machine: 000249573100

0.303 secs in measured interval
Cpu utilization:  55.3%

Most Active Segments
------------------------------------------------------------------------
  #MBs  #rpgs  #wpgs  segid  segtype             volume:inode
------------------------------------------------------------------------
   0.1    26     0    0984   persistent          /dev/hd1:25
   0.0     1     0    34ba   .indirect           /dev/hd1:4

Most Active Logical Volumes
------------------------------------------------------------------------
  util  #rblk  #wblk   KB/s  volume              description
------------------------------------------------------------------------
  0.66   216     0    357.0  /dev/hd1            /home

Most Active Physical Volumes
------------------------------------------------------------------------
  util  #rblk  #wblk   KB/s  volume              description
------------------------------------------------------------------------
  0.65   216     0    357.0  /dev/hdisk1         320   MB SCSI


------------------------------------------------------------------------
Detailed VM Segment Stats   (4096 byte pages)
------------------------------------------------------------------------

SEGMENT: 0984  segtype: persistent  volume: /dev/hd1  inode: 25
segment flags:          pers
reads:                  26      (0 errs)
  read times (msec):    avg  45.644 min    9.115 max 101.388 sdev  33.045
  read sequences:       3
  read seq. lengths:    avg    8.7 min     1 max      22 sdev     9.5
SEGMENT: 34ba  segtype: .indirect  volume: /dev/hd1  inode: 4
segment flags:          pers jnld sys
reads:                  1       (0 errs)
  read times (msec):    avg  16.375 min 16.375 max  16.375 sdev   0.000
  read sequences:       1
  read seq. lengths:    avg    1.0 min     1 max       1 sdev     0.0


------------------------------------------------------------------------
Detailed Logical Volume Stats   (512 byte blocks)
------------------------------------------------------------------------

VOLUME: /dev/hd1  description: /home
```

```
reads:                    27      (0 errs)
  read sizes (blks):      avg     8.0 min       8 max       8 sdev     0.0
  read times (msec):      avg  44.316 min   8.907 max 101.112 sdev  32.893
  read sequences:         12
  read seq. lengths:      avg    18.0 min       8 max      64 sdev    15.4
seeks:                    12      (44.4%)
  seek dist (blks):       init    512
                          avg   312.0 min       8 max    1760 sdev   494.9
time to next req(msec): avg     8.085 min   0.012 max  64.877 sdev  17.383
throughput:               357.0 KB/sec
utilization:              0.66
------------------------------------------------------------------------
Detailed Physical Volume Stats   (512 byte blocks)
------------------------------------------------------------------------

VOLUME: /dev/hdisk1  description: 320  MB SCSI
reads:                    14      (0 errs)
  read sizes (blks):      avg    15.4 min       8 max      32 sdev     8.3
  read times (msec):      avg  13.989 min   5.667 max  25.369 sdev   5.608
  read sequences:         12
  read seq. lengths:      avg    18.0 min       8 max      64 sdev    15.4
seeks:                    12      (85.7%)
  seek dist (blks):       init 263168,
                          avg   312.0 min       8 max    1760 sdev   494.9
  seek dist (cyls):       init    399
                          avg     0.5 min       0 max       2 sdev     0.8
time to next req(msec): avg    27.302 min   3.313 max  64.856 sdev  22.295
throughput:               357.0 KB/sec
utilization:              0.65
```

The Most Active Segments report lists the most active files. To identify unknown files, you could translate the logical volume name, **/dev/hd1**, to the mount point of the file system, **/home**, and use the **find** command:

```
# find /home -inum 25 -print
```

which returns:

```
/home/waters/smit.log
```

Using **filemon** in systems with real workloads would result in much larger reports and might require more trace buffer space. **filemon**'s space and CPU time consumption can degrade system performance to some extent. You should experiment with **filemon** on a nonproduction system before starting it in a production environment.

Note: Although **filemon** reports average, minimum, maximum, and standard deviation in its detailed-statistics sections, the results should not be used to develop confidence intervals or other formal statistical inferences. In general, the distribution of data points is neither random nor symmetrical.

Disk-Limited Programs

Disk sensitivity can come in a number of forms, with different resolutions:

- If large, I/O-intensive background jobs are interfering with interactive response time, you may want to activate I/O pacing.
- If it appears that a small number of files are being read over and over again, you should consider whether additional real memory would allow those files to be buffered more effectively.
- If **iostat** indicates that your workload I/O activity is not evenly distributed among the system disk drives, and the utilization of one or more disk drives is often 70–80% or more, consider reorganizing file systems.
- If the workload's access pattern is predominantly random, you may want to consider adding disks and distributing the randomly accessed files across more drives.
- If the workload's access pattern is predominantly sequential and involves multiple disk drives, you may want to consider adding one or more disk adapters. It may also be appropriate to consider building a striped logical volume to accommodate large, performance-critical sequential files.

Expanding the Configuration

Unfortunately, every performance-tuning effort ultimately does reach a point of diminishing returns. The question then becomes, "What hardware do I need, how much of it, and how do I make the best use of it?" That question is especially tricky with disk-limited workloads because of the large number of variables. Changes that might improve the performance of a disk-limited workload include:

- Adding disk drives and spreading the existing data across them. This divides the I/O load among more accessors
- Acquiring faster disk drives to supplement or replace existing ones for high-usage data
- Adding one or more disk SCSI adapters to attach the current and/or new disk drives
- Adding RAM to the system and increasing the VMM's **minperm** and **maxperm** parameters to improve the in-memory caching of high-usage data

Precisely because this question is complex and highly dependent on the workload and configuration, and because the absolute and relative speeds of disks, adapters, and processors are changing so rapidly, we can't give a prescription, only some "rules of thumb."

- If you are seeking maximum sequential-access performance:
    - Attach no more than three 1.0GB (new) drives to a given SCSI-2 disk adapter.

    The maximum sustained sequential performance per SCSI-2 disk adapter, under ideal conditions, is approximately 6.8MB/sec.

- If you are seeking maximum random-access performance:
  - Attach no more than six 1.0GB (new) drives to a given SCSI-2 disk adapter.

  The maximum sustained random performance (on 4KB pages) per SCSI-2 disk adapter, under ideal conditions, is approximately 435 pages/sec.

For more guidance more closely focused on your configuration and workload, you could use a measurement-driven simulator, such as BEST/1.

Background Information

The following other sections contain information that may help you understand I/O performance:

- "Performance Overview of the Virtual Memory Manager (VMM)" on page 17
- "Memory-Limited Programs" on page 64
- "Placement and Sizes of Paging Spaces" on page 69

Tuning Sequential Read Ahead

The VMM's sequential read-ahead feature, described in "Sequential-Access Read Ahead" on page 27, can improve the performance of programs that access large files sequentially.

Occasions when tuning the sequential read-ahead feature (or turning it off) will improve performance are rare. Nevertheless, the performance analyst should understand how this feature interacts with the application and with other disk-I/O tuning parameters. The figure "Sequential Read Ahead Example" illustrates a typical situation.

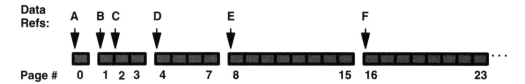

Figure 13: Sequential Read Ahead Example

In this example, **minpgahead** is 2 and **maxpgahead** is 8—the defaults. The program is processing the file sequentially. Only the data references that have significance to the read-ahead mechanism are shown, designated by A through F. The sequence of steps is:

A   The first access to the file causes the first page (page 0) of the file to be read. At this point the VMM makes no assumptions about random or sequential access.

B   When the program accesses the first byte of the next page (page 1), with no intervening accesses to other pages of the file, the VMM concludes that the program is accessing sequentially. It schedules **minpgahead** (2)

	additional pages (pages 2 and 3) to be read. Thus access B causes a total of 3 pages to be read.
C	When the program accesses the first byte of the first page that has been read ahead (page 2), the VMM doubles the page-ahead value to 4 and schedules pages 4 through 7 to be read.
D	When the program accesses the first byte of the first page that has been read ahead (page 4), the VMM doubles the page-ahead value to 8 and schedules pages 8 through 15 to be read.
E	When the program accesses the first byte of the first page that has been read ahead (page 8), the VMM determines that the page-ahead value is equal to **maxpgahead** and schedules pages 16 through 23 to be read.
F	The VMM continues reading **maxpgahead** pages when the program accesses the first byte of the previous group of read-ahead pages until the file ends.

(If the program were to deviate from the sequential-access pattern and access a page of the file out of order, sequential read ahead would be terminated. It would be resumed with **minpgahead** pages if the VMM detected a resumption of sequential access by the program.)

The **minpgahead** and **maxpgahead** values can be changed with the **vmtune** command. If you are contemplating changing these values, keep in mind:

- The values should be from the set: 0, 1, 2, 4, 8, 16. The use of other values may have adverse performance or functional effects.
  - Values should be powers of 2 because of the doubling algorithm of the VMM.
  - Values of **maxpgahead** greater than 16 (reads ahead of more then 64KB) exceed the capabilities of some disk device drivers.
  - Higher values of **maxpgahead** can be used in systems where the sequential performance of striped logical volumes is of paramount importance.
- A **minpgahead** value of 0 effectively defeats the mechanism. This may have serious adverse consequences for performance.
- The default **maxpgahead** value of 8 yields the maximum possible sequential I/O performance for currently supported disk drives.
- The ramp-up of the read-ahead value from **minpgahead** to **maxpgahead** is quick enough that for most file sizes there would be no advantage to increasing **minpgahead**.

Use Of Disk-I/O Pacing

Disk-I/O pacing is intended to prevent programs that generate very large amounts of output from saturating the system's I/O facilities and causing the response times of less-demanding programs to deteriorate. Disk-I/O pacing enforces per-segment (which effectively means per-file) high- and low-water marks on the sum of all pending I/Os.

When a process tries to write to a file that already has "high-water mark" pending writes, the process is put to sleep until enough I/Os have completed to make the number of pending writes less than or equal to "low-water mark." The logic of I/O-request handling does not change. The output from high-volume processes is just slowed down somewhat. The high- and low-water marks are set with **smit** by selecting **System Environments –> Change / Show Characteristics of Operating System** and then entering the number of pages for the high- and low-water marks. The default value for the high- and low-water marks is 0, which disables pacing. New I/O pacing parameters normally take effect immediately and last until they are explicitly changed.

Example

The effect of pacing on performance can be demonstrated with an experiment that consists of starting a **vi** session on a new file while another process is **cp**ing a 64MB file. The file is copied from `disk1` to `disk0` and the **vi** executable is located on `disk0`. For the **vi** session to start, it must page itself in as well as perform a few other I/Os, which it does randomly one page at a time. This takes about 50 physical I/Os, which can be completed in .71 seconds when there is no contention for the disk. With the high-water mark set to the default of 0, the logical writes from **cp** run ahead of the physical writes, and a large queue builds up. Each I/O started by **vi** must wait its turn in the queue before the next I/O can be issued, and thus **vi** is not able to complete its needed I/O until after **cp** finishes. The figure "I/O Pacing Test Results" shows the the elapsed times for **cp** execution and **vi** initialization with different pacing parameters. This experiment was run on a Model 530 with two 857MB disks and 32MB of RAM.

High-Water Mark	Low-Water Mark	cp (sec)	vi (sec)
0	0	50.0	**vi** not done
0	0	50.2	**vi** finished after **cp** had finished
9	6	76.8	2.7
17	12	57.9	3.6
17	8	63.9	3.4
33	24	52.0	9.0
33	16	55.1	4.9

Figure 14: I/O-Pacing-Test Results

It is important to notice that the **cp** duration is always longer when pacing is set. Pacing sacrifices some throughput on I/O-intensive programs to improve the response time of other programs. The challenge for a system administrator is to choose settings that result in a throughput/response-time trade-off that is consistent with the organization's priorities.

The high- and low-water marks were chosen by trial and error, based on our knowledge of the I/O path. Choosing them is not straightforward because of the combination of write-behind and asynchronous writes. High-water marks of 4x + 1 work particularly well, because of the following interaction:

- The write-behind feature sends the previous four pages to disk when a logical write occurs to the first byte of the fifth page.
- If the pacing high-water mark were a multiple of 4 (say, 8), a process would hit the high-water mark when it requested a write that extended into the 9th page. It would then be put to sleep—*before* the write-behind algorithm had a chance to detect that the fourth dirty page is complete and the four pages were ready to be written.
- The process would then sleep with four full pages of output until its outstanding writes fell below the pacing low-water mark.
- If, on the other hand, the high-water mark had been set to 9, write-behind would get to schedule the four pages for output before the process was suspended.

One limitation of pacing is that it does not offer as much control when a process writes buffers larger than 4KB. If, when a write is sent to the VMM, the high-water mark has not been met, the VMM performs Start I/Os on all pages in the buffer, even if that results in exceeding the high-water mark. Pacing works well on **cp** because **cp** writes 4KB at a time; but if **cp** wrote larger buffers, the times in the figure "I/O Pacing Test Results" for starting **vi** would increase.

Disk-I/O pacing is a tuning parameter that can improve interactive response time in some situations where foreground or background programs that write large volumes of data are interfering with foreground requests. If not used properly, however, it can reduce throughput excessively. The settings in the figure I/O Pacing Test Results are a good place to start, but some experimenting will be needed to find the best settings for your workload.

Programs whose presence in a workload may make imposition of disk-I/O pacing necessary include:

- Programs that generate large amounts of output algorithmically, and thus are not constrained by the time required to read input. Some such programs may need pacing on comparatively fast processors and not need it on comparatively slow processors.
- Programs that write large, possibly somewhat modified, files that have been read in their entirety shortly before writing begins—by a previous command, for example.
- Filters, such as the **tar** command, that read a file and write it out again with little processing. The need for pacing can be exacerbated if the input is being read from a faster disk drive than the output is being written to.

Logical Volume Striping

Striping is a technique for spreading the data in a logical volume across several disk drives in such a way that the I/O capacity of the disk drives can be used in parallel to access data on the logical volume. (The ability to create striped logical volumes is not available on

AIX Version 3.2.5.) The primary objective of striping is very high-performance reading and writing of large sequential files. The figure "Striped Logical Volume" **/dev/lvs0** gives a simple example.

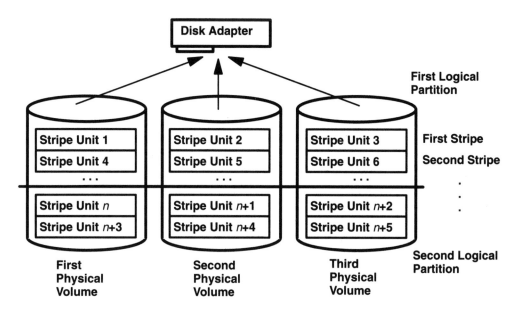

Figure 15: Striped Logical Volume /dev/lvs0

In an ordinary logical volume, the data addresses correspond to the sequence of blocks in the underlying physical partitions. In a striped logical volume, the data addresses follow the sequence of stripe units. A complete stripe consists of one stripe unit on each of the physical devices that contains part of the striped logical volume. The LVM determines which physical blocks on which physical drives correspond to a block being read or written. If more than one drive is involved, the necessary I/O operations are scheduled for all drives simultaneously.

As an example, suppose that the hypothetical **lvs0** has a stripe-unit size of 64KB, consists of six 2MB partitions, and contains a journaled file system (JFS). If an application is reading a large sequential file and read-ahead has reached a steady state, each read will result in two or three I/Os being scheduled to each of the disk drives to read a total of eight pages (assuming that the file is on consecutive blocks in the logical volume). The read operations are performed in the order determined by the disk device driver. The requested data is assembled from the various pieces of input and returned to the application.

Although each disk device will have a different initial latency, depending on where its accessor was at the beginning of the operation, once the process reaches a steady state, all three disks should be reading at close to their maximum speed.

Designing a Striped Logical Volume

When a striped logical volume is defined, you specify:

drives Obviously, at least two physical drives are required. The drives used should have little other activity when the performance-critical sequential I/O is taking place.

Some combinations of disk adapter and disk drive will require dividing the workload of a striped logical volume between two or more adapters.

stripe unit size Although this can be any power of 2 from 4KB through 128KB, you should take sequential read ahead into account, since that will be the mechanism that issues most of the reads. The objective is to have each read-ahead operation result in at least one I/O, ideally an equal number, to each disk drive.

size The number of physical partitions allocated to the logical volume must be an integral multiple of the number of disk drives used.

attributes Cannot be mirrored; that is, copies = 1.

Tuning for Striped Logical Volume I/O

In benchmarking situations, the following techniques have yielded the highest levels of sequential I/O throughput:

- Stripe unit size of 64KB.
- **max_coalesce** of 64KB (the default). Equal to the stripe unit size.
- **minpgahead** of 2
- **maxpgahead** of (16 times the number of disk drives). This causes page ahead to be done in units of the stripe unit size (64KB) times the number of disk drives, resulting in the reading of one stripe unit from each disk drive for each read ahead operation.
- I/O requests for (64KB times the number of disk drives). This is equal to the **maxpgahead** value.
- Modify **maxfree** to accommodate the change in **maxpgahead**. See "Choosing **minfree** and **maxfree** Settings", on page 126.
- 64-byte aligned I/O buffers. If the logical volume will occupy physical drives that are connected to two or more disk adapters, the I/O buffers used should be allocated on 64-byte boundaries. This avoids having the LVM serialize the I/Os to the different disks. The following code would yield a 64-byte-aligned buffer pointer:

```
char *buffer;
buffer = malloc(MAXBLKSIZE+64);
buffer = ((int)buffer + 64) & ~0x3f;
```

File-System Fragment Size

The *fragments* feature (in AIX Version 4.1 only) allows the space in a file system to be allocated in less than 4KB chunks. When a file system is created, the system administrator can specify the size of the fragments in the file system. The allowable sizes are 512, 1024, 2048, and 4096 bytes (the default). Files smaller than a fragment are stored in a single fragment, conserving disk space, which is the primary objective.

Files smaller than 4096 bytes are stored in the minimum necessary number of contiguous fragments. Files whose size is between 4096 bytes and 32KB (inclusive) are stored in one or more (4KB) full blocks and in as many fragments as are required to hold the remainder. Files that contain more than 32KB of data are stored entirely in full blocks.

Whatever the fragment size, a full block is still considered to be 4096 bytes. In a file system with a fragment size less than 4096, however, a need for a full block can be satisfied by any contiguous sequence of fragments totalling 4096 bytes. It doesn't have to begin on a multiple-of-4096-byte boundary.

The file system tries to allocate space for files in contiguous fragments whenever possible. In pursuit of that objective, it spreads the files themselves across the logical volume to minimize inter-file allocation interference and fragmentation.

The primary performance hazard for file systems with small fragment sizes is space fragmentation. The existence of small files scattered across the logical volume can make it impossible to allocate contiguous or closely spaced blocks for a large file. The performance of accessing the large file suffers. Carried to an extreme, space fragmentation can make it impossible to allocate space for a file, even though there are many individual free fragments.

Part of a decision to create a small-fragment file system should be a policy for defragmenting the space in that file system with the **defragfs** command. This policy also has to take into account the performance cost of running **defragfs**.

Compression

When a file is written into a file system for which compression is specified, the compression algorithm compresses the data 4096 bytes (a page) at a time, and the compressed data is then written in the minimum necessary number of contiguous fragments. Obviously, if the fragment size of the file system is 4KB, there is no disk-space payback for the effort of compressing the data. (Compression and fragments smaller than 4KB are new in AIX Version 4.1.)

Although compression should result in conserving space overall, there are at least two reasons for leaving some space in the file system unused:

- Since the degree to which each 4096-byte block of data will compress is not known in advance, the file system initially reserves a full block of space. The unneeded fragments are released after compression, but the conservative initial allocation policy may lead to premature "out of space" indications.
- Some free space is necessary to allow the **defragfs** command to operate.

Asynchronous Disk I/O

Applications can use the **aio_read** and **aio_write** subroutines to perform asynchronous disk I/O. Control returns to the application from the subroutine as soon as the request has been queued. The application can then continue processing while the disk operation is being performed.

Although the application can continue processing, a kernel process (kproc) called a *server* is in charge of each request from the time it is taken off the queue until it completes. The number of servers limits the number of asynchronous disk I/O operations that can be in progress in the system simultaneously. The number of servers can be set with **smit** (**smit**–>Devices–>Asynchronous I/O–>Change/Show Characteristics of Asynchronous I/O–>{MINIMUM|MAXIMUM} number of servers or **smit aio**) or with **chdev**. The minimum number of servers is the number to be started at system boot. The maximum limits the number that can be started in response to large numbers of simultaneous requests.

The default values are **minservers=1** and **maxservers=10**. In systems that seldom run applications that use asynchronous I/O, this is usually adequate. For environments with many disk drives and key applications that use asynchronous I/O, the default is far too low. The result of a deficiency of servers is that disk I/O seems much slower than it should be. Not only do requests spend inordinate lengths of time in the queue, the low ratio of servers to disk drives means that the seek-optimization algorithms have too few requests to work with for each drive.

For environments in which the performance of asynchronous disk I/O is critical and the volume of requests is high, we recommend that:

- **maxservers** should be set to at least 10*(number of disks accessed asynchronously)
- **minservers** should be set to **maxservers**/2.

This could be achieved for a system with 3 asynchronously accessed disks with:

```
# chdev -l aio0 -a minservers='15' -a maxservers='30'
```

Using Raw Disk I/O

There are three ways in which a program might access disk in raw mode:

1. Block raw-disk-device special files have names of the form **/dev/hdisk**n, and are used by some subsystems. These devices should not be used by application programs.

2. Character raw-disk-device special files have names of the form **/dev/rhdisk**n. Use of these devices by application programs is not recommended. If you decide to use this technique, make sure that no AIX logical volumes occupy any part of the physical disk drive being accessed. The performance effect of interaction

between raw access and file-system access to the same physical drive is unpredictable.

3. A logical volume on which no file system has been created can be accessed in raw mode. All **write**s, **read**s, **lseek**s, etc. must be in multiples of 512 bytes. The least important consequence of violating this rule is serious performance degradation.

Using sync/fsync

Forced synchronization of the contents of real memory and disk takes place in several ways:

- An application program makes an **fsync()** call for a specified file. This causes all of the pages that contain modified data for that file to be written to disk. The writing is complete when the **fsync()** call returns to the program.
- An application program makes a **sync()** call. This causes all of the file pages in memory that contain modified data to be scheduled for writing to disk. The writing is *not necessarily* complete when the **sync()** call returns to the program.
- A user can enter the **sync** command, which in turn issues a **sync()** call. Again, some of the writes may not be complete when the user is prompted for input (or the next command in a shell script is processed).
- The sync daemon, **/usr/sbin/syncd**, issues a **sync()** call at regular intervals—usually every 60 seconds. This ensures that the system does not accumulate large amounts of data that exists only in volatile RAM.

A sync operation has several effects, aside from its small CPU consumption:

- It causes writes to be clumped, rather than spread out.
- It causes at least 28KB of system data to be written, even if there has been no I/O activity since the previous sync.
- It accelerates the writing of data to disk, defeating the write-behind algorithm. This effect is significant mainly in programs that issue an **fsync()** after every write.

Modifying the SCSI Device Driver max_coalesce Parameter

When there are multiple disk-I/O requests in the SCSI device driver's queue, it attempts to coalesce those requests into a smaller number of large requests. The largest request (in terms of data transmitted) that the SCSI device driver will build is limited by the **max_coalesce** parameter. Normally, **max_coalesce** has a value of 64KB.

To make maximum use of striped logical volumes and disk arrays, it may be desirable to increase the size of **max_coalesce**. To do so, it is necessary to have a stanza in the PdAt ODM database that specifies the new **max_coalesce** value. If you have already added such a stanza, you can obtain the current version with:

```
# odmget -q \
"uniquetype=disk/scsi/osdisk AND attribute=max_coalesce" \
PdAt > foo
```

If there is no such stanza already, use an editor to create the file foo with the following content:

```
PdAt:
        uniquetype = "disk/scsi/osdisk"
        attribute = "max_coalesce"
        deflt = "0x20000"
        values = "0x20000"
        width = ""
        type = "R"
        generic = ""
        rep = "n"
        nls_index = 0
```

Note that **max_coalesce**, in bytes, is expressed as a hexadecimal number. The deflt and values field values of 0x20000 will set **max_coalesce** to 128KB. Then replace the old stanza in PdAt, if any, with foo, using:

```
# odmdelete -o PdAt \
-q "uniquetype=/disk/scsi/osdisk AND attribute=max_coalesce"
# odmadd < foo
```

To put the change into effect, you must rebuild the kernel and reboot, with:

```
# bosboot -a -d hdisk0
# shutdown -rF
```

Setting SCSI-Adapter and Disk-Device Queue Limits

AIX has the ability to enforce limits on the number of I/O requests that can be outstanding from the SCSI adapter to a given SCSI bus or disk drive. These limits are intended to exploit the hardware's ability to handle multiple requests while ensuring that the seek-optimization algorithms in the device drivers are able to operate effectively.

For non-IBM devices, it is sometimes appropriate to modify AIX default queue-limit values that have been chosen to handle the worst possible case. The following sections describe situations in which the defaults should be changed and the recommended new values.

Non-IBM Disk Drive

For IBM disk drives, the default number of requests that can be outstanding at any given time is 3. This value is based on complex performance considerations, and no direct interface is provided for changing it. The default hardware queue depth for non-IBM disk drives is 1. If a specific non-IBM disk drive does have the ability to buffer multiple requests, the system's description of that device should be changed accordingly.

As an example, the default characteristics of a non-IBM disk drive are displayed with the **lsattr** command:

```
$ lsattr -D -c disk -s scsi -t osdisk
pvid          none Physical volume identifier     False
clr_q         no   Device CLEARS its Queue on error
q_err         yes  Use QERR bit
q_type        none Queuing TYPE
queue_depth   1    Queue DEPTH
reassign_to   120  REASSIGN time out value
rw_timeout    30   READ/WRITE time out value
start_timeout 60   START unit time out value
```

The ability to change these parameters is provided through **smit** (the fast path is **chgdsk**) and via the **chdev** command. For example, if your system contained a non-IBM SCSI disk drive **hdisk5**, the command:

```
# chdev -l hdisk5 -a q_type=simple -a queue_depth=3
```

would enable queuing for that device and set its queue depth to 3.

Non-IBM Disk Array

A disk array appears to AIX as a single, rather large, disk drive. A non-IBM disk array, like a non-IBM disk drive, is of class **disk**, subclass **scsi**, type **osdisk** (which stands for "Other SCSI Disk Drive"). Since a disk array actually contains a number of physical disk drives, each of which can handle multiple requests, the queue depth for the disk array device has to be set to a value high enough to allow efficient use of all of the physical devices. For example, if **hdisk7** were an eight-disk non-IBM disk array, an appropriate change would be:

```
# chdev -l hdisk7 -a q_type=simple -a queue_depth=24
```

If the disk array is attached via a SCSI-2 Fast/Wide SCSI adapter bus, it may also be necessary to change the outstanding-request limit for that bus.

Disk Adapter Outstanding-Request Limits

The SCSI-2 Fast/Wide Adapter supports two SCSI buses; one for internal devices and one for external devices. A limit on the total number of outstanding requests is defined for each bus. The default value of that limit is 40 and the maximum is 128. If an IBM disk array is attached to a SCSI-2 Fast/Wide Adapter bus, the outstanding-request limit for the bus is increased to accommodate the queue depth of the disk array. For a non-IBM disk array, this change must be performed manually. For example, to set the outstanding-request limit of adapter **scsi3** to 70, you would use:

```
# chdev -l scsi3 -a num_cmd_elems=70
```

In the SCSI-2 High Performance Controller, the maximum number of queued requests is 30. That limit cannot be changed. For that reason, you should ensure that the sum of the queue depths of the devices attached to a SCSI-2 High Performance Controller does not exceed 30.

The original RISC System/6000 SCSI adapter does not support queueing. It is inappropriate to attach a disk array device to such an adapter.

Controlling the Number of System pbufs

The Logical Volume Manager (LVM) uses a construct called a "pbuf" to control a pending disk I/O. In AIX Version 3, one pbuf is required for each page being read or written. In systems that do large amounts of sequential I/O, this can result in depletion of the pool of pbufs. The **vmtune** command can be used to increase the number of pbufs to compensate for this effect.

In AIX Version 4, a single pbuf is used for each sequential I/O request, regardless of the number of pages involved. This greatly decreases the probability of running out of pbufs.

9

Monitoring and Tuning Communications I/O

UDP/TCP/IP Performance Overview

To understand the performance characteristics of UDP and TCP/IP, you must first understand some of the underlying architecture. Figure 16, "UDP/TCP/IP Data Flow," illustrates the structure that will be discussed in this chapter.

Figure 16 shows the path of data from an application in one system to another application in a remote system. The processing at each of the layers will be discussed in detail later, but briefly (ignoring error handling and buffer limits):

- The application's write request causes the data to be copied from the application's working segment to the socket send buffer.
- The socket layer or subsystem gives the data to UDP or TCP.
- If the size of the data is larger than the maximum transfer unit (MTU) of the LAN,
  - TCP breaks the output into segments that comply with the MTU limit.
  - UDP leaves the breaking up of the output to the IP layer.
- If necessary, IP fragments the output into pieces that comply with the MTU.
- The Interface layer ensures that no outgoing packet exceeds the MTU limit.
- The packets are put on the device output queue and transmitted by the LAN adapter to the receiving system.
- Arriving packets are placed on the device driver's receive queue, and pass through the Interface layer to IP.
- If IP in the receiving system determines that IP in the sending system had fragmented a block of data, it coalesces the fragments into their original form and passes the data to TCP or UDP.

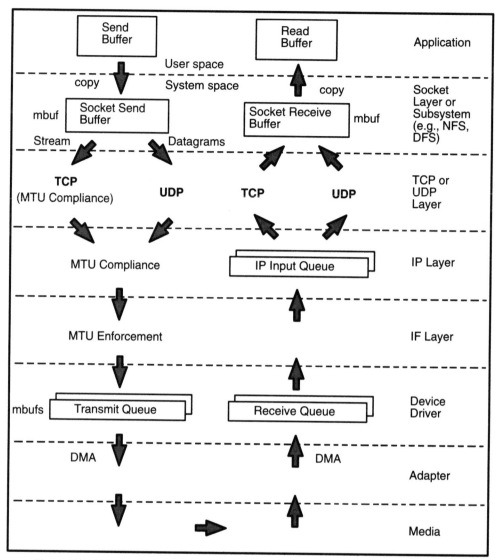

Figure 16: UDP/TCP/IP Data Flow

- TCP reassembles the original segments and places the input in the socket receive buffer.
- UDP simply passes the input on to the socket receive buffer.
- When the application makes a read request, the appropriate data is copied from the socket receive buffer in kernel memory into the buffer in the application's working segment.

Communication Subsystem Memory (mbuf) Management

To avoid fragmentation of kernel memory and the overhead of numerous calls to **xmalloc()**, common buffer pools are shared by the various layers of the communication subsystem. The mbuf management facility controls two pools of buffers: a pool of small buffers (256 bytes each), which are simply called *mbufs*, and a pool of large buffers (4096 bytes each), which are usually called *mbuf clusters* or just *clusters*. These pools are usually referred to collectively as "mbufs." The pools consist of pinned pieces of kernel virtual memory; this means that they always reside in physical memory and are never paged out. The result is that the real memory available for paging in application programs and data has been decreased by the amount that the mbuf pools have been increased.

In addition to avoiding duplication, sharing the mbuf and cluster pools allows the various layers to pass pointers to one another, reducing mbuf management calls and copying of data.

Socket Layer

Sockets provide the application program interface (API) to the communication subsystem. There are several types of sockets that provide various levels of service by using different communication protocols. Sockets of type SOCK_DGRAM use the UDP protocol. Sockets of type SOCK_STREAM use the TCP protocol.

The semantics of opening, reading, and writing to sockets are similar to those for manipulating files.

The sizes of the buffers in system virtual memory (that is, the total number of bytes from the mbuf pools) that are used by the input and output sides of each socket are limited by system-wide default values (which can be overridden for a given socket by a call to the **setsockopt()** subroutine):

udp_sendspace and **udp_recvspace**
> The buffer sizes for datagram sockets. The defaults are 9216 and 41600, respectively.

tcp_sendspace and **tcp_recvspace**
> The buffer sizes for stream sockets. The defaults for both values are 16384.

> These values can be displayed with

```
$ no -a
```

and set (by `root`) with, for example:

```
# no -o udp_sendspace=NewValue
```

The NewValue parameter must be less than or equal to the **sb_max** parameter, which controls the maximum amount of space that can be used by a socket's send or receive buffer. **sb_max** is displayed with **no –a** and set (*before* attempting to exceed its current value) with the **no** command:

```
# no -o sb_max=NewLimit
```

Note: Socket send or receive buffer sizes are limited to no more than **sb_max** bytes, because **sb_max** is a ceiling on buffer space consumption. The two quantities are not measured in the same way, however. The socket buffer size limits the amount of *data* that can be held in the socket buffers. **sb_max** limits the number of *bytes of mbufs* that can be in the socket buffer at any given time. In an Ethernet environment, for example, each 4096-byte mbuf cluster might hold just 1500 bytes of data. In that case, **sb_max** would have to be 2.73 times larger than the specified socket buffer size to allow the buffer to reach its specified capacity. Our rule of thumb is that **sb_max** should be set to at least twice the size of the largest socket buffer.

Send Flow

As an application writes to a socket, the data is copied from user space into the socket send buffer in kernel space. Depending on the amount of data being copied into the socket send buffer, the socket puts the data into either mbufs or clusters. Once the data is copied into the socket send buffer, the socket layer calls the *transport layer* (either TCP or UDP), passing it a pointer to the linked list of mbufs (an *mbuf chain*).

Receive Flow

On the receive side, an application opens a socket and attempts to read data from it. If there is no data in the socket receive buffer, the socket layer causes the application thread to go to the sleep state (blocking) until data arrives. When data arrives, it is put on the receive socket buffer queue and the application thread is made dispatchable. The data is then copied into the application's buffer in user space, the mbuf chain is freed, and control is returned to the application.

Relative Level of Function in UDP and TCP

The following two sections contain descriptions of the function of UDP and TCP. To facilitate comparison of UDP and TCP, both descriptions are divided into subsections on: connection, error detection, error recovery, flow control, data size, and MTU handling.

UDP Layer

UDP provides a low-cost protocol for applications that have the facilities to deal with communication failures. UDP is most suitable for "request-response" applications. Since such an application has to handle a failure to respond anyway, it is little additional effort to handle communication error as one of the causes of failure to respond. For this reason, and because of its low overhead, subsystems such as NFS, ONC RPC, DCE RPC, and DFS use UDP.

Connection   None. UDP is essentially a stateless protocol. Each request received from the caller is handled independent of those that precede or follow it. (If the **connect()** subroutine is called for a datagram socket, the information about the destination is considered a hint to cache the resolved address for future use. It does not actually bind the socket to that address or affect UDP on the receiving system.)

Error detection   Checksum creation and verification. The sending UDP builds the checksum and the receiving UDP checks it. If the check fails, the packet is dropped.

Error recovery	None. UDP does not acknowledge receipt of packets, nor does it detect their loss in transmission or through buffer-pool overflow. Consequently, UDP never retransmits a packet. Recovery must be performed by the application.
Flow control	None. When UDP is asked to send, it sends the packet to IP. When a packet arrives from IP, it is placed in the socket-receive buffer. If either the device driver/adapter buffer queue or the socket-receive buffer is full when the packet arrives there, the packet is dropped without an error indication. The application or subsystem that sent the packet must detect the failure by timeout and retry the transmission.
Data size	Must fit in one buffer. This means that the buffer pools on both sides of UDP must have buffer sizes that are adequate for the applications' requirements. The maximum size of a UDP packet is 64KB. Of course, an application that builds large blocks can break them into multiple datagrams itself—DCE is an example—but it is simpler to use TCP.
MTU handling	None. Dealing with data larger than the maximum transfer unit (MTU) size for the interface is left to IP. If IP has to fragment the data to make it fit the MTU, loss of one of the fragments becomes an error that the application or subsystem must deal with.

Send Flow

If **udp_sendspace** is large enough to hold the datagram, the application's data is copied into mbufs in kernel memory. If the datagram is larger than **udp_sendspace**, an error is returned to the application.

   If the datagram is larger than or equal to 936 bytes, it is copied into one or more 4KB clusters. The remainder (and any complete datagram) of less than 936 bytes is copied into 1–4 mbufs. For example, a write of 8704 bytes is copied into two clusters and the remainder into three mbufs. UDP adds the UDP header (in the same mbuf, if possible), checksums the data, and calls the IP **ip_output** routine.

Receive Flow

UDP verifies the checksum and queues the data onto the proper socket. If the **udp_recvspace** limit is exceeded, the packet is discarded. (A count of these discards is reported by **netstat –s** under "udp:" as "socket buffer overflows.") If the application is waiting on a **receive** or **read** on the socket, it is put on the run queue. This causes the **receive** to copy the datagram into the user's address space and release the mbufs, and the **receive** is complete. Normally, the receiver will respond to the sender to acknowledge the receipt and also return a response message.

TCP Layer

TCP provides a reliable-transmission protocol. TCP is most suitable for applications that, at least for periods of time, are mostly output or mostly input. With TCP ensuring that packets reach their destination, the application is freed from error detection and recovery responsibilities. Applications that use TCP transport include **ftp**, **rcp**, and **telnet**. DCE can use TCP if it is configured to use a connection-oriented protocol.

Connection Explicit. The instance of TCP that receives the connection request from an application (we will call it the *initiator*) establishes a session with its counterpart on the other system, which we will call the *listener*. All exchanges of data and control packets are within the context of that session.

Error detection Checksum creation and verification. The sending TCP builds the checksum and the receiving TCP checks it. If checksum verification fails, the receiver does not acknowledge receipt of the packet.

Error recovery Full. TCP detects checksum failures and loss of a packet or fragment through timeout. In error situations TCP retransmits the data until it is received correctly (or notifies the application of an unrecoverable error).

Flow control Enforced. TCP uses a discipline called a sliding window to ensure delivery to the receiving application. The sliding window concept is illustrated in the figure called "TCP Sliding Window." (The records shown in the figure are for clarity only. TCP processes data as a stream of bytes and does not keep track of record boundaries, which are application-defined.)

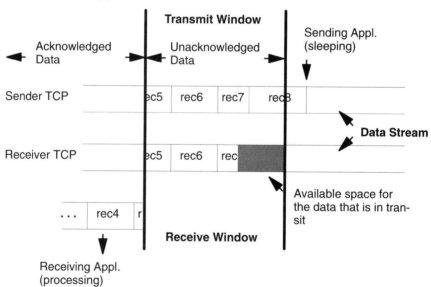

Figure 17: TCP Sliding Window

In the figure, the sending application is sleeping because it has attempted to write data that would cause TCP to exceed the send socket buffer space (i.e., **tcp_sendspace**). The sending TCP still has the last part of rec5, all of rec6 and rec7, and the beginning of rec8. The receiving TCP has not yet received the last part of rec7 or any of rec8.

The receiving application got rec4 and the beginning of rec5 when it last read the socket, and it is now processing that data. When the receiving application next reads the socket, it will receive (assuming a large enough read), the rest of rec5, rec6, and as much of rec7 and rec8 as has arrived by that time.

Once the next read occurs, the receiving TCP will be able to acknowledge that data, the sending TCP will be able to discard the data, the pending write will complete, and the sending application will wake up. (To avoid excessive LAN traffic when the application is reading in tiny amounts, TCP delays acknowledgement until the receiving application has read a total amount of data that is at least half the receive window size or twice the maximum segment size.)

In the course of establishing a session, the initiator and the listener converse to determine their respective capacities for buffering input and output data. The smaller of the two sizes defines the size of the window. As data is written to the socket, it is moved into the sender's buffer. When the receiver indicates that it has space available, the sender transmits enough data to fill that space (assuming that it has that much data). When the receiving application reads from the socket, the receiving TCP returns as much data as it has in its buffer. It then informs the sender that the data has been successfully delivered. Only then does the sender discard the data from its own buffer, effectively moving the window to the right by the amount of data delivered. If the window is full because the receiving application has fallen behind, the sending thread will be blocked (or receive a specific **errno**) when it tries to write to the socket.

The figure "TCP Window Sizes" shows the relationship between the socket buffer sizes and the window size.

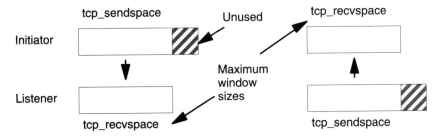

Figure 18: TCP Window Sizes

tcp_recvspace in both of these systems is smaller than **tcp_sendspace** to illustrate a point: since the moving-window technique requires that the two systems be able to buffer the same amount of data, the window size is set to the lesser value in both directions. The nominally available extra space for buffering output shown in the figure is never used.

	If the **rfc1323** parameter is 1, the maximum TCP window size is 4GB (instead of 64KB).
Data size	Indefinite. TCP does not process records or blocks, it processes a stream of bytes. If a send buffer is larger than the receiver can handle, it is segmented into MTU-size packets. Because it handles shortages of buffer space under the covers, TCP does not guarantee that the number and size of data receives will be the same as the number and size of sends. It is the responsibility of the two sides of the application to identify record or block boundaries, if any, within the stream of data.

Note: When using TCP to exchange request/response messages, the application must use **setsockopt** to turn on the TCP_NODELAY option. This causes TCP to send the message immediately (within the constraints of the sliding window), even though it is less than MTU-size. Otherwise, TCP would wait for up to 200 milliseconds for more data to send before transmitting the message. The consequences for performance are obvious.

MTU handling	Handled by segmentation in TCP. When the connection is established, the initiator and the listener negotiate a maximum segment size (MSS) to be used. The MSS is normally smaller than the MTU (see "Tuning TCP Maximum Segment Size (MSS)" on page 165). If the output packet size exceeds the MSS, TCP does the segmentation, thus making fragmentation in IP unnecessary. The receiving TCP normally puts the segments on the socket receive queue as they arrive. If the receiving TCP detects the loss of a segment, it withholds acknowledgement and holds back the succeeding segments until the missing segment has been received successfully.

There is, of course, no such thing as free function. The additional operations performed by TCP to ensure a reliable connection result in about 7 to 12% higher processor cost than in UDP.

Send Flow

When the TCP layer receives a write request from the socket layer, it allocates a new mbuf for its header information and copies the data in the socket-send buffer either into the TCP-header mbuf, if there is room, or into a newly allocated mbuf chain. If the data being copied is in clusters, the data is not actually copied into new clusters. Instead, a pointer field in the new mbuf header (this header is part of the mbuf structure and is unrelated to the TCP header) is set to point to the clusters containing the data, thereby avoiding the overhead of one or more 4KB copies. TCP then checksums the data, updates its various state variables, which are used for flow control and other services, and finally calls the IP layer with the header mbuf now linked to the new mbuf chain.

Receive Flow

When the TCP input routine receives input data from IP, it checksums the TCP header and data for corruption detection, determines which connection this data is for, removes its header information, links the mbuf chain onto the socket-receive buffer associated with this connection, and uses a socket service to wake up the application (if it is sleeping as described earlier).

IP Layer

The Internet Protocol provides a basic datagram service to the higher layers. If it is given a packet larger than the MTU of the interface, it fragments the packet and sends the fragments to the receiving system, which reassembles them into the original packet. If one of the fragments is lost in transmission, the incomplete packet is ultimately discarded by the receiver. The length of time IP waits for a missing fragment is controlled by the **ipfragttl** parameter, which is set and displayed with **no**.

The maximum size of IP's queue of packets received from the network interface is controlled by the **ipqmaxlen** parameter, which is set and displayed with **no**. If the size of the input queue reaches this number, subsequent packets are dropped.

Send Flow

When the IP output routine receives a packet from UDP or TCP, it identifies the interface to which the mbuf chain should be sent, updates and checksums the IP part of the header, and passes the packet to the interface (IF) layer.

IP determines the proper device driver and adapter to use, based on the network number. The driver interface table defines the maximum MTU for this network. If the datagram is less than the MTU size, IP adds the IP header in the existing mbuf, checksums the IP header and calls the driver to send the frame. If the driver send queue is full, an EAGAIN error is returned to IP which simply returns it to UDP which returns it to the sending application. The sender should delay and try again.

If the datagram is larger than the MTU size (which only happens in UDP) IP fragments the datagram into MTU-size fragments, appends a IP header (in an mbuf) to each, and calls the driver once for each fragment frame. If the driver's send queue is full, an EAGAIN error is returned to IP. IP discards all remaining unsent fragments associated with this datagram and returns EAGAIN to UDP. UDP returns EAGAIN the the sending application. Since IP and UDP do not queue messages, it is up to the application to delay and try the send again.

Receive Flow

In AIX Version 3, when the IP input routine receives control as the result of an IF-scheduled off-level interrupt, it dequeues the mbuf chain, checks the IP header checksum to make sure the header was not corrupted, and determines if the packet is for this system. If so, and the frame is not a fragment, IP passes the mbuf chain to the TCP or UDP input routine.

In AIX Version 4, the demux layer (called the IF layer in Version 3) calls IP on the interrupt thread. There is no longer any scheduling or queuing/dequeuing activity. IP checks the IP header checksum to make sure the header was not corrupted and determines if the packet is for this system. If so, and the frame is not a fragment, IP passes the mbuf chain to the TCP or UDP input routine.

If the received frame is a fragment of a larger datagram (which only happens in UDP), IP holds onto the frame. When the other fragments arrive, they are merged into a logical datagram and given to UDP when the datagram is complete. IP holds the fragments of an incomplete datagram until the **ipfragttl** time (as specified by **no**) expires. The default **ipfragttl** time is 60 seconds. If any fragments are lost due to problems such as network errors, lack of mbufs, or transmit queue overruns, IP never receives them. When **ipfragttl** expires, IP discards the fragments it did receive. This is reported by **netstat –s** under "`ip:`" as "`fragments dropped after timeout.`"

IF Layer (Demux Layer in AIX Version 4)

Send Flow

When the IF layer receives a packet from IP, it attaches the link-layer header information to the beginning of the packet, checks the format of the mbufs to make sure they conform to the device driver's input specifications, and then calls the device driver write routine.

Receive Flow

In AIX Version 3, when the IF layer receives a packet from the device driver, it removes the link header and enqueues the mbuf chain (done with pointers, not copying) on the IP input queue and schedules an off-level interrupt to do the IP input processing.

In AIX Version 4, when the demux layer receives a packet from the device driver, it calls IP on the interrupt thread to perform IP input processing.

LAN Adapters and Device Drivers

Many different kinds of LAN adapters are supported in the AIX environment. These adapters differ, not only in the communications protocol and transmission medium they support, but also in their interface to the the I/O bus and the processor. Similarly, the device drivers vary in the technique used to convey the data between memory and the adapter. The following high-level description applies to most adapters and device drivers, but details vary.

Send Flow

At the device-driver layer, the mbuf chain containing the packet is enqueued on the transmit queue. The maximum total number of output buffers that can be queued is controlled by the system parameter **xmt_que_size**. In some cases, the data is copied into driver-owned DMA buffers. The adapter is then signaled to start DMA operations.

At this point, control returns back up the path to the TCP or UDP output routine, which continues sending as long as it has more to send. When all data has been sent, control returns to the application, which then runs asynchronously while the adapter transmits data. When the adapter has completed transmission, it interrupts the system, and the device interrupt routines are called to adjust the transmit queues and free the mbufs that held the transmitted data.

Receive Flow

When frames are received by an adapter, they are transferred from the adapter into a driver-managed receive queue. The receive queue may consist of mbufs or the device driver may manage a separate pool of buffers for the device; in either case, the data is in an mbuf chain when it is passed from the device driver to the IF layer.

Some drivers receive frames via DMA into a pinned area of memory and then allocate mbufs and copy the data into them. Drivers/adapters that receive large-MTU frames may have the frames DMA'd directly into cluster mbufs. The driver hands off the frame to the proper network protocol (IP in this example) by calling a demultiplexing function that identifies the packet type and puts the mbuf containing the buffer on the input queue for that network protocol. If no mbufs are available or if the higher-level input queue is full, the incoming frames are discarded.

TCP and UDP Performance Tuning

The optimal settings of the tunable communications parameters vary with the type of LAN as well as with the communications-I/O characteristics of the predominant system and application programs. The following sections describe the global principles of communications tuning, followed by specific recommendations for the different types of LAN.

Overall Recommendations

You can choose to tune primarily either for maximum throughput or for minimum memory use. Some recommendations apply to one or the other; some apply to both.

Maximizing Throughput

Request-Response Protocols

- For maximum number of transactions per second, use the smallest feasible messages.
- For maximum bytes per second, use messages that are at least 1000 bytes and equal to or just less than a multiple of 4096 bytes.
- If the requests and responses are fixed-size and fit into one datagram, use UDP.
  - If possible, make the write sizes equal to (a multiple of the MTU size minus 28 bytes to allow for standard IP and UDP headers).
  - In general, it is more efficient for the application to write large messages and have them fragmented and reassembled by IP, than to have the application write multiple times.
  - Whenever possible, use the **connect** subroutine to associate an address with the UDP socket. This may not be possible on a server that is communicating with a number of clients via a single socket.

- If the requests or responses are variable-size, use TCP with the TCP_NODELAY option. Our measurements indicate that the overhead of TCP compared with UDP is negligible, especially if optimum write sizes are used.
  - To avoid data copies in the kernel, make write sizes greater than 936 bytes.
  - Make writes equal to or slightly less than, a multiple of MTU size. This will avoid the sending of a segment (packet) with just a few bytes in it.

Streaming

- TCP provides higher throughput than UDP and ensures reliable delivery.
- Writes should be in multiples of 4096 bytes. If possible, writes should be the size of the MSS (see "Tuning TCP Maximum Segment Size (MSS)", below).

Minimizing Memory

- If your traffic is predominantly local, use the largest MTU size that is supported by your LAN type. This minimizes the fragmentation of packets exchanged by local systems. The offsetting cost is fragmentation in gateways that connect your LAN to other LANS with smaller MTUs (see "Tuning TCP Maximum Segment Size (MSS)", below).
- Whenever possible, application programs should read and write in quantities of either:
  - Less than or equal to 935 bytes, or
  - Slightly less than or equal to 4096 bytes (or multiples thereof)

  The former will be placed in one to four mbufs; the latter will make efficient use of the 4096-byte clusters that are used for writes larger than 935 bytes. Writing 936 bytes would result in 3160 bytes of wasted space per write. The application could hit the **udp_recvspace** default value of 65536 with just 16 writes totalling 14976 bytes of data.

  If the application were using TCP, this would waste time as well as memory. TCP tries to form outbound data into MTU-sized packets. If the MTU of the LAN were larger than 14976 bytes, TCP would put the sending thread to sleep when the **tcp_sendspace** limit was reached. It would take a timeout ACK from the receiver to force the data to be written.

Note: When the **no** command is used to change parameters, the change is in effect only until the next system boot. At that point all parameters are initially reset to their defaults. To make the change permanent, you should put the appropriate **no** command in the **/etc/rc.net** file.

Regardless of Tuning Priorities

- Always set **xmt_que_size** to the maximum—150. This does not consume any additional space unless the memory is really needed for data.

  The appropriate command is:

```
# chdev -l ifname -a xmt_que_size=150
```

> If the LAN adapter is already in use, you must take it offline temporarily to change this parameter. For a Token-Ring adapter, for example, the appropriate sequence of commands would be:

```
# ifconfig tr0 detach
# chdev -l tok0 -a xmt_que_size=150
# ifconfig tr0 hostname up
```

Tuning TCP Maximum Segment Size (MSS)

The TCP protocol includes a mechanism for both ends of a connection to negotiate the maximum segment size (MSS) to be used over the connection. Each end uses the OPTIONS field in the TCP header to advertise a proposed MSS. The MSS that is chosen is the smaller of the values provided by the two ends.

The purpose of this negotiation is to avoid the delays and throughput reductions caused by fragmentation of the packets when they pass through routers or gateways and reassembly at the destination host.

The value of MSS advertised by the TCP software during connection setup depends on whether the other end is a *local* system on the same physical network (that is, the systems have the same network number) or whether it is on a different, *remote*, network.

Local Network

If the other end is local, the MSS advertised by TCP is based on the MTU (maximum transfer unit) of the local network interface:

> TCP MSS = MTU – TCP header size – IP header size.

Since this is the largest possible MSS that can be accommodated without IP fragmentation, this value is inherently optimal, so no MSS tuning is required for local networks.

Remote Network

When the other end is on a remote network, TCP in AIX defaults to advertising an MSS of 512 bytes. This conservative value is based on a requirement that all IP routers support an MTU of at least 576 bytes.

The optimal MSS for remote networks is based on the smallest MTU of the intervening networks in the route between source and destination. In general, this is a dynamic quantity and could only be ascertained by some form of path MTU discovery. The TCP protocol does not provide any mechanism for doing this, which is why a conservative value is the default.

While this default is appropriate in the general Internet, it can be unnecessarily restrictive for private internets within an administrative domain. In such an environment, MTU sizes of the component physical networks are known and the minimum MTU and optimal MSS can be determined by the administrator. AIX provides several ways in which TCP can be persuaded to use this optimal MSS. Both source and destination hosts must support these features. In a heterogeneous, multi-vendor environment, the availability of the feature on both systems may determine the choice of solution.

Static Routes

The default MSS of 512 can be overridden by specifying a static route to a specific remote network and using the **–mtu** option of the **route** command to specify the MTU to that network. In this case, you would specify the actual minimum MTU of the route, rather than calculating an MSS value.

In a small, stable environment, this method allows precise control of MSS on a network-by-network basis. The disadvantages of this approach are:

- It does not work with dynamic routing.
- It becomes impractical when the number of remote networks increases.
- Static routes must be set at both ends to ensure that both ends negotiate with a larger-than-default MSS.

Use the tcp_mssdflt Option of the no Command

The default value of 512 that TCP uses for remote networks can be changed via the **no** command by changing the **tcp_mssdflt** parameter. This change is a systemwide change.

The value specified to override the MSS default should be the minimum MTU value less 40 to allow for the normal length of the TCP and IP headers.

In an environment with a larger-than-default MTU, this method has the advantage that the MSS does not need to be set on a per-network basis. The disadvantages are:

- Increasing the default can lead to IP router fragmentation if the destination is on a network that is truly remote and the MTUs of the intervening networks are not known.
- The **tcp_mssdflt** parameter must be set to the same value on the destination host.

Subnetting and the subnetsarelocal Option of the no Command

Several physical networks can be made to share the same network number by subnetting. The **no** option **subnetsarelocal** specifies, on a system-wide basis, whether subnets are to be considered local or remote networks. With **subnetsarelocal=1** (the default), Host A on subnet 1 considers Host B on subnet 2 to be on the same physical network.

The consequence of this is that when Host A and Host B establish a connection, they negotiate the MSS assuming they are on the same network. Each host advertises an MSS based on the MTU of its network interface. This usually leads to an optimal MSS being chosen.

This approach has several advantages:

- It does not require any static bindings; MSS is automatically negotiated.
- It does not disable or override the TCP MSS negotiation, so that small differences in the MTU between adjacent subnets can be handled appropriately.

The disadvantages are:

- Potential IP router fragmentation when two high-MTU networks are linked through a lower-MTU network. The figure "Inter-Subnet Fragmentation" illustrates this problem.

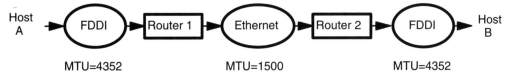

Figure 19: Inter-Subnet Fragmentation

In this scenario, Hosts A and B would establish a connection based on a common MTU of 4352. A packet going from A to B would fragmented by Router 1 and defragmented by Router 2, and the reverse would occur going from B to A.

- Source and destination must both consider subnets to be local.

IP Protocol Performance Tuning Recommendations

At the IP layer, the only tunable parameter is **ipqmaxlen,** which controls the length of the IP input queue discussed earlier (which exists only in AIX Version 3). Packets may arrive very quickly and overrun the IP input queue. In the AIX operating system, there is no simple way to determine if this is happening. However an overflow counter can be viewed using the **crash** command. To check this value, start the **crash** command and when the prompt appears, type `knlist ipintrq`. This command returns a hexadecimal value, which may vary from system to system. Next, add `10` (hex) to this value, and then use it as an argument for the **od** subcommand. For example:

```
# crash
> knlist ipintrq
 ipintrq: 0x0149ba68
> od 0149ba78 1
0149ba78: 00000000 <--   This is the value of the IP input queue
          overflow counter
>quit
```

If the number returned is greater than 0, overflows have occurred. The maximum length of this queue is set using the **no** command. For example:

```
no -o ipqmaxlen=100
```

allows 100 packets to be queued up. The exact value to use is determined by the maximum burst rate received. If this cannot be determined, using the number of overflows can help determine what the increase should be. No additional memory is used by increasing the queue length. However, an increase may result in more time spent in the off-level interrupt handler, since IP will have more packets to process on its input queue. This could adversely affect processes needing CPU time. The tradeoff is reduced packet dropping versus CPU availability for other processing. It is best to increase **ipqmaxlen** by moderate increments if the tradeoff is a concern.

Ethernet Performance Tuning Recommendations

Ethernet is one of the contributors to the "least common denominator" algorithm of MTU choice. If a configuration includes Ethernets and other LANs, and there is extensive traffic among them, the MTUs of all of the LANs may need to be set to 1500 bytes to avoid fragmentation when data enters an Ethernet.

- The default (and maximum) MTU of 1500 bytes should not be changed.
- Application block size should be in multiples of 4096 bytes.
- Socket space settings can be left at the default values.
- If the workload includes extensive use of services that use UDP, such as NFS or RPC, **sb_max** should be increased to allow for the fact that each 1500-byte MTU uses a 4096-byte buffer.

Token Ring (4Mb) Performance Tuning Recommendations

The default MTU of 1492 bytes is appropriate for Token Rings that interconnect to Ethernets or to heterogeneous networks in which the minimum MTU is not known.

- Unless the LAN has extensive traffic to outside networks, the MTU should be raised to the maximum of 3900 bytes.
- Application block size should be in multiples of 4096 bytes.
- Socket space settings can be left at the default values.
- If the workload includes extensive use of services that use UDP, such as NFS or RPC, **sb_max** should be increased to allow for the fact that each 1492-byte MTU uses a 4096-byte buffer.

Token Ring (16Mb) Performance Tuning Recommendations

The default MTU of 1492 bytes is appropriate for Token Rings that interconnect to Ethernets or to heterogeneous networks in which the minimum MTU is not known.

- Unless the LAN has extensive traffic to outside networks, the MTU should be increased to 8500 bytes. This allows NFS 8KB packets to fit in one MTU. Further increasing the MTU to the maximum of 17000 bytes seldom results in corresponding throughput improvement.
- Application block size should be in multiples of 4096 bytes.
- Socket space settings can be left at the default values.
- If the workload includes extensive use of services that use UDP, such as NFS or RPC, and the MTU must be left at the default because of interconnections, **sb_max** should be increased to allow for the fact that each 1492-byte MTU uses a 4096-byte buffer.

FDDI Performance Tuning Recommendations

Despite the comparatively low MTU, this high-speed medium benefits from substantial increases in socket buffer size.

- Unless the LAN has extensive traffic to outside networks, the default MTU of 4352 bytes should be retained.
- Where possible, an application using TCP should write multiples of 4096 bytes at a time (preferably 8KB or 16KB) for maximum throughput.
- Use **no –o sb_max=**(*2*NewSize*) to raise the ceiling on socket buffer space.
- Use **no –o *_*space=***NewSize* to set the TCP and UDP socket send and receive space defaults to *NewSpace* bytes. *NewSpace* should be at least 57344 bytes (56KB).
- For RISC System/6000 Model *90 or faster, use **no –o rfc1323=1** to allow socket buffer sizes to be set to more than 64KB. Then use the previous procedure with *NewSize* of at least 128KB.

ATM Performance Tuning Recommendations

- Unless the LAN has extensive traffic to outside networks, the default MTU of 9180 bytes should be retained.
- Where possible, an application using TCP should write multiples of 4096 bytes at a time (preferably 8KB or 16KB) for maximum throughput.
- Use **no –o sb_max=**(*2*NewSize*) to raise the ceiling on socket buffer space.
- Use **no –o *_*space=***NewSize* to set the TCP and UDP socket send and receive space defaults to *NewSpace* bytes. *NewSpace* should be at least 57344 bytes (56KB).
- For RISC System/6000 Model *90 or faster, use **no –o rfc1323=1** to allow socket buffer sizes to be set to more than 64KB. Then use the previous procedure with *NewSize* of at least 128KB.

SOCC Performance Tuning Recommendations

- The default MTU 61428 bytes should not be changed.
- Where possible, an application using TCP should write 28672 bytes (28KB) at a time for maximum throughput.
- TCP and UDP socket send and receive space defaults should be set to 57344 bytes.

HIPPI Performance Tuning Recommendations

- The default MTU of 65536 bytes should not be changed.
- Where possible, an application using TCP should write 65536 bytes at a time for maximum throughput.

- Set **sb_max** to a value greater than 2*655360.
- TCP and UDP socket send and receive space defaults should be set to 655360 bytes. Use **no –o rfc1323=1** to allow socket buffer sizes to be set to more than 64KB.

AIX Version 3.2.5 mbuf Pool Performance Tuning

Note: This section applies only to AIX Version 3.2.5. The mbuf allocation mechanism in AIX Version 4.1 is substantially different. At this writing, there are no recommended tuning techniques for AIX Version 4.1 mbuf management.

The network subsystem uses a memory management facility that revolves around a data structure called an *mbuf*. Mbufs are mostly used to store data for incoming and outbound network traffic. Having mbuf pools of the right size can have a very positive effect on network performance. If the mbuf pools are configured improperly, both network and system performance can suffer. The AIX operating system offers the capability for run-time mbuf pool configuration. With this convenience comes the responsibility for knowing when the pools need adjusting and how much they should be adjusted.

Overview of the mbuf Management Facility

The mbuf management facility controls two pools of buffers: a pool of small buffers (256 bytes each), which are simply called *mbufs*, and a pool of large buffers (4096 bytes each), which are usually called *mbuf clusters* or just *clusters*. The pools are created from system memory by making an allocation request to the Virtual Memory Manager (VMM). The pools consist of pinned pieces of virtual memory; this means that they always reside in physical memory and are never paged out. The result is that the real memory available for paging in application programs and data has been decreased by the amount that the mbuf pools have been increased. This is a nontrivial cost that must always be taken into account when considering an increase in the size of the mbuf pools.

The initial size of the mbuf pools is system-dependent. There is a minimum number of (small) mbufs and clusters allocated for each system, but these minimums are increased by an amount that depends on the specific system configuration. One factor affecting how much they are increased is the number of communications adapters in the system. The default pool sizes are initially configured to handle small- to medium-size network loads (network traffic of 100–500 packets/second). The pool sizes dynamically increase as network loads increase. The cluster pool shrinks if network loads decrease (the mbuf pool is never reduced). To optimize network performance, the administrator should balance mbuf pool sizes with network loads (packets/second). If the network load is particularly oriented towards UDP traffic (as it would be on an NFS server, for example) the size of the mbuf pool should be two times the packet/second rate. This is due to UDP traffic consuming an extra small mbuf.

To provide an efficient mbuf allocation service, an attempt is made to maintain a minimum number of free buffers in the pools at all times. The **lowmbuf** and **lowclust** network parameters (which can be manipulated using the **no** command) are used to define these lower limits.

The **lowmbuf** parameter controls the minimum number of free buffers for the mbuf pool. The **lowclust** parameter controls the minimum number of free buffers for the cluster pool. When the number of buffers in the pools drops below the **lowmbuf** or **lowclust** thresholds the pools are expanded by some amount. The expansion of the mbuf pools is not done immediately, but is scheduled to be done by a kernel service named **netm**. When the **netm** kernel service is dispatched, the pools are expanded to meet the minimum requirements of **lowclust** and **lowmbuf**. Having a kernel process do this work is required by the structure of the VMM.

An additional function that the **netm** kernel service provides is to limit the growth of the cluster pool. The **mb_cl_hiwat** network parameter defines this maximum value.

The **mb_cl_hiwat** parameter controls the maximum number of free buffers the cluster pool can contain. When the number of free clusters in the pool exceeds **mb_cl_hiwat**, **netm** is scheduled to release some of the clusters back to the VMM.

The **netm** kernel system runs at a very favored priority (fixed 37). Because of this, excessive **netm** kernel system dispatching can cause not only poor network performance but also poor system performance because of contention with other system and user processes. Improperly configured pools can result in **netm** "thrashing" due to conflicting network traffic needs and improperly tuned thresholds. The **netm** kernel system dispatching can be minimized by properly configuring the mbuf pools to match system and networking needs.

The last network parameter that is used by the mbuf management facility is **thewall**.

The **thewall** parameter controls the maximum amount of RAM (in kilobytes) that the mbuf management facility can allocate from the VMM. This parameter is used to prevent unbalanced VMM resources which result in poor system performance.

When to Tune the mbuf Pools

When and how much to tune the mbuf pools is directly related to the network load to which a given machine is being subjected. A server machine that is supporting many clients is a good candidate for having the mbuf pools tuned to optimize network performance. It is important for the system administrator to understand the networking load for a given system.

By using the **netstat** command you can get a rough idea of the network load in packets/second. For example:

```
netstat -I tr0 5
```

reports the input and output traffic both for the `tr0` adapter and for all LAN adapters on the system. The output below shows the activity caused by a large **ftp** command operation:

```
$ netstat -I tr0 2
   input    (tr0)     output                 input   (Total)     output
 packets  errs  packets  errs colls       packets  errs  packets  errs colls
   20615   227     3345     0    0          20905   227     3635     0    0
      17     0        1     0    0             17     0        1     0    0
     174     0      320     0    0            174     0      320     0    0
     248     0      443     0    0            248     0      443     0    0
     210     0      404     0    0            210     0      404     0    0
     239     0      461     0    0            239     0      461     0    0
     253     1      454     0    0            253     1      454     0    0
     246     0      467     0    0            246     0      467     0    0
      99     1      145     0    0             99     1      145     0    0
      13     0        1     0    0             13     0        1     0    0
```

The **netstat** command also has a flag, **–m**, that gives detailed information about the use and availability of the mbufs and clusters:

```
253 mbufs in use:
50 mbufs allocated to data
1 mbufs allocated to packet headers
76 mbufs allocated to socket structures
100 mbufs allocated to protocol control blocks
10 mbufs allocated to routing table entries
14 mbufs allocated to socket names and addresses
2 mbufs allocated to interface addresses
16/64 mapped pages in use
319 Kbytes allocated to network (39% in use)
0 requests for memory denied
0 requests for memory delayed
0 calls to protocol drain routines
```

The line `16/64 mapped pages in use` indicates that there are 64 pinned clusters, of which 16 are currently in use.

This report can be compared to the existing system parameters by issuing a **no –a** command. The following lines from the report are of interest:

```
  lowclust = 29
   lowmbuf = 88
   thewall = 2048
mb_cl_hiwat = 58
```

It is clear that on the test system, the `319 Kbytes allocated to network` is considerably short of **thewall** value of 2048KB and the (64 – 16 = 48) free clusters are short of the **mb_cl_hiwat** limit of 58.

The `requests for memory denied` counter is maintained by the mbuf management facility and is incremented each time a request for an mbuf allocation cannot be satisfied. Normally the `requests for memory denied` value will be 0. If a system experiences a high burst of network traffic, the default configured mbuf pools may not be sufficient to meet the demand of the incoming burst, causing the error counter to be incremented once for each mbuf allocation request that fails. Usually this is in the thousands due to the large number of packets arriving in a short interval. The `requests for memory denied` statistic will correspond to dropped packets on the network.

Dropped network packets mean retransmissions, resulting in degraded network performance. If the `requests for memory denied` value is greater than zero, it may be appropriate to tune the mbuf parameters—see "How to Tune the mbuf Pools", below.

The `Kbytes allocated to the network` statistic is maintained by the mbuf management facility and represents the current amount of system memory that has been allocated to both mbuf pools. The upper bound of this statistic set by **thewall** is used to prevent the mbuf management facility from consuming too much of a system's physical memory. The default value for **thewall** limits the mbuf management facility to 2048KB (as shown in the report generated by the **no –a** command). If the `Kbytes allocated to the network` value approaches **thewall**, it may be appropriate to tune the mbuf parameters. See "How to Tune the mbuf Pools", below.

There are cases where the above indicators suggest that the mbuf pools may need to be expanded, when in fact there is a system problem that should be corrected first. For example:

- mbuf memory leak
- Queued data not being read from socket or other internal queuing structure

An mbuf memory leak is a situation in which some kernel or kernel-extension code has neglected to release an mbuf resource and has destroyed the pointer to its memory location, thereby losing the address of the mbuf forever. If this occurs repeatedly, eventually all the mbuf resources will be used up. If the **netstat** mbuf statistics show a gradual increase in usage that never decreases or high mbuf usage on a relatively idle system, there may be an mbuf memory leak. Developers of kernel extensions that use mbufs should always include checks for memory leaks in their testing.

It is also possible to have a large number of mbufs queued at the socket layer because of an application defect. Normally an application program would read data from the socket, causing the mbufs to be returned to the mbuf management facility. An administrator can monitor the statistics generated by the **netstat –m** command and look for high mbuf usage while there is no expected network traffic. The administrator can also view the current list of running processes (by entering `ps -ef`) and scan for those that use the network subsystem with large amounts of CPU time being used. If this behavior is observed, the suspected application defect should be isolated and fixed.

How to Tune the mbuf Pools

With an understanding of how the mbuf pools are organized and managed, tuning the mbuf pools is simple in the AIX operating system and can be done at run time. The **no** command can be used by the root user to modify the mbuf pool parameters. Some guidelines are:

- When adjusting the **lowclust** and **lowmbuf** attributes, **thewall** may need to be increased first to prevent pool expansions from hitting **thewall**.
- The value of the **mb_cl_hiwat** attribute should be at least two times greater than the **lowclust** attribute at all times. This will prevent the **netm** thrashing discussed earlier.

- When adjusting **lowclust, lowmbuf** should be adjusted by at least the same amount. For every cluster there will exist an mbuf that points to that cluster.
- After expanding the pools, use the **vmstat** command to ensure that paging rates have not increased. If you cannot expand the pools to the necessary levels without adversely affecting the paging rates, additional memory may be required.

The following is an example shell script that might be run at the end of **/etc/rc.net** to tune the mbuf pools for an NFS server that experiences a network traffic load of approximately 1500 packets/sec.

```
#!/bin/ksh
# echo "Tuning mbuf pools..."
# set maximum amount of memory to allow for allocation (10MB)
no -o thewall=10240

# set minimum number of small mbufs
no -o lowmbuf=3000

# generate network traffic to force small mbuf pool expansion
ping 127.0.0.1  1000 1 >/dev/null

# set minimum number of small mbufs back to default to prevent netm from
# running unnecessarily
no -d lowmbuf

# set maximum number of free clusters before expanding pool
# (about 6MB)
no -o mb_cl_hiwat=1500

# gradually expand cluster pool
N=10
while [ $N -lt 1500 ]
do
  no -o lowclust=$N
  ping 127.0.0.1 1000 1 >/dev/null
  let N=N+10
done

# set minimum number of clusters back to default to prevent netm
# from running unnecessarily
no -d lowclust
```

You can use `netstat -m` following the above script to verify the size of the pool of clusters (which the **netstat** command calls mapped pages). To verify the size of the pool of mbufs you can use the **crash** command to examine a kernel data structure, **mbstat** (see the **/usr/include/sys/mbuf.h** file). The kernel address of **mbstat** can be displayed while in **crash** using the **od mbstat** command. You will then need to enter `od <kernel`

address> to dump the first word in the **mbstat** structure, which contains the size of the mbuf pool. The dialog would be similar to the following:

```
$ crash
> od mbstat
000e2be0: 001f7008
> od 1f7008
001f7008: 00000180
> quit
```

The size of the mbuf pool is therefore 180_{16} (384_{10}).

UDP, TCP/IP, and mbuf Tuning Parameters Summary

The following paragraphs summarize the attributes and tuning techniques for each of the communications tuning parameters.

thewall

Purpose:	Provide an absolute upper bound on the amount of real memory that can be used by the communication subsystem.
Values:	Default: 25% of real memory. Range: up to 50% of real memory
Display:	**no –a** or **no –o thewall**
Change:	**no –o thewall=***newvalue*
	newvalue is in KB, not bytes
	Change takes effect immediately for new connections.
	Change is effective until the next system boot.
Diagnosis:	None.
Tuning:	Increase size, preferably to multiple of 4(KB).
Refer to:	"AIX Version 3.2.5 mbuf Pool Performance Tuning" on page 170.

sb_max

Purpose:	Provide an absolute upper bound on the size of TCP and UDP socket buffers. Limits **setsockopt()**, **udp_sendspace, udp_recvspace, tcp_sendspace**, and **tcp_recvspace**.
Values:	Default: 65536 Range: N/A
Display:	**no –a** or **no –o sb_max**
Change:	**no –o sb_max=***newvalue*
	Change takes effect immediately for new connections.
	Change is effective until the next system boot.
Diagnosis:	None.
Tuning:	Increase size, preferably to multiple of 4096. Should be about twice the largest socket buffer limit.
Refer to:	"Socket Layer" on page 155.

rfc1323

Purpose:	Value of 1 indicates that **tcp_sendspace** and **tcp_recvspace** can exceed 64KB.
Values:	Default: 0 Range: 0 or 1
Display:	**no –a** or **no –o rfc1323**
Change:	**no –o rfc1323=***newvalue*
	Change takes effect immediately.
	Change is effective until the next system boot.
Diagnosis:	None.
Tuning:	Change before attempting to set **tcp_sendspace** and **tcp_recvspace** to more than 64KB.
Refer to:	"TCP Layer" on page 157.

udp_sendspace

Purpose:	Provide the default value for the size of the UDP socket send buffer.
Values:	Default: 9216 Range: 0 to 65536
	Must be less than or equal to **sb_max**.
Display:	**no –a** or **no –o udp_sendspace**
Change:	**no –o udp_sendspace=***newvalue*
	Change takes effect immediately for new connections.
	Change is effective until the next system boot.
Diagnosis:	None.
Tuning:	Increase size, preferably to multiple of 4096.
Refer to:	"Socket Layer" on page 155.

udp_recvspace

Purpose:	Provide the default value of the size of the UDP socket receive buffer.
Values:	Default: 41600 Range: N/A
	Must be less than or equal to **sb_max**.
Display:	**no –a** or **no –o udp_recvspace**
Change:	**no –o udp_recvspace=***newvalue*
	Change takes effect immediately for new connections.
	Change is effective until the next system boot.
Diagnosis:	Nonzero *n* in **netstat –s** report of **udp:** *n* **socket buffer overflows**
Tuning:	Increase size, preferably to multiple of 4096.
Refer to:	"Socket Layer" on page 155.

tcp_sendspace

Purpose:	Provide the default value of the size of the TCP socket send buffer.
Values:	Default: 16384 Range: 0 to 64KB if **rfc1323=0**,
	Range: 0 to 4GB if **rfc1323=1**.
	Must be less than or equal to **sb_max**.
	Should be equal to **tcp_recvspace** and uniform on all frequently accessed AIX systems.
Display:	**no –a** or **no –o tcp_sendspace**
Change:	**no –o tcp_sendspace=**_newvalue_
	Change takes effect immediately for new connections.
	Change is effective until the next system boot.
Diagnosis:	Poor throughput.
Tuning:	Increase size, preferably to multiple of 4096.
Refer to:	"Socket Layer" on page 155.

tcp_recvspace

Purpose:	Provide the default value of the size of the TCP socket receive buffer.
Values:	Default: 16384 Range: 0 to 64KB if **rfc1323=0**,
	Range: 0 to 4GB if **rfc1323=1**.
	Must be less than or equal to **sb_max**.
	Should be equal to **tcp_sendspace** and uniform on all frequently accessed AIX systems.
Display:	**no –a** or **no –o tcp_recvspace**
Change:	**no –o tcp_recvspace=**_newvalue_
	Change takes effect immediately for new connections.
	Change is effective until the next system boot.
Diagnosis:	Poor throughput.
Tuning:	Increase size, preferably to multiple of 4096.
Refer to:	"Socket Layer" on page 155.

ipqmaxlen

Purpose:	Specify the maximum number of entries on the IP input queue.
Values:	Default: 50 Range: N/A
Display:	**no –a** or **no –o ipqmaxlen**
Change:	**no –o ipqmaxlen=**_newvalue_
	Change takes effect immediately.
	Change is effective until the next system boot.
Diagnosis:	Use **crash** to access IP input queue overflow counter.
Tuning:	Increase size.
Refer to:	"IP Protocol Performance Tuning Recommendations" on page 167.

xmt_que_size

Purpose:	Specifies the maximum number of send buffers that can be queued up for the device.
Values:	Default: 30 Range: 20 to 150
Display:	**lsattr −E −l tok0 −a xmt_que_size**
Change:	**ifconfig tr0 detach**
	chdev −I tok0 −a xmt_que_size=_newvalue_
	ifconfig tr0 _hostname_ **up**
	Change is effective across system boots.
Diagnosis:	**netstat −i**
	`Oerr > 0`
Tuning:	Increase size. Should be set to 150 as a matter of course on network-oriented systems, especially servers.
Refer to:	"LAN Adapters and Device Drivers" on page 162.

rec_que_size

Purpose:	(Tunable only in AIX Version 3.) Specifies the maximum number of receive buffers that can be queued up for the interface.
Values:	Default: 30 Range: 20 to 150
Display:	**lsattr −E −l tok$n$ −a rec_que_size**
Change:	**ifconfig tr0 detach**
	chdev −I tok$n$ −a rec_que_size=_newvalue_
	ifconfig tr0 _hostname_ **up**
	Change is effective across system boots.
Diagnosis:	None.
Tuning:	Increase size. Should be set to 150 as a matter of course on network-oriented systems, especially servers.
Refer to:	"LAN Adapters and Device Drivers" on page 162.

MTU

Purpose:	Limits the size of packets that are transmitted on the network.
Values:	**tr***n* (4Mb): Default: 1492, Range: 60 to 3900
	tr*n* (16Mb): Default: 1492, Range: 60 to 17960
	en*n*: Default: 1500, Range: 60 to 1500
	fi*n*: Default: 4352, Range: 60 to 4352
	hi*n*: Default: 65536, Range: 60 to 65536
	so*n*: Default: 61428, Range: 60 to 61428
	lo*n*: Default: 1500 (3.2.5), 16896 (4.1), Range: 60 to 65536
Display:	**lsattr –E –l tr***n*
Change:	**chdev –l tr***n* **–a mtu=***NewValue*
	Cannot be changed while the interface is in use. Because all systems on a LAN must have the same MTU, they must all change simultaneously. Change is effective across boots.
Diagnosis:	Packet fragmentation stats
Tuning:	Increase MTU size for the Token-Ring interfaces:
	tr*n* (4Mb): 4056
	tr*n* (16Mb): 8500
	For the loopback interface **lo***n* in Version 3.2.5, increase to 16896
	For other interfaces, the default should be kept.
Refer to:	"LAN Adapters and Device Drivers", on page 162.

NFS Tuning

NFS allows programs on one system to access files on another system transparently by **mount**ing the remote directory. Normally, when the server is booted, directories are made available by the **exportfs** command, and the daemons to handle remote access (**nfsd**s) are started. Similarly, the **mount**s of the remote directories and the initiation of the appropriate numbers of **biod**s to handle remote access are performed during client system boot.

The figure "NFS Client-Server Interaction" illustrates the structure of the dialog between NFS clients and a server. When a thread in a client system attempts to read or write a file in an NFS-mounted directory, the request is redirected from the normal I/O mechanism to one of the client's NFS block I/O daemons (**biod**s). The **biod** sends the request to the appropriate server, where it is assigned to one of the server's NFS daemons (**nfsd**s). While that request is being processed, neither the **biod** nor the **nfsd** involved do any other work.

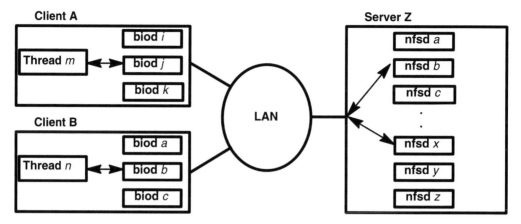

Figure 20: NFS Client-Server Interaction

How Many biods and nfsds Are Needed for Good Performance?

Because **biod**s and **nfsd**s handle one request at a time, and because NFS response time is often the largest component of overall response time, it is undesirable to have threads blocked for lack of a **biod** or **nfsd**. The general considerations for configuring NFS daemons are:

- Increasing the number of daemons cannot compensate for inadequate client or server processor power or memory, or inadequate server disk bandwidth. Before changing the number of daemons, you should check server and client resource-utilization levels with **iostat** and **vmstat**.
- NFS daemons are comparatively cheap. A **biod** costs 36KB of memory (9 pages total, 4 of them pinned), while an **nfsd** costs 28KB (7 pages total, 2 of them pinned). Of course, the unpinned pages are only in real memory if the **nfsd** or **biod** has been active recently. Further, idle AIX **nfsd**s do not consume CPU time.
- All NFS requests go through an **nfsd**; only reads and writes go through a **biod**.

Choosing Initial Numbers of nfsds and biods

Determining the best numbers of **nfsd**s and **biod**s is an iterative process. Rules of thumb can give you no more than a reasonable starting point.

By default there are six **biod**s on a client and eight **nfsd**s on a server. The defaults are a good starting point for small systems, but should probably be increased for client systems with more than two users or servers with more than 2 clients. A few guidelines are:

- In each client, estimate the maximum number of files that will be written simultaneously. Configure at least two **biod**s per file. If the files are large (more than 32KB), you may want to start with four **biod**s per file to support read-ahead or write-behind activity. It is common for up to five **biod**s to be busy writing to a single large file.

- In each server, start by configuring as many **nfsd**s as the sum of the numbers of **biod**s that you have configured on the clients to handle files *from that server*. Add 20% to allow for non-read/write NFS requests.

- If you have fast client workstations connected to a slower server, you may have to constrain the rate at which the clients generate NFS requests. The best solution is to reduce the number of **biod**s on the clients, with due attention to the relative importance of each client's workload and response time.

Tuning the Numbers of nfsds and biods

After you have arrived at an initial number of **biod**s and **nfsd**s, or have changed one or the other:

- First, recheck the affected systems for CPU or I/O saturation with **vmstat** and **iostat**. If the server is now saturated, you need to reduce its load or increase its power, or both.

- Use **netstat –s** to determine if any system is experiencing UDP socket buffer overflows. If so, use **no –a** to verify that the recommendations in "Tuning Other Layers to Improve NFS Performance" on page 183 have been implemented. If so, and the system is not saturated, you should increase the number of **biod**s or **nfsd**s.

The numbers of **nfsd**s and **biod**s are changed with the **chnfs** command. To change the number of **nfsd**s on a server to 10, both immediately and at each subsequent system boot, you would use:

```
# chnfs -n 10
```

To change the number of **biod**s on a client to 8 temporarily, with no permanent change (that is, the change happens now but is lost at the next system boot), you would use:

```
# chnfs -N -b 8
```

To change both the number of **biod**s and the number of **nfsd**s on a system to 9, with the change delayed until the next system boot (that is, the next IPL), you would use:

```
# chnfs -I -b 9 -n 9
```

In extreme cases of a client overrunning the server, it may be necessary to reduce the client to one **biod**. This can be done with:

```
# stopsrc -s biod
```

This leaves the client with the kproc **biod** still running.

Performance Implications of Hard or Soft NFS Mounts

One of the choices you make when configuring NFS-mounted directories is whether the mounts will be hard or soft. When, after a successful mount, an access to a soft-mounted directory encounters an error (typically, a timeout), the error is immediately reported to the program that requested the remote access. When an access to a hard-mounted directory encounters an error, NFS retries the operation.

A persistent error accessing a hard-mounted directory can escalate into a perceived performance problem because the default number of retries (1000) and the default timeout value (.7 second), combined with an algorithm that increases the timeout value for successive retries, mean that NFS will try practically forever (subjectively) to complete the operation.

It is technically possible to reduce the number of retries, or increase the timeout value, or both, using options of the **mount** command. Unfortunately, changing these values sufficiently to remove the perceived performance problem might lead to unnecessary reported hard errors. Instead, hard-mounted directories should be mounted with the **intr** option, which allows the user to interrupt from the keyboard a process that is in a retry loop.

Although soft-mounting the directories would cause the error to be detected sooner, it runs a serious risk of data corruption. In general, read/write directories should be hard mounted.

Tuning to Avoid Retransmits

Related to the hard-versus-soft mount question is the question of the appropriate timeout duration for a given network configuration. If the server is heavily loaded, is separated from the client by one or more bridges or gateways, or is connected to the client by a WAN, the default timeout criterion may be unrealistic. If so, both server and client will be burdened with unnecessary retransmits. For example, if

```
$ nfsstat -cr
```

reports a significant number (> 5% of the total) of both timeouts and badxids, you could increase the **timeo** parameter with:

```
# smit chnfsmnt
```

Identify the directory you want to change, and enter a new value on the line "NFS TIMEOUT. In tenths of a second." For LAN-to-LAN traffic via a bridge, try 50 (tenths of seconds). For WAN connections, try 200. Check the NFS statistics again after at least one day. If they still indicate excessive retransmits, increase **timeo** by 50% and try again. You will also want to look at the server workload and the loads on the intervening bridges and gateways to see if any element is being saturated by other traffic.

Tuning the NFS File-Attribute Cache

NFS maintains a cache on each client system of the attributes of recently accessed directories and files. Five parameters that can be set in the **/etc/filesystems** file control how long a given entry is kept in the cache. They are:

actimeo   Absolute time for which file and directory entries are kept in the file-attribute cache after an update. If specified, this value overrides the following *min and *max values, effectively setting them all to the **actimeo** value.

acregmin	Minimum time after an update that file entries will be retained. The default is 3 seconds.
acregmax	Maximum time after an update that file entries will be retained. The default is 60 seconds.
acdirmin	Minimum time after an update that directory entries will be retained. The default is 30 seconds.
acdirmax	Maximum time after an update that directory entries will be retained. The default is 60 seconds.

Each time the file or directory is updated, its removal is postponed for at least **acregmin** or **acdirmin** seconds. If this is the second or subsequent update, the entry is kept at least as long as the interval between the last two updates, but not more than **acregmax** or **acdirmax** seconds.

Disabling Unused NFS ACL Support

If your workload does not use the NFS ACL support on a mounted file system, you can reduce the workload on both client and server to some extent by specifying:

```
options = noacl
```

as part of the client's **/etc/filesystems** stanza for that file system.

Tuning for Maximum Caching of NFS Data

NFS does not have a data caching function, but the AIX Virtual Memory Manager caches pages of NFS data just as it caches pages of disk data. If a system is essentially a dedicated NFS server, it may be appropriate to permit the VMM to use as much memory as necessary for data caching. This is accomplished by setting the **maxperm** parameter, which controls the maximum percentage of memory occupied by file pages, to 100% with:

```
# vmtune -P 100
```

The same technique could be used on NFS clients, but would only be appropriate if the clients were running workloads that had very little need for working-segment pages.

Tuning Other Layers to Improve NFS Performance

NFS uses UDP to perform its network I/O. You should be sure that the tuning techniques described in "TCP and UDP Performance Tuning" on page 163 and "AIX Version 3.2.5

mbuf Pool Performance Tuning" on page 170 have been applied. In particular, you should:

- Ensure that the LAN adapter transmit and receive queues are set to the maximum (150).
- Increase the maximum socket buffer size (**sb_max**) to at least 131072. If the MTU size is not 4096 bytes or larger, set **sb_max** to at least 262144. Set the UDP socket buffer sizes (**udp_sendspace** and **udp_recvspace**) to 131072 also.
- If possible, increase the MTU size on the LAN. On a 16Mb Token Ring, for example, an increase in MTU size from the default 1492 bytes to 8500 bytes allows a complete 8KB NFS read or write request to be transmitted without fragmentation. It also makes much more efficient use of mbuf space, reducing the probability of overruns.

Increasing NFS Socket Buffer Size

In the course of tuning UDP, you may find that the command:

```
$ netstat -s
```

shows a significant number of UDP socket buffer overflows. As with ordinary UDP tuning, you should increase the **sb_max** value. You also need to increase the value of **nfs_chars**, which specifies the size of the NFS socket buffer. The sequence:

```
# no -o sb_max=131072
# nfso -o nfs_chars=130000
# stopsrc -s nfsd
# startsrc -s nfsd
```

sets **sb_max** to a value at least 100 bytes larger than the desired value of **nfs_chars**, sets **nfs_chars** to 130972, then stops and restarts the **nfsd**s to put the new values into effect. If you determine that this change improves performance, you should put the **no** and **nfso** commands in **/etc/rc.nfs**, just before the **startsrc** command that starts the **nfsd**s.

NFS Server Disk Configuration

NFS servers that experience high levels of write activity can benefit from configuring the journal logical volume on a separate physical volume from the data volumes. This technique is discussed in "Disk Pre-Installation Guidelines" on page 67.

Hardware Accelerators

Prestoserve

The objective of the Prestoserve product is to reduce NFS write latency by providing a faster method than disk I/O of satisfying the NFS requirement for synchronous writes. It provides nonvolatile RAM into which NFS can write data. The data is then considered "safe," and NFS can allow the client to proceed. The data is later written to disk as device availability allows. Ultimately, it is impossible to exceed the long-term bandwidth of the disk, but since much NFS traffic is in bursts, Prestoserve is able to smooth out the workload on the disk with sometimes dramatic performance effects.

Interphase Network Coprocessor

This product handles NFS protocol processing on Ethernets, reducing the load on the CPU. NFS protocol processing is particularly onerous on Ethernets because NFS blocks must be broken down to fit within Ethernet's maximum MTU size of 1500 bytes.

Misuses of NFS That Affect Performance

Many of the misuses of NFS occur because people don't realize that the files they are accessing are at the other end of an expensive communication path. A few examples we have seen are:

- A COBOL application running on one AIX system doing random updates of an NFS-mounted inventory file—supporting a real-time retail cash register application.
- A development environment in which a source code directory on each system was NFS-mounted on all of the other systems in the environment, with developers logging onto arbitrary systems to do editing and compiles. This practically guaranteed that all of the compiles would be obtaining their source code from, and writing their output to, remote systems.
- Running the **ld** command on one system to transform **.o** files in an NFS-mounted directory into an **a.out** file in the same directory.

It can be argued that these are valid uses of the transparency provided by NFS. Perhaps so, but these uses cost processor time and LAN bandwidth and degrade response time. When a system configuration involves NFS access as part of the standard pattern of operation, the configuration designers should be prepared to defend the consequent costs with offsetting technical or business advantages, such as:

- Placing all of the data or source code on a server, rather than on individual workstations, will improve source-code control and simplify centralized backups.
- A number of different systems access the same data, making a dedicated server more efficient than one or more systems combining client and server roles.

Serving Diskless Workstations

Diskless systems potentially offer excellent processor power coupled with low cost, low noise and space requirements, and centralized data management. As tantalizing as these advantages seem, diskless workstations are not the best solution for every desktop. This section sheds some light on the workings of AIX diskless workstations, the kinds of loads they present to their servers, and the resulting performance of different kinds of programs. Much of the NFS background in this section also applies to serving requests from workstations with disks.

How a Diskless System Is Different

In a system with local disks (also referred to as a *diskful* system), the operating system and the programs needed to do the most basic functions are contained on one or more local disks. When the system is started, the operating system is loaded from local disk. When the system is fully operational, the files accessible to users are usually on local disk. The software that manages the local disks is the journaled file system (JFS).

In a diskless system, the operating system must be booted from a server using bootstrap code that is in the diskless machine's read-only storage. The loading takes place over a local area network: an Ethernet or a Token Ring. When the system is fully operational, the files accessible to users are located on disks on one or more server systems.

The primary mechanism used by diskless workstations to access files is the Network File System (NFS). NFS makes remote files seem to be located on the diskless system. NFS is not exclusive to diskless systems. Diskful systems can also mount remote file systems. Diskless systems, or diskful systems that depend on servers for files, are usually called *clients*.

Normally, several diskless clients are attached to each server, so they contend for the server's resources. The difference in performance between otherwise identical diskless and diskful systems is a function of file systems (NFS versus JFS), the network speed, and the server resources.

NFS Considerations

The Network File System lets multiple clients access remotely mounted data in a consistent manner. It provides primitives for basic file-system functions such as create, read, write, and remove. NFS also provides support for directory operations such as making a directory, removing a directory, reading and setting attributes, and path-name lookup.

The protocol used by NFS is stateless, that is, no request to the server depends on any previous request. This adds to the robustness of the protocol. It also introduces performance problems. Consider the case of writing a file. As the file is written, the modified data is either in the client memory or on the server. The NFS protocol requires that data written from the client to the server must be committed to nonvolatile storage, normally disk, before the write operation is considered complete. That way, if the server crashes, the data the client had written can be recovered after system restart. Data that was being written and was not committed to the disk would be rewritten by the client to the server until the write was successful. Because NFS does not allow write buffering in the server, each NFS write requires one or more synchronous disk writes. For example, if a new file of 1 byte is written by the client, the completion of that write would entail three disk I/Os on the server. The first would be the data itself. The second would be the journal record, a feature of JFS to maintain file-system integrity. The third is a flush of the file-allocation data. Because disks can only write 50 to 100 times a second, total write throughput is limited by the number of and type of disks on the server system.

Read and write requests used by AIX clients are 4096 bytes or 8192 bytes in length. These requests generally require more server resources to process than other request types.

Because remote files and file attributes may be cached in the memory of the client, the NFS protocol provides mechanisms for ensuring that the client version of file-system information is current. For example, if a 1-byte file is read, the file data will be cached as long as the space it occupies in the client is not needed for another activity. If a program in the client reads the file again later, the client ensures that the data in the local copy of the file is current. This is accomplished by a Get Attribute call to the server to find out if the file has been modified since it was last read.

Path-name resolution is the process of following the directory tree to a file. For example, opening the file /u/x/y/z normally requires examining /u, x, y, and z in that order. If any component of the path does not exist, the file cannot exist as named. One of NFS's caches is used to cache frequently used names, reducing the number of requests actually going to the server.

Obviously, the server receives some mix of read or write and smaller requests during any time interval. This mix is hard to predict. Workloads that move large files frequently will be dominated by read/write requests. Support of multiple diskless workstations will tend to generate a larger proportion of small NFS requests, although it depends greatly on the workload.

When a Program Runs on a Diskless Workstation

To better understand the flow of NFS requests in a diskless client, let's look at the Korn shell execution of the trivial C program:

```
#include <stdio.h>
main()
{
printf("This is a test program\n");
}
```

The program is compiled, yielding an executable named a.out. Now if the **PATH** environment variable is /usr/bin:/usr/bin/X11:. (the period representing the current working directory is at the end of the path) and the command a.out is entered at the command line, the following sequence of operations occurs:

	Request type	Component	Bytes Sent and Received
1	NFS_LOOKUP	usr (called by statx)	(send 178, rcv 70)
2	NFS_LOOKUP	bin	
3	NFS_LOOKUP	a.out	(Not found)
4	NFS_LOOKUP	usr (called by statx)	
5	NFS_LOOKUP	bin	
6	NFS_LOOKUP	X11	(send 174, rcv 156)
7	NFS_LOOKUP	a.out (Not found)	(send 174, rcv 70)
8	NFS_LOOKUP	. (called by statx)	(send 174, rcv 156)
9	NFS_LOOKUP	.	

187

```
10    NFS_LOOKUP       a.out                              (send 178, rcv 156)
11    NFS_LOOKUP       . (called by accessx)
12    NFS_LOOKUP       a.out
13    NFS_GETATTR      a.out
14    NFS_LOOKUP       .
15    NFS_LOOKUP       a.out                              (send 170, rcv 104,
                                                           send 190, rcv 168)
16    fork
17    exec
18    NFS_LOOKUP       usr
19    NFS_LOOKUP       bin
20    NFS_LOOKUP       a.out (Not found)                  (send 178, rcv 70)
21    NFS_LOOKUP       usr
22    NFS_LOOKUP       bin
23    NFS_LOOKUP       X11
24    NFS_LOOKUP       a.out (Not found)                  (send 178, rcv 70)
25    NFS_LOOKUP       .
26    NFS_LOOKUP       a.out
27    NFS_OPEN                                            (send 166, rcv 138)
28    NFS_GETATTR      a.out
29    NFS_ACCESS                                          (send 170, rcv 104,
                                                           send 190, rcv 182)
30    NFS_GETATTR      a.out
31    FS_GETATTR       a.out
32    NFS_READ         a.out (Read executable)            (send 178, rcv 1514,
                                                           rcv 1514, rcv 84)
33    NFS_GETATTR      a.out
34    NFS_LOOKUP       usr (Access library)
35    NFS_LOOKUP       lib
36    NFS_LOOKUP       libc.a
37    NFS_READLINK     libc.a                             (send 166, rcv 80)
38    NFS_LOOKUP       usr
39    NFS_LOOKUP       ccs
40    NFS_LOOKUP       lib
41    NFS_LOOKUP       libc.a
42    NFS_OPEN         libc.a                             (send 166, rcv 124)
43    NFS_GETATTR      libc.a
44    NFS_ACCESS       libc.a                             (send 170, rcv 104,
                                                           send 190, rcv 178)
45    NFS_GETATTR      libc.a
46    NFS_GETATTR      libc.a
47    NFS_CLOSE        libc.a
48    _exit
```

If the **PATH** were different, the series of NFS operations would be different. For example, a **PATH** of `.:/usr/bin:/usr/bin/X11:` would allow the program `a.out` to be found much sooner. The negative side of this **PATH** would be that most commands would be slower to execute since most of them are in `/usr/bin`. Another fast way to execute the program would be by entering `./a.out`, since no lookup is needed on the executable (although library resolution still is needed). Adding a lot of seldom-used directories to the **PATH** will slow down command execution. This applies to all environments, but is particularly significant in diskless environments.

Another factor to consider in program development is minimizing the number of libraries referenced. Obviously, the more libraries that need to be loaded, the slower the program execution becomes. Also the **LIBPATH** environment variable can affect the speed of program loading, so use it carefully if at all.

National Language Support can also be a factor in program execution. The above example was run in the "C" locale, the most efficient. Running in other locales can cause additional overhead to access message catalogs.

At first look, the NFS activity for a small program seems intimidating. Actually, the performance of the above example is quite acceptable. Remember that the path resolution for file accesses also takes place in JFS file systems, so the total number of operations is similar. The NFS cache ensures that not all NFS operations result in network traffic. Finally, the latency for network operations is usually small, so the aggregate increase in elapsed time for the command is not great—unless the server itself is overloaded.

Paging

AIX diskless systems perform paging via the NFS protocol. Paging is the process by which working storage such as program variables may be written to and read from disk. Paging occurs when the sum of the memory requirements of the processes running in a system is larger than the system memory. (See "Performance Overview of the Virtual Memory Manager (VMM)" on page 17.)

Paging is a mixed blessing in any system. It does allow memory to be overcommitted, but performance usually suffers. In fact, there is a narrow range of paging that will allow acceptable response time in a workstation environment.

In the diskless environment, paging is particularly slow. This is a result of the NFS protocol forcing writes to disk. In fact, one can expect each page out (write) operation to be at best two to three times slower than on a diskful system. Because of paging performance, it is important that diskless systems contain enough memory that the application mix being executed does not normally page. (See "Memory-Limited Programs" on page 64.)

AIXwindows-based desktop products encourage behavior that can lead to periods of intense paging in systems with inadequate memory. For example, a user may have two programs running in different windows: a large spreadsheet and a database. The user recalculates a spreadsheet, waits for the calculation to complete, then switches windows to the database and begins a query. Although the spreadsheet is not currently running, it occupies a substantial amount of storage. Running the database query also requires lots of storage. Unless real memory is large enough to hold both of these programs, the virtual-memory pages of the spreadsheet are paged out, and the database is paged in. The next time the user interacts with the spreadsheet, memory occupied by the database must be paged out, and the spreadsheet must be paged back in. Clearly user tolerance of this situation will be determined by how often windows are switched and how loaded the server becomes.

Resource Requirements of Diskless Workstations

Several AIX services can be used to measure client-server workloads. The number of NFS requests processed by a system is available via **nfsstat**. This command details the NFS-request counts by category. The **netstat** command allows analysis of total packet counts and bytes transferred to a network device. The **iostat** command details processor utilization and disk utilization, which are useful for measuring server systems. Finally, the AIX trace facility allows the collection of very detailed performance data.

Capacity planning for diskless networks is often complicated by the "burstiness" of client I/O requests—the characteristic pattern of short periods of high request rates interspersed with longer periods of low request rates. This phenomenon is common in systems where people act as the primary drivers of applications.

The capacity, or number of clients supported by a server and network for a particular workload, is determined by request statistics and end-user requirements. Several questions should be asked.

- How often do users really execute this workload? Normally, a user spends a large percentage of his or her day on things other than compiling and linking programs. Assuming that all of the users will spend all of their time interacting with their workstations at top speed can lead to over-conservative estimates of the number of users that can be supported.
- What is the acceptable average network utilization? For Ethernets, it is usually 30% to 60%, depending on site concerns.
- What is the probability that a large number of clients will encounter a period in which their network utilizations peak simultaneously? During these periods, response time will suffer. How often do concurrent peaks occur, and how long do they last?

Sometimes remote execution is more appropriate for running large applications. One example is the InfoExplorer online documentation system. InfoExplorer has a large memory requirement. By running the application on the server, via a remote window, the client is able to take advantage of the memory of the server system and the fact that multiple instances of InfoExplorer from different clients could share pages of code and document files. If the application is run in the client, swapping behavior as described previously would dramatically affect response time. Other uses, such as large, disk-intensive **make** or **cp** operations, can also benefit by moving the application closer to the hard disks.

When configuring networks and servers for diskless clients, application measurement should be performed whenever possible. Don't forget to measure server processor utilization and disk utilization. They are more likely to present bottlenecks than either Ethernet or 16Mb Token-Ring networks.

Tuning for Performance

The capacity of a client/server configuration may be thought of in terms of supply and demand. The supply of resources is constrained by the type of network and the server configuration. The demand is the sum of all client requirements on the server. When a configuration produces unacceptable performance, improvement can be obtained by changing the client demand or by increasing the server supply of resource.

Utilization is the percentage of time a device is in use. Devices with utilizations greater than 70% will see rapidly increasing response times because incoming requests have to wait for previous requests to complete. Maximum acceptable utilizations are a trade-off of response time for throughput. In interactive systems, utilizations of devices should generally not exceed 70–80% for acceptable response times. Batch systems, where throughput on multiple job streams is important, can run close to 100% utilization. Obviously, with mixtures of batch and interactive users, care must be taken to keep interactive response time acceptable.

Client Tuning

Client tuning can involve any combination of:

- Adding client memory
- Increasing the number of client NFS **biod** daemons
- Changing client network configuration
- Adding a disk to the client configuration

If a client contains insufficient memory, the end result is working-storage paging. This can be detected by looking at the output of **vmstat –s**. If a client experiences continual working-storage paging, adding memory to the client will almost always improve the client's performance.

The number of block I/O daemons (**biod**s) configured on a client limits the number of outstanding NFS read and write requests. In a diskless system without NFS explicitly activated, only a few **biod**s are available. If NFS is activated, the number increases. Normally, the default number of **biod**s available with NFS activated is sufficient for a diskless workstation.

Both the Ethernet and Token Ring device drivers have parameters defining the transmit queue size and receive queue size for the device. These parameters can have performance implications in the client. See the section on "Tuning Other Layers to Improve NFS Performance" on page 183.

Adding a disk to a diskless machine should not be considered heresy. In fact, marketing studies indicate that diskless systems are usually upgraded to having a disk within a year of purchase. Adding a disk does not necessarily nullify the chief advantage of diskless systems—centralized file maintenance. A disk may be added for paging only. This is usually called a *dataless* system. Other combinations exist. For example a disk may contain both paging space and temporary file space.

Network Tuning

The network bandwidth of Ethernet is nominally 10 megabits/second. In practice, contention among the users of the Ethernet makes it impossible to use the full nominal bandwidth. Considering that an IBM SCSI disk can provide up to 32 megabits/second, it is alarming to consider a number of clients sharing about one-fourth the bandwidth of a disk. This comparison is only valid, however, for applications that do sequential disk I/O. Most workloads are dominated by random I/O, which is seek and rotational-latency limited. Since most SCSI disks have sustainable throughputs of 50 – 85 random I/O operations per second, the effective random I/O rate of a disk is 2 – 3 megabits/second. Therefore, an Ethernet bandwidth is roughly equivalent to about two disks doing random I/O. There is a lesson here. Applications that do sequential I/O on large files should be run on the system to which the disks are attached, not on a diskless workstation.

Although the maximum transfer unit (MTU) of a LAN can be changed using SMIT, diskless workstations are limited to using the default sizes.

Server Tuning

Server configuration involves:

- Server CPU
- Server disk configuration
- Server NFS configuration
- Server memory configuration
- Server network configuration

The server CPU processing power is significant because all server requests require CPU service. Generally, the CPU processing required for read and write requests is significantly more than for other requests.

Server disk configuration is usually the first bottleneck encountered. One obvious tuning hint is to balance the disk I/O, so that no one disk's utilization is much greater than the others. Another is to maximize the number of disks. For example, two 400MB disks will provide almost twice the random I/Os per second of a single 857MB disk. Additionally, with AIX it is possible to place a journal log on another device. By doing this, the multiple-write NFS sequence is improved as follows:

- Write data on file disk
- Write journal log on log disk (no disk seek)
- Write file allocation data on file disk (small seek)

By not having the journal on the file disk, one or two potentially long disk-seek operations are avoided. (If the file and the journal log were on the same lightly loaded disk, the accessor would be continually seeking back-and-forth between file area and journal log.)

The number of instances of the NFS daemon (**nfsd**) running on the server limits the number of NFS requests that the server can be executing concurrently. The default number of **nfsd**s is only 8, which is probably insufficient for all but low-end servers. The number of **nfsd**s started at each boot can be changed via **smit nfs** (**Network File System (NFS)** -> **Configure NFS on This System**).

The server memory size is significant only for NFS read operations. Since writes cannot be cached, memory size has no effect on write performance. On the other hand, assuming that some files are used repetitively, the larger the server memory, the higher the probability that a read can be satisfied from memory, avoiding disk I/O. Avoiding disk I/O has the threefold benefit of reducing disk utilization, improving response time for the read, and decreasing server CPU utilization. You can observe server disk activity using **iostat**. The following cues may indicate that additional memory could improve the performance of the server:

- One or more of the disk drives is operating close to its limit (40–85 random I/Os per second, see "Disk Pre-Installation Guidelines" on page 67).
- Over a period of minutes or longer, the number of bytes read is significantly greater than the number of bytes written.

As in the client, both the Ethernet and Token-Ring device drivers have limits on the number of buffers available for sending data. See "Tuning Other Layers to Improve NFS Performance" on page 183.

Commands Performance

AIX commands experience the same kinds of behavior we observed when running a trivial program (see "When a Program Runs on a Diskless Workstation" on page 187). The behavior of commands can be predicted based on the type and number of file-system operations required in their execution. Commands that do numerous file lookup operations, such as **find**, or lots of read and/or write operations, such as a large **cp**, will run much slower on a diskless system. The figure "Test Results" should give you a sense of the diskless performance of some frequently used commands.

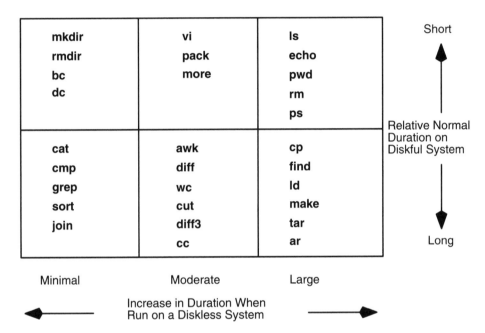

Figure 21: Test Results

The penalty experienced by a command on a diskless client is expressed as a ratio of elapsed time diskful to elapsed time diskless. This ratio is interesting, but not always important. For example, if a command executes in 0.05 seconds diskful and 0.2 seconds diskless, the diskless penalty is four. But does an end user care? The 0.2 second response is well within human tolerance. On the other hand, if the command is used in a shell script and executed 100 times, the shell script response time might increase from 5 seconds to 20 seconds. For this reason, a good rule of thumb is to avoid diskless workstations for users who have complex, frequently executed shell scripts.

Case Study 1—An Office Workload

As an example of client I/O characteristics, we measured a workload that is representative of a single-user-per-client office environment on a 16MB diskless RISC System/6000 Model 220. The workload creates a file, using the **vi** editor, at a typing rate of 6 characters per second. **nroff**, **spell**, and **cat** utilities are run against the document. The document is **tftp**ed to the server. Additional commands include **cal**, **calendar**, **rm**, **mail**, and a small program to do telephone number lookup. Simulated "think time" is included between commands.

The figure "Office Server CPU Utilization" and the figure "Office Server Disk Utilization" show server-CPU and server-disk resource utilization for the office workload. The server is a Model 530H with a single 857MB hard disk. The client running the office workload is a single Model 220. The workload is "bursty"—the peaks of utilization are much higher than the average utilization.

The figure "Office Ethernet Packets/Second" shows the I/O-request pattern on the Ethernet over the period of the workload execution. The average NFS request count is 9.5 requests/second, with a peak of 249 requests/second. The figure "Office Ethernet Bytes/second" shows the total bytes transferred per second, including protocol overhead. The average transfer rate is 4000 bytes/second, with a peak of 114,341 bytes/second. This workload consumes an average of 1/300th of the nominal bandwidth of an Ethernet, with a peak of 1/11 utilization.

Since the average per-client server-CPU utilization is 2%, the average server-disk utilization per client is 2.8%, and the average Ethernet utilization is 0.3%, the disk will probably be the critical resource when a number of copies of this workload are using a single server.

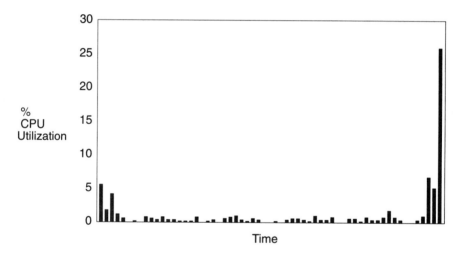

Figure 22: Office Server CPU Utilization

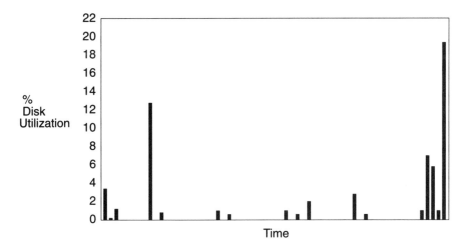

Figure 23: Office Server Disk Utilization

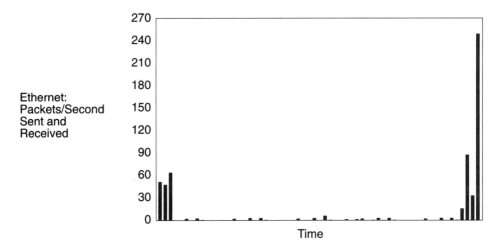

Figure 24: Office Ethernet Packets/Second

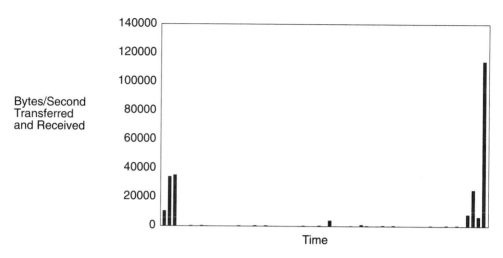

Figure 25: Office Ethernet Bytes/Second

Case Study 2—A Software-Development Workload

As another example of client-I/O characteristics, we measured a compile/link/execute workload on a 16MB diskless RISC System/6000 Model 220. This is a very heavy workload compared with the office case just described. The workload combines a number of AIX services commonly used in software development in a single-user-per-client environment. Simulated "think time" is included to mimic typing delays.

The figures "Software Development Server CPU Utilization" and "Software Development Server Disk Utilization" show the server-resource utilization for this workload. The same configuration as the previous case study was used.

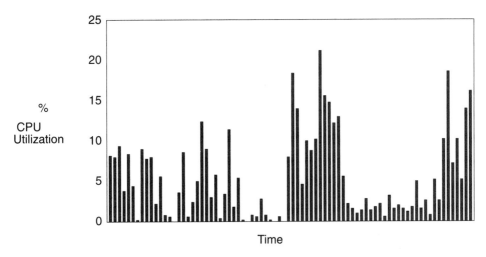

Figure 26: Software Development Server CPU Utilization

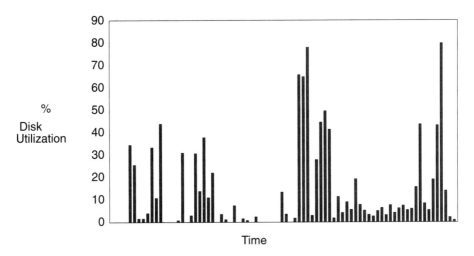

Figure 27: Software Development Server Disk Utilization

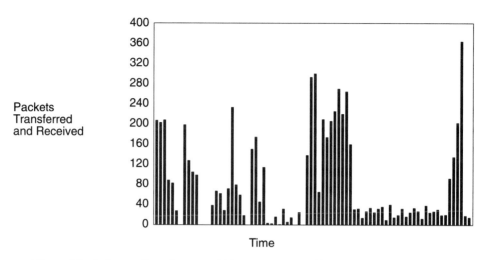

Figure 28: Software Development Ethernet Packets/Second

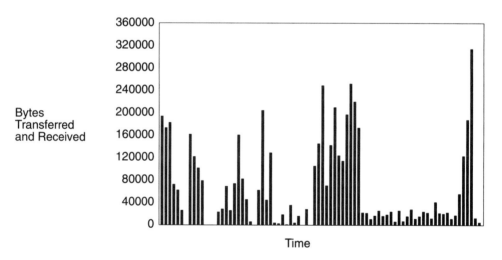

Figure 29: Software Development Ethernet Bytes/Second

The figure "Software Development Ethernet Packets/Second" shows the I/O request pattern on the Ethernet over the period of the workload execution. The average NFS request count is 82 requests/second, with a peak of 364 requests/second. The figure "Software Development Ethernet Bytes/Second" shows the total bytes transferred per second, including protocol overhead. The average transfer rate is 67,540 bytes/second, with a peak of 314,750 bytes/second. This workload consumes an average of 1/18th of the nominal bandwidth of an Ethernet, with a peak of 1/4 utilization.

Since the average per-client server-CPU utilization is 4.2%, the average server-disk utilization per client is 8.9%, and the average Ethernet utilization is 5.3%, the disk will probably be the critical resource when a number of copies of this workload are using a single server. However, if a second disk were added to the server configuration, the Ethernet would probably be the next resource to saturate. There's always a "next bottleneck."

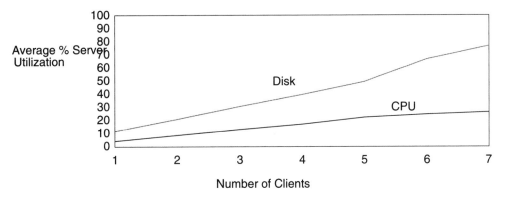

Figure 30: Average Server Utilization

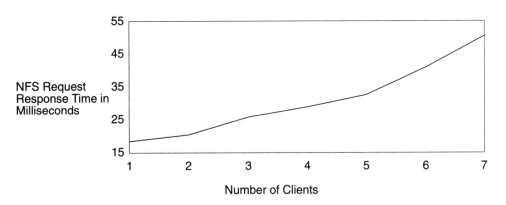

Figure 31: NFS Request Response Time

Given that the disk bottleneck occurs at a small number of clients for this workload, it is easily measured. The figure "Average Server Utilization" shows the average CPU utilization and average disk utilization (one-disk server) of the server as clients are added. The figure "NFS Request Response Time" shows the measured response time for NFS requests as the number of clients is increased.

Tuning Asynchronous Connections for High-Speed Transfers

Async ports permit the connection to a computer of optional devices such as terminals, printers, fax machines, and modems. Async ports are provided by adapter devices such as the 8-, 16-, or 64-port IBM adapters or the 128-port Digiboard adapter, which reside on the Micro Channel and provide multiple asynchronous connections, typically RS232 or RS422. Many adapters, such as the three IBM async adapters mentioned above, were originally designed for servicing terminals and printers, and so are optimized for output (sends). Input processing (receives) is not as well optimized, perhaps because the assumption was once made that users could not type very fast. This is not a great concern when data transmission is slow and irregular, as with keyboard input. It becomes a problem with raw-mode applications, where massive chunks of input are transmitted by other computers and by devices such as fax machines.

This section discusses the performance of the various adapters when receiving and sending raw-mode file transfers. While some adapters have inherent limitations, we provide some guidelines and methods that can squeeze out better performance from those adapters for raw-mode transfers.

Measurement Objectives and Configurations

Our measurements had two objectives: to evaluate throughput, effective baud rate, and CPU utilization at various baud rates for the adapters and to determine the maximum number of ports that could be supported by each device at each baud rate.

Note: Our throughput measurements were made using raw-mode file-transfer workloads and are mainly useful for estimating performance of raw-mode devices, like fax machines and modems. These measurements do not apply to commercial multiuser configurations, which may incur significant CPU overhead for database accesses or screen control and are often gated by disk-I/O limitations.

In raw-mode processing, data is treated as a continuous stream; input bytes are not assembled into lines, and erase and kill processing are disabled. A minimum data-block size and a read timer are used to determine how the operating system processes the bytes received before passing them to the application.

Measurements were performed on the native, 8-, 16-, and 64-port adapters at 2400-, 9600-, 19,200- and 38,400-baud line speeds. (Because RISC System/6000 native async ports, the 8-port adapter, and the 16-port adapter are all serviced by the same device driver and have similar performance, they are referred to as one, the 8/16-port adapter.) The 128-port adapter was measured only at 19,200 and 38,400 baud.

All ports tested were configured and optimized as fast ports for raw-mode transfers (see the `fastport.s` shell script on page 205). A 128,000-character file was written on each TTY line by the driver, a RISC System/6000 Model 530, and simultaneously read by the system under test, another 530. Each 530 was configured with 32MB of RAM and a single 857MB disk drive.

The AIX performance-monitoring command, **iostat** (or **sar**, in the case of the 128-port adapter), was run in the background at a predetermined frequency to monitor system performance. Measurements were taken upon reaching steady state for a fixed interval of time in the flat portion of the throughput curve. In each test, the system load was gradually increased by adding active ports up to some maximum or until 100% CPU utilization was reached.

Three metrics that best describe peak performance characteristics—aggregate character throughput per second (char/sec) averaged over the measured interval, effective per-line baud rate, and CPU utilization—were measured for half-duplex receive and half-duplex send.

XON/XOFF pacing (async handshaking, no relation to AIX disk-I/O pacing), RTS/CTS pacing, and no pacing were tested. Pacing and handshaking refer to hardware or software mechanisms used in data communication to turn off transmission when the receiving device is unable to store the data it is receiving. We found that XON/XOFF pacing was appropriate for the 8/16-port adapters when receiving and for the 128-port adapter both sending and receiving. RTS/CTS was better for the 64-port adapter when receiving. No pacing was better for the 8/16- and 64-port adapters when sending.

Character throughput is the aggregate number of characters transmitted per second across all the lines. Line speeds (or baud rates) of 2400, 9600, 19,200, and 38,400, which are set through the software, are the optimum speed settings for transfer of data over TTY lines. While the baud rate is the peak line speed, measured in bits/second, the *effective* baud rate is always less, and is calculated as 10 times the character throughput divided by the number of lines. (The factor 10X is used because it takes 10 bits to transfer one 8-bit character.)

Results

The following table summarizes our results. "Max ports:" is the number of ports that can be supported by the adapter when the effective baud rate most closely approaches the line speed.

Line Speed	8/16-port:		64-port:	128-port:		
	Send	Receive	Send	Receive	Send	Receive
2400 baud						
Max ports:	32	16	64	64	N/A	N/A
Char/sec	7700	3800	15200	14720		
Eff. Kb/sec:	2.4	2.4	2.3	2.3		
CPU util. %:	5	32	9	76		
9600 baud						
Max ports:	32	12	56	20	128	128
Char/sec	30700	11500	53200	19200	122200	122700
Eff. Kb/sec:	9.6	9.6	9.5	9.6	9,6	9.6
CPU util. %:	17	96	25	99	21	27
19,200 baud						
Max ports:	32	6	32	10	128	128
Char/sec	48900	11090	51200	18000	245400	245900
Eff. Kb/sec:	15.3	18.5	16	18	19.2	19.2
CPU util. %:	35	93	23	92	39	39

38400 baud

Max ports:	32	4	24	7	75	75
Char/sec	78400	10550	50400	15750	255200	255600
Eff. Kb/sec:	24.5	26.4	21	22.5	34	34
CPU util. %:	68	98	23	81	40	37

The 8/16 Async Port Adapter

8/16 Half-Duplex Send

The 8/16 half-duplex send measurements were made with no pacing, allowing the unimpeded outbound transmission of data. For the 8/16-port adapter, the RISC System/6000 processes approximately 1400 char/sec per 1% CPU utilization. The peak throughput of a single 16-port adapter is 48,000 char/sec.

8/16 Half-Duplex Receive

In this configuration, using XON/XOFF pacing, the RISC System/6000 processes about 120 char/sec per 1% CPU. The peak bandwidth is 11,000 char/sec at 100% CPU utilization for the 16-port async adapter.

The 64-Port Async Adapter

The limiting device in 64-port async adapter systems is typically the 16-port concentrator box, of which there can be up to four. Concentrator saturation is a concern because as the concentrator box approaches overload, no additional throughput is accepted. The effective baud rate is lowered, and there is a noticeable slowdown in work. For the following measurements, four 16-port concentrators were connected to the 64 RS232 ports.

64 Half-Duplex Receive

The 64-port half-duplex receive measurements used RTS/CTS hardware pacing. In this configuration, the RISC System/6000 processes about 195 char/sec per 1% CPU. The peak bandwidth is 19,500 char/sec at 100% CPU utilization.

For half-duplex receive, a single 16-port concentrator box saturates at 8450 char/sec with 44% CPU. Once the concentrator is saturated, no additional throughput is possible until another concentrator is added. At 38,400 baud, the single-concentrator saturation point is four active ports with an effective rate of 22.5 Kbaud. At 19,200 baud the saturation point is five ports with an effective baud rate of 17 Kbaud. At 9600 baud saturation is at nine ports with an effective baud rate of 9.6 Kbaud. At 2400 baud the system supports all 64 ports with an effective baud rate of 2.3 Kbaud with no saturation point. Peak throughput is 14,800 chars/sec.

64 Half-Duplex Send

The 64-port half-duplex send measurements were made with no pacing, allowing the unimpeded outbound transmission of data with no flow-control restrictions. For the

64-port adapter, the RISC System/6000 processes approximately 2200 char/sec per 1% CPU utilization. The peak throughput of the 64-port adapter using all four concentrators is 54,500 char/sec.

A single concentrator box saturates at 13300 char/sec with 6% CPU. At 38,400 baud it supports six ports with an effective baud rate of approximately 22 Kbaud. At 19,200 baud it supports eight ports with an effective baud rate of approximately 16.3 Kbaud.

The 128-Port Async Adapter

Up to seven 128-port Digiboard async adapters can be connected to a given RISC System/6000, for a total of 896 ports.

There are two synchronous-data-link-control (SDLC) links per adapter, with a combined capacity of 2.4 Mbaud. (The 64-port adapter has a four-channel SDLC with a combined capacity of 768 Kbaud.)

Other 128-port features that favorably affect data transmission speed and reduce CPU utilization are:

- The polling algorithm piggybacks the clock interrupt, so there are no additional host interrupts. Polling rates can be changed by the application on a per-port basis.
- The device driver detects raw-mode I/O and moves data from adapter memory to user space, bypassing the host line discipline.
- The concentrator processes most line-discipline options. An exception is cooked mode, in which all processing is done by the host.
- Adapter microcode reallocates memory buffers based on the number of concentrators and the available memory.

No concentrator saturation occurs in the 128-port async adapters, giving this adapter the advantage over the 64-port async-adapter systems.

For the measurements, eight 16-port concentrator boxes were connected to the 128 RS232 ports.

128 Half-Duplex Receive

Using XON/XOFF software pacing, this configuration processes about 6908 char/sec per 1% CPU. The peak throughput is 255,600 char/sec at 37% CPU utilization.

128 Half-Duplex Send

With no pacing the maximum rate at which this configuration can send data to a TTY device is approximately 5800 char/sec per 1% CPU utilization. The peak throughput of the 128-port adapter is 255,200 char/sec.

Async Port Tuning Techniques

The test configurations in this study used a number of hardware and software flow-control mechanisms and additional software techniques to optimize character-transmission rates.

The guidelines below discuss these techniques. (A shell script containing appropriate **stty** commands to implement most of the techniques is given at the end of the section.)

- Increase the value of the *vmin* variable for each TTY from the default of 4. The *vmin* variable value is the minimum number of bytes that should be received when the read is successful. The value chosen for the *vmin* variable should be the lesser of the application data-block size or 255 (the maximum allowed). If the application block size is variable or unknown, *vmin* should be set to 255. Setting the *vmin* variable to 255 will result in fewer read executions and will reduce CPU utilization by 15–20% for file-transfer programs.

- Except on the 128-port adapter, set *vtime* > 0 to prevent an indefinite block on read. If the *vtime* variable is set to zero on the 128-port adapter, POSIX line-discipline processing will be offloaded to the adapter hardware, reducing CPU processing significantly.

- For raw-mode sends where output translations are not needed, turn off the **opost** option in the POSIX line discipline. This will help the CPU performance by reducing the output path length. For file-transfer applications, which move large amounts of data on TTY lines, this can reduce CPU utilization by 3X. Example:

```
# stty -opost < /dev/ttyn
```

- Because the 64-port adapter is prone to unpredictable data overruns at higher baud rates when XON/XOFF is used for pacing, use RTS/CTS hardware pacing instead. This avoids the risk of losing data.

- Since the 64-port-adapter concentrator boxes have a limited bandwidth and saturate at higher baud rates, adding more ports to a saturated concentrator will decrease the performance of all ports connected. Instead, add another concentrator and keep going until it is saturated or you have run out of CPU.

- For input processing, using the **echo** option is expensive, as it increases the time per character. Character echo is useful for canonical user input but is probably not necessary for most raw-mode applications. Example:

```
# stty -echo < /dev/ttyn
```

fastport for Fast File Transfers

The `fastport.s` script is intended to condition a TTY port for fast file transfers in raw mode; for example, when a FAX machine is to be connected. Using the script may improve CPU performance by a factor of 3 at 38,400 baud. `fastport.s` is not intended for the canonical processing that is used when interacting with a user at an async terminal, because canonical processing cannot be easily buffered. The bandwidth of the canonical read is too small for the fast-port settings to make a perceptible difference.

Any TTY port can be configured as a fast port. The improved performance is the result of reducing the number of interrupts to the CPU during the read cycle on a given TTY line.

1. Create a TTY for the port using SMIT (**Devices** –> **TTY** –> **Add a TTY**), with Enable LOGIN=disable and BAUD rate=38,400.

2. Create the Korn shell script named `fastport.s`, as follows:

```
#*******************************************************************
#
#     Configures a fastport for "raw" async I/O.
#
#*******************************************************************
set -x
sync;sync
i=$1

if [ $i -le 100 ]
then
# for the native async ports and the 8-, 16-, and 64-port adapters
# set vmin=255 and vtime=0.5 secs with the following stty
 stty -g </dev/tty$i |awk ' BEGIN { FS=":";OFS=":" }
  { $5="ff";$6=5;print $0 } ' >foo
# for a 128-port adapter, remove the preceding stty, then
# uncomment and use the
# following stty instead to
# set vmin=255 and vtime=0 to offload line discipline processing
# stty -g </dev/tty$i |awk ' BEGIN { FS=":";OFS=":" }
#  { $5="ff";$6=0;print $0 } ' >foo
 stty `cat foo ` </dev/tty$i
 sleep 2

# set raw mode with minimal input and output processing
 stty -opost -icanon -isig -icrnl -echo -onlcr</dev/tty$i
rm foo
 sync;sync
else
echo "Usage is fastport.s < TTY number >"
fi
```

3. Invoke the script for TTY *number* with the command:

```
fastport.s number
```

Using netpmon to Evaluate Network Performance

The **netpmon** command uses the trace facility to obtain a detailed picture of network activity during a time interval. Since it uses the trace facility, **netpmon** can be run only by `root` or by a member of the `system` group.

In AIX Version 4.1, the **netpmon** command is packaged as part of the Performance Toolbox for AIX. To determine whether **netpmon** is available, use:

```
lslpp -lI perfagent.tools
```

If this package has been installed, **netpmon** is available.

Tracing is started by the **netpmon** command, optionally suspended with **trcoff** and resumed with **trcon**, and terminated with **trcstop**. As soon as tracing is terminated, **netpmon** writes its report to **stdout**. The following sequence of commands gives a simple example of **netpmon** use:

```
# netpmon -o nm.test.out ; ping xactive 256 5 ; trcstop
```

The report (somewhat condensed) produced by this sequence, in an otherwise idle system, was:

```
Wed Jan 12 14:33:25 1994
System: AIX alborz Node: 3 Machine: 000249573100
4.155 secs in measured interval
========================================================================
Process CPU Usage Statistics:
-----------------------------

                                                      Network
Process (top 20)           PID  CPU Time   CPU %      CPU %
------------------------------------------------------------

ping                     12699    0.0573   1.380      0.033
trcstop                  12700    0.0150   0.360      0.000
ksh                      13457    0.0150   0.360      0.000
rlogind                   6321    0.0127   0.306      0.088
netpmon                  12690    0.0064   0.153      0.000
netw                       771    0.0047   0.113      0.113
netpmon                  10650    0.0037   0.090      0.000
trace                    10643    0.0023   0.055      0.000
swapper                      0    0.0022   0.053      0.000
writesrv                  1632    0.0009   0.021      0.000
------------------------------------------------------------

Total (all processes)             0.1201   2.891      0.234
Idle time                         3.8904  93.639
========================================================================
First Level Interrupt Handler CPU Usage Statistics:
---------------------------------------------------

                                                      Network
FLIH                            CPU Time   CPU %      CPU %
------------------------------------------------------------

external device                   0.0573   1.379      0.890
data page fault                   0.0368   0.887      0.000
floating point                    0.0001   0.003      0.000
------------------------------------------------------------

Total (all FLIHs)                 0.0943   2.269      0.890
========================================================================
Second Level Interrupt Handler CPU Usage Statistics:
----------------------------------------------------

                                                      Network
SLIH                            CPU Time   CPU %      CPU %
------------------------------------------------------------

clock                             0.0415   0.998      0.000
tokdd                             0.0064   0.154      0.154
<addr=0x00022140>                 0.0008   0.019      0.000
```

```
---------------------------------------------------------------
Total (all SLIHs)              0.0486  1.171  0.154
===============================================================
Network Device-Driver Statistics (by Device):
---------------------------------------------

               ---------- Xmit ----------  ----- Recv ----
Device        Pkts/s  Bytes/s  Util  QLen  Pkts/s  Bytes/s
---------------------------------------------------------------
/dev/tok0      3.37     629  0.005 0.005  16.85     1900
===============================================================
Network Device-Driver Transmit Statistics (by Destination Host):
---------------------------------------------------------------
Host                   Pkts/s  Bytes/s
---------------------------------------
xactive.austin.ibm.com  1.44      390
===============================================================
Detailed Second Level Interrupt Handler CPU Usage Statistics:
---------------------------------------------------------------
SLIH: tokdd
count:               84
  cpu time (msec):   avg 0.076   min 0.058   max 0.097   sdev 0.009
===============================================================
Detailed Network Device-Driver Statistics:
-------------------------------------------
DEVICE: /dev/tok0
recv packets:        70
  recv sizes (bytes): avg 112.8   min 68    max 324    sdev 75.2
  recv times (msec):  avg 0.226   min 0.158 max 0.449  sdev 0.056
xmit packets:        14
  xmit sizes (bytes): avg 186.6   min 52    max 314    sdev 100.0
  xmit times (msec):  avg 1.552   min 1.127 max 2.532  sdev 0.380
===============================================================
Detailed Network Device-Driver Transmit Statistics (by Host):
---------------------------------------------------------------
HOST: xactive.austin.ibm.com
xmit packets:        6
  xmit sizes (bytes): avg 270.3   min 52    max 314    sdev 97.6
  xmit times (msec):  avg 1.772   min 1.516 max 2.532  sdev 0.346
```

Using iptrace to Analyze Performance Problems

There are many tools for observing the activity, both normal and pathological, on the network. Some run under AIX, others run on dedicated hardware. One tool that can be used to obtain a detailed, packet-by-packet description of the LAN activity generated by a workload is the combination of the **iptrace** daemon and the **ipreport** command. The **iptrace** daemon can only be started by root.

By default, **iptrace** traces all packets. An option (**–a**) allows exclusion of address resolution protocol (ARP) packets. Other options can narrow the scope of tracing to a particular source host (**–s**), destination host (**–d**), or protocol (**–p**). See *AIX Version 4.1*

Commands Reference, Volume 2. Because **iptrace** can consume significant amounts of processor time, you should be as specific as possible in describing the packets you want traced.

Since **iptrace** is a daemon, it should be started with a **startsrc** command rather that directly from the command line. This makes it easier to control and shut down cleanly. A typical invocation would be:

```
# startsrc -s iptrace -a "-i tr0 /home/user/iptrace/log1"
```

This command starts the **iptrace** daemon with directions to trace all activity on the Token-Ring interface, tr0, and place the trace data in /home/user/iptrace/log1. To stop the daemon, use:

```
# stopsrc -s iptrace
```

If you hadn't started it with **startsrc**, you would have to find its process ID with **ps** and **kill** it.

The **ipreport** command is a formatter for the log file. Its output is written to stdout. Options allow recognition and formatting of RPC packets (**–r**), identifying each packet with a number (**–n**), and prefixing each line with a 3-character string that identifies the protocol (**–s**). A typical **ipreport** command to format the log1 file just created (which is owned by root) would be:

```
# ipreport -ns log1 >log1_formatted
```

This would result in a sequence of packet reports similar to the following examples. The first packet is the first half of a **ping**. The fields of most interest are: the source (SRC) and destination (DST) host address, both in dotted decimal and in ASCII; the IP packet length (ip_len); and the indication of the higher-level protocol in use (ip_p).

```
Packet Number 131
TOK: =====( packet transmitted on interface tr0 )=====Fri Dec 10 08:42:07
1993
TOK: 802.5 packet
TOK: 802.5 MAC header:
TOK: access control field = 0, frame control field = 40
TOK: [ src = 90:00:5a:a8:88:81, dst = 10:00:5a:4f:35:82]
TOK: routing control field = 0830,  3 routing segments
TOK: routing segments [ ef31 ce61 ba30  ]
TOK: 802.2 LLC header:
TOK: dsap aa, ssap aa, ctrl 3, proto 0:0:0, type 800 (IP)
IP:     < SRC =  129.35.145.140 >  (alborz.austin.ibm.com)
IP:     < DST =  129.35.145.135 >  (xactive.austin.ibm.com)
IP:     ip_v=4, ip_hl=20, ip_tos=0, ip_len=84, ip_id=38892, ip_off=0
IP:     ip_ttl=255, ip_sum=fe61, ip_p = 1 (ICMP)
ICMP:   icmp_type=8 (ECHO_REQUEST)   icmp_id=5923   icmp_seq=0
ICMP: 00000000    2d088abf 00054599 08090a0b 0c0d0e0f |-.....E.........|
ICMP: 00000010    10111213 14151617 18191a1b 1c1d1e1f |................|
ICMP: 00000020    20212223 24252627 28292a2b 2c2d2e2f | !"#$%&'()*+,-./|
ICMP: 00000030    30313233 34353637                   |01234567        |
```

The next example is a frame from an **ftp** operation. Note that the IP packet is the size of the MTU for this LAN—1492 bytes.

```
Packet Number 501
TOK: =====( packet received on interface tr0 )=====Fri Dec 10 08:42:51
1993
TOK: 802.5 packet
TOK: 802.5 MAC header:
TOK: access control field = 18, frame control field = 40
TOK: [ src = 90:00:5a:4f:35:82, dst = 10:00:5a:a8:88:81]
TOK: routing control field = 08b0,  3 routing segments
TOK: routing segments [ ef31 ce61 ba30  ]
TOK: 802.2 LLC header:
TOK: dsap aa, ssap aa, ctrl 3, proto 0:0:0, type 800 (IP)
IP:     < SRC =  129.35.145.135 >  (xactive.austin.ibm.com)
IP:     < DST =  129.35.145.140 >  (alborz.austin.ibm.com)
IP:     ip_v=4, ip_hl=20, ip_tos=0, ip_len=1492, ip_id=34233, ip_off=0
IP:     ip_ttl=60, ip_sum=5ac, ip_p = 6 (TCP)
TCP:    <source port=20(ftp-data), destination port=1032 >
TCP:    th_seq=445e4e02, th_ack=ed8aae02
TCP:    th_off=5, flags<ACK |>
TCP:    th_win=15972, th_sum=0, th_urp=0
TCP: 00000000     01df0007 2cd6c07c 00004635 000002c2 |....,..|..F5....|
TCP: 00000010     00481002 010b0001 000021b4 00000d60 |.H........!....`|
             --------- Lots of uninteresting data omitted -----------
TCP: 00000590     63e40000 3860000f 4800177d 80410014 |c...8`..H..}.A..|
TCP: 000005a0     82220008 30610038 30910020          |.".0a.80..     |
```

10

DFS Performance Tuning

Note: The following recommendations are based on performance experiments using AIX Version 3.2.5. At the time this book was written, the degree to which these recommendations would apply to AIX Version 4.1 was not known.

From the performance standpoint, the most important difference between DFS and NFS is the client data-caching capability of DFS, so it is not surprising that the most important performance-tuning techniques for DFS involve choosing the attributes of the client cache.

DFS Caching on Disk or Memory?

To assess the disk versus memory trade-off in your environment, consider the following points:

- If the system being tuned, or another system with similar workload, is already running DFS with a disk cache, you can estimate the required size of a memory cache by issuing the following command toward the end of a period of peak workload:

```
cm getcachesize
```

    Divide the number of 1KB blocks being used by .9 to determine the memory cache size needed to accommodate the same amount of data. (About 10% of the blocks in the cache are used for DFS record keeping.)
- If the data being handled is frequently reaccessed, the greater potential capacity of a disk cache is probably appropriate.
- If the data being handled is so extensive that it would overflow the largest feasible disk cache, or if the data is frequently changed by another client, a memory cache is probably more appropriate because of its greater effect on RPC performance.
- The size of a memory cache should not exceed 10% of the real memory size of the machine. The recommended size is about 5% of real memory. Because DFS

exploits the memory caching capability of the AIX VMM, most of a DFS memory cache is used to hold directory and mount-point information.

- If your system shows any sign of being memory-bound, as evidenced by nonzero values in the `pi` or `po` columns of a **vmstat** report, you should not use a memory cache for DFS.
- As a feasibility check, you could temporarily reduce, using **rmss**, the effective memory size of the machine by the amount of memory you are considering using for a memory cache. If you observe paging activity, or diminished performance, or both, you should not use a memory cache. See "Assessing Memory Requirements via the **rmss** Command" on page 115.

DFS Cache Size

Determining the appropriate DFS cache size for a particular system will take some experimentation. You might begin by estimating the sum of:

- The sizes of the set of DFS-resident data files that are read at least once a day.
- The amount of DFS-resident data that is generated by the users of the system each day.
- The sizes of the DFS-resident programs that are executed more than once a day.

If the users' home directories are in DFS, you will want to make an allowance for the frequency with which the home directory is accessed, and the effect on perceived responsiveness of the system.

The size of the client cache is specified in the **CacheInfo** file and can be overridden with the **dfsd –blocks** n option, where n is the number of KB in the cache. This parameter applies to both memory and disk caches.

DFS Cache Chunk Size

The DFS cache chunk size can range from 8KB to 256KB. For large files (several MB), sequential read and write performance increases as chunk size increases, up to about 64KB. For very large files (100MB or more) a chunk size of 256KB yields the best read performance.

The chunk size is specified with the **dfsd –chunksize** n option, where n is an integer from 13 to 18, inclusive. The cache size is $2**n$ bytes, and so ranges from 8KB ($2**13$) to 256KB($2**18$). This parameter applies to both memory and disk caches. The default size is 8KB for memory caches and 64KB for disk caches.

Number of DFS Cache Chunks

This parameter only applies to disk caches. For memory caches, the number of chunks is already specified by the combination of cache size and chunk size. For disk caches, the default number of chunks is computed as the number of cache blocks divided by 8. If a **du** of the cache directory indicates that the space is less than 90% full, increase the number of cache chunks with the **dfsd –files** *n* option, where *n* is the number of chunks to be accommodated. This allows better utilization of the available cache space in applications that use many small files. Since multiple files cannot share a chunk, the number of chunks determines the maximum number of files the cache can accommodate.

Location of DFS Disk Cache

The disk cache should be in a logical volume that is:

- In the `outer_edge` area, if it is on a 200MB, 540MB, or 1.0GB disk drive.
- In the `center` area, if it is on any other disk drive.
- Not in the `rootvg` volume group.
- Not on the same physical volume as a paging space.
- Primarily or exclusively for use by the disk cache.
- Large enough to hold the specified disk cache without encroachment by other contents.

Cache Status-Buffer Size

The status-buffer size limits the maximum number of files that can be in the cache at one time. One entry is required for each file. If the status buffer is full, new files will displace old files in the cache, even though there is enough disk space to hold them. If your workload consists mostly of files that are equal to or smaller than the chunk size, the status buffer should have as many entries as there are chunks in the cache.

The status-buffer size is specified with the **dfsd –stat** *n* option, where *n* is the number of entries in the status buffer. The default value of *n* is 300.

Effect of Application Read/Write Size

Sequential read and write performance are affected by the size of the records being read or written by the application. In general, read throughput increases with record size up to 4KB, above which it levels off. Write throughput increases with record size up to 2KB, above which it levels off or decreases slightly.

Communications Parameter Settings for DFS

DFS uses UDP as its communications protocol. The recommendations for tuning DFS communications for servers and multiuser client systems parallel those for tuning communications in general (see "UDP, TCP/IP, and mbuf Tuning Parameters Summary" on page 175):

- Set the network adapter transmit and receive queue sizes to 150 (the maximum). This can be done with **smit commodev** –> (adapter type) –> Adapter –> Change / Show Characteristics of a (adapter type) Adapter. These parameters cannot be changed while the adapter is in operation. SMIT allows you to specify the change to take effect when the system is next restarted.

  You can also use **chdev** to set these parameters, if you take the adapter offline first. For example, for a Token-Ring adapter, the sequence of commands would be:

```
# ifconfig tr0 detach
# chdev -l tok0 -a xmt_que_size=150 -a rec_que_size=150
# ifconfig tr0 hostname up
```

You can observe the effect of the change with:

```
$ lsattr -E -l tok0
```

- If a **netstat -s** command reports a nonzero number in udp: n socket buffer overflows, increasing the **sb_max** and **udp_recvspace** parameters with the **no** command will only solve the problem if an application other than DFS is experiencing the overflows. DFS sets its own values (176KB) for **sb_max** and **udp_recvspace**. These values are not displayed or changed by the **no** command.

DFS File Server Tuning

On high-speed servers, it may be desirable to increase the number of **–mainprocs** and **–tokenprocs** (in the **fxd** command), to ensure that all of the available CPU capacity can be used effectively.

- A good level to start with is **–mainprocs 10 –tokenprocs 4**.
- Run **vmstat** during periods of heavy load. If a considerable level of CPU I/O wait is being experienced, try increasing the **–mainprocs** and **–tokenprocs** values further.

DCE LFS Tuning for DFS Performance

The following should be considered when setting up a DCE LFS aggregate (using the **newaggr** command) on a DFS server:

- If most of the files will be large, set the **–blocksize** parameter to the largest permitted value that is less than the typical file size. The **–blocksize** parameter can any power of 2 in the range from 4KB to 64KB.
- If most of the files will be several times larger than the **–blocksize** parameter, set the **–fragsize** parameter equal to the **–blocksize** parameter. This may use some additional disk space, but will streamline processing.
- If the aggregate is smaller than 100MB, use the **–logsize** parameter to ensure that the log is larger than the default (1% of the aggregate size). In general, **logsize** should never be less than 1000 blocks.

11

Performance Analysis with the Trace Facility

The AIX trace facility is a powerful system observation tool. The trace facility captures a sequential flow of time-stamped system events, providing a fine level of detail on system activity. Events are shown in time sequence and in the context of other events. Trace is a valuable tool for observing system and application execution. Where other tools provide high-level statistics, such as CPU utilization or I/O-wait time, the trace facility is useful in expanding the information to understand who, when, how, and why.

The operating system is instrumented to provide general visibility to system execution. Users can extend visibility into their applications by inserting additional events and providing formatting rules.

Care was taken in the design and implementation of this facility to make the collection of trace data efficient, so that system performance and flow would be minimally altered by activating trace. Because of this, the facility is extremely useful as a performance-analysis tool and as a problem-determination tool.

Understanding the Trace Facility

The trace facility is more flexible than traditional system-monitor services that access and present statistics maintained by the system. With traditional monitor services, data reduction (conversion of system events to statistics) is largely coupled to the system instrumentation. For example, many systems maintain the minimum, maximum, and average elapsed time observed for executions of task A and permit this information to be extracted.

The AIX trace facility does not strongly couple data reduction to instrumentation, but provides a stream of trace event records (usually abbreviated to *events*). It is not necessary to decide in advance what statistics will be needed; data reduction is to a large degree separated from the instrumentation. The user may choose to determine the minimum, maximum and average time for task A from the flow of events. But it is also possible to extract the average time for task A when called by process B; or the average time for task A when conditions XYZ are met; or calculate the standard deviation of run time for task A; or even decide that some other task, recognized by a stream of events, is more meaningful to summarize. This flexibility is invaluable for diagnosing performance or functional problems.

In addition to providing detailed information about system activity, the trace facility allows application programs to be instrumented and their trace events collected in addition to system events. The trace file then contains a complete record of the application and system activity, in the correct sequence and with precise time stamps.

Limiting the Amount of Trace Data Collected

The trace facility generates large volumes of data. This data cannot be captured for extended periods of time without overflowing the storage device. There are two ways that the trace facility can be used efficiently:

- The trace facility can be turned on and off in multiple ways to capture snippets of system activity. It is practical to capture in this way seconds to minutes of system activity for post processing. This is enough time to characterize major application transactions or interesting sections of a long task.
- The trace facility can be configured to direct the event stream to standard output. This allows a real-time process to connect to the event stream and provide data reduction as the events are recorded, thereby creating long-term monitoring capability. A logical extension for specialized instrumentation is to direct the data stream to an auxiliary device that can either store massive amounts of data or provide dynamic data reduction. This technique is used by the performance tools **tprof**, **netpmon**, and **filemon**.

Starting and Controlling Trace

The trace facility provides three distinct modes of use:

- Subcommand Mode. Trace is started with a shell command (**trace**) and carries on a dialog with the user via subcommands. The workload being traced must be provided by other processes, because the original shell process is in use.
- Command Mode. Trace is started with a shell command (**trace –a**) that includes a flag which specifies that the trace facility is to run asynchronously. The original shell process is free to run ordinary commands, interspersed with trace-control commands.
- Application-Controlled Mode. Trace is started (with **trcstart()**) and controlled by subroutine calls (such as **trcon()**, **trcoff()**) from an application program.

Formatting Trace Data

A general-purpose trace report facility is provided by the **trcrpt** command. The report facility provides little data reduction, but converts the raw binary event stream to a readable ASCII listing. Data can be visually extracted by a reader, or tools can be developed to further reduce the data.

The report facility displays text and data for each event according to rules provided in the trace format file. The default trace format file is **/etc/trcfmt**. It contains a stanza for each event ID. The stanza for the event provides the report facility with formatting rules for that event. This technique allows users to add their own events to programs and insert corresponding event stanzas in the format file to specify how the new events should be formatted.

Viewing Trace Data

When trace data is formatted, all data for a given event is usually placed on a single line. Additional lines may contain explanatory information. Depending on the fields included, the formatted lines can easily exceed 80 characters. It is best to view the reports on an output device that supports 132 columns.

An Example of Trace Facility Use

Obtaining a Sample Trace File

Trace data accumulates rapidly. We want to bracket the data collection as closely around the area of interest as possible. One technique for doing this is to issue several commands on the same command line. For example:

```
$ trace -a -k "20e,20f" -o ./trc_raw ; cp ../bin/track /tmp/junk ; trcstop
```

captures the execution of the **cp** command. We have used two features of the trace command. The `-k "20e,20f"` option suppresses the collection of events from the **lockl** and **unlockl** functions. These calls are numerous and add volume to the report without adding understanding at the level we're interested in. The `-o ./trc_raw` option causes the raw trace output file to be written in our local directory.

Note: This example is more educational if the input file is not already cached in system memory. Choose as the source file any file that is about 50KB and has not been touched recently.

Formatting the Sample Trace

We use the following form of the **trcrpt** command for our report:

```
$ trcrpt -O "exec=on,pid=on" trc_raw > cp.rpt
```

This reports both the fully qualified name of the file that is **exec**ed and the process ID that is assigned to it.

A quick look at the report file shows us that there are numerous VMM page assign and delete events in the trace, like the following sequence:

```
1B1 ksh      8525    0.003109888    0.162816    VMM page delete:   V.S=00
00.150E ppage=1F7F

                                               delete_in_progress proce
ss_private working_storage
```

```
1B0 ksh      8525    0.003141376    0.031488      VMM page assign:   V.S=00
00.2F33 ppage=1F7F
                             delete_in_progress process_private working_storage
```

We are not interested in this level of VMM activity detail at the moment, so we reformat the trace with:

```
$ trcrpt -k "1b0,1b1" -O "exec=on,pid=on" trc_raw > cp.rpt2
```

The −k "1b0,1b1" option suppresses the unwanted VMM events in the formatted output. It saves us from having to retrace the workload to suppress unwanted events. We could have used the **−k** function of **trcrpt** instead of that of the **trace** command to suppress the **lockl** and **unlockl** events, if we had believed that we might need to look at the lock activity at some point. If we had been interested in only a small set of events, we could have specified **−d** "*hookid1,hookid2*" to produce a report with only those events. Since the hook ID is the left-most column of the report, you can quickly compile a list of hooks to include or exclude.

A comprehensive list of Trace hook IDs is available in InfoExplorer. The hook IDs are defined in **/usr/include/sys/trchkid.h**.

Reading a Trace Report

The header of the trace report tells you when and where the trace was taken, as well as the command that was used to produce it:

```
Fri Nov 19 12:12:49 1993
System: AIX ptool Node: 3
Machine: 000168281000
Internet Address: 00000000 0.0.0.0
trace -ak 20e 20f -o -o ./trc_raw
```

The body of the report looks approximately as follows:

```
ID   PROCESS NAME  PID   ELAPSED_SEC  DELTA_MSEC  APPL   SYSCALL KERNEL
INTERRUPT
101 ksh            8525  0.005833472  0.107008           kfork
101 ksh            7214  0.012820224  0.031744           execve
134 cp             7214  0.014451456  0.030464           exec cp
../bin/trk/junk
```

In cp.rpt you can see the following phenomena:

- The **fork**, **exec**, and page fault activities of the **cp** process
- The opening of the input file for reading and the creation of the /tmp/junk file
- The successive **read/write** system calls to accomplish the copy
- The process **cp** becoming blocked while waiting for I/O completion, and the **wait** process being dispatched
- How logical-volume requests are translated to physical-volume requests
- The files are mapped rather than buffered in traditional kernel buffers, and the read accesses cause page faults that must be resolved by the Virtual Memory Manager.
- The Virtual Memory Manager senses sequential access and begins to prefetch the file pages.

- The size of the prefetch becomes larger as sequential access continues.
- When possible, the disk device driver coalesces multiple file requests into one I/O request to the drive.

The trace output looks a little overwhelming at first. This is a good example to use as a learning aid. If you can discern the activities described, you are well on your way to being able to use the trace facility to diagnose system-performance problems.

Filtering of the Trace Report

The full detail of the trace data may not be required. You can choose specific events of interest to be shown. For example, it is sometimes useful to find the number of times a certain event occurred. To answer the question "How many **open**s occurred in the copy example?" first find the event ID for the **open** system call. This can be done as follows:

```
$ trcrpt -j | grep -i open
```

You should be able to see that event ID 15b is the **open** event. Now, process the data from the copy example as follows:

```
$ trcrpt -d 15b -O "exec=on" trc_raw
```

The report is written to standard output, and you can determine the number of **open** subroutines that occurred. If you want to see only the **open** subroutines that were performed by the **cp** process, run the report command again using the following:

```
$ trcrpt -d 15b -p cp -O "exec=on" trc_raw
```

Starting and Controlling Trace from the Command Line

The trace facility is configured and data collection optionally started by the **trace** command, the detailed syntax of which is described in *AIX Version 4.1 Commands Reference, Volume 5*.

After trace is configured by the **trace** command, there are controls to turn data collection on and off and to stop the trace facility (stop deconfigures trace and unpins buffers). There are several ways to invoke the controls: subcommands, commands, subroutines, and **ioctl** calls. The subroutine and **ioctl** interfaces are described in "Starting and Controlling Trace from a Program" on page 219.

Controlling Trace in Subcommand Mode

If the trace routine is configured without the **–a** option, it runs in subcommand mode. Instead of the normal shell prompt, a prompt of ">" is given. In this mode the following subcommands are recognized:

trcon	Starts or resumes collection of event data.
trcoff	Suspends collection of event data.
q or quit	Stops collection of event data and terminates the trace routine.
!command	Runs the specified shell *command*.

Controlling Trace by Commands

If the trace routine is configured to run asynchronously (**trace –a**), trace can be controlled by the following commands:

trcon   Starts or resumes collection of event data.

trcoff   Suspends collection of event data.

trcstop   Stops collection of event data and terminates the trace routine.

Starting and Controlling Trace from a Program

The AIX trace facility can be started from a program, via a subroutine call. The subroutine is **trcstart** and is in the **librts.a** library. The syntax of the **trcstart** subroutine is:

int trcstart(char *args)

where *args* is simply the options list that you would have entered for the **trace** command. By default, the system trace (channel 0) is started. If you want to start a generic trace, you should include a **–g** option in the *args* string. On successful completion, the **trcstart** subroutine returns the channel ID. For generic tracing this channel ID can be used to record to the private generic channel.

When compiling a program using this subroutine, the link to the **librts.a** library must be specifically requested (use **–l rts** as a compile option).

Controlling Trace with Trace Subroutine Calls

The controls for the trace routine are available as subroutines from the **librts.a** library. The subroutines return zero on successful completion. The subroutines are:

int trcon()   Begins or resumes collection of trace data.

int trcoff()   Suspends collection of trace data.

int trcstop() Stops collection of trace data and terminates the trace routine.

Controlling Trace with ioctl Calls

Each of the above subroutines for controlling trace:

- **open**s the trace control device (**/dev/systrctl**)
- Issues the appropriate **ioctl**
- **close**s the control device
- Returns to the calling program

To turn tracing on and off around individual sections of code, it may be more efficient for a program to issue the **ioctl** controls directly. This avoids the repetitive opening and closing of the trace control device. To use the **ioctl** interface in a program, include **<sys/trcctl.h>** to define the **ioctl** commands. The syntax of the **ioctl** is as follows:

ioctl (*fd, CMD, Channel*)

where:

fd	is the file descriptor returned from opening **/dev/systrctl**
CMD	is one of: TRCON, TRCOFF, or TRCSTOP
Channel	is the trace channel (0 for system trace)

The following code example shows how to start a trace from a program and only trace around a specified section of code:

```
#include <fcntl.h>
#include <sys/trcctl.h>
extern int trcstart(char *arg);
char *ctl_dev ="/dev/systrctl";
int ctl_fd;
main()
{
      printf("configuring trace collection \n");
      if (trcstart("-ad")){
         perror("trcstart");
         exit(1);
      }
      printf("opening the trace device \n");
      if((ctl_fd =open (ctl_dev,O_RDWR))<0){
         perror("open ctl_dev");
         exit(1);
      }
      printf("turning data collection on \n");
      if(ioctl(ctl_fd,TRCON,0)){
         perror("TRCON");
         exit(1);
      }

      /* *** code here will be traced *** */
      printf("The code to print this line will be traced.");

      printf("turning data collection off\n");
      if (ioctl(ctl_fd,TRCOFF,0)){
         perror("TRCOFF");
         exit(1);
      }
      printf("stopping the trace daemon \n");
      if (trcstop(0)){
         perror("trcstop");
         exit(1);
      }
      exit(0);
}
```

Since no output file was specified in the parameter to the **trcstart()** subroutine, the output of the trace will be in **/var/adm/ras/trcfile**, which is also the default input file of the **trcrpt** command.

Adding New Trace Events

The operating system is shipped instrumented with key events. The user need only activate trace to capture the flow of events from the operating system. Application developers may want to instrument their application code during development for tuning purposes. This provides them with insight into how their applications are interacting with the system.

To add a trace event you have to design the trace records generated by your program in accordance with trace interface conventions. You then add trace-hook macros to the program at the appropriate locations. Traces can then be taken via any of the standard ways of invoking and controlling trace (commands, subcommands, or subroutine calls). To use the **trcrpt** program to format your traces, you need to add stanzas describing each new trace record and its formatting requirements to the trace format file.

Possible Forms of a Trace Event Record

A trace event can take several forms. An event consists of a hook word, optional data words, and an optional time stamp, as shown in the figure "Format of a Trace Event Record" on page 221. A four-bit type is defined for each form the event record can take. The type field is imposed by the recording routine so that the report facility can always skip from event to event when processing the data, even if the formatting rules in the trace format file are incorrect or missing for that event.

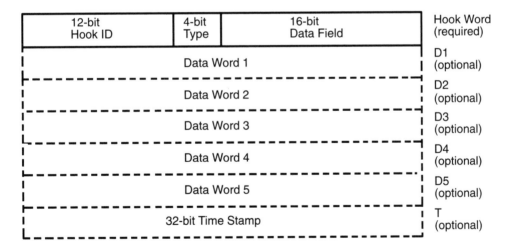

Figure 32: Format of a Trace Event Record

An event record should be as short as possible. Many system events use only the hook word and time stamp. There is another event type that is mentioned but should seldom be used because it is less efficient and is intrusive. It is a long format that allows the user to record a variable length of data. In this long form, the 16-bit data field of the hook word is converted to a *length* field that describes the length of the event record.

Trace Channels

The trace facility can accommodate up to eight simultaneous channels of trace-hook activity, which are numbered 0–7. Channel 0 is always used for system events, but application events can also use it. The other seven channels, called *generic channels*, can be used for tracing application-program activity.

When trace is started, channel 0 is used by default. A **trace** *−n* command (where *n* is the channel number) starts trace to a generic channel. Use of the generic channels has some limitations.

- The interface to the generic channels costs more CPU time than the interface to channel 0 because of the need to distinguish between channels and because generic channels record variable-length records.
- Events recorded on channel 0 and on the generic channels can be correlated only by time stamp, not by sequence, so there may be situations in which it is not possible to determine which event occurred first.

Macros for Recording Trace Events

There is a macro to record each possible type of event record. The macros are defined in **/usr/include/sys/trcmacros.h**. The event IDs are defined in **/usr/include/sys/trchkid.h**. These two files should be included by any program that is recording trace events.

The macros to record events on channel 0 with a time stamp are:

TRCHKL0T(*hw*)

TRCHKL1T(*hw,D1*)

TRCHKL2T(*hw,D1,D2*)

TRCHKL3T(*hw,D1,D2,D3*)

TRCHKL4T(*hw,D1,D2,D3,D4*)

TRCHKL5T(*hw,D1,D2,D3,D4,D5*)

Similarly, to record events on channel 0 without a time stamp, use:

TRCHKL0(*hw*)

TRCHKL1(*hw,D1*)

TRCHKL2(*hw,D1,D2*)

TRCHKL3(*hw,D1,D2,D3*)

TRCHKL4(*hw,D1,D2,D3,D4*)

TRCHKL5(*hw,D1,D2,D3,D4,D5*)

The *type* field of the trace event record is set to the value that corresponds to the macro used, regardless of the value of those 4 bits in the *hw* parameter.

There are only two macros to record events to one of the generic channels (1–7). These are as follows:

TRCGEN(*ch,hw,D1,len,buf*)

TRCGENT(*ch,hw,D1,len,buf*)

These macros record in the event stream specified by the channel parameter (*ch*) a hook word (*hw*), a data word (*D1*) and *len* bytes from the user's data segment beginning at the location specified by *buf*.

Use of Event IDs

The event ID in a trace record identifies that record as belonging to a particular class of records. The event ID is the basis on which the trace mechanism records or ignores trace hooks, as well as the basis on which the **trcrpt** command includes or excludes trace records in the formatted report.

Event IDs are 12 bits (three hexadecimal digits) for a possible 4096 IDs. Event IDs that are permanently left in and shipped with code are permanently assigned by IBM to avoid duplication. To allow users to define events in their environments or during development, the range of event IDs from hex 010 through hex 0FF has been set aside for temporary use. Users can freely use IDs in this range *in their own environment* (that is, any set of systems within which the users are prepared to ensure that the same event ID is not used ambiguously).

Warning: It is important that users who make use of this event range do not let the code leave their environment. If you ship code instrumented with temporary hook IDs to an environment in which you do not control the use of IDs, you risk collision with other programs that already use the same IDs in that environment.

Event IDs should be conserved because there are so few of them, but they can be extended by using the 16-bit Data Field. This yields a possible 65536 distinguishable events for every formal hook ID. The only reason to have a unique ID is that an ID is the level at which collection and report filtering are available in the trace facility.

A user-added event can be formatted by the **trcrpt** command if there is a stanza for the event in the specified trace format file. The trace format file is an editable ASCII file—see "Syntax of Stanzas in the Trace Format File", below.

Examples of Coding and Formatting Events

The following example shows the use of trace events to time the execution of a program loop:

```
#include <sys/trcctl.h>
#include <sys/trcmacros.h>
#include <sys/trchkid.h>
char *ctl_file = "/dev/systrctl";
int ctlfd;
int i;
main()
{
  printf("configuring trace collection \n");
  if (trcstart("-ad")){
    perror("trcstart");
    exit(1);
  }
```

```
    printf("opening the trace device  \n");
    if((ctlfd = open(ctl_file,0))<0){
      perror(ctl_file);
      exit(1);
    }

    printf("turning  trace on \n");
    if(ioctl(ctlfd,TRCON,0)){
      perror("TRCON");
      exit(1);
    }

    for(i=1;i<11;i++){
      TRCHKL1T(HKWD_USER1,i);

      /* The code being measured goes here. The interval */
      /* between occurrences of HKWD_USER1 in the trace  */
      /* file is the total time for one iteration.       */
    }

    printf("turning trace off\n");
    if(ioctl(ctlfd,TRCSTOP,0)){
      perror("TRCOFF");
      exit(1);
    }
    printf("stopping the trace daemon \n");
    if (trcstop(0)){
      perror("trcstop");
      exit(1);
    }

  exit(0);
}
```

When you compile the sample program, you need to link to the **librts.a** library as follows:

```
$ xlc -O3 sample.c -o sample -l rts
```

HKWD_USER1 is event ID 010 hexadecimal (you can verify this by looking at **/usr/include/sys/trchkid.h**). The report facility does not know how to format the HKWD_USER1 event, unless rules are provided in the trace format file. The following example of a stanza for HKWD_USER1 could be used.

```
# User event HKWD_USER1 Formatting Rules Stanza
# An example that will format the event usage of the sample program
010 1.0 L=APPL "USER EVENT - HKWD_USER1" O2.0        \n \
              "The # of loop iterations =" U4        \n \
              "The elapsed time of the last loop = " \
                endtimer(0x010,0x010) starttimer(0x010,0x010)
```

When entering the example stanza, do not modify the master format file **/etc/trcfmt**, but instead make a copy and keep it in your own directory (assume you name it `mytrcfmt`). When you run the sample program, the raw event data is captured in the default log file since no other log file was specified to the **trcstart** subroutine. You probably want to filter the output report to get only your events. To do this, run the **trcrpt** command as follows:

```
trcrpt -d 010 -t mytrcfmt -O "exec=on" > sample.rpt
```

You can browse `sample.rpt` to see the result.

Syntax for Stanzas in the Trace Format File

The intent of the trace format file is to provide rules for presentation and display of the expected data for each event ID. This allows new events to be formatted without changing the report facility. Rules for new events are simply added to the format file. The syntax of the rules provides flexibility in the presentation of the data.

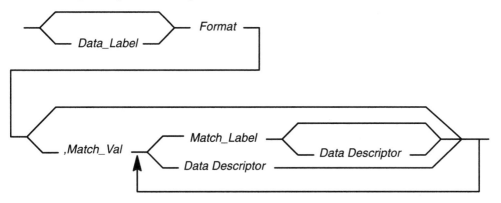

where a *Data_Descriptor* has the syntax:

Figure 33: Syntax of a Stanza in a Trace Format File

The figure "Syntax of a Stanza in a Trace Format File" illustrates the syntax for a given event. A trace format stanza can be as long as required to describe the rules for any particular event. The stanza can be continued to the next line by terminating the present line with a '\' character. The fields are:

event_id   Each stanza begins with the three-digit hexadecimal event ID that the stanza describes, followed by a space.

V.R   Describes the version (*V*) and release (*R*) in which the event was first assigned. Any integers will work for *V* and *R*, and users may want to keep their own tracking mechanism.

L=   Specifies text indentation level. The text description of an event can begin at various indentation levels. This improves the readability of the report output. The indentation levels correspond to the level at which the system is executing. The recognized levels are application level (**APPL**), a transitioning system call (**SVC**), kernel level (**KERN**), and interrupt (**INT**).

event_label Specifies an ASCII text string that describes the overall use of the event ID. This is used by the **–j** option of the **trcrpt** command to provide a listing of events and their first-level description. The *event_label* also appears in the formatted output for the event unless the *event_label* starts with an @ character.

\n The event stanza describes how to parse, label, and present the data contained in an event record. The **\n** (newline) function can be imbedded in the event stanza to force presentation of the data to a new line. This allows the presentation of the data for an event to be several lines long.

\t Inserts a tab at the point where it is encountered in parsing the description. This is similar to the way the **\n** function inserts new lines. Spacing can also be inserted by spaces in the *data_label* or *match_label* fields.

starttimer(*timerID***), endtimer(***timerID***)**

The *timerID* is a unique identifier that associates a particular **starttimer** with a later **endtimer** that has the same identifier. By (unenforced) convention, the *timerID* is of the form:

ID of starting event, ID of ending event

When the report facility encounters a **starttimer** directive while parsing an event, it associates the starting event's time with the specified *timerID*. When an **endtimer** with the same *timerID* is encountered, the report facility shows the delta time (in brackets) that elapsed between the starting event and ending event. The begin- and end-system-call events make use of this capability. On the return from a system-call event, a delta time indicates how long the system call took.

data_descriptor Describes how the data should be consumed, labeled, and presented by the report facility. The syntax of the *data_descriptor* field is expanded in the second part of the figure "Syntax of a Stanza in a Trace Format File" on page 225. The various fields of the *data_descriptor* are described as follows:

format The user can think of the report facility as having a pointer into the data portion of an event. This data pointer is initialized to point to the beginning of the event data (the 16-bit data field in the hook word). The *format* field describes how much data the report facility should consume from this point and how the data should be considered. For example, a *format* field of **B***m.n* tells the report facility to consume *m* bytes and *n* bits of data and to consider it as binary data. (The possible format fields are described in following sections.) If the format field is not followed by a comma, the report facility outputs the consumed data in the format specified. If, however, the format field is followed by a comma, it signifies that the data is not to be displayed but instead compared against the following *match_values*. The data descriptor associated with the matching *match_value* is then applied to the remainder of the data.

data_label   The *data_label* is an ASCII string that can optionally precede the output of data consumed by the format field.

match_value   The *match_value* is data of the same format described by the preceding format fields. Several *match_value*s typically follow a format field that is being matched. The successive match fields are separated by commas. The last match value is not followed by a comma. A * is used as a pattern-matching character to match anything. A pattern-matching character is frequently used as the last *match_value* field to specify default rules if the preceding *match_values* field did not occur.

match_label   The *match_label* is an ASCII string that will be output for the corresponding match.

All of the possible format fields are described in the comments of the **/etc/trcfmt** file. A brief introduction to the possibilities is provided here:

Format Field Descriptions

A*m.n*   Specifies that *m* bytes of data should be consumed as ASCII text and that the text should be displayed in an output field that is *n* characters wide. The data pointer is moved *m* bytes.

S1, S2, S4   Specifies left-justified string. The length of the field is defined as 1 byte (**S1**), 2 bytes (**S2**), or 4 bytes (**S4**). The data pointer is moved accordingly.

B*m.n*   Specifies binary data of *m* bytes and *n* bits. The data pointer is moved accordingly.

X*m*   Specifies hexadecimal data of *m* bytes. The data pointer is moved accordingly.

D2, D4   Specifies signed decimal format. Data length of 2 (**D2**) bytes or 4 (**D4**) bytes is consumed.

U2, U4   Specifies unsigned decimal format. Data length of 2 or 4 bytes is consumed.

F4, F8   Specifies floating point of 4 or 8 bytes.

G*m.n*   Specifies that the data pointer should be positioned *m* bytes and *n* bits into the data.

O*m.n*   Omits, from the current location of the data pointer, the next *m* bytes and *n* bits.

R*m*   Reverses the data pointer *m* bytes.

Some macros are provided that can be used as format fields to quickly access data. For example:

$HD, $D1, $D2, $D3, $D4, $D5

Access the 16-bit data field of the hook word and data words 1 through

5 of the event record, respectively. The data pointer is not moved. The data accessed by a macro is hexadecimal by default. A macro can be cast to a different data type (X, D, U, B) by using a "%" character followed by the new format code. For example:

```
$D1%B2.3
```

This macro causes data word 1 to be accessed but to be considered as 2 bytes and 3 bits of binary data.

The comments in the **/etc/trcfmt** file describe other format and macro possibilities and describe how a user can define additional macros.

12

Performance Diagnostic Tool (PDT)

PDT assesses the current state of a system and tracks changes in workload and performance. It attempts to identify incipient problems and suggest solutions before the problems become critical. PDT is available only on AIX Version 4.1.

For the most part, PDT functions with no required user input. PDT data collection and reporting are easily enabled, and then no further administrator activity is required. Periodically, data is collected and recorded for historical analysis, and a report is produced and mailed to the adm userid. Normally, only the most significant apparent problems are recorded on the report. If there are no significant problems, that fact is reported. PDT can also be customized to direct its report to a different user or to report apparent problems of a lower severity level.

Structure of PDT

As shown in the figure "PDT Component Structure," the PDT application consists of three components:

- The collection component comprises a set of programs that periodically collect and record data.
- The retention component periodically reviews the collected data and discards data that is obsolete.
- The reporting component periodically produces a diagnostic report from the current set of historical data.

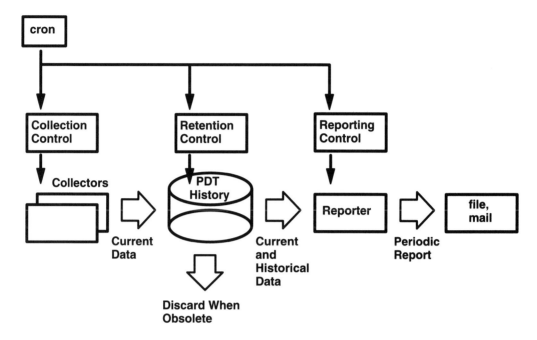

Figure 34: PDT Component Structure

PDT considers various aspects of a system's configuration, availability, and delivered performance in making its assessment. In particular, areas of configuration imbalance are sought out (such as I/O-configuration balance, paging-configuration balance) as well as other configuration problems (for example, disks not allocated to volume groups). A wide variety of trending assessments is made, including file sizes, file-system sizes, paging-area usage, network delays and workload-related delays.

Scope of PDT Analysis

PDT collects configuration, availability, workload, and performance data on a daily basis. This data is maintained in a historical record. Approximately a month's worth of data is kept in this way. Also on a daily basis, PDT generates a diagnostic report. The report is mailed to user adm.

In addition to mailing the report, PDT stores a copy in **/var/perf/tmp/PDT_RE-PORT.** Before the new report is written, the previous report is renamed **/var/perf/tmp/PDT_REPORT.last.**

While many common system performance problems are of a specific nature—a system may have too little memory—PDT also attempts to apply some general concepts of well-performing systems to its search for problems.

Balanced Use of Resources

In general, if there are several resources of the same type, then a balanced use of those resources produces better performance.

- Comparable numbers of physical volumes (disks) on each disk adapter
- Paging space distributed across multiple physical volumes
- Roughly equal measured load on different physical volumes

Operation within Bounds

Resources have limits to their use. Trends that would attempt to exceed those limits should be detected and reported.

- A disk drive cannot be utilized more than 100% of the time.
- File and file-system sizes cannot exceed the allocated space.

Identify Workload Trends

Trends can indicate a change in the nature of the workload as well as increases in the amount of resource used:

- Number of users logged on.
- Total number of processes
- CPU-idle percentage

Error-Free Operation

Hardware or software errors often produce performance problems.

- Check the hardware and software error logs.
- Report bad VMM pages.

Changes Should be Investigated

New workloads or processes that start to consume resources may be the first sign of a problem.

- Appearance of new processes that consume lots of CPU or memory resources.

Appropriate Setting of System Parameters

There are many parameters in a system. Are all of them set appropriately?

- Is **maxuproc** set too low?
- How about the memory-load-control-parameter settings?

The PDT report consists of several sections (see the example, below). After the header information, the Alerts section contains identified violations of the concepts noted above. If no alerts are found, the section is not present in the report. The next two sections are for upward trends and downward trends. These two sections focus on problem anticipation, rather than on the identification of existing problems. In general, the same concepts are applied—but with a view toward projecting when violations will occur. If no upward or downward trends are detected, these sections are not present in the report.

Sample PDT Report

```
Performance Diagnostic Facility 1.0

Report printed: Tue Aug 3 10:00:01 1993
Host name: test.austin.ibm.com
Range of analysis is from:  Hour 16 on Monday, July 5th, 1993
to: Hour 9 on Tuesday, August 3rd, 1993.

[To disable/modify/enable collection or reporting, execute the pdt_config
script]

-------------------- Alerts --------------------
  I/O BALANCE
    - Phys. vol. hdisk0 is significantly busier than others
        volume cd0, mean util. = 0.00
        volume hdisk0, mean util. = 11.75
        volume hdisk1, mean util. = 0.00
  PAGE SPACE AND MEMORY
    - Mean page space used = 46.85 MB
        System has 32MB memory; may be inadequate.
        Consider further investigations to determine if memory is a
bottleneck

------------------ Upward Trends ----------------
  FILE SYSTEMS
    - File system hd2 (/usr) PERCENTAGE FULL
        now, 45.00 % full, and growing an avg. of 2.0 %/day
        At this rate, hd2 will be full in about 15 days
  PAGE SPACE
    - Page space hd6 USE
        now, 44.80 MB and growing an avg. of 1.81 MB/day
        At this rate, hd6 will be full in about 30 days
  WORKLOAD TRACKING
    - Workload nusers indicator is increasing;
        now 23, and growing an avg. of 1.2 per day
```

```
---------------------- System Health ---------------
SYSTEM HEALTH
  -  Current process state breakdown:
       2.00 [ 3.0 %] : waiting for the cpu
      64.00 [ 97.0 %] : sleeping
      66.00 = TOTAL
      [based on 1 measurement consisting of 10 2-second samples]

----------------- Summary -----------------------
  This is a severity level 2 report
  Further details are available at severity levels > 2
```

In the above example, the header section indicates the release number of PDT, the date the report was printed, the host from which the data was collected, and the range of dates of the data that fed the analysis.

The next section, Alerts, indicates suspicious configuration and load conditions. In the example, it appears that, of the three disks on the system, one is getting essentially all of the I/O activity. Clearly, I/O load is not distributed in such a way as to best make use of the available resources. The next message, PAGE SPACE AND MEMORY, suggests that the system may be underconfigured in memory.

The Upward Trends section in the example identifies two possible trends. The first is that the file system on logical volume **hd2** (the **/usr** file system) is growing at an average rate of 2% per day. An estimated date at which the file system will be full is provided, based on an assumption of continued linear growth.

The second trend is the apparent systematic growth in the utilization level of one of the paging areas. Information about its rate of increase and expected fill-date is given. Knowledge of growing file systems and paging spaces approaching their limits is potentially very important (especially if the rate is high or the expected fill-date is imminent), since a full file system or paging space can cause system or application failure.

The third trend is a change in one of the workload indicators. The following indicators are tracked by PDT for trends:

Keyword	Indicator
nusers	Total number of logged-on users.
loadavg	15-minute load average.
nprocesses	Total number of processes.
STAT_A	Number of active processes.
STAT_W	Number of swapped processes.
STAT_Z	Number of zombie processes.
STAT_I	Number of idle processes.
STAT_T	Number of processes stopped after receiving a signal.
STAT_x	Number of processes reported by the **ps** command as being in state x, where x is a state not listed above.
cp	Time to copy a 40KB file.
idle_pct_cpu0	CPU-idle percentage.
idle_pct_avg	CPU-idle percentage.

The next section, System Health, uses a number of the workload indicators to assess how processes are spending their time.

The final section of the report (Summary) indicates the selected severity level, and whether or not additional detail can be obtained by changing that level. (The highest severity level is 1, which is the default level reported. The lowest level is 3.)

Any message (excluding header and summary information) occurring in the PDT report should be investigated. The indicated problem should be corrected or an explanation for the condition obtained. Possible responses to specific messages are covered in "Responding to PDT-Report Messages" on page 238.

Installing and Enabling PDT

PDT is installed via **installp** as the **bos.perf.diag_tool** option of the AIX 4.1 BOS LPP.

PDT must be enabled in order to begin data collection and report writing. PDT is enabled by executing the script **/usr/sbin/perf/diag_tool/pdt_config.** Only the root userid is permitted to run this script. When executed, the following message is displayed:

```
# /usr/sbin/perf/diag_tool/pdt_config
_____PDT customization menu_____

1) show current   PDT report recipient and severity level
2) modify/enable PDT reporting
3) disable        PDT reporting
4) modify/enable PDT collection
5) disable        PDT collection
6) de-install     PDT
7) exit pdt_config
Please enter a number:
```

When you respond with 4, default PDT collection and reporting is enabled. The crontab entry for user adm is updated to add the PDT entries. Actual collection occurs when the cron jobs are run by **cron**. Respond with 7 to terminate the **pdt_config** program.

Option 5 should be selected to disable collection.

Customizing PDT

Certain aspects of PDT can be customized. For example, any user can be designated as the regular recipient of PDT reports, and the retention period for data in PDT's historical record can be modified. All customization is performed either by modifying one of the PDT files in **/var/perf/cfg/diag_tool/** or by executing the **/usr/sbin/perf/diag_tool/ pdt_config** script.

We recommend that no changes be made until after PDT has produced several reports, and a certain familiarity with PDT has been acquired.

Changing the PDT Report Recipient and Severity Level

By default, PDT reports are generated with severity level 1. This means that only the most serious problems are identified. There are other severity levels (2,3) at which more detailed information is frequently available. Further, whenever a PDT report is produced, it is mailed to userid `adm`. It might be desirable to have the report mailed elsewhere or not mailed at all.

Both of these parameters are controlled with the **pdt_config** script. The following dialog changes the user and the severity level :

```
# /usr/sbin/perf/diag_tool/pdt_config
_____PDT customization menu_____

1) show current  PDT report recipient and severity level
2) modify/enable PDT reporting
3) terminate     PDT reporting
4) modify/enable PDT collection
5) terminate     PDT collection
6) de-install    PDT
7) exit pdt_config
Please enter a number: 1
adm 1
Please enter a number: 2
enter id@host for recipient of report : rsmith
enter severity level for report (1-3): 2
Please enter a number: 1
rsmith 2
Please enter a number: 7
#
```

In the above example, the recipient is changed to user `rsmith`, and the severity is changed to 2. This means that user `rsmith` will receive the PDT report, and that both severity 1 and 2 messages will be included. Note the use of option 1 to determine the current PDT report recipient and report severity level.

To terminate reporting (but allow collection to continue), option 3 is selected, for example:

```
Please enter a number: 3
Please enter a number: 1
reporting has been disabled (file .reporting.list not found).
Please enter a number: 7
#
```

PDT Severity Levels

The following lists indicate the possible problems associated with each severity level. Remember that selecting Severity n results in the reporting of all problems of severity less than or equal to n.

Severity 1 Problems

- JFS file system becomes unavailable
- JFS file system nearly full
- Physical volume not allocated to a volume group
- All paging spaces defined on one physical volume
- System appears to have too little memory for current workload.

- Page space nearly full
- Possible problems in the settings of load control parameters
- VMM-detected bad memory frames
- Any host in **.nodes** becomes unreachable

Severity 2 Problems

- Imbalance in the I/O configuration (e.g., disks per adapter)
- Imbalance in allocation of paging space on physical volumes with paging space
- Fragmentation of a paging space in a volume group
- Significant imbalance in measured I/O load to physical volumes
- New process is identified as a heavy memory or CPU consumer
- A file in **.files** exhibits systematic growth (or decline) in size
- A file system or page space exhibits systematic growth (or decline) in space utilization
- A host in **.nodes** exhibits degradation in **ping** delays or packet loss percentage
- A getty process consumes too much CPU time
- A process with high CPU or memory consumption exhibits systematic growth (or decline) in resource use

Severity 3 Messages:

- Severity 3 messages provide additional detail about problems identified at severity levels 1 and 2. This includes the data-collection characteristics, such as number of samples, for severity 1 and 2 messages.

Obtaining a PDT Report on Demand

As an alternative to using the periodic report, any user can request a current report from the existing data by executing **/usr/sbin/perf/diag_tool/pdt_report** [*SeverityNum*]. The report is produced with the given severity (if none is provided, *SeverityNum* defaults to 1) and written to **stdout**. Generating a report in this way does not cause any change to the **/var/perf/tmp/PDT_REPORT** or **/var/perf/tmp/PDT_REPORT.last** files.

PDT Error Reporting

Errors can occur within each of the different PDT components. In general, an error does not terminate PDT. Instead, a message is output to PDT's standard error file: **/var/perf/tmp/.stderr**, and that phase of processing terminates.

Users experiencing unexpected behavior, such as the PDT report not being produced as expected, should examine **/var/perf/tmp/.stderr**.

De-Installing PDT

It is not possible to de-install PDT directly using **pdt_config**, but if option 6 is requested, a message describes the steps necessary to remove PDT from the system:

```
# /usr/sbin/perf/diag_tool/pdt_config
_____PDT customization menu_____

1) show current  PDT report recipient and severity level
2) modify/enable PDT reporting
3) terminate     PDT reporting
4) modify/enable PDT collection
5) terminate     PDT collection
6) de-install    PDT
7) exit pdt_config
Please enter a number: 6

  PDT is installed as package bos.perf.diag_tool in the bos lpp.
  Use the installp facility to remove the package
Please enter a number: 7
#
```

Modifying the List of Files Monitored by PDT

PDT analyzes files and directories for systematic growth in size. It examines only those files and directories listed in the file **/var/perf/cfg/diag_tool/.files**. The format of the **.files** file is one file/directory name per line. The default content is:

```
/usr/adm/wtmp
/var/spool/qdaemon/
/var/adm/ras/
/tmp/
```

You can modify this file with an editor to track files and directories that are important to your system.

Modifying the List of Hosts That PDT Monitors

PDT tracks the average **ping** delay to hosts whose names are listed in **/var/perf/cfg/diag_tool/.nodes**. This file is not shipped with PDT (which means that no host analysis is performed by default), but may be created by the administrator. The format of the **.nodes** file is one host name per line in the file.

Changing the Historical-Record Retention Period

Periodically, a retention shell script is run that discards entries in PDT's historical record that are older than the designated retention period. The retention of all data is governed by the same retention policy. This policy is described in the **/var/perf/cfg/diag_tool/.reten-tion.list** file. The default **.retention.list** content is:

```
* * * 35
```

which causes all data to be retained no more than 35 days. The number 35 can be replaced by any unsigned integer.

PDT uses the historical record to assess trends and identify system changes. Extending the retention period increases the scope of this analysis at the cost of additional disk storage and PDT processing time.

PDT's historical record is maintained in **/var/perf/tmp/.SM**. The retention script creates a copy of this file in **/var/perf/tmp/.SM.last** prior to performing the retention operation. In addition, historical data that is discarded is appended to **/var/perf/tmp/.SM.discards**.

The existence of **/var/perf/tmp/.SM.last** provides limited backup, but the administrator should ensure that the **/var/perf/tmp/.SM** file is regularly backed up. If the file is lost, PDT continues to function, but without the historical information. Over time, the historical record will grow again as new data is collected.

Modifying the Collection, Retention, and Reporting Times

Collection, reporting and retention are driven by three entries in user adm's **cron** table. Collection occurs on every weekday at 9 a.m. Reporting occurs every weekday at 10 a.m. The retention analysis is performed once a week, on Saturday evening at 9 p.m. The cron entries (created by executing the **/usr/sbin/perf/diag_tool/pdt_config** script and selecting option 2) are shown below:

```
0  9 * * 1-5   /usr/sbin/perf/diag_tool/Driver_ daily
0 10 * * 1-5   /usr/sbin/perf/diag_tool/Driver_ daily2
0 21 * * 6     /usr/sbin/perf/diag_tool/Driver_ offweekly
```

While it is possible to modify these times by editing adm's **cron** table, this is not recommended.

Responding to PDT-Report Messages

PDT identifies many types of problems. Responses to these indications depends on the individual organization's available resources and set of priorities. The following samples suggest some possibilities:

Problem: **JFS file system becomes unavailable**
Response: Investigate why file system is unavailable.
Useful cmds: **lsfs** (to determine file system status)

Problem: **JFS file system nearly full**
Response: Look for large files in the file system, possibly caused by a runaway process. Has this file system exhibited long term growth trend (look at the rest of the PDT report—or past PDT reports—to check this)?
Useful cmds: **du, ls, lvedit**

Problem: **Physical volume not allocated to a volume group**
Response: Volume should be defined in a volume group; otherwise, it is inaccessible to AIX and is being wasted.
Useful cmds: **lspv** (to confirm that the volume is not allocated)
             smit (to manipulate volume groups)

Problem:	**All paging spaces defined on one physical volume**
Response:	The system has more than one physical volume, yet all paging space is defined on a single volume. If the system experiences paging, this configuration will result in reduced performance.
Useful cmds:	**smit** (to modify paging spaces)
Problem:	**Apparently too little memory for current workload**
Response:	If the system is paging heavily, more memory may be required on the system for good performance.
Useful cmds:	**lsps −a**, **vmstat**
Problem:	**Page space nearly full**
Response:	The system's paging space may need to be enlarged, unless the problem is due to a process with a memory leak, in which case that process should be identified and the application fixed.
Useful cmds:	**ps aucg** (to examine process activity)
	smit (to modify page space characteristics)
Problem:	**Possible problems in the settings of load control parameters**
Response:	The memory-load-control parameters are evaluated in relation to current paging activity. For example, if thrashing is occurring and load control is not enabled, it may be appropriate to enable load control.
Useful cmds	**schedtune**
Problem:	**VMM-detected bad memory frames**
Response:	It may be necessary to have the memory analyzed. Compare the amount of installed memory with the memory actually accessible; if the latter is less than the former, then bad memory has been identified.
	You can use **/usr/sbin/perf/diag_tool/getvmparms** and look at the value of numframes to determine the actual number of 4KB memory frames.
Useful cmds:	**lscfg | grep mem** (to obtain installed memory size in MB)
Problem:	**Any host in .nodes becomes unreachable**
Response:	Determine if problem is with current host (has a change in the **/etc/hosts** file been made?), with the remote host (is it down?), or with the network (is the nameserver down?).
Useful cmds:	**ping**
Problem:	**Imbalance in the I/O configuration (number of disks per adapter)**
Response:	Consider moving disks around so that an individual SCSI adapter is not overloaded.
Useful cmds:	**lscfg** (to examine the current configuration)
	iostat (to determine if the actual load on the adapters is out of balance)
Problem:	**Imbalance in allocation of paging space on physical volumes with paging space**
Response:	Consider making paging spaces the same size, except for a few extra megabytes (say, 4) on the primary paging space (**hd6**). A substantial

imbalance in the sizes of paging spaces can cause performance problems.

Useful cmds: **smit**

Problem: **Fragmentation of a paging space in a volume group**

Response: Paging performance is better if paging areas are contiguous on a physical volume. However, when paging areas are enlarged, it is possible to create fragments that are scattered across the disk surface.

Useful cmds: **lspv –p hdisk***n* for each physical volume in the volume group. Look for more than one PP Range with the same LVNAME and a TYPE of "paging."

Problem: **Significant imbalance in measured I/O load to physical volumes**

Response: If one physical volume seems to be getting little I/O activity, consider moving data from busier physical volumes onto less busy volumes. In general, the more evenly the I/O is distributed, the better the performance.

Useful cmds: **iostat –d 2 20** (to view the current distribution of I/O across physical volumes)

Problem: **New process is a heavy consumer of memory or CPU**

Response: Top CPU and memory consumers are regularly identified by PDT. If any of these processes haven't been seen before, they are highlighted in a problem report. These processes should be examined for unusual behavior. Note that PDT simply looks at the process ID. If a known heavy user terminates, then is resumed (with a different process id), it will be identified here as a NEW heavy user.

Useful cmds: **ps aucg** (To view all processes and their activity)

Problem: **Any file in .files exhibits systematic growth (or decline) in size**

Response: Look at the current size. Consider the projected growth rate. What user or application is generating the data? For example, the **/var/adm/wtmp** file is liable to grow unbounded. If it gets too large, login times can increase. In some cases, the solution is to delete the file. In most cases, it is important to identify the user causing the growth and work with that user to correct the problem.

Useful cmds: **ls –al** (to view file/directory sizes)

Problem: **Any file system or paging space exhibits systematic growth (or decline) in space used**

Response: Consider the projected growth rate and expected time to fill. It may be necessary to enlarge the file system (or page space). On the other hand, the growth may be an undesirable effect (for example, a process having a memory leak).

Useful cmds: **smit** (to manipulate file systems/page spaces)
ps aucg, **svmon** (to view process virtual memory activity)
filemon (to view file system activity)

Problem:	**Degradation in ping response time or packet loss percentage for any host in .nodes**
Response:	Is the host in question experiencing performance problems? Is the network having performance problems?
Useful cmds:	**ping**, **rlogin**, **rsh** (to time known workloads on remote host)
Problem:	**A getty process that consumes too much CPU time**
Response:	Getty processes that use more than just a few percent of the CPU may be in error. It is possible in certain situations for these processes to consume system CPU, even though no users are actually logged on. In general, the solution is to terminate the process.
Useful cmds:	**ps aucg** (to see how much CPU is being used)
Problem:	**A process that is a top consumer of CPU or memory resources exhibits systematic growth or decline in consumption**
Response:	Known large consumers of CPU and memory resources are tracked over time to see if their demands grow. As major consumers, a steady growth in their demand is of interest from several perspectives. If the growth is normal, this represents useful capacity planning information. If the growth is unexpected, then the workload should be evaluated for a change (or a chronic problem, such as a memory leak).
Useful cmds:	**ps aucg**
Problem:	**maxuproc indicated as being possibly too low for a particular userid**
Response:	it is likely that this user is hitting the **maxuproc** threshold. **maxuproc** is a system-wide parameter that limits the number of processes that nonroot users are allowed to have simultaneously active. If the limit is too low, the user's work can be delayed or terminated. On the other hand, the user might be accidently creating more processes than needed or appropriate. Further investigation is warranted in either case. The user should be consulted in order to understand more clearly what is happening.
Useful cmds:	**lsattr –E –l sys0	grep maxuproc** to determine the current value of **maxuproc** (although it is also reported directly in the PDT message). **chdev –l sys0 –a maxuproc=100** to change **maxuproc** to 100 (for example). Root authority is required.
Problem:	**A WORKLOAD TRACKING indicator shows an upward trend.**
Response:	The response depends on which workload indicator shows the trend: **loadavg** – 15-minute load average In general, the level of contention in the system is growing. Examine the rest of the PDT report for indicators of system bottlenecks (for example, substantial page space use may indicate a memory shortage; I/O imbalances may indicate that the I/O subsystem requires attention). **nusers** – total number of logged users

The number of users on the system is growing. This is important from a capacity planning perspective. Is the growth expected? Can it be explained?

nprocesses – total number of processes

The total number of processes on the system is growing. Are there users bumping up against the maxuproc limitation? Perhaps there are "runaway" applications forking too many processes.

STAT_A – number of active processes

A trend here indicates processes are spending more time waiting for the CPU.

STAT_W – number of swapped processes

A trend here indicates that processes are contending excessively for memory.

STAT_Z – number of zombie processes

Zombies should not stay around for a long time. If the number of zombies on a system is growing, this may be cause for concern.

STAT_I – number of idle processes

This might not be of much concern.

STAT_T – number of processes stopped after receiving a signal

A trend here might indicate a programming error.

STAT_x – (where x is any valid character in the **ps** command output indicating a process state that has not been listed above)

The interpretation of a trend here depends on the the meaning of the character x.

cp – time required to copy a 40KB file

A trend in the time to do a file copy suggests that degradation in the I/O subsystem is evident.

idle_pct_cpu0 – idle percentage for processor 0

An upward trend in the idle percentage might indicate increased contention in non-CPU resources such as paging or I/O. Such an increase is of interest because it suggests the CPU resource is not being well-utilized.

idle_pct_avg – average idle percentage for all processors

An upward trend in the idle percentage might indicate increased contention in non-CPU resources such as paging or I/O. Such an increase is of interest because it suggests the CPU resource is not being well-utilized.

13

Handling a Possible AIX Performance Bug

If you believe that you have found a possible performance problem in AIX, there are tools and procedures for reporting the problem and supplying problem-analysis data. They are intended to ensure that you get a prompt and accurate response with a minimum of effort and time on your part.

Measuring the Baseline

Performance problems are often reported right after some change to the system's hardware or software. Unless there is a pre-change baseline measurement with which to compare post-change performance, quantification of the problem is impossible. Still better would be collection of a full set of performance and configuration information using the PerfPMR package, as recommended in "Check Before You Change" on page 80.

Having the Performance Diagnostic Tool (PDT) installed and operational also provides a baseline of overall system performance.

Reporting the Problem

You should report suspected AIX performance problems to the IBM Software Service organization. Use your normal software problem-reporting channel. If you are not familiar with the correct problem-reporting channel for your organization, check with your IBM representative.

When you report the problem, you should supply the following basic information:

- A description of the problem that can be used to search the problem-history database to see if a similar problem has already been reported.
- What aspect of your analysis led you to conclude that the problem is due to a defect in AIX?
- What is the hardware/software configuration in which the problem is occurring?

- Is the problem confined to a single system, or does it affect multiple systems?
- What are the models, memory sizes, and number and size of disks on the affected system(s)?
- What kinds of LAN and other communications media are connected to the system(s)?
- Does the overall configuration include non-AIX systems? Non-UNIX systems?

- What are the characteristics of the program or workload that is experiencing the problem?
  - Does an analysis with **time**, **iostat**, and **vmstat** indicate that it CPU-limited or I/O-limited?
  - Are the workloads being run on the affected system(s): workstation, server, multiuser, or a mixture?
- What are the performance objectives that are not being met?
  - Is the primary objective in terms of console or terminal response time, throughput, or real-time responsiveness?
  - Were the objectives derived from measurements on another AIX system? If so, what was its configuration?

If this is the first report of the problem, you will receive a PMR number for use in identifying any additional data you supply and for future reference.

You will probably be asked to provide data to help IBM analyze the problem. An IBM-provided tools package called PerfPMR can collect the necessary data. On AIX Version 3.2.5, PerfPMR is an informal tool available from your IBM representative. On AIX Version 4.1, PerfPMR is an optionally installable package on the AIX Base Operating System distribution medium.

Obtaining and Installing AIX Version 3.2.5 PerfPMR

Your IBM representative can obtain a copy of AIX Version 3.2.5 PerfPMR on suitable media. To install PerfPMR you:

- Log in as `root` or use the **su** command to obtain root authority.
- Create the **perfpmr** directory and move to that directory (this example assumes the directory built is under **/tmp**).

```
# cd /tmp
# mkdir perfpmr
# cd perfpmr
```

- Copy the compressed **tar** file from diskette (this example assumes the diskette drive used is **fd0**):

```
# tar -xvf/dev/fd0 perfpmr.tarbinz
```

- Rename the compressed **tar** file:

```
# mv perfpmr.tarbinz perfpmr.tarbin.Z
```

- Uncompress the **tar** file with:

```
# uncompress perfpmr.tarbin.Z
```

- Extract the shell scripts from the **tar** file with:

```
# tar -xvf perfpmr.tarbin
```

- Install the shell scripts with:

```
# ./Install
```

Installing AIX Version 4.1 PerfPMR

If you are not sure whether or not PerfPMR is installed on the system, enter:

```
# lslpp -lI bos.perf.pmr
```

To install PerfPMR from a high-density tape, enter:

```
# installp -acd/dev/rmt0.1 bos.perf.pmr
```

If the Base Operating System is on low-density tape, use `rmt0.5` as the device.

The installation process places the PerfPMR package in a directory called **/usr/sbin/perf/pmr**. The package takes approximately 200KB of disk space.

Problem-Analysis Data

All of the following items should be included when the supporting information for the PMR is first gathered:

- A means of reproducing the problem
    - If possible, a program or shell script that demonstrates the problem should be included.
    - At a minimum, a detailed description of the conditions under which the problem occurs is needed.
- Data collected by the PerfPMR tools
    - On each system involved
    - At the same time
    - While the performance problem is occurring
- The application experiencing the problem
    - If the application is, or depends on, a software product, the exact version and release of that product should be identified, even if the software is not an IBM product.
    - If the source code of a user-written application cannot be released, the exact set of compiler parameters used to create the executable should be documented.

Capturing the Data

To capture and package the data in usable form, perform the following steps on each of the systems involved with the problem. If possible, step 6 should be performed on all of the systems at (approximately) the same time.

1. Login as, or **su** to, `root`.
2. PerfPMR captures more information if the **tprof**, **filemon**, and **netpmon** performance tools are available. In AIX Version 4.1, these tools are packaged as

part of the Performance Toolbox for AIX. To determine whether the performance tools have been installed on the system, check with:

```
$ lslpp -lI perfagent.tools
```

If this package has been installed, the tools are available.

3. Make sure that your PATH variable includes the directory that contains the PerfPMR executables.

In AIX Version 4, add **/usr/sbin/perf/pmr** to the PATH. For example:

```
# echo $PATH
/usr/bin:/etc:/usr/local/bin:/usr/ucb:.:
# PATH=$PATH:/usr/sbin/perf/pmr:
# export PATH
```

In Version 3, add to the PATH the directory in which you installed PerfPMR (in place of **/usr/sbin/perf/pmr**) and the directory for the performance tools, **/usr/lpp/bosperf**.

4. In Version 4, the output of **perfpmr** will be written to **/var/perf/tmp**. In Version 3, you should:

   a. **cd** to a suitable directory, such as **/tmp**, in a file system that has at least 5MB of free space.

   b. Create a subdirectory to hold the data and switch to it, with:

```
# mkdir perfdata
# cd perfdata
```

5. Track system activity for 1 hour with:

```
# perfpmr 3600
```

(in Version 3, **perfpmr** is named **perfpmr.sh**.)

6. Combine the files into one compressed **tar** file with:

```
# cd ..
# tar -cvf pmrnumber.tarbin perfdata
# compress pmrnumber.tarbin
```

Where *pmrnumber* is the number assigned to the PMR by Software Service.

7. Put the file on a diskette (or other portable volume) with, for example:

```
# tar -cvf /dev/fd0 pmrnumber.tarbin.Z
```

8. Label the portable volume with:
   - PMR number
   - Date the information was gathered
   - Command and flags that should be used to remove the data from the portable volume, for example:

```
# tar -xvf /dev/fd0
```

9. Within the United States, send the data to:

IBM Corporation
Dept. J65, Zip 2900, Building 042
11400 Burnet Road
Austin, TX 78758
Attn: V4DEFECT   (or V3DEFECT, as appropriate)

Outside the United States, send the data to your IBM Software Service organization.

Appendix A

AIX Performance Monitoring and Tuning Commands

Performance tools for the AIX environment fall into two general categories: those that tell you what is going on and those that let you do something about it. A few do both. This appendix lists these performance-related commands. Many of them are discussed in the chapters on tuning specific aspects of the system. The details of the syntax and functions of most of these commands are documented in the *AIX Version 4.1 Commands Reference*. The **schedtune**, **pdt_config**, **pdt_report**, and **vmtune** commands are documented later in this appendix.

Some of the performance-related commands are packaged as part of the Performance Toolbox for AIX (PTX), rather than the AIX Base Operating System. Those commands are identified with (PTX). You can determine whether the PTX tools have been installed with:

```
$ lslpp -lI perfagent.tools
```

If this package is listed as AVAILABLE, the PTX tools can be used.

Performance Reporting and Analysis Commands

These tools give you information on the performance of one or more aspects of the system or on one or more of the parameters that affect performance.

Command	Function
bf, **bfrpt**	(PTX) Provides detailed reports of the memory-access patterns of applications.
filemon	(PTX) Uses the trace facility to report on the I/O activity of physical volumes, logical volumes, individual files, and the Virtual Memory Manager.
fileplace	(PTX) Displays the physical or logical placement of the blocks that constitute a file within the physical or logical volume on which they reside.

gprof	Reports the flow of control among the subroutines of a program and the amount of CPU time consumed by each subroutine. This command is documented in *AIX Version 4.1 Commands Reference, Volume 2*.
iostat	Displays utilization data for: • Terminals • CPU • Disks
lockstat	(PTX) Displays information about kernel lock contention.
lsattr	Displays attributes of the system that affect performance, such as: • Size of the caches • Size of real memory • Maximum number of pages in the block I/O buffer cache • Maximum number of kilobytes of memory allowed for mbufs • High- and low-water marks for disk-I/O pacing
lslv	Displays information about a logical volume.
netpmon	(PTX) Uses the trace facility to report on network activity, including: • CPU consumption • Data rates • Response time
netstat	Displays a wide variety of configuration information and statistics on communications activity, such as: • Current status of the mbuf pool • Routing tables • Cumulative statistics on network activity
nfso	Displays (or changes) the values of NFS options
nfsstat	Displays statistics on Network File System (NFS) and Remote Procedure Call (RPC) server and client activity
no	Displays (or changes) the values of network options, such as: • Default send and receive socket buffer sizes • Maximum total amount of memory used in mbuf and cluster pools
pdt_config	Starts, stops, or changes the parameters of the Performance Diagnostic Tool.
pdt_report	Generates a PDT report based on the current historical data.
ps	Displays statistics and status information about the processes in the system, such as: • Process ID • I/O activity • CPU utilization

sar	Displays statistics on operating-system activity such as: • Directory accesses • Read and write system calls • Forks and execs • Paging activity
schedtune	Displays (or changes) the values of VMM memory-load-control parameters, the CPU-time-slice duration, and the paging-space-low retry interval.
smit	Displays (or changes) system-management parameters.
stem	(PTX) Supports the entry and exit instrumentation of executable programs without requiring access to the source code of the executable.
svmon	(PTX) Reports on the status of memory at system, process, and segment levels
syscalls	(PTX) Records and counts system calls
time	Prints the elapsed and CPU time used by the execution of a command
tprof	(PTX) Uses the trace facility to report the CPU consumption of kernel services, library subroutines, application-program modules, and individual lines of source code in the application program
trace	Writes a file that records the exact sequence of activities within the system
vmstat	Displays VMM data, such as: • Number of processes that are dispatchable or waiting • Page-frame free-list size • Page-fault activity • CPU utilization
vmtune	Displays (or changes) the Virtual Memory Manager page-replacement algorithm parameters.

Performance Tuning Commands

The following tools allow you to change one or more performance-related aspects of the system.

Command	Function
fdpr	(PTX) Optimizes executable files for a specific workload.
lvedit	(PTX) Permits the system administrator to make detailed changes to the location and attributes of logical volumes
nfso	Changes (or displays) the values of NFS options
nice	Executes a command at a specified priority
no	Changes (or displays) the values of network options

renice	Changes the priority of running processes
reorgvg	Reorganizes elements of a volume group.
rmss	(PTX) Temporarily reduces the effective RAM size of a system to assess the probable performance of a workload on a smaller machine or to ascertain the memory requirement of one element of a workload.
schedtune	Changes (or displays) the values of VMM memory load control parameters, the CPU-time-slice duration, and the paging-space-low retry interval.
smit	Changes (or displays) system-management parameters.
vmtune	Changes (or displays) the Virtual Memory Manager page-replacement algorithm parameters.

schedtune Command

Purpose

Sets parameters for CPU scheduler and Virtual Memory Manager processing.

Syntax

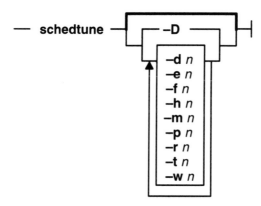

Description

Priority-Calculation Parameters

The priority of most user processes varies with the amount of CPU time the process has used recently. The CPU scheduler's priority calculations are based on two parameters that are set with **schedtune**: **–r** and **–d**. The r and d values are in thirty-seconds (1/32); that is, the formula used by the scheduler to calculate the amount to be added to a process's priority value as a penalty for recent CPU use is:

CPU penalty = (recently used CPU value of the process) * $(r/32)$

and the once-per-second recalculation of the recently used CPU value of each process is:

new recently used CPU value =
(old recently used CPU value of the process) * $(d/32)$

Both r and d have default values of 16. This maintains the CPU scheduling behavior of previous versions of AIX. Before experimenting with these values, you should be familiar with "Tuning the Process-Priority-Value Calculation with schedtune", on page 107.

Memory-Load-Control Parameters

The AIX scheduler performs memory load control by suspending processes when memory is overcommitted. The system does not swap out processes; instead pages are "stolen" as they are needed to fulfill the current memory requirements. Typically, pages are stolen from suspended processes. Memory is considered overcommitted when the following condition is met:

$p * h > s$ where p is the number of pages written to paging space in the last second, h is an integer specified by the **–h** flag, and s is the number of page steals that have occurred in the last second.

A process is suspended when memory is overcommitted and the following condition is met:

$r * p > f$ where r is the number of repages that the process has accumulated in the last second, p is an integer specified by the **–p** flag, and f is the number of page faults that the process has experienced in the last second.

In addition, fixed-priority processes and kernel processes are exempt from being suspended.

The term "repages" refers to the number of pages belonging to the process, which were reclaimed and are soon after referenced again by the process.

The user also can specify a minimum multiprogramming level with the **–m** flag. Doing so ensures that a minimum number of processes remain active throughout the process-suspension period. Active processes are those that are runnable and waiting for page I/O. Processes that are waiting for events and processes that are suspended are not considered active, nor is the wait process considered active.

Suspended processes can be added back into the mix when the system has stayed below the overcommitted threshold for n seconds, where n is specified by the **–w** flag. Processes are added back into the system based, first, on their priority and, second, on the length of their suspension period.

Before experimenting with these values, you should be thoroughly familiar with "Tuning VMM Memory Load Control" on page 124.

Time-Slice-Increment Parameter

The **schedtune** command can also be used to change the amount of time the operating system allows a given process to run before the dispatcher is called to choose another process to run (the *time slice*). The default value for this interval is a single clock tick (10 milliseconds). The **–t** flag of the **schedtune** command allows the user to specify the number of clock ticks by which the time slice length is to be increased.

In AIX Version 4.1, this parameter only applies to threads with the SCHED_RR scheduling policy. See "Scheduling Policy for Threads with Local or Global Contention Scope" on page 15.

fork() Retry Interval Parameter

If a **fork()** subroutine call fails because there is not enough paging space available to create a new process, the system retries the call after waiting for a specified period of time. That interval is set with the **schedtune –f** flag.

schedtune Limitations

schedtune can only be executed by `root`. Changes made by the **schedtune** command last until the next reboot of the system. If a permanent change in VMM or time-slice parameters is needed, an appropriate **schedtune** command should be put in **/etc/inittab**.

Warning: Misuse of this command can cause performance degradation or operating-system failure. Be sure that you have studied the appropriate tuning sections before using **schedtune** to change system parameters.

Flags

If no flags are specified, the current values are printed.

–D Restores the default values (**h**=6, **p**=4, **w**=1, **m**=2, **e**=2, **f**=10, **t**=0, **r**=16, **d**=16).

–d *d* Each process's recently used CPU value is multiplied by *d*/32 once a second.

–e *n* Specifies that a recently resumed suspended process is eligible to be suspended again when it has been active for at least *n* seconds.

–f *n* Specifies the number of (10-millisecond) clock ticks to delay before retrying a **fork** call that has failed because of insufficient paging space. The system retries the **fork** call up to five times.

–h *n* Specifies the systemwide criterion for determining when process suspension begins and ends. A value of zero effectively turns off memory load control.

–m *n* Sets the minimum multiprogramming level.

–p *n* Specifies the per-process criterion for determining which processes to suspend.

–r *r* A process's recently used CPU value is multiplied by *r*/32 when the process's priority value is recalculated.

–t *n* Increases the duration of the time slice—the maximum amount of time before another process is scheduled to run. The default time-slice duration is 10 milliseconds. The parameter *n* is in units of 10 milliseconds each. If *n*=0, the time-slice duration is 10 milliseconds. If n=2, the time-slice duration is 30 milliseconds. In AIX Version 4.1, this parameter only applies to threads with the SCHED_RR scheduling policy

–w *n* Specifies the number of seconds to wait, after thrashing ends, before reactivating any suspended processes.

–? Displays a brief description of the command and its parameters.

Related Information

"Real-Memory management" on page 17
"Tuning the Process-Priority-Value Calculation with **schedtune**" on page 107
"Tuning VMM Memory Load Control" on page 124.

vmtune Command

Purpose

Changes operational parameters of the Virtual Memory Manager and other AIX components.

Syntax

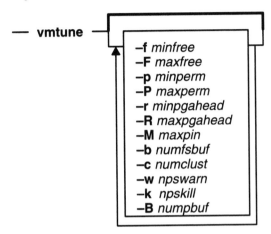

```
— vmtune ┬─────────────────┬
          │  -f minfree     │
          │  -F maxfree     │
          │  -p minperm     │
          │  -P maxperm     │
          │  -r minpgahead  │
          │  -R maxpgahead  │
          │  -M maxpin      │
          │  -b numfsbuf    │
          │  -c numclust    │
          │  -w npswarn     │
          │  -k npskill     │
          │  -B numpbuf     │
          └─────────────────┘
```

Description

The Virtual Memory Manager (VMM) maintains a list of free real-memory page frames. These page frames are available to hold virtual-memory pages needed to satisfy a page fault. When the number of pages on the free list falls below that specified by the *minfree* parameter, the VMM begins to steal pages to add to the free list. The VMM continues to steal pages until the free list has at least the number of pages specified by the *maxfree* parameter.

If the number of file pages (permanent pages) in memory is less than the number specified by the *minperm* parameter, the VMM steals frames from either computational or file pages, regardless of repage rates. If the number of file pages is greater than the number specified by the *maxperm* parameter, the VMM steals frames only from file pages. Between the two, the VMM normally steals only file pages, but if the repage rate for file pages is higher than the repage rate for computational pages, computational pages are stolen as well.

If a process appears to be reading sequentially from a file, the values specified by the *minpgahead* parameter determine the number of pages to be read ahead when the condition is first detected. The value specified by the *maxpgahead* parameter sets the maximum number of pages that will be read ahead, regardless of the number of preceding sequential reads.

In AIX Version 3.2.5, no more than 80% of real memory can be pinned. In AIX Version 4.1, the *maxpin* parameter allows you to specify the upper limit on the percentage of memory that is pinned.

AIX Version 4.1 allows tuning of the number of file system `bufstructs` (*numfsbuf*) and the amount of data processed by the write-behind algorithm (*numclust*).

In AIX Version 4.1 you can also modify the thresholds that are used to decide when the system is running out of paging space. The *npswarn* parameter specifies the number of paging-space pages available at which the system begins warning processes that paging space is low. The *npskill* parameter specifies the number of paging-space pages available at which the system begins killing processes to release paging space.

vmtune can only be executed by `root`. Changes made by the **vmtune** command last until the next reboot of the system. If a permanent change in VMM parameters is needed, an appropriate **vmtune** command should be put in **inittab**.

Warning: Misuse of this command can cause performance degradation or operating-system failure. Before experimenting with **vmtune**, you should be thoroughly familiar with both "Performance Overview of the Virtual Memory Manager (VMM)", beginning on page 17, and "Tuning VMM Page Replacement" on page 126.

Flags

–b *numfsbuf*	Specifies the number of file system `bufstructs`. The default value is 64.
–B *numpbuf*	Specifies the number of pbufs used by the LVM. The maximum value is 128. In AIX Version 3, the number of pbufs may need to be increased in systems doing many large, sequential I/O operations.
–c *numclust*	Specifies the number of 16KB clusters processed by write behind. The default value is 1.
–f *minfree*	Specifies the minimum number of frames on the free list. This number can range from 8 to 204800.
–F *maxfree*	Specifies the number of frames on the free list at which page stealing is to stop. This number can range from 16 to 204800 but must be greater than the number specified by the *minfree* parameter by at least the value of *maxpgahead*.
–k *npskill*	Specifies the number of free paging-space pages at which AIX begins killing processes. The default value is 128.
–M *maxpin*	Specifies the maximum percentage of real memory that can be pinned. The default value is 80. If this value is changed, the new value should ensure that at least 4MB of real memory will be left unpinned for use by the kernel.
–p *minperm*	Specifies the point below which file pages are protected from the repage algorithm. This value is a percentage of the total real-memory page frames in the system. The specified value must be greater than or equal to 5.

–P *maxperm*	Specifies the point above which the page stealing algorithm steals only file pages. This value is expressed as a percentage of the total real-memory page frames in the system. The specified value must be greater than or equal to 5.
–r *minpgahead*	Specifies the number of pages with which sequential read-ahead starts. This value can range from 0 through 4096. It should be a power of 2.
–R *maxpgahead*	Specifies the maximum number of pages to be read ahead. This value can range from 0 through 4096. It should be a power of 2 and should be greater than or equal to *minpgahead*.
–w *npswarn*	Specifies the number of free paging-space pages at which AIX begins sending the SIGDANGER signal to processes. The default value is 512.

pdt_config Script

Purpose

Controls the operation of the Performance Diagnostic Tool (PDT).

Syntax

— pdt_config —

Description

The **pdt_config** script is interactive. When invoked, it displays the following menu:

```
# /usr/sbin/perf/diag_tool/pdt_config
_____PDT customization menu_____

1) show current  PDT report recipient and severity level
2) modify/enable PDT reporting
3) disable       PDT reporting
4) modify/enable PDT collection
5) disable       PDT collection
6) de-install    PDT
7) exit pdt_config
Please enter a number:
```

Menu items are selected by typing the corresponding number and pressing Enter.

The directory **/usr/sbin/perf/diag_tool** must be in the search path, or the script can be invoked with **/usr/sbin/perf/diag_tool/pdt_config**.

The **pdt_config** script can only be run by root.

Flags

None

Related Information

Chapter 12. "Performance Diagnostic Tool (PDT)"

pdt_report Script

Purpose

Generates a Performance Diagnostic Tool (PDT) report based on the current historical information.

Syntax

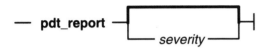

Description

PDT periodically samples the performance of the system and adds the data to a historical database. Normally, PDT generates a report daily at a set time. The **pdt_report** script creates such a report on demand. The report is written to **stdout**. Error messages are directed to **stderr**.

Messages from PDT can range in severity from 1 to 3 (with 1 being the most severe). By default, only messages of severity 1 are included in the report. Optionally, **pdt_report** can be instructed to include messages of lower severity.

The directory **/usr/sbin/perf/diag_tool** must be in the search path, or the script can be invoked with **/usr/sbin/perf/diag_tool/pdt_report**

Flags

severity   The lowest severity messages to be included in the report. Can range from 1 to 3.

Related Information

Chapter 12. "Performance Diagnostic Tool (PDT)"

Appendix B

Performance-Related Subroutines

The following subroutines can be used in monitoring and tuning performance:

Subroutines	Function
getpri	Determines the scheduling priority of a running process.
getpriority	Determines the nice value of a running process
getrusage	Retrieves information about the use of system resources.
nice	Increments the nice value of the current process.
psdanger	Retrieves information about paging space use.
setpri	Changes the priority of a running process to a fixed priority.
setpriority	Sets the nice value of a running process.

Appendix C

Cache and Addressing Considerations

Because efficient use of caches is a major factor in achieving high processor performance, software developers should understand what constitutes appropriate and inappropriate coding technique from the standpoint of cache use. Achieving that understanding requires some knowledge of the RISC System/6000 cache architectures.

Disclaimer

The following discussion is for the benefit of programmers who are interested in the effect of caches and virtual addressing on the performance of their programs. Engineers who are interested in the details of the electronic logic and packaging of the RISC System/6000 will find it oversimplified, and the distinctions among the POWER, PowerPC, and POWER2 architectures blurred.

Addressing

Figure 35, "Successive Transformations of a Memory Address," shows the stages by which a 32-bit data virtual-memory address generated by a program is transformed into a real-memory address. The exact bit numbers vary by model. Models differ in detail but not in principle.

When the program requests that a register be loaded with the contents of a portion of memory, the memory location is specified by a 32-bit virtual address. The high-order 4 bits of this address are used to index into the bank of 16 segment registers. The segment registers are maintained by the operating system, and at any given time contain the 24-bit segment IDs that have been assigned to the currently executing process. Those segment IDs are unique, unless the process is sharing a segment with one or more other processes. The 24-bit segment ID from the selected segment register is combined with the 28 low-order bits of the data address to form the 52-bit virtual address of the data item to be loaded. Since the offset within the segment is 28 bits, each segment is 256MB long.

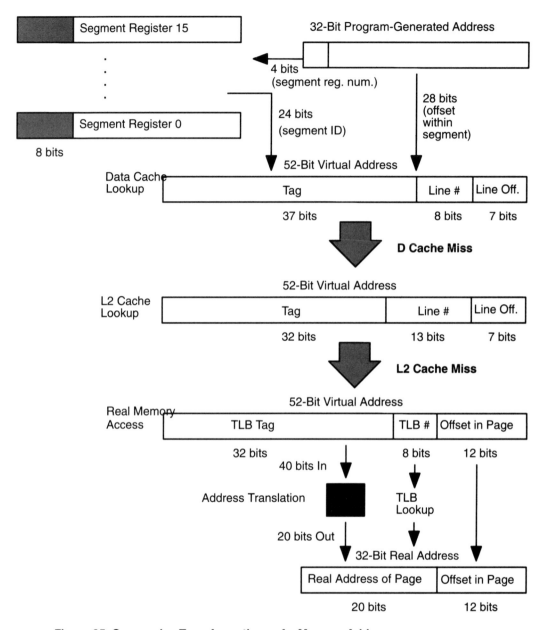

Figure 35: Successive Transformations of a Memory Address

Cache Lookup

The 52-bit virtual address is used for the data cache lookup, as shown in the figure "Data Cache Lookup" on page 263 . Since the lines in the cache are 128 bytes long, the low-order 7 bits of the address represent the offset within the cache line. The data cache contains 128KB of space, and is four-way set associative. Thus each bank of the cache contains 256 128-byte lines (128KB/(128*4) = 256), and so the next higher-order 8 bits represent the line number (0–255). Each bank of the cache has a line with that number, and the four lines with the same number form the congruence class, that is, the four possible locations for the data being sought. This is a *four-way set-associative cache*. If the congruence class had two members, we would speak of the cache as two-way set-associative. If there were exactly one cache line corresponding to a given address, the cache would be *direct-mapped*.

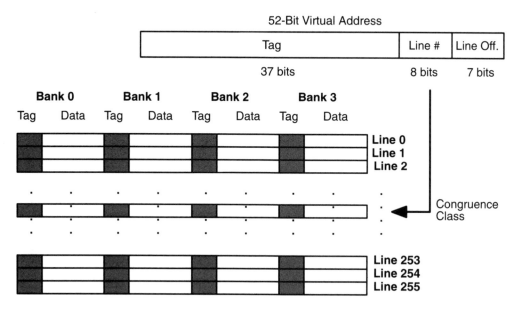

Figure 36: Data Cache Lookup

Associated with each line of the cache is a 37-bit tag, which is the high-order part of the 52-bit address from which the cache line was originally loaded. If one of the tags of the four lines in the congruence set matches the high-order 37 bits of the 52-bit virtual address just generated, we have a *cache hit*. The data from the cache line is loaded into the register, and no access to the RAM (and so no real address) is required.

If none of the four tags in the congruence set matches the tag of the data to be loaded, there is a data cache miss. In this machine there is an L2 cache, so a cache lookup similar to the one in the data cache is performed. The primary difference between the data cache lookup and the L2 cache lookup is that the L2 is direct mapped. The lines are 128 bytes long, and the cache can hold 1MB. There are therefore 8192 lines. The low-order 7 bits of the 52-bit address are still the offset within the line. The next 13 bits constitute the cache line number. Each line is associated with a single 32-bit tag. If that tag matches the high-order 32 bits of the 52-bit address, there is an L2 cache hit. If not, the real address of the data must be determined and the data obtained from RAM.

Different implementations of the POWER architectures have different sizes and geometries of caches; some have no L2 cache, some have combined instruction and data caches, some have different line lengths. The precise size and position of the fields in the 52-bit address may differ, but the principles of cache lookup are the same.

TLB Lookup

The data translation lookaside buffer (TLB) is a cache of addresses. The TLB tag is the high-order 32 bits of the 52-bit virtual address. The next 8 bits of the 52-bit virtual address are the line number in the TLB, which has 512 entries and is two-way set-associative (so each bank has 256 entries). The low-order 12 bits of the 52-bit address are the offset within the 4096-byte page. The data portion of each TLB line is the 20 high-order bits of the 32-bit real address of the page (see the figure "Data TLB Lookup"). If there is a TLB hit, the 20 high-order bits from the TLB entry are combined with the low-order 12 bits of offset within the page to form the 32-bit real address of the data.

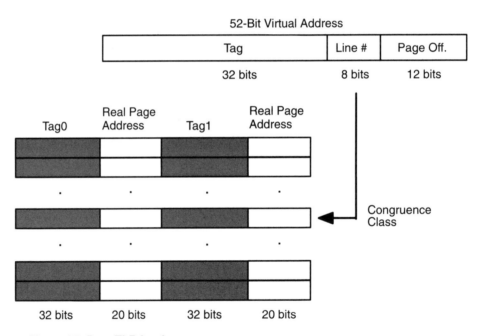

Figure 37: Data TLB Lookup

If there is a TLB miss, the hardware determines the real address of the data using the page tables via an algorithm that is beyond the scope of this book. Obtaining the real address from the page tables takes several dozen processor cycles. When the 32-bit real address has been calculated, its 20-bit page-address portion is cached in the appropriate TLB entry, and the tag for that entry is updated appropriately.

RAM Access

However derived, the 32-bit real address of the data is used to issue a request to RAM. Normally, there is a latency of at least eight processor cycles between the issuing of the

RAM request and the return of the first 16-byte (128 bits—the width of the memory bus) section of data, which includes the data being loaded. At this point the processor can resume operation. The RAM access continues for a further seven processor cycles to load the appropriate data cache line with its full 128 bytes, 16 bytes at a time. Thus, a cache miss entails at least 16 processor cycles from beginning to end. The tag of the cache line is updated with the high-order 37 bits of the data address. The previous content of the cache line is lost.

Implications

Several kinds of pathological addressing patterns can cause incessant cache or TLB misses, greatly slowing the effective rate of execution. For example, if the program accesses an array larger than the cache with a stride of exactly 128 bytes, it will incur a cache miss for each access. If the program presents the processor with a series of requests for the same cache line number but in different pages, a series of congruence-set collisions will occur, resulting in numerous cache misses even though the full capacity of the cache is not being used. The fact that the cache is four-way set-associative makes it unlikely that this will happen by chance, but a particularly unfortunate choice of offsets for data items could make a specific program particularly slow.

Large arrays can also cause problems. The figure "Array Layout in Memory" shows the storage layout of arrays in C and in FORTRAN. C arrays are row-major, while FORTRAN arrays are column-major. If the innermost loop of a C program indexes by column, or a FORTRAN program by row, a sufficiently large array (for example, 512x512 double-precision floating point) can cause a TLB miss on *every* access. For a further discussion of these phenomena, see "A (Synthetic) Cautionary Example" beginning on page 95.

FORTRAN Array				
	Column 1	Column 2	. . . .	Column n	

C Array				
	Row 1	Row 2	. . . .	Row n	

Figure 38: Array Layout in Memory

Appendix D

Efficient Use of the ld Command

The AIX binder (invoked as the final stage of a compile or directly via the **ld** command) has functions that are not found in the typical UNIX linker. This can result in longer linking times if the additional power of the AIX binder is not exploited. This section describes some techniques for more efficient use of the binder.

Rebindable Executables

The formal documentation of the binder refers to the ability of the binder to take an executable (a *load module*) as input. Exploitation of this function can significantly improve the overall performance of the system with software-development workloads, as well as the response time of individual **ld**s.

In most typical UNIX systems, the **ld** command always takes as input a set of files containing object code, either from individual **.o** files or from archived libraries of **.o** files. The **ld** command then resolves the external references among these files and writes an executable with the default name of **a.out**. The **a.out** file can only be executed. If a bug is found in one of the modules that was included in the **a.out** file, the defective source code is changed and recompiled, and then the entire **ld** process must be repeated, starting from the full set of **.o** files.

In the AIX operating system, however, the binder can accept both **.o** and **a.out** files as input, because the binder includes resolved External Symbol Dictionary (ESD) and Relocation Dictionary (RLD) information in the executable file. This means that the user has the ability to rebind an existing executable to replace a single modified **.o** file, rather than build a new executable from the beginning. Since the binding process consumes storage and processor cycles partly in proportion to the number of different files being accessed and the number of different references to symbols that have to be resolved, rebinding an executable with a new version of one module is much quicker than binding it from scratch.

Prebound Subroutine Libraries

Equally important in some environments is the ability to bind an entire subroutine library in advance of its use. The system subroutine libraries such as **libc.a** are, in effect, shipped in binder-output format, rather than as an archive file of **.o** files. This saves the user considerable processing time when binding an application with the required system libraries, since only the references from the application to the library subroutines have to be resolved. References among the system library routines themselves have already been resolved during the system-build process.

Many third-party subroutine libraries, however, are routinely shipped in archive form as raw **.o** files. When users bind applications with such libraries, the binder has to do symbol resolution for the entire library each time the application is bound. This results in long bind times in environments where applications are being bound with large libraries on small machines.

The performance difference between bound and unbound libraries is dramatic, especially in minimum configurations. One user reported **ld** command execution times on the order of 11 *minutes* in an 8MB Model 320 when binding a small FORTRAN program with an 8+MB subroutine library that had been built in the usual archive form. When the subroutine library was prebound, the time required to bind the FORTRAN program fell to approximately 1.7 minutes. When the resulting **a.out** file was rebound with a new FORTRAN **.o** file, simulating the handling of a trivial bug fix, the bind time fell to approximately 4 seconds.

Examples

1. To prebind a library, use the following command on the archive file:

```
ld -r libfoo.a -o libfooa.o
```

2. The compile and bind of the FORTRAN program **something.f** is then:

```
xlf something.f libfooa.o
```

Notice that the prebound library is treated as another ordinary input file, *not* with the usual library identification syntax (**–lfoo**).

3. To recompile the module and rebind the executable after fixing a bug, use:

```
xlf something.f a.out
```

4. However, if the bug fix had resulted in a call to a different subroutine in the library, the bind would fail. The following Korn shell script tests for a failure return code and recovers:

```
# !/usr/bin/ksh
# Shell script for source file replacement bind
#
xlf something.f a.out
rc=$?
if [ "$rc" != 0 ]
then
    echo "New function added ... using libfooa.o"
    xlf something.o libfooa.o
fi
```

Appendix E

Performance of the Performance Tools

Occasionally, the AIX Performance Group is asked about the "overhead" of the performance tools. This is certainly a meaningful question, because some of the tools can add significantly to system workload. It is also a difficult question to answer, because the cost of running the tools is often proportional to some aspect of the workload. The following sections contain brief, informal discussions of the speed and resource use of the main performance monitoring and tuning facilities. These discussions are intended to give a general sense of the relative cost of various tools—not to constitute a rigorous description of tool performance. Most of the experiments were performed on AIX Version 3.2.5 on a RISC System/6000 Model 320. Exceptions are noted where they occur.

filemon

Most of **filemon**'s load on the system is its CPU-time consumption. In a CPU-saturated environment with little I/O, **filemon** slowed a large compile by about 1%. In a CPU-saturated environment with a high disk-output rate, **filemon** slowed the writing program by about 5%.

fileplace

Most variations of this command use less than .3 seconds of CPU time.

iostat

This command uses about 20 milliseconds of CPU time for each periodic report generated.

lsattr

This command is I/O-limited. The first time it is run, it may take 2 to 4 seconds to read the necessary data. Subsequent executions on a lightly loaded system will use about .5 seconds of CPU time.

lslv

This command is CPU-limited. As an example, the command:

```
lslv -p hdisk0 hd1
```

consumes about .5 seconds of CPU time.

netpmon

With a moderate, network-oriented workload, **netpmon** increases overall CPU utilization by 3–5%. In a CPU-saturated environment with little I/O of any kind, **netpmon** slowed a large compile by about 3.5%.

netstat

Most of the variations of this command use less than .2 seconds of CPU time.

nfsstat

Most of the variations of this command use less than .1 seconds of CPU time.

PDT

Daily data collection takes several elapsed minutes, but most of that time is spent sleeping. Total CPU consumption is normally less than 30 seconds.

ps

The CPU time consumed by this command varies with the number of processes to be displayed, but usually does not exceed .3 seconds.

svmon

The **svmon –G** command uses about 3.2 seconds of CPU time. An **svmon** command for a single process (**svmon –P** *processid*), takes about .7 seconds of CPU time.

tprof

Since **tprof** uses **trace**, it causes some system overhead. **tprof** only enables one trace hook, however, so its overhead is less than that of a full trace. For example, **tprof** degraded the performance of a large compile by less than 2%.

trace

The overhead added by **trace** varies widely, depending on the workload and the number of hook IDs being collected. As an extreme case, a long-running, CPU-intensive job in an otherwise idle system took 3.2% longer when **trace** was running with all hooks enabled.

vmstat

This command uses about 40 milliseconds of CPU time for each report generated. The **vmstat –s** command requires about 90 milliseconds of CPU time.

Appendix F

Application Memory Management—malloc and realloc

AIX acquired a new memory-management algorithm in Version 3.2, which is retained in Version 4.1. The previous algorithm, which is widely used in UNIX systems, rounded up the size of all **malloc** requests to the next power of 2. The result was considerable virtual- and real-memory fragmentation and poor locality of reference. The Version 3.2 algorithm allocates exactly the amount of space requested and is more efficient about reclaiming previously used blocks of memory.

Unfortunately, a certain number of existing application programs depended inadvertently on the previous algorithm for acceptable performance or even for correct functioning. For example, if a program depends on the additional space provided by the rounding-up process because it actually overruns the end of an array, it will probably fail when used with the Version 3.2 **malloc**.

As another example, because of the inefficient space reclamation of the Version 3.1 routine, the application program almost always receives space that has been set to zeros (when a process touches a given page in its working segment for the first time, that page is set to zeros). Applications may depend on this side effect for correct execution. In fact, zeroing out of the allocated space is not a specified function of **malloc** and would result in an unnecessary performance penalty for programs that initialize only as required and possibly not to zeros. Because the Version 3.2 **malloc** is more aggressive about reusing space, programs that are dependent on receiving zeroed storage from **malloc** will probably fail in Version 3.2 or later systems.

Similarly, if a program continually **realloc**s a structure to a slightly greater size, in Version 3.1 **realloc** may not need to move the structure very often. In many cases **realloc** can make use of the extra space provided by the rounding. In Version 3.2, **realloc** will usually have to move the structure to a slightly larger area because something else has been **malloc**ed just above it. This has the appearance of a deterioration in **realloc** performance, when in fact it is the surfacing of a cost that is implicit in the application program's structure.

The possibility that existing AIX programs, and programs ported from other UNIX systems, might depend on side effects of the Version 3.1 **malloc** subroutine was foreseen. The Version 3.1 algorithm can be reinvoked by entering:

```
MALLOCTYPE=3.1; export MALLOCTYPE
```

Thereafter, all programs run by the shell will use the previous version of the **malloc** subroutine. Setting MALLOCTYPE to anything other than 3.1 causes the shell to revert to Version 3.2 behavior.

Appendix G

Performance Effects of Shared Libraries

The shared-library capability sometimes provides an opportunity to make time and memory trade-offs.

Advantages and Disadvantages of Shared Libraries

The idea behind shared libraries is to have only one copy of commonly used routines and to maintain this common copy in a unique shared-library segment. This can significantly reduce the size of executables, thereby saving disk space. In addition, since these common routines are used by many processes in a multiuser environment, the routine may already be in real memory when you first reference it. In that case, the time it takes to page fault the subroutine into real memory and the page frame it would occupy are saved. Another advantage to shared libraries is that the routines are not statically bound to the application but are dynamically bound when the application is loaded. This permits applications to automatically inherit changes to the shared libraries, without recompiling or rebinding.

There are, however, possible disadvantages to the use of shared libraries. From a performance viewpoint, there is "glue code" that is required in the executable to access the shared segment. This code adds a number of cycles per call to a shared-library segment. A more subtle effect is a reduction in "locality of reference." You may be interested in only a few of the routines in a library, and these routines may be scattered widely in the virtual address space of the library. Thus, the total number of pages you need to touch in order to access all of your routines is significantly higher than if these routines were all bound directly into your executable. One impact of this is that, if you are the only user of these routines, you experience more page faults to get them all into real memory. In addition, since more pages are touched, there is a greater likelihood of causing an instruction translation lookaside buffer (TLB) miss.

How to Build Executables Shared or Nonshared

The **cc** command defaults to the shared-library option. To override the default, use the **–bnso** option as follows:

```
cc xxx.c -o xxx.noshr -O -bnso -bI:/lib/syscalls.exp
```

How to Determine If Nonshared Will Help

The obvious method of determining whether your application is sensitive to the shared-library approach is to recompile your executable using the nonshare option. If the performance is significantly better, you may want to consider trading off the other advantages of shared libraries for the performance gain. Be sure to measure performance in an authentic environment, however. A program that had been bound nonshared might run faster as a single instance in a lightly loaded machine. That same program, when used by a number of users simultaneously, might increase real memory usage enough to slow down the whole workload.

Appendix H

Accessing the Processor Timer

Attempts to measure very small time intervals in AIX are often frustrated by the intermittent background activity that is part of the operating system and by the processing time consumed by the system time routines. One approach to solving this problem is to access the processor timer directly to determine the beginning and ending times of measurement intervals, run the measurements repeatedly, and then filter the results to remove periods when an interrupt intervened.

The POWER and POWER2 architectures implement the processor timer as a pair of special-purpose registers. The PowerPC architecture defines a 64-bit register called the Time Base. These registers can only be accessed by assembler-language programs.

Warning: The time measured by the processor timer is the absolute *wall-clock* time. If an interrupt occurs between accesses to the timer, the calculated duration will include the processing of the interrupt and possibly other processes being dispatched before control is returned to the code being timed. The time from the processor timer is the *raw* time and should never be used in situations in which it will not be subjected to a reasonableness test.

In AIX Version 4.1, a pair of library subroutines has been added to the system to make accessing of these registers easier and architecture-independent. The subroutines are **read_real_time** and **time_base_to_time**. The **read_real_time** subroutine obtains the current time from the appropriate source and stores it as two 32-bit values. The **time_base_to_time** subroutine ensures that the time values are in seconds and nanoseconds, performing any necessary conversion from the TimeBase format. The reason for the separation of the time-acquisition and time-conversion functions is to minimize the overhead of time acquisition.

The following example shows how these new subroutines could be used to measure the elapsed time for a specific piece of code:

```
#include <stdio.h>
#include <sys/time.h>

int main(void) {
    timebasestruct_t start, finish;
    int val = 3;
    int w1, w2;
    double time;

    /* get the time before the operation begins */
    read_real_time(&start, TIMEBASE_SZ);

    /* begin code to be timed */
    printf("This is a sample line %d \n", val);
    /* end code to be timed    */

    /* get the time after the operation is complete
    read_real_time(&finish, TIMEBASE_SZ);

    /* call the conversion routines unconditionally, to ensure    */
    /* that both values are in seconds and nanoseconds regardless */
    /* of the hardware platform.                                  */
    time_base_to_time(&start, TIMEBASE_SZ);
    time_base_to_time(&finish, TIMEBASE_SZ);

    /* subtract the starting time from the ending time */
    w1 = finish.tb_high - start.tb_high; /* probably zero */
    w2 = finish.tb_low - start.tb_low;

    /* if there was a carry from low-order to high-order during */
    /* the measurement, we may have to undo it.                 */
    if (w2 < 0) {
        w1--;
        w2 += 1000000000;
    }

    /* convert the net elapsed time to floating point microseconds */
    time = ((double) w2)/1000.0;
    if (w1 > 0)
        time += ((double) w1)*1000000.0;

    printf("Time was %9.3f microseconds \n", time);
    exit(0);
}
```

To minimize the overhead of calling and returning from the timer routines, the analyst may want to experiment with binding the benchmark nonshared (see Appendix G).

If this were a real performance benchmark, we would perform the code to be measured repeatedly. If we timed a number of consecutive repetitions collectively, we could calculate an average time for the operation, but it might include interrupt handling or other extraneous activity. If we timed a number of repetitions individually, we could inspect the individual times for reasonableness, but the overhead of the timing routines would be included in each measurement. It may be desirable to use both techniques and compare the results. In any case, the analyst will want to consider the purpose of the measurements in choosing the method.

POWER-Architecture-Unique Timer Access

Warning: The following discussion applies only to the POWER and POWER2 architectures (and the IBM 601 processor chip). The code examples will *function* correctly in a PowerPC system(that is, they won't blow up), but some of the instructions will be simulated. Since the purpose of accessing the processor timer is to obtain high-precision times with low overhead, simulation makes the results much less useful.

The POWER and POWER2 processor architectures include two special-purpose registers (an upper register and a lower register) that contain a high-resolution timer. The upper register contains time in seconds, and the lower register contains a count of fractional seconds in nanoseconds. The actual precision of the time in the lower register depends on its update frequency, which is model-specific.

Assembler Routines to Access the POWER Timer Registers

The following assembler-language module (**timer.s**) provides routines (rtc_upper and rtc_lower) to access the upper and lower registers of the timer.

```
            .globl  .rtc_upper
.rtc_upper: mfspr   3,4         # copy RTCU to return register
            br

            .globl  .rtc_lower
.rtc_lower: mfspr   3,5         # copy RTCL to return register
            br
```

C Subroutine to Supply the Time in Seconds

The following module (**second.c**) contains a C routine that calls the **timer.s** routines to access the upper and lower register contents and returns a double-precision real value of time in seconds.

```
double second()
{
  int ts, tl, tu;

  ts = rtc_upper();     /* seconds                        */
  tl = rtc_lower();     /* nanoseconds                    */
  tu = rtc_upper();     /* Check for a carry from         */
  if (ts != tu)         /* the lower reg to the upper.    */
    tl = rtc_lower();   /* Recover from the race condition. */
  return ( tu + (double)tl/1000000000 );
}
```

The subroutine **second**, can be called from either a C routine or a FORTRAN routine.

Note: Depending on the length of time since the last system reset, **second.c** may yield a varying amount of precision. The longer the time since reset, the larger the number of bits of precision consumed by the (probably uninteresting) whole-seconds part of the number. The technique shown in the first part of this Appendix avoids this problem by performing the subtraction required to obtain an elapsed time before converting to floating point.

Accessing Timer Registers in PowerPC-Architecture Systems

The PowerPC processor architecture includes a 64-bit Time Base register, which is logically divided into 32-bit upper and lower fields (TBU and TBL). The Time Base register is incremented at a frequency that is hardware and software implementation dependent and may vary from time to time. Transforming the values from Time Base into seconds is a more complex task than in the POWER architecture. We strongly recommend using the **read_real_time** and **time_base_to_time** interfaces to obtain time values in PowerPC systems.

Example Use of the second Routine

An example (**main.c**) of a C program using the **second** subroutine is:

```
#include <stdio.h>
double second();
main()
{
    double t1,t2;

    t1 = second();
    my_favorite_function();
    t2 = second();

    printf("my_favorite_function time: %7.9f\n",t2 - t1);
    exit();
}
```

An example (**main.f**) of a FORTRAN program using the **second** subroutine is:

```
    double precision t1
    double precision t2

    t1 = second()
    my_favorite_subroutine()
    t2 = second()
    write(6,11) (t2 - t1)
11  format(f20.12)
    end
```

To compile and use either **main.c** or **main.f**, use the following:

```
xlc -O3 -c second.c timer.s
xlf -O3 -o mainF main.f second.o timer.o
xlc -O3 -o mainC main.c second.o timer.o
```

Appendix I

National Language Support— Locale vs Speed

AIX National Language Support (NLS) facilitates the use of AIX in various language environments. Because informed use of NLS is increasingly important in obtaining optimum performance from the system, a brief review of NLS is in order.

NLS allows AIX to be tailored to the individual user's language and cultural expectations. A *locale* is a specific combination of language and geographic or cultural requirements that is identified by a compound name, such as en_US (English as used in the United States). For each supported locale, there is a set of message catalogs, collation value tables, and other information that defines the requirements of that locale. When AIX is installed, the system administrator can choose what locale information should be installed. Thereafter, the individual users can control the locale of each shell by changing the **LANG** and **LC_ALL** variables.

The one locale that does not conform to the structure just described is the C (or POSIX) locale. The C locale is the system default locale unless the user explicitly chooses another. It is also the locale in which each newly forked process starts. Running in the C locale is the nearest equivalent in AIX to running in the original, unilingual form of UNIX. There are no C message catalogs. Instead, programs that attempt to get a message from the catalog are given back the default message that is compiled into the program. Some commands, such as the **sort** command, revert to their original, character-set-specific algorithms.

Our measurements show that the performance of NLS falls into three bands. The C locale is generally the fastest for the execution of commands, followed by the single-byte (Latin alphabet) locales such as en_US, with the multibyte locales resulting in the slowest command execution.

Programming Considerations

Historically, the C language has displayed a certain amount of provinciality in its interchangeable use of the words *byte* and *character*. Thus, an array declared `char` `foo[10]` is an array of 10 bytes. But not all of the languages in the world are written with characters that can be expressed in a single byte. Japanese and Chinese, for example, require two or more bytes to identify a particular graphic to be displayed. Therefore, in AIX we distinguish between a *byte*, which is 8 bits of data, and a *character*, which is the amount of information needed to represent a single graphic.

Two characteristics of each locale are the maximum number of bytes required to express a character in that locale and the maximum number of output display positions a single character can occupy. These values can be obtained with the **MB_CUR_MAX** and **MAX_DISP_WIDTH** macros. If *both* values are 1, the locale is one in which the equivalence of byte and character still holds. If either value is greater than 1, programs that do character-by-character processing, or that keep track of the number of display positions used, will need to use internationalization functions to do so.

Since the multibyte encodings consist of variable numbers of bytes per character, they cannot be processed as arrays of characters. To allow efficient coding in situations where each character has to receive extensive processing, a fixed-byte-width data type, **wchar_t**, has been defined. A **wchar_t** is wide enough to contain a translated form of any supported character encoding. Programmers can therefore declare arrays of **wchar_t** and process them with (roughly) the same logic they would have used on an array of **char**, using the wide-character analogs of the traditional **libc** functions. Unfortunately, the translation from the multibyte form in which text is entered, stored on disk, or written to the display, to the **wchar_t** form, is computationally quite expensive. It should only be performed in situations in which the processing efficiency of the **wchar_t** form will more than compensate for the cost of translation to and from the **wchar_t** form.

Some Simplifying Rules

It is possible to write a slow, multilingual application program if the programmer is unaware of some constraints on the design of multibyte character sets that allow many programs to run efficiently in a multibyte locale with little use of internationalization functions. For example:

- In all code sets supported by IBM, the character codes 0x00 through 0x3F are unique and encode the ASCII standard characters. Being unique means that these bit combinations never appear as one of the bytes of a multibyte character. Since the null character is part of this set, the **strlen**, **strcpy**, and **strcat** functions work on multibyte as well as single-byte strings. The programmer must remember that the value returned by **strlen** is the number of *bytes* in the string, not the number of *characters*.

- Similarly, the standard string function `strchr(foostr, '/')` works correctly in all locales, since the / (slash) is part of the unique code-point range. In fact, most of the standard delimiters are in the 0x00 to 0x3F range, so most parsing can be accomplished without recourse to internationalization functions or translation to **wchar_t** form.

- Comparisons between strings fall into two classes: equal and unequal. Comparisons for equality can and should be done with the standard **strcmp** function. When we write

```
if (strcmp(foostr,"a rose") == 0)
```

we are not looking for "a rose" by any other name; we are looking for that set of bits only. If `foostr` contains "a rosé" we are not interested.

- Unequal comparisons occur when we are attempting to arrange strings in the locale-defined collation sequence. In that case, we would use

```
if (strcoll(foostr,barstr) > 0)
```

and pay the performance cost of obtaining the collation information about each character.

- When a program is **exec**ed, it always starts in the C locale. If it will use one or more internationalization functions, including accessing message catalogs, it must execute:

```
setlocale(LC_ALL, "");
```

to switch to the locale of its parent process before calling any internationalization function.

Controlling Locale

The command sequence:

```
LANG=C
export LANG
```

sets the *default* locale to C (that is, C is used unless a given variable, such as **LC_COLLATE**, is explicitly set to something else).

The sequence:

```
LC_ALL=C
export LC_ALL
```

forcibly sets *all* the locale variables to C, regardless of previous settings.

For a report on the current settings of the locale variables, type `locale`.

Appendix J

Summary of Tunable AIX Parameters

Each of the following sections describes one of the AIX parameters that can affect performance. The parameters are described in alphabetical order.

arpt_killc

Purpose:	Time before an inactive, complete ARP entry is deleted.
Values:	Default: 20 (minutes), Range: N/A
Display:	**no –a** or **no –o arpt_killc**
Change:	**no –o arpt_killc=***NewValue*
	Change takes effect immediately. Change is effective until next boot. Permanent change is made by adding **no** command to **/etc/rc.net**.
Diagnosis:	N/A
Tuning:	To reduce ARP activity in a stable network, **arpt_killc** can be increased. This is not a large effect.
Refer to:	N/A

biod Count

Purpose:	Number of **biod** processes available to handle NFS requests on a client.
Values:	Default: 6, Range: 1 to any positive integer
Display:	**ps –ef	grep biod**
Change:	**chnfs –b** *NewValue*
	Change normally takes effect immediately and is permanent. The **–N** flag causes an immediate, temporary change. The **–I** flag causes a change that takes effect at the next boot.
Diagnosis:	**netstat –s** to look for UDP socket buffer overflows.
Tuning:	Increase number until socket buffer overflows cease.
Refer to:	"How Many **biod**s and **nfsd**s Are Needed for Good Performance?" on page 180.

Disk Adapter Outstanding-Requests Limit

Purpose: Maximum number of requests that can be outstanding on a SCSI bus. (Applies only to the SCSI–2 Fast/Wide Adapter.)

Values: Default: 40, Range: 40 to 128

Display: **lsattr –E –l scsi*n* –a num_cmd_elems**

Change: **chdev –l scsi*n* –a num_cmd_elems=***NewValue*

Change is effective immediately and is permanent. If the **–T** flag is used, the change is immediate and lasts until the next boot. If the **–P** flag is used, the change is deferred until the next boot, and is permanent.

Diagnosis: N/A

Tuning: Value should equal the number of physical drives (including those in disk arrays) on the SCSI bus, times the queue depth of the individual drives.

Refer to: "Setting SCSI-Adapter and Disk-Device Queue Limits" on page 150.

Disk Drive Queue Depth

Purpose: Maximum number of requests the disk device can hold in its queue.

Values: Default: IBM disks=3, Range: N/A

Default: Non-IBM disks=0, Range: specified by manufacturer.

Display: **lsattr –E –l hdisk*n***

Change: **chdev –l hdisk*n* –a q_type=simple –a queue_depth=***NewValue*

Change is effective immediately and is permanent. If the **–T** flag is used, the change is immediate and lasts until the next boot. If the **–P** flag is used, the change is deferred until the next boot, and is permanent.

Diagnosis: N/A

Tuning: If the non-IBM disk drive is capable of request queuing, this change should be made to ensure that the operating system takes advantage of the capability.

Refer to: "Setting SCSI-Adapter and Disk-Device Queue Limits" on page 150.

dog_ticks

Purpose: Timer granularity for IfWatchdog routines. This value is not used in AIX.

Values: Default: 60

Display: N/A

Change: N/A

Diagnosis: N/A

Tuning: N/A

Refer to: N/A

fork() Retry Interval

Purpose:	Specify the amount of time to wait to retry a **fork** that has failed for lack of paging space.
Values:	Default: 10 (10-millisecond clock ticks), Range: 10 to *n* clock ticks
Display:	**schedtune**
Change:	**schedtune –f** *NewValue*
	Change takes effect immediately. Change is effective until next boot. Permanent change is made by adding **schedtune** command to **/etc/inittab**.
Diagnosis:	If processes have been killed for lack of paging space, monitor the situation with the **sigdanger()** subroutine.
Tuning:	If the paging-space-low condition is only due to brief, sporadic workload peaks, increasing the retry interval may allow processes to delay long enough for paging space to be released. Otherwise, make the paging spaces larger.
Refer to:	N/A

ipforwarding

Purpose:	Specifies whether the kernel forwards IP packets.
Values:	Default: 0 (no), Range: 0 to 1
Display:	**no –a** or **no –o ipforwarding**
Change:	**no –o ipforwarding=***NewValue*
	Change takes effect immediately. Change is effective until next boot. Permanent change is made by adding **no** command to **/etc/rc.net**.
Diagnosis:	N/A
Tuning:	This is a configuration decision with performance consequences.
Refer to:	N/A

ipfragttl

Purpose:	Time to live for IP packet fragments.
Values:	Default: 60 (seconds), Range: 60 to *n*
Display:	**no –a** or **no –o ipfragttl**
Change:	**no –o ipfragttl=***NewValue*
	Change takes effect immediately. Change is effective until next boot. Permanent change is made by adding **no** command to **/etc/rc.net**.
Diagnosis:	**netstat –s**
Tuning:	If value of IP: fragments dropped after timeout is nonzero, increasing **ipfragttl** may reduce retransmissions.
Refer to:	N/A

ipqmaxlen

Purpose:	Specify the maximum number of entries on the IP input queue.
Values:	Default: 50, Range: 50 to *n*
Display:	**no –a** or **no –o ipqmaxlen**
Change:	**no –o ipqmaxlen=***NewValue*
	Change takes effect immediately. Change is effective until next boot.
	Permanent change is made by adding **no** command to **/etc/rc.net**.
Diagnosis:	Use **crash** to access IP input queue overflow counter.
Tuning:	Increase size.
Refer to:	"IP Protocol Performance Tuning Recommendations" on page 167.

ipsendredirects

Purpose:	Specifies whether the kernel sends redirect signals.
Values:	Default: 1 (yes), Range: 0 to 1
Display:	**no –a** or **no –o ipsendredirects**
Change:	**no –o ipsendredirects=***NewValue*
	Change takes effect immediately. Change is effective until next boot.
	Permanent change is made by adding **no** command to **/etc/rc.net**.
Diagnosis:	N/A
Tuning:	N/A. This is a configuration decision with performance consequences.
Refer to:	N/A

loop_check_sum (3.2.5 only)

Purpose:	Specifies whether checksums are built and verified on a loopback interface. (This function does not exist in AIX Version 4.1.)
Values:	Default: 1 (yes), Range: 0 to 1
Display:	**no –a** or **no –o loop_check_sum**
Change:	**no –o loop_check_sum=0**
	Change takes effect immediately. Change is effective until next boot.
	Permanent change is made by adding **no** command to **/etc/rc.net**.
Diagnosis:	N/A
Tuning:	Turning checksum verification off (**loop_check_sum=0**) is recommended.
Refer to:	N/A

lowclust (3.2.5 only)

Purpose:	Specifies the low-water mark for the mbuf cluster pool.
Values:	Default: configuration-dependent, Range: 5 to *n*
Display:	**no –a** or **no –o lowclust**
Change:	**no –o lowclust=***NewValue*
	Change takes effect immediately. Change is effective until next boot.
	Permanent change is made by adding **no** command to **/etc/rc.net**.
Diagnosis:	**netstat –m**
Tuning:	If "requests for memory denied" is nonzero, increase **lowclust**.
Refer to:	"AIX Version 3.2.5 mbuf Pool Performance Tuning" on page 170.

lowmbuf (3.2.5 only)

Purpose:	Specifies the low-water mark for the mbuf pool
Values:	Default: configuration-dependent, Range: 64 to n
Display:	**no –a** or **no –o lowmbuf**
Change:	**no –o lowmbuf=***NewValue*
	Change takes effect immediately. Change is effective until next boot. Permanent change is made by adding **no** command to **/etc/rc.net**.
Diagnosis:	**netstat –m**
Tuning:	If "requests for memory denied" is nonzero, increase **lowmbuf**.
Refer to:	"AIX Version 3.2.5 mbuf Pool Performance Tuning" on page 170.

maxbuf

Purpose:	Number of (4KB) pages in the block-I/O buffer cache.
Values:	Default: 20, Range: x to y
Display:	**lsattr –E –l sys0 –a maxbuf**
Change:	**chdev –l sys0 –a maxbuf=***NewValue*
	Change is effective immediately and is permanent. If the **–T** flag is used, the change is immediate and lasts until the next boot. If the **–P** flag is used, the change is deferred until the next boot and is permanent.
Diagnosis:	N/A
Tuning:	This parameter normally has little performance effect on an AIX system, since ordinary I/O does not use the block-I/O buffer cache.
Refer to:	N/A

max_coalesce

Purpose:	Specifies the maximum size, in bytes, of requests that the SCSI device driver will coalesce from the requests in its queue.
Values:	Default: 64KB, Range: 64KB to 2GB
Display:	**odmget**
Change:	**odmdelete**, **odmadd**, **bosboot**
	Change takes effect at next boot and is permanent.
Diagnosis:	N/A
Tuning:	Increase if striped logical volumes or disk arrays are in use.
Refer to:	"Modifying the SCSI Device Driver **max_coalesce** Parameter" on page 149.

maxfree

Purpose:	The maximum size to which the VMM page-frame free list will grow by page stealing.
Values:	Default: configuration-dependent, Range: 16 to 204800 (4KB frames)
Display:	**vmtune**
Change:	**vmtune –F** *NewValue* Change takes effect immediately. Change is effective until next boot. Permanent change is made by adding **vmtune** command to **/etc/inittab**.
Diagnosis:	Observe free-list-size changes with **vmstat** *n*.
Tuning:	If **vmstat** *n* shows free-list size frequently driven below **minfree** by application demands, increase **maxfree** to reduce calls to replenish free list. Generally, keep **maxfree – minfree** <= 100.
Refer to:	"Tuning VMM Page Replacement" on page 126.

maxperm

Purpose:	The percentage of memory page frames occupied by permanent pages above which only permanent pages will have their frames stolen.
Values:	Default: 80% of (memory size – 4MB), Range: 5 to 100
Display:	**vmtune**
Change:	**vmtune –P** *NewValue* Change takes effect immediately. Change is effective until next boot. Permanent change is made by adding **vmtune** command to **/etc/inittab**.
Diagnosis:	Monitor disk I/O with **iostat** *n*.
Tuning:	If some files are known to be read repetitively, and I/O rates do not decrease with time from startup, **maxperm** may be too low.
Refer to:	"Tuning VMM Page Replacement" on page 126.

maxpgahead

Purpose:	The upper limit on the number of pages the VMM will read ahead when processing a sequentially accessed file.
Values:	Default: 8, Range: 0 to 16
Display:	**vmtune**
Change:	**vmtune –R** *NewValue* Change takes effect immediately. Change is effective until next boot. Permanent change is made by adding **vmtune** command to **/etc/inittab**.
Diagnosis:	Observe the elapsed execution time of critical sequential-I/O-dependent applications with **time** command.
Tuning:	If execution time decreases with higher **maxpgahead**, observe other applications to ensure that their performance has not deteriorated.
Refer to:	"Tuning Sequential Read Ahead" on page 141.

maxpin (4.1 only)

Purpose:	The maximum percentage of real memory that can be pinned.
Values:	Default: 80 (% of RAM), Range: At least 4MB pinnable to at least 4MB unpinnable.
Display:	**vmtune**
Change:	**vmtune –M** *NewValue*
	Change takes effect immediately. Change is effective until next boot.
Diagnosis:	N/A
Tuning:	Only change for extreme situations, such as maximum-load benchmarking.
Refer to:	**vmtune** command on page 255.

maxpout

Purpose:	Specifies the maximum number of pending I/Os to a file.
Values:	Default: 0 (no checking), Range: 0 to *n* (*n* should be a multiple of 4, plus 1)
Display:	**lsattr –E –l sys0 –a maxpout**
Change:	**chdev –l sys0 –a maxpout=***NewValue*
	Change is effective immediately and is permanent. If the **–T** flag is used, the change is immediate and lasts until the next boot. If the **–P** flag is used, the change is deferred until the next boot and is permanent.
Diagnosis:	If foreground response time sometimes deteriorates when programs with large amounts of sequential disk output are running, sequential output may need to be paced.
Tuning:	Set **maxpout** to 33 and **minpout** to 16. If sequential performance deteriorates unacceptably, increase one or both. If foreground performance is still unacceptable, decrease both.
Refer to:	"Use of Disk-I/O Pacing" on page 142.

maxttl

Purpose:	Time to live for Routing Information Protocol (RIP) packets.
Values:	Default: 255, Range: N/A
Display:	**no –a** or **no –o maxttl**
Change:	**no –o maxttl=***NewValue*
	Change takes effect immediately. Change is effective until next boot. Permanent change is made by adding **no** command to **/etc/rc.net**.
Diagnosis:	N/A
Tuning:	N/A
Refer to:	N/A

mb_cl_hiwat (3.2.5 only)

Purpose: Specifies the high-water mark for the mbuf cluster pool

Values: Default: configuration-dependent, Range: N/A

Display: **no –a** or **no –o mb_cl_hiwat**

Change: **no –o mb_cl_hiwat=**_NewValue_

     Change takes effect immediately. Change is effective until next boot.

     Permanent change is made by adding **no** command to **/etc/rc.net**.

Diagnosis: **netstat –m**

Tuning: If the number of mbuf clusters (called "mapped pages" by **netstat**) is regularly greater than **mb_cl_hiwat**, increase **mb_cl_hiwat**.

Refer to: "AIX Version 3.2.5 mbuf Pool Performance Tuning" on page 170.

Memory-Load-Control Parameters

Purpose: Customize the VMM memory-load-control facility to maximize use of the system while avoiding thrashing. The most frequently used parameters are:

         h *H*igh memory-overcommitment threshold

         p *P*rocess memory-overcommitment threshold

         m *M*inimum level of multiprogramming

Values: h Default: 6, Range: 0 to any positive integer

         p Default: 4, Range: 0 to any positive integer

         m Default: 2, Range: 0 to any positive integer

Display: **schedtune**

Change: **schedtune** [**–h** _NewValue_] [**–p** _NewValue_] [**–m** _NewValue_]

     Change takes effect immediately. Change is effective until next boot.

     Permanent change is made by adding **schedtune** command to **/etc/inittab**.

Diagnosis: Heavy memory loads cause wide variations in response time.

Tuning: **schedtune –h 0** turns off memory load control.

     schedtune –p 2 requires a higher level of repaging by a given process before it is a candidate for suspension by memory load control.

     schedtune –m 10 requires that memory load control always leave at least 10 user processes running when it is suspending processes.

Refer to: "VMM Memory Load Control Facility" on page 21 and "Tuning VMM Memory Load Control" on page 124.

minfree

Purpose: The VMM page-frame free-list size at which the VMM starts to steal pages to replenish the free list.

Values: Default: configuration-dependent, Range: x to any positive integer

Display: **vmtune**

Change: **vmtune –f** _NewValue_

     Change takes effect immediately. Change is effective until next boot.

     Permanent change is made by adding **vmtune** command to **/etc/inittab**.

Diagnosis: **vmstat** n

Tuning: If processes are being delayed by page stealing, increase **minfree** to improve response time. Increase **maxfree** by an equal or greater amount.

Refer to: "Tuning VMM Page Replacement" on page 126.

minperm

Purpose: The percentage of page frames occupied by permanent pages below which the VMM steals frames from both permanent and working pages without regard to repage rates.

Values: Default: 20% of (memory size − 4MB), Range: 5 to 100

Display: **vmtune**

Change: **vmtune −P** *NewValue*
Change takes effect immediately. Change is effective until next boot. Permanent change is made by adding **vmtune** command to **/etc/inittab**.

Diagnosis: Monitor disk I/O with **iostat** *n*.

Tuning: If some files are known to be read repetitively, and I/O rates do not decrease with time from startup, **minperm** may be too low.

Refer to: "Tuning VMM Page Replacement" on page 126.

minpgahead

Purpose: The number of pages the VMM reads ahead when it first detects sequential access.

Values: Default: 2, Range: 0 to 16

Display: **vmtune**

Change: **vmtune −r** *NewValue*
Change takes effect immediately. Change is effective until next boot. Permanent change is made by adding **vmtune** command to **/etc/inittab**.

Diagnosis: Observe the elapsed execution time of critical sequential-I/O-dependent applications with **time** command.

Tuning: If execution time decreases with higher **minpgahead**, observe other applications to ensure that their performance has not deteriorated.

Refer to: "Tuning Sequential Read Ahead" on page 141.

minpout

Purpose: Specifies the point at which programs that have hit **maxpout** can resume writing to the file.

Values: Default: 0 (no checking), Range: 0 to *n* (*n* should be a multiple of 4 and should be at least 4 less than **maxpout**)

Display: **lsattr −E −l sys0 −a minpout**

Change: **chdev −l sys0 −a minpout=***NewValue*
Change is effective immediately and is permanent. If the **−T** flag is used, the change is immediate and lasts until the next boot. If the **−P** flag is used, the change is deferred until the next boot and is permanent.

Diagnosis: If foreground response time sometimes deteriorates when programs with large amounts of sequential disk output are running, sequential output may need to be paced.

Tuning: Set **maxpout** to 33 and **minpout** to 16. If sequential performance deteriorates unacceptably, increase one or both. If foreground performance is still unacceptable, decrease both.

Refer to: "Use of Disk-I/O Pacing" on page 142.

MTU

Purpose: Limits the size of packets that are transmitted on the network.

Values: **tr**n (4Mb): Default: 1492, Range: 60 to 3900

tr$n$ (16Mb): Default: 1492, Range: 60 to 17960

en$n$: Default: 1500, Range: 60 to 1500

fi$n$: Default: 4352, Range: 60 to 4352

hi$n$: Default: 65536, Range: 60 to 65536

so$n$: Default: 61428, Range: 60 to 61428

lo$n$: Default: 1500 (3.2.5) 16896 (4.1), Range: 60 to 65536

Display: **lsattr –E –l tr**n

Change: **chdev –l tr**n **–a mtu=**$NewValue$

Cannot be changed while the interface is in use. Because all systems on a LAN must have the same MTU, they must all change simultaneously. Change is effective across boots.

Diagnosis: Packet fragmentation stats

Tuning: Increase MTU size for the Token Ring interfaces:

tr$n$ (4Mb): 4056

tr$n$ (16Mb): 8500

For the loopback interface **lo**n in Version 3.2.5, increase to 16896. For other interfaces, the default should be kept.

Refer to: "LAN Adapters and Device Drivers" on page 162.

nfs_chars (3.2.5), nfs_socketsize (4.1)

Purpose: The size of the NFS UDP socket buffer.

Values: Default: 60000, Range: 60000 to (**sb_max** −128)

Display: **nfso –a** or **nfso –o nfs_chars** (In 4.1, **nfso –o nfs_socketsize**)

Change: **nfso –o nfs_chars=**$NewValue$

(In 4.1, **nfso –o nfs_socketsize=**$NewValue$)

stopsrc –g nfs

startsrc –g nfs

Change takes effect immediately. Change is effective until next boot. Permanent change is made by adding **nfso** command to **/etc/rc.nfs** or **/etc/rc.net**. **sb_max** must change appropriately first.

Diagnosis: **netstat –s**

Tuning: If the "UDP: socket buffer overflows" count is nonzero, increase **sb_max** and **nfs_chars**.

Refer to: "NFS Tuning" on page 179.

nfsd Count

Purpose:	Number of **nfsd** processes available to handle NFS requests on a server.
Values:	Default: 8, Range: 1 to *n*
Display:	**ps −ef	grep nfsd**
Change:	**chnfs −n** *NewValue*
	Change normally takes effect immediately and is permanent. The **−N** flag causes an immediate, temporary change. The **−I** flag causes a change that takes effect at the next boot.
Diagnosis:	**netstat −s** to look for UDP socket buffer overflows.
Tuning:	Increase number until socket buffer overflows cease.
Refer to:	"How Many **biod**s and **nfsd**s Are Needed for Good Performance?" on page 180.

nfs_gather_threshold (4.1 only)

Purpose:	Minimum size of a write that sleeps before syncing. Used to disable scatter/gather of writes to the same vnode.
Values:	Default: 4096, Range: x to y
Display:	**nfso −a** or **nfso −o nfs_gather_threshold**
Change:	**nfso −o nfs_gather_threshold=***NewValue*
	Change takes effect immediately.
	Change is effective until next boot.
Diagnosis:	N/A
Tuning:	N/A
Refer to:	N/A

nfs_portmon (3.2.5), portcheck (4.1)

Purpose:	Specifies that NFS is to check whether or not requests come from privileged ports.
Values:	Default: 0 (no), Range: 0 to 1
Display:	**nfso −a** or **nfso −o nfs_portmon**
Change:	**nfso −o nfs_portmon=***NewValue*
	Change takes effect immediately. Change is effective until next boot.
	Permanent change is made by adding **nfso** command to **/etc/rc.nfs**.
Diagnosis:	N/A
Tuning:	This is a configuration decision with minimal performance consequences.
Refer to:	N/A

nfs_repeat_messages (4.1 only)

Purpose:	Should messages written by NFS be repeated?
Values:	Default: 1 (yes), Range: 0 to 1
Display:	**nfso −a** or **nfso −o nfs_repeat_messages**
Change:	**nfso −o nfs_repeat_messages=***NewValue*
	Change takes effect immediately.
	Change is effective until next boot.
Diagnosis:	N/A
Tuning:	N/A
Refer to:	N/A

nfs_setattr_error (4.1 only)

Purpose:	Specifies that NFS is to ignore NFS errors due to illegal PC setattrs.
Values:	Default: 1, Range: 0 to 1
Display:	**nfso –a**
Change:	**nfso –o nfs_setattr_error=**_NewValue_
	Change takes effect immediately.
	Change is effective until next boot.
Diagnosis:	N/A
Tuning:	N/A
Refer to:	N/A

nfsudpcksum (3.2.5), udpchecksum (4.1)

Purpose:	Specifies that NFS is to use UDP checksum processing.
Values:	Default: 1 (yes), Range: 0 to 1
Display:	**nfso –a** or **nfso –o nfsudpcksum**
Change:	**nfso –o nfsudpcksum=**_NewValue_
	Change takes effect immediately. Change is effective until next boot.
	Permanent change is made by adding **nfso** command to **/etc/rc.nfs**.
Diagnosis:	N/A
Tuning:	Turning checksum processing off may save some processing time but increases the risk of undetected data errors.
Refer to:	N/A

nonlocsrcroute

Purpose:	Indicates that strict-source-routed IP packets can be addressed to hosts outside the local ring. (Loose source routing is not affected.)
Values:	Default: 1 (yes), Range: 0 to 1
Display:	**no –a** or **no –o nonlocsrcroute**
Change:	**no –o nonlocsrcroute=**_NewValue_
	Change takes effect immediately. Change is effective until next boot.
	Permanent change is made by adding **no** command to **/etc/rc.net**.
Diagnosis:	N/A
Tuning:	This is a configuration decision with minimal performance consequences.
Refer to:	N/A

npskill (4.1 only)

Purpose:	The number of free paging-space pages at which processes begin to be killed.
Values:	Default: 128, Range: 0 to the number of pages in real memory.
Display:	**vmtune**
Change:	**vmtune –k** _NewValue_
	Change takes effect immediately. Change is effective until next boot.
Diagnosis:	N/A
Tuning:	N/A
Refer to:	**vmtune** command on page 255.

npswarn (4.1 only)

Purpose:	The number of free paging-space pages at which processes begin to receive SIGDANGER.
Values:	Default: 512, Range: At least **npskill** to the number of pages in real memory.
Display:	**vmtune**
Change:	**vmtune –w** *NewValue* Change takes effect immediately. Change is effective until next boot.
Diagnosis:	N/A
Tuning:	Increase if you experience processes being killed for low paging space.
Refer to:	**vmtune** command on page 255.

numclust (4.1 only)

Purpose:	The number of 16KB clusters processed by write behind.
Values:	Default: 1, Range: 1 to any positive integer
Display:	**vmtune**
Change:	**vmtune –c** *NewValue* Change takes effect immediately. Change is effective until next boot.
Diagnosis:	N/A
Tuning:	May be appropriate to increase if striped logical volumes or disk arrays are being used.
Refer to:	**vmtune** command on page 255.

numfsbuf (4.1 only)

Purpose:	The number of file-system `bufstructs`.
Values:	Default: 64, Range: 64 to any positive integer
Display:	**vmtune**
Change:	**vmtune –b** *NewValue* Change takes effect immediately. Change is effective until next boot.
Diagnosis:	N/A
Tuning:	May be appropriate to increase if striped logical volumes or disk arrays are being used.
Refer to:	**vmtune** command on page 255.

Paging Space Size

Purpose:	The amount of disk space required to hold pages of working storage.
Values:	Default: configuration-dependent, Range: 16MB to *n*MB
Display:	**lsps –a**
Change:	**mkps** or **chps** or **smit pgsp** Change takes effect immediately and is permanent. Paging space is not necessarily put into use immediately, however.
Diagnosis:	**lsps –a** If processes have been killed for lack of paging space, monitor the situation with the **psdanger()** subroutine.
Tuning:	If it appears that there is not enough paging space to handle the normal workload, add a new paging space on another physical volume or make the existing paging spaces larger.
Refer to:	"Placement and Sizes of Paging Spaces" on page 69.

Process-Priority Calculation

Purpose: Specify the amount by which a process's priority value will be increased by its recent CPU usage, and the rate at which the recent-CPU-usage value decays. The parameters are called r and d.

Values: Default: 16, Range: 0 to 32 (**Note:** When applied to the calculation, the values of r and d are divided by 32. Thus the effective range of factors is from 0 to 1 in increments of .03125.)

Display: **schedtune**

Change: **schedtune –r** or **schedtune –d**
Change takes effect immediately. Change is effective until next boot. Permanent change is made by adding **schedtune** command to **/etc/inittab**.

Diagnosis: **ps al** If you find that the PRI column has priority values for foreground processes (those with NI values of 20) that are higher than the PRI values of some background processes (NI values > 20), you may want to reduce the r value.

Tuning: Decreasing r makes it easier for foreground processes to compete. Decreasing d enables foreground processes to avoid competition with background processes for a longer time. **schedtune –r 2** would ensure that any new foreground process would receive at least .5 seconds of CPU time before it had to compete with any process with NI >= 24.

Refer to: "Tuning the Process-Priority-Value Calculation with schedtune" on page 107.

rec_que_size

Purpose: (Tunable only in AIX Version 3.) Specifies the maximum number of receive buffers that can be queued up for the interface.

Values: Default: 30, Range: 20 to 150

Display: **lsattr –E –l tok***n* **–a rec_que_size**

Change: **ifconfig tr0 detach**
chdev –I tok*n* **–a rec_que_size=***NewValue*
ifconfig tr0 *hostname* **up**
Change is effective across boots.

Diagnosis: N/A

Tuning: Increase size. Should be set to 150 as a matter of course on network-oriented systems, especially servers.

Refer to: "LAN Adapters and Device Drivers" on page 162.

rfc1122addrchk

Purpose:	Specifies whether address validation is performed between communications layers.
Values:	Default: 0 (no), Range: 0 to 1
Display:	**no –a** or **no –o rfc1122addrchk**
Change:	**no –o rfc1122addrchk=**_NewValue_
	Change takes effect immediately. Change is effective until next boot. Permanent change is made by adding **no** command to **/etc/rc.net**.
Diagnosis:	N/A
Tuning:	This value should not be changed.
Refer to:	N/A

rfc1323

Purpose:	Value of 1 indicates that **tcp_sendspace** and **tcp_recvspace** can exceed 64KB.
Values:	Default: 0, Range: 0 or 1
Display:	**no –a** or **no –o rfc1323**
Change:	**no –o rfc1323=**_NewValue_
	Change takes effect immediately. Change is effective until next boot. Permanent change is made by adding **no** command to **/etc/rc.net**.
Diagnosis:	None.
Tuning:	Change before attempting to set **tcp_sendspace** and **tcp_recvspace** to more than 64KB.
Refer to:	"TCP Layer" on page 157.

sb_max

Purpose:	Provide an absolute upper bound on the size of TCP and UDP socket buffers. Limits **setsockopt()**, **udp_sendspace, udp_recvspace, tcp_sendspace**, and **tcp_recvspace**.
Values:	Default: 65536, Range: N/A
Display:	**no –a** or **no –o sb_max**
Change:	**no –o sb_max=**_NewValue_
	Change takes effect immediately for new connections. Change is effective until next boot. Permanent change is made by adding **no** command to **/etc/rc.net**.
Diagnosis:	None.
Tuning:	Increase size, preferably to multiple of 4096. Should be about twice the largest socket buffer limit.
Refer to:	"Socket Layer" on page 155

subnetsarelocal

Purpose:	Specifies that all subnets that match the subnet mask are to be considered local for purposes of establishing, for example, the TCP maximum segment size.
Values:	Default: 1 (yes), Range: 0 to 1
Display:	**no –a** or **no –o subnetsarelocal**
Change:	**no –o subnetsarelocal=***NewValue*
	Change takes effect immediately. Change is effective until next boot. Permanent change is made by adding **no** command to **/etc/rc.net**.
Diagnosis:	N/A
Tuning:	This is a configuration decision with performance consequences. If the subnets do not all have the same MTU, fragmentation at bridges may degrade performance. If the subnets do have the same MTU, and **subnetsarelocal** is 0, TCP sessions may use an unnecessarily small MSS.
Refer to:	"Tuning TCP Maximum Segment Size (MSS)" on page 165.

syncd Interval

Purpose:	The time between **sync()** calls by **syncd**.
Values:	Default: 60 (seconds), Range: 1 to any positive integer
Display:	**grep syncd /sbin/rc.boot**
Change:	**vi /sbin/rc.boot**
	Change takes effect at next boot and is permanent.
Diagnosis:	N/A
Tuning:	At its default level, this parameter has little performance cost. No change is recommended. Significant reductions in the **syncd** interval in the interests of data integrity could have adverse consequences.
Refer to:	"Performance Implications of sync/fsync" on page 149.

tcp_keepidle

Purpose:	Total length of time to keep an idle TCP connection alive.
Values:	Default: 14400 (half-seconds) = 2 hours, Range: any positive integer
Display:	**no –a** or **no –o tcp_keepidle**
Change:	**no –o tcp_keepidle=***NewValue*
	Change takes effect immediately. Change is effective until next boot. Permanent change is made by adding **no** command to **/etc/rc.net**.
Diagnosis:	N/A
Tuning:	This is a configuration decision with minimal performance consequences. No change is recommended.
Refer to:	N/A

tcp_keepintvl

Purpose:	Interval between packets sent to validate the TCP connection.
Values:	Default: 150 (half-seconds) = 75 seconds, Range: any positive integer
Display:	**no –a** or **no –o tcp_keepintvl**
Change:	**no –o tcp_keepintvl=***NewValue*
	Change takes effect immediately. Change is effective until next boot.
	Permanent change is made by adding **no** command to **/etc/rc.net**.
Diagnosis:	N/A
Tuning:	This is a configuration decision with minimal performance consequences. No change is recommended. If the interval were shortened significantly, processing and bandwidth costs might become significant.
Refer to:	N/A

tcp_mssdflt

Purpose:	Default maximum segment size used in communicating with remote networks.
Values:	Default: 512, Range: 512 to (MTU of local net – 64)
Display:	**no –a** or **no –o tcp_mssdflt**
Change:	**no –o tcp_mssdflt=***NewValue*
	Change takes effect immediately. Change is effective until next boot.
	Permanent change is made by adding **no** command to **/etc/rc.net**.
Diagnosis:	N/A
Tuning:	Increase, if practical.
Refer to:	"Tuning TCP Maximum Segment Size (MSS)" on page 165.

tcp_recvspace

Purpose:	Provide the default value of the size of the TCP socket receive buffer.
Values:	Default: 16384, Range: 0 to 64KB if **rfc1323=0,**
	Range: 0 to 4GB if **rfc1323=1**.
	Must be less than or equal to **sb_max**.
	Should be equal to **tcp_sendspace** and uniform on all frequently accessed AIX systems.
Display:	**no –a** or **no –o tcp_recvspace**
Change:	**no –o tcp_recvspace=***NewValue*
	Change takes effect immediately for new connections. Change is effective until next boot. Permanent change is made by adding **no** command to **/etc/rc.net**.
Diagnosis:	Poor throughput.
Tuning:	Increase size, preferably to multiple of 4096.
Refer to:	"Socket Layer" on page 155.

tcp_sendspace

Purpose:	Provide the default value of the size of the TCP socket send buffer.
Values:	Default: 16384, Range: 0 to 64KB if **rfc1323=0,** Range: 0 to 4GB if **rfc1323=1**. Must be less than or equal to **sb_max**. Should be equal to **tcp_recvspace** and uniform on all frequently accessed AIX systems.
Display:	**no –a** or **no –o tcp_sendspace**
Change:	**no –o tcp_sendspace=***NewValue* Change takes effect immediately for new connections. Change is effective until next boot. Permanent change is made by adding **no** command to **/etc/rc.net**.
Diagnosis:	Poor throughput.
Tuning:	Increase size, preferably to multiple of 4096.
Refer to:	"Socket Layer" on page 155.

tcp_ttl

Purpose:	Time to live for TCP packets.
Values:	Default: 60 (10-millisecond processor ticks), Range: any positive integer
Display:	**no –a** or **no –o tcp_ttl**
Change:	**no –o tcp_ttl=***NewValue* Change takes effect immediately. Change is effective until next boot. Permanent change is made by adding **no** command to **/etc/rc.net**.
Diagnosis:	**netstat –s**
Tuning:	If the system is experiencing TCP timeouts, increasing **tcp_ttl** may reduce retransmissions.
Refer to:	N/A

thewall

Purpose:	Provide an absolute upper bound on the amount of real memory that can be used by the communications subsystem.
Values:	Default: 25% of real memory, Range: 0 to 50% of real memory
Display:	**no –a** or **no –o thewall**
Change:	**no –o thewall=***NewValue NewValue* is in KB, not bytes. Change takes effect immediately for new connections. Change is effective until next boot. Permanent change is made by adding **no** command to **/etc/rc.net**.
Diagnosis:	None.
Tuning:	Increase size, preferably to multiple of 4(KB).
Refer to:	"AIX Version 3.2.5 mbuf Pool Performance Tuning" on page 170

Time-Slice Expansion Amount

Purpose: The number of 10 millisecond clock ticks by which the default 10
            millisecond time slice is to be increased.
Values: Default: 0, Range: 0 to any positive integer
Display: **schedtune**
Change: **schedtune –t** *NewValue*
            Change takes effect immediately. Change is effective until next boot.
            Permanent change is made by adding **schedtune** command to **/etc/inittab**.
Diagnosis: N/A
Tuning: In general, this parameter should not be changed. If the workload consists
            almost entirely of very long-running, CPU-intensive programs, increasing
            this parameter may have some positive effect.
Refer to: "Modifying the Scheduler Time Slice" on page 109.

udp_recvspace

Purpose: Provide the default value of the size of the UDP socket receive buffer.
Values: Default: 41600, Range: N/A
            Must be less than or equal to **sb_max**.
Display: **no –a** or **no –o udp_recvspace**
Change: **no –o udp_recvspace=***NewValue*
            Change takes effect immediately for new connections. Change is effective
            until next boot. Permanent change is made by adding **no** command to
            /etc/rc.net.
Diagnosis: Nonzero *n* in **netstat –s** report of **udp:** *n* **socket buffer overflows**
Tuning: Increase size, preferably to multiple of 4096.
Refer to: "Socket Layer" on page 155

udp_sendspace

Purpose: Provide the default value for the size of the UDP socket send buffer.
Values: Default: 9216, Range: 0 to 65536
            Must be less than or equal to **sb_max**.
Display: **no –a** or **no –o udp_sendspace**
Change: **no –o udp_sendspace=***NewValue*
            Change takes effect immediately for new connections. Change is effective
            until next boot. Permanent change is made by adding **no** command to
            /etc/rc.net.
Diagnosis: N/A
Tuning: Increase size, preferably to multiple of 4096.
Refer to: "Socket Layer" on page 155

udp_ttl

Purpose:	Time to live for UDP packets.
Values:	Default: 30 (10-millisecond timer ticks), Range: any positive integer
Display:	**no –a** or **no –o udp_ttl**
Change:	**no –o udp_ttl=**_NewValue_
	Change takes effect immediately. Change is effective until next boot.
	Permanent change is made by adding **no** command to **/etc/rc.net**.
Diagnosis:	N/A
Tuning:	N/A
Refer to:	N/A

xmt_que_size

Purpose:	Specifies the maximum number of send buffers that can be queued up for the device.
Values:	Default: 30, Range: 20 to 150
Display:	**lsattr –E –l tok0 –a xmt_que_size**
Change:	**ifconfig tr0 detach**
	chdev –I tok0 –a xmt_que_size=_NewValue_
	ifconfig tr0 _hostname_ **up**
	Change is effective across boots.
Diagnosis:	**netstat –i**
	`Oerr > 0`
Tuning:	Increase size. Should be set to 150 as a matter of course on network-oriented systems, especially servers.
Refer to:	"LAN Adapters and Device Drivers" on page 162

Bibliography

For the reader who is interested in attaining a deeper understanding of computer and operating system performance, the following sources may be useful:

- Leffler, McKusick, Karels, and Quarterman, *The Design and Implementation of the 4.3 BSD Unix Operating System*, Reading: Addison-Wesley, 1989.
- Comer, D., *Internetworking with TCP/IP Vol I*, 2nd ed., Englewood Cliffs: Prentice-Hall, 1991.
- Ferrari, D., Serazzi, G., and Zeigner, A., *Measurement and Tuning of Computer Systems*, New York: Prentice-Hall, 1983.
- Smith, C. U., *Performance Engineering of Software Systems*, Reading: Addison-Wesley, 1990.
- Lazowska, D., Zahorjan, J., Graham, G., and Sevchik, K., *Quantitative System Performance*, New York: Prentice-Hall, 1984.
- Stern, H., *Managing NFS and NIS*, Sebastopol: O'Reilly, 1992.
- *Optimization and Tuning Guide for XL Fortran, XL C and XL C++*, IBM Order Number SC09-1705
- *AIX and Related Products Documentation Overview*, IBM Order Number SC23-2456.
- *AIX Version 4.1 Topic Index and Glossary*, IBM Order Number SC23-2513.
- *RISC System/6000 System Overview and Planning*, IBM Order Number GC23-2406.
- *AIX Version 4.1 Technical Reference, Volume 1: Base Operating System and Extensions*, IBM Order Number SC23-2614.
- *AIX Version 4.1 Commands Reference*, IBM Order Number SBOF-1851.
- *AIX Version 4.1 System Management Guide: Operating System and Devices*, IBM Order Number SC23-2525.
- *AIX Version 4.1 System Management Guide: Communications and Networks*, IBM Order Number SC23-2526.
- *IBM Engineering and Scientific Subroutine Library Guide and Reference*, IBM Order Number SC23-0184.
- *Performance Toolbox 1.2 and 2.1 for AIX: User's Guide*, IBM Order Number SC23-2625.

References

- Auslander, M., Chibib, A., Hoagland, C., and Kravetz, M., "Dynamic Linking and Loading in the AIX System," *IBM RISC System/6000 Technology*, SA23-2619, IBM Corporation, 1990, p. 150.

Glossary

The purpose of this glossary is to help you understand AIX performance tuning. In some cases, the definitions apply specifically to AIX or to the tuning of a production system, rather than to the universe of all computers or to measurement under laboratory conditions.

baud. Technically, the number of changes in signal levels, frequency, or phase per second on a communications channel. Informally (as used by programmers) synonymous with "bits per second." (Named for J. Baudot, 1845–1903, French inventor.)

benchmark. The combination of a rigorously specified workload and a method of quantifying the performance of a system when processing that workload. The performance metric is usually derived from the time required to process the workload.

binding. In a multiprocessor context, constraining a thread to a specific physical processor to gain the benefit of processor affinity.

cache. 1. High-speed storage that can deliver data or instructions faster than the storage medium on which that information usually resides. 2. A (usually software) technique whereby high-speed storage that is not immediately required for other purposes is used to retain data that has been loaded into it once, in the hope that another request for the data will occur before the high-speed storage must be reassigned.

cache coherency. The need to ensure that multiple threads on multiple processors changing a single cache line do not create inconsistent versions of the cache line in the different caches.

cache hit. A processor storage reference that is satisfied by information from a cache.

cache line. The cache component that is normally loaded, stored, and interrogated during cache lookup.

cache line tag. The information kept with each cache line to identify the part of virtual storage it contains.

cache lookup. The process of determining whether or not a cache contains the information necessary to satisfy a storage reference. A defined set of bits in the address being referenced identifies the line or lines to be interrogated.

cache miss. A processor storage reference that cannot be satisfied from a cache and therefore requires a RAM access.

cluster. 1) a group of LAN-connected systems that share workload, 2) a page-size (4096-byte) buffer provided by the mbuf management facility to the various layers of communication software in AIX. Also called "cluster mbuf," "mbuf cluster," and "mapped page."

combined I and D cache. A cache that contains both instructions and data, distinguishable only by the cache line tag.

computational memory. The set of all virtual-memory pages in real memory that are part of working-storage or program-text segments.

congruence class. The set of lines in a set-associative cache that must be interrogated to determine whether or not the cache contains the required information.

contention scope. The group of threads against which a given thread must compete for the CPU. If *local*, the thread competes against other threads in the same process. If *global*, the thread competes against all other threads in the system.

critical resource. The system resource whose speed and/or size limits the speed with which a particular workload can be processed.

data cache. A cache for providing data to the processor faster than it can be obtained from RAM.

direct-mapped cache. A cache in which exactly one line corresponds to each possible value of the virtual-address field that identifies the line to be interrogated.

effective rate. The average sustained speed at which a device operates under real-world conditions, when processing a representative workload.

executable. A file that can be loaded into memory and executed as a program. An executable is produced by the binder (**ld**) from one or more object (**.o**) files. The default processing of compilation commands includes invoking the binder to produce an executable whose name is **a.out**.

FDDI. Fiber distributed data interface. A 100 Mbit/sec optical LAN interface.

file memory. Virtual-memory pages that are currently in real memory that are not part of computational memory. Normally these are pages of nonexecutable files.

fragment. A unit of disk storage that is smaller that a (4KB) page.

free list. The set of real-memory page frames that are available for immediate allocation.

funnelling. Forcing device drivers and kernel extensions that are not known to be MP safe to run only on the master processor.

industry-standard benchmark. A benchmark that has been adopted by consensus or by some (presumably neutral) sponsoring organization as constituting a meaningful measure of some aspect of computer-system performance. There are many counter-examples to the assumption that an improvement in industry-standard benchmark performance corresponds to an improvement in the performance experienced by users.

instruction cache. A cache for providing program instructions to the processor faster than they can be obtained from RAM.

L1 cache. The first cache accessed when a storage reference occurs.

L2 cache. The cache that is accessed, on certain RISC System/6000 models, if the L1 cache lookup results in a cache miss. Normally, the L2 cache is larger and slower than the L1 cache, but faster than RAM.

latency. The time from the initiation of an operation until something actually starts happening (for example, data transmission begins).

line of memory. The section of memory that corresponds to a cache line, which corresponds to a single virtual-memory address tag.

load module. See executable.

locality of reference. The degree to which a running program makes use of a compact range of addresses for instructions and/or data.

logical partition (LP). A fixed-size portion of a logical volume. A logical partition is the same size as the physical partitions in its volume group. Unless the logical volume of which it is a part is mirrored, each logical partition corresponds to—and its contents are stored on—a single physical partition.

logical resource. A software construct, such as a lock or a buffer, that is required for the execution of a program and is in limited supply.

logical volume (LV). A virtual disk drive made up of one or more logical partitions, each of which is stored on one or more physical partitions from one or more of the physical volumes of a given volume group. A logical volume has a device name of the form /dev/hd*n* and contains a single file system.

master processor. The first processor started at boot time in a multiprocessor system.

mbuf. A small (256-byte) buffer provided by the mbuf management facility to the various layers of communication software in AIX.

memory leak. A software bug in which the program allocates memory, loses track of it, and then allocates some more. If the program is long-running, it can eventually tie up large amounts of real memory and paging space. System performance gradually deteriorates and the program that finally fails due to lack of resource may not be the culprit. Memory leaks in kernel extensions that allocate pinned memory may be particularly costly.

memory load control. A VMM facility that detects memory overcommitment and temporarily reduces the number of running processes, thus avoiding thrashing.

memory overcommitment. A condition in which the number of virtual-memory pages being used by the currently running programs exceeds the number of real-memory page frames available to hold them. If the overcommitment is large or sustained, system performance suffers.

MTU (maximum transfer unit). The largest amount of data that can be transmitted in a single frame for a particular network interface.

mutex. Jargon for *mutual exclusion lock*. Use of this type of lock excludes all threads other than the lock holder from any access whatsoever to the locked resource.

object file. The primary output of a compiler or assembler, which can be processed by the binder (**ld**) to produce an executable file. The names of object files normally end in **.o**.

page. A 4096-contiguous-byte portion of a virtual-memory segment. The offset of each page from the beginning of the segment is an integral multiple of 4096.

page fault. An interrupt that occurs when the processor attempts to access a virtual-memory page that is not in real memory.

page frame. A 4096-contiguous-byte portion of real memory that is used to hold a virtual-memory page.

peak rate. The maximum speed at which a device could operate under ideal conditions, if its designer were choosing the workload.

persistent segment. A segment whose pages have permanent locations on disk, rather than temporary slots in the paging space.

physical partition (PP). A fixed-size portion of a physical volume. One or more physical partitions constitute the underlying physical storage medium for a logical partition.

physical volume (PV). The actual storage space provided by a single hard-disk drive. Physical volumes normally have names of the form /dev/hdisk*n*

priority. The importance or urgency of a process.

priority value. A number maintained by the AIX scheduler for each process, that indicates the priority of that process. The smaller the *priority value* of the process, the higher its *priority.*

process concurrency. The degree to which a given process has multiple dispatchable threads at all times.

processor affinity. The degree to which a thread is likely to be dispatched to the same physical processor on which it last ran.

program-text segment. A virtual-memory segment that contains the executable instructions of an application program. A program-text segment is identified by the occurrence of an instruction-cache miss in that segment.

repage fault. A page fault on a virtual-memory page that is known to have been read from disk "recently."

response time. The time from the initiation of an operation until its initiator has enough information to proceed

RW lock. Abbreviation for *read shared/write exclusive lock.* Any number of threads can hold the lock simultaneously for reading, but if a thread holds the lock for writing, all other threads are excluded from reading or writing the locked resource.

scalability. The ability of a workload to benefit from a multiprocessor environment.

scaling factor. The throughput of a workload on a multiprocessor divided by the throughput of that workload on a comparable uniprocessor (*not* on a single-processor SMP system).

scheduling policy. The set of rules that govern when a thread will lose control of the CPU and which thread will get control next.

segment. The information that can be addressed via a single, unique segment-register value. A segment is up to 256MB long.

set-associative cache. A cache in which two or four (or more) lines correspond to each possible value of the virtual-address field that identifies the line to be interrogated during cache lookup.

single-processor SMP. A system designed to handle two or more processors, running the SMP version of the operating system, which has been configured with a single processor. (This is in contrast to a true "uniprocessor" system)

SLA. Serial link adapter. *See* SOCC.

SMP efficient. Avoidance in a program of any action that would cause functional or performance problems in an SMP environment. A program that is described as SMP efficient is generally assumed to be SMP safe as well. An SMP-efficient program has usually undergone additional changes to minimize incipient bottlenecks.

SMP exploiting. Adding features to a program that are specifically intended to make effective use of an SMP environment. A program that is described as SMP exploiting is generally assumed to be SMP safe and SMP efficient as well.

SMP safe. Avoidance in a program of any action, such as unserialized access to shared data, that would cause functional problems in an SMP environment. This term, when used alone, usually refers to a program that has undergone only the minimum changes necessary for correct functioning in an SMP environment.

steal (a page frame). The act (by the Virtual Memory Manager) of reallocating a real-memory page frame that contains a virtual-memory page that is being used by a currently executing program.

SOCC. Serial optical channel converter. A 220 Mbit/sec optical point-to-point link.

thrashing. A condition, caused by a high level of memory overcommitment, in which the system is spending almost all of its time writing out virtual-memory pages and reading them back in. The application programs make no progress because their pages don't stay in memory long enough to be used. Memory load control is intended to avoid or quash thrashing.

thread. The dispatchable entity in AIX Version 4. Each thread represents the current execution state of a single instance of a program. Each user thread runs in the environment provided by a specific process, but multiple threads may share the resources owned by that process.

throughput. The *number* of workload operations that can be accomplished per unit of time

time slice. The interval between scheduled checks by the CPU scheduler to see if a different thread should be dispatched. Unscheduled checks may occur as a result of interrupts or system calls.

uniprocessor. A system containing a single processor. As used in this book, the phrase "comparable uniprocessor" means a system designed to have only a single processor, with the same CPU-clock speed and cache capacity as the SMP system being discussed, running a uniprocessor version of the operating system. (This is in contrast to a single-processor SMP system—see above.)

volume group (VG). A set of one or more physical volumes from which space can be allocated to one or more logical volumes.

working segment. A segment whose pages are backed by slots in the disk paging space rather than by a permanent location on disk.

working set. The parts of a program's executable code and/or data areas that are being used intensively and are therefore important to keep in the fastest possible type of storage. Thus a program's "instruction cache working set" is the set of program cache lines that need to be kept in the instruction cache if the program is to run at near-maximum speed.

workload. A sequence of requests—such as commands, I/O operations, and subroutine-library calls—that constitute the work being done by a system. In performance analysis the term normally refers to a workload that has been captured in such a way as to be repeatable (via shell scripts, remote terminal emulators), so that it can be used to measure the performance effect of changes to the system.

workload concurrency. The degree to which the system approaches the ideal of always having as many dispatchable threads as there are processors.

Index

Symbols

#pragma disjoint, 59

#pragma for C program, 59

#pragma isolated_call, 60

A

a.out input to ld command, 266

AIX Performance Toolbox, checking availability, 248

AIX problem reporting. *See* PerfPMR

architecture-specific compilation, 58

arrays
    C, 98
    storage layout, 265

async connections
    fastport script, 205
    tuning for high-speed input, 200

ATM, tuning recommendations, 169

B

benchmark, industry-standard, 2

BEST/1, xiv

BigFoot tool, 115

binder. *See* ld (binder)

binding subroutine libraries, 266

biod daemon, 180, 283

C

C arrays, 98

C compiler speed, 63

cache
    architecture, 261
    direct mapped, 263
    four-way set associative, 263
    hit, 5, 263
    line refill, 265
    miss, 5, 263

calloc subroutine use, 65

cc command run time, 63

character, multibyte, 280

cluster
    description, 170

lowclust, 170

mb_cl_hiwat, 171

mbuf, 155

code optimization. *See* optimization

coding
    effective use of preprocessor and compiler, 57
    efficient C and C++ style, 62
    pageable code style, 65
    string subroutines, 62

communications
    See also network
    installation and tuning recommendations summary, 175

compilation, architecture-specific, 58

compiler speed, 63

compression, file system, 147

configuration
    disk recommendations, 67
    recording a performance baseline before changing, 80
    size and location of paging spaces, 69

contention scope, 15
    See also thread

CPU. *See* processor

CPU hot spots, finding in a program, 94

CPU usage. *See* priority

critical resource. *See* resource

cycles per instruction, 7

D

DFS tuning, 210

disk array, 29

disk-dependent applications, 83

diskless workstation, 186
    NFS activity for simple program execution, 187
    paging over NFS, 189
    performance difference from diskful, 194
    resource requirements, 189
    tuning considerations, 190

disks

adapter outstanding-requests limit, 284
assessing performance with iostat, 130
block size, 26
expanding and enhancing configuration, 140
file-system compression, 147
filemon command, 137
fragment allocation, 147
fragmentation, 26
    reducing, 134
I/O pacing, 29, 142
    maxpout parameter, 289
    minpout parameter, 291
journaled file system (JFS), 26
logical partition, 26
logical volume (LV)
    definition, 26
    mirror write consistency, 71
management overview, 25
mapped files, 28
paging space. *See* paging space
physical partition (PP), 26
physical placement of a file, 133
physical placement of logical volume, 131
physical volume (PV), 25
planning physical and logical configuration, 67
queue depth, 284
raw device, 148
read ahead, 27
relative speeds, 68
reorganizing, 134, 135
striping, 144
sync/fsync, 149
tuning sequential read ahead, 141
volume group (VG), 26
write behind, 28
write verify, 71
dog_ticks, 284

E

early allocation of paging space slots, 25
environment variable
    LANG, 282
    LC_ALL, 282
    MALLOCTYPE, 272
    PATH, 188

Ethernet, tuning recommendations, 168
executable files, 266

F

FDDI, tuning recommendations, 169
filemon command, 137
    availability, 137
files. *See* disks
fixed disk. *See* disks
fixed priority. *See* priority
fork, retry interval, 285
fragmentation, disk. *See* disks
fragments, file system, 147
free list, 18
    changing size, 126
    maxfree parameter, 288
    minfree parameter, 290
free subroutine
    avoiding memory leaks, 114
    unnecessary use, 114
fsync subroutine, 149

G

global contention scope, 15

H

HIPPI, tuning recommendations, 169

I

I/O pacing. *See* disks
initial thread, 41
installation
    configuration and setup guidelines, 66
    disk recommendations, 67
interface (IF) layer
    receive flow, 162
    send flow, 162
International Language Support (ILS), 280
    coding hints, 281
    environment variable
        LANG, 282
        LC_ALL, 282
Interphase Network Coprocessor, 185
interrupt handlers, 6
intrusiveness, of the performance tools, 268

iostat command
    performance monitoring, 73
    sample shell script, 130
    sample summary reports, 81

IP
    functional overview, 161
    ipforwarding parameter, 285
    ipfragttl parameter, 285
    ipqmaxlen parameter, 286
    ipsendredirects parameter, 286
    maxttl, 289
    nonlocsrcroute parameter, 294
    receive flow, 161
    send flow, 161
    tuning recommendations, 167

IP input queue overrun, 167

ipqmaxlen, summary, 177

ipreport command, 208

iptrace
    report formatting, 208
    sample output, 208, 209
    starting and stopping, 208
    use on performance problems, 207

J

journaled file system (JFS). *See* disks

L

LAN adapter device driver
    receive flow, 163
    send flow, 162

LANG. *See* International Language Support
    (ILS)

late allocation of paging space slots, 25

latency
    definition, 4
    RAM, 5
    rotational, 4
    seek, 4

LC_ALL. *See* International Language Support (ILS)

ld (binder) use, 266

libc.a, 99

libraries. *See* shared libraries

loader, 5

local contention scope, 15

locale, 280

locality of reference
    definition, 54
    example, 7

location on disk. *See* disks

lockstat command, 83

logical partition. *See* disks

logical volume (LV). *See* disks

Logical Volume Manager, 7

logical volume striping, 144

lowclust, 286
    See also cluster

lowmbuf, 287
    See also mbuf

M

malloc
    AIX 3.1 vs AIX 3.2, 271
    efficient use of, 65
    memory leaks, 114
    paging-space slot allocation, 25

MALLOCTYPE environment variable, 272

matrix operations, 56

maxbuf, 287

maxfree. *See* free list

maxperm, 288
    changing, 128
    overview, 21

maxpgahead, 288

maxpout, 289

mb_cl_hiwat. *See* cluster

mbuf
    description, 170
    lowclust, 170, 286
    lowmbuf, 170, 287
    management overview, 155
    mb_cl_hiwat, 171, 290
    tuning guidelines, 173
    verifying current pool size, 174

mbuf cluster, 155
    See also cluster

memory
    assessing application requirements, 118

computational, 19
file, 19
size reduction, 86

memory load control
description, 21
parameters summary, 290
schedtune command, 252
tuning for large real memories, 126

minfree. *See* free list

minperm, 291
changing, 128
overview, 21

minpgahead, 291

minpout, 291

mirror write consistency. *See* disks

monitoring
continuous, 72
overhead, 268
with iostat, netstat, and/or vmstat, 73
with the Performance Diagnostic Tool, 74

MTU, 179, 292

multiuser workload. *See* workload

N

National Language Support (NLS). *See* International Language Support (ILS)

netpmon command, 205
availability, 205

netstat command
–m option for reporting mbuf usage, 172
performance monitoring, 73
use in tuning mbuf pools, 171

network
arpt_killc parameter, 283
iptrace, 207
loop_check_sum parameter, 286
netpmon command, 205

NFS
ACL support, 183
biod count, 283
data caching, 183
file attribute cache, 183
hard vs soft mounts, 182
hardware accelerators, 185

nfs_chars parameter, 292
nfs_gather_threshold parameter, 293
nfs_portmon parameter, 293
nfs_repeat_messages parameter, 293
nfs_setattr_error parameter, 294
nfs_udpcksum parameter, 294
number of biods and nfsds, 180
overview, 180
relationship to lower layers, 184
server disk configuration, 68
socket buffer size, 184
timeo parameter, 182

nfsd daemon, 180, 293

nice command
See also priority
clarification of syntax, 107
examples of use, 104

nice value. *See* priority

non-fixed priority. *See* priority

O

optimization
architecture-specific, 58
effect on compile time, 63
levels, 61
XL compilers, 57

overhead, of monitoring tools, 268

overrun IP input queues, 167

P

pacing
See also disks
disk I/O. *See* disks

page fault
example of, 4
latency, 64
new, 20
repage, 20

page out, 19

page replacement, 255

page-replacement algorithm
description, 21
tuning, 126

pages, 17

paging space, 19
early allocation of slots, 25
insufficient paging space retry parameter, 254, 285

late allocation of slots, 25
placement and sizes, 69
psdanger() subroutine, 69
size, 295

paging statistics, 84

parameters, tunable, summary, 283

path length, 7

pathname resolution, 187

pdt_config script, 258

pdt_report script, 259

Performance Diagnostic Tool (PDT), 74

performance monitoring. *See* monitoring

performance problem solving
communications, 153
CPU, 88
disk, 130
general, 75
memory, 111

performance requirements, 44

Performance Toolbox (PTX), xv, 74
checking availability, 248

performance tools, 248, 250

performance-tuning process, steps, 8

PerfPMR
data capture, 245
for AIX Version 3, 244
installation, 245
reporting a possible AIX performance
bug, 243
use in performance diagnosis, 78

physical partition. *See* disks

physical volume. *See* disks

pinned storage, 66

placement on disk. *See* disks

POWER architectures, 58

pragma. *See* #pragma

Prestoserve, 185

printf subroutine performance, 101

priority
components
CPU usage, 16
nice value, 16
user-thread minimum, 16

displaying with ps, 106
fixed, 15
displaying with ps, 106
setting with setpri, 105
modifying with renice, 106
nice command, 16
non-fixed, 15, 104
priority value, 15
renice command, 16
running a command with nice, 104
setpri subroutine, 16
tuning the calculation algorithm, 296

problem reporting. *See* PerfPMR

processor
accessing the hardware timer, 275
control of contention with priority, 104
identifying heavy users with the ps
command, 91
measuring use with the time command,
89
monitoring with vmstat, 88
profiling a program for hot spots, 94
time slice, 17, 109
virtual addressing scheme, 261

ps command
displaying process priority, 106
flags specifying what columns to display, 93
flags specifying what processes to report on, 92
identifying CPU-intensive programs, 91
list of columns that can be displayed, 93
memory reporting, 112

psdanger() subroutine, 69

PTX, xv
checking availability, 248

R

RAID, 29

RAM, measuring requirements with rmss.
See memory

raw devices, disk. *See* disks

read ahead. *See* disks

realloc subroutine, 114

realloc subroutine usage, 271

rebinding executable files, 266

rec_que_size, 296

summary, 178

renice command
See also priority
clarification of syntax, 107
example of use, 106

reorganizing disk data. *See* disks

repage fault, 20

repage history buffer, 20

reporting and analysis tools, 248

requirements
performance, 44
resource. *See* resource

resource
additional, 12, 140
critical, 9
estimation, 45, 50
logical, 9
measurement, 47
real, 9

response time, 2

rfc1122addrchk, 297

rfc1323, 297
summary, 176

rmss command
changing effective machine size, 86
examples of use, 116, 118
memory size simulation, 115

S

safe interval, 22

sb_max, 297
summary, 175

schedtune command, 126, 252
incrementing time slice, 17, 109
warning, 125

schedulers, 14

scheduling policy, 15
See also thread

seek latency, 4

segment
client, 19
deferred, 19
journaled, 19
persistent, 18, 26

virtual memory, 261
working, 19

segment registers, 261

sequential read ahead. *See* disks

server workload. *See* workload

setpri subroutine
See also priority
example of use, 105

shared libraries, 273
assessing CPU usage, 99

SMIT
creating a TTY port, 205
setting disk I/O pacing parameters, 143
setting number of nfsd daemons started
at boot, 192

SOCC, tuning recommendations, 169

socket
buffer size. *See* NFS
buffer size limits, 155
receive flow, 156
send flow, 156

sort, performance in C and non-C locales,
280

STEM tool, control flow analysis example,
101

string subroutines, 62

strip mining, 56

striping, 144

subnetsarelocal, 298

subroutine libraries, 266

svmon command, examples of use, 112

sync command or subroutine, 149

syncd interval, 298

system activity, analysis with the trace facility, 214

System Management Interface Tool. *See*
SMIT

T

TCP
functional overview, 157
receive flow, 160
send flow, 160
tuning recommendations, 163
window illustration, 158

TCP/IP
See also IP; TCP
data flow illustration, 153
iptrace, 207

tcp_keepidle, 298

tcp_keepintvl, 299

tcp_mssdflt, 299

tcp_recvspace, 299
summary, 177

tcp_sendspace, 300
summary, 177

tcp_ttl, 300

thewall, 300
summary, 175

thewall description. See mbuf, cluster

thrashing, avoidance, 124

thread
contention scope, 15
global contention scope, 15
local contention scope, 15
scheduling policy, 15

thread support, overview, 14

throughput, 2

time command, measuring CPU use, 89

time slice, 17
effect of, 17
expansion amount, 301
modification of with schedtune, 17, 109

timer (hardware), accessing, 275

TLB. See translation lookaside buffer (TLB)

token ring (16Mb), tuning recommendations, 168

token ring (4Mb), tuning recommendations,
168

toolbox, xv
checking availability, 248

tprof command, extended example of use,
95

trace
adding new events, 221
channels, 222
control commands, 219
control ioctl calls, 219
control subroutines, 219

event IDs, 223
event record format, 221
example of user event, 223
facility introduction, 214
format-file-stanza syntax, 225
macros, 222
subcommands, 218

translation lookaside buffer (TLB)
hit, 264
miss, 5, 264

trcstart subroutine, 219

tunable AIX parameters, summary of, 283

tuning system performance, steps in the process, 8

tuning tools, 250

U

UDP
data flow illustration, 153
functional overview, 156
receive flow, 157
send flow, 157
tuning recommendations, 163

UDP, TCP/IP, and mbuf tuning parameters,
175

udp_recvspace, 301
summary, 176

udp_sendspace, 301
summary, 176

udp_ttl, 302

V

Virtual Memory Manager
definition, 17
description, 7

VMM memory load control. See memory
load control

vmstat command
memory reporting, 111
monitoring CPU use, 88
performance monitoring, 73
reporting CPU and I/O activity, 80
reporting on memory, 84

vmstatit shell script, 84

vmtune, overview, 20

vmtune command, 255

using, 126
warning, 126
volume group (VG). *See* disks

W

working set definition, 54
workload
    identifying, 9
    multiuser, 8
    server, 8

workload management, 87
workstation workload, 8
write behind. *See* disks
write verify. *See* disks

X

xlc command run time, 63
xmt_que_size, 302
    summary, 178